THE READER'S COMPANION TO
CUBA

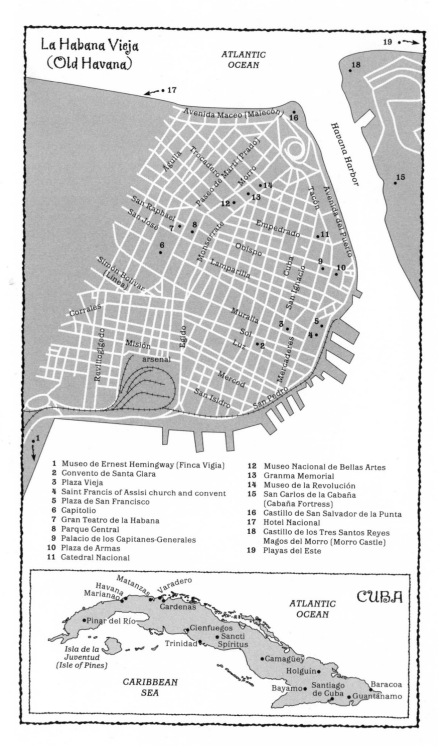

La Habana Vieja (Old Havana)

ATLANTIC OCEAN

Avenida Maceo (Malecón)

Águila
Trocadero
Paseo de Martí (Prado)
Morro
San Raphael
San José
Monserrate
Obispo
Lamparilla
Simón Bolívar (Línea)
Corrales
Revillagigedo
Misión
arsenal
Egido
Muralla
Sol
Luz
Merced
San Isidro
San Pedro
Empedrado
Tacón
Cuba
San Ignacio
Mercaderes
Avenida del Puerto
Havana Harbor

ATLANTIC OCEAN

1 Museo de Ernest Hemingway (Finca Vigia)
2 Convento de Santa Clara
3 Plaza Vieja
4 Saint Francis of Assisi church and convent
5 Plaza de San Francisco
6 Capitolio
7 Gran Teatro de la Habana
8 Parque Central
9 Palacio de los Capitanes-Generales
10 Plaza de Armas
11 Catedral Nacional

12 Museo Nacional de Bellas Artes
13 Granma Memorial
14 Museo de la Revolución
15 San Carlos de la Cabaña (Cabaña Fortress)
16 Castillo de San Salvador de la Punta
17 Hotel Nacional
18 Castillo de los Tres Santos Reyes Magos del Morro (Morro Castle)
19 Playas del Este

CUBA

Matanzas
Havana
Marianao
Varadero
Cardenas
Pinar del Río
Cienfuegos
Trinidad
Sancti Spíritus
Isla de la Juventud (Isle of Pines)
Camagüey
Holguín
CARIBBEAN SEA
Bayamo
Santiago de Cuba
Baracoa
Guantánamo

ATLANTIC OCEAN

THE READER'S COMPANION TO
CUBA

EDITED BY **ALAN RYAN**

A Harvest Original
Harcourt Brace & Company
SAN DIEGO   NEW YORK   LONDON

Requests for permission to make copies of any part of
the work should be mailed to:
Permissions Department, Harcourt Brace & Company,
6277 Sea Harbor Drive, Orlando, Florida 32887-6777.

Library of Congress Cataloging-in-Publication Data
The reader's companion to Cuba/edited by Alan Ryan. — 1st ed.
      p.   cm.
   "A Harvest original."
   ISBN 0-15-600367-8
   1. Cuba — Description and travel.   2. Havana (Cuba) —
Description and travel.   3. Cuba — Social life and customs.
4. Havana (Cuba) — Social life and customs.   5. Visitors,
Foreign — Cuba — Attitudes. 6. Travelers — Cuba —
Attitudes.   I. Ryan, Alan.
F1763.R43   1997
917.29104'64 — dc21   96-47363

Text set in Fairfield Medium
Designed by Ivan Holmes
Printed in the United States of America
First Edition
E D C B A

Permission acknowledgments appear
on pages 390–92, which constitute a continuation of
the copyright page.

THIS BOOK IS DEDICATED TO
JOHN COYNE
FOR MAKING ME AN NPCV
AND FOR OTHER GOOD DEEDS

CUBA SEEMS TO HAVE THE SAME EFFECT ON AMERICAN ADMINISTRATIONS THAT THE FULL MOON USED TO HAVE ON WEREWOLVES.

—WAYNE S. SMITH
PORTRAIT OF CUBA

CONTENTS

and seething and shuffling in a dazzling confusion, until the town became a universal *Conga* under a heaving roof of lanterns and streamers and confetti, and stars."

young Cuban, asking questions, shaking his hand, taking pictures, getting autographs."

INTRODUCTION

"I'LL SEE YOU IN C-U-B-A," WENT THE WORDS
of an Irving Berlin song in the early years of the twentieth century. Later on, Louis Armstrong would be singing a tune about
a girl who was "the daughter of a planter from Havana / and a
young Americana." And in 1941, Carmen Miranda was asking
the musical question to which there was only one sensible answer: "How would you like to spend the weekend in Havana?"

A guidebook published in the United States in the 1920s
reflected one popular attitude toward Cuba, although the book
might just as easily have appeared in the forties or fifties. Written in a jocular tone, by Basil Woon, it was called *When It's
Cocktail Time in Cuba*.

It was, in fact, cocktail time in Cuba for half a century.
But it was Americans who were drinking the cocktails and Cubans who were being told to hurry up and bring them.

For better *and* for worse, Cuba and the United States have
been closely entangled for more than a century and a half. In
the 1830s, Cuba was as much a burning political issue in

Washington as it is today. Senators and congressmen, many of them strongly influenced by the desires of wealthy supporters, were pounding the podium on Capitol Hill, just as they did last week and will do again next week. The United States should buy Cuba! The United States should annex Cuba! The United States should conquer Cuba! The United States should just damn well *take* Cuba from Spain and be done with it! Common courtesy did not influence the debate; no one seemed to consider that the Spaniards and possibly even the Cubans themselves might hold views of their own on the subject.

There were, it almost goes without saying, economic reasons. Cuba, bursting with sugar and rum, was part of that triangle of trade we all studied in grammar school, although the parts about rum and slaves may have been glossed over.

But the psychological appeal of Cuba for Americans may have been even more basic. In the middle years of the nineteenth century, the United States was growing steadily. The French had been bought out of the south. The Mexicans were driven out of Texas and California. The Indians were being conquered and relegated to reservations. And, though it was dubbed Seward's Folly at the time, even distant Alaska had been bought from the Russians.

But not Cuba . . . Cuba, the largest island in the Caribbean, where the sun shone all the time and the land was beautiful and the fertile soil produced endless tropical riches: sugar and coffee and tobacco and oranges and bananas and pineapples. And—to use the phrase heard so often in the U.S. in the last four decades—it was only ninety miles away. Only ninety miles away . . . and it wasn't ours.

Then, in the second half of the nineteenth century, the Cubans themselves—just like Americans in the second half of the eighteenth century—began to feel strongly that their colonial status was inconvenient and unfair, and an anachronism besides. A revolutionary movement began, based, like all good Cuban revolutionary movements, in the Sierra Maestra mountain range of Oriente province, at the eastern end of the island. Giving impetus to the movement, a great patriotic leader, José Martí, came to the fore and was quickly martyred. The revolution was on.

This was a perfect chance for American firebrands and adventurers like Theodore Roosevelt and newspaper magnate William Randolph Hearst to demand that the U.S. leap into the fray and seize, as Roosevelt later wrote, "this opportunity of driving the Spaniard from the Western World." Then the U.S. battleship *Maine* mysteriously exploded in Havana harbor. It must have been the Spaniards! And off went American forces, Roosevelt the loudest among them, to invade the island's eastern end, near the city of Santiago de Cuba, where most of the Spanish forces were gathered. The energetic Americans made short work of the disorganized Spaniards, and the victory flag was hoisted over the city of Santiago.

But the flag was American, not Cuban. Indeed, the Cuban residents of Santiago were banished from their city for the occasion, so the Americans could enjoy their victory to the fullest. (Among the people sent away was the family of Desi Arnaz, whose father, a prominent doctor in Santiago, had attended some of the American wounded.)

The U.S. flag flew over Cuba until 1902, when the Platt Amendment went into effect. In brief, the Platt Amendment permitted the Cubans to run their own affairs but gave the U.S. the right to intervene if the Cubans didn't seem to be going about things properly. Also, the U.S. got forty-five square miles of Cuban land for a naval base at Guantánamo Bay, for a nominal rental and in perpetuity.

Cocktail time had begun.

For the next half century American influence flourished in Cuba; by the 1950s even Havana's electricity was supplied by an American company. And at the same time, Cuba's homegrown corruption also flourished, often tied to American interests. Much of this, including the role played by the American Mafia, is outlined in the headnotes that introduce the selections in this book.

Finally, by the 1950s, with cocktail time reaching its frenzied heights, and with the dictatorship of Fulgencio Batista reaching even lower depths of corruption than his predecessors had achieved, it all got to be too much for the Cubans. Another revolutionary movement began stirring, again based in the Sierra Maestra, and led this time by a dynamic Jesuit-educated political activist and sometime baseball pitcher, Fidel Castro. Cocktail time came to an abrupt end when the revolutionary forces reached the streets of Havana, ironically, but perhaps symbolically, near midnight on New Year's Eve, December 31, 1958.

Think of *The Reader's Companion to Cuba* as a multi-screen, time-lapse portrait of Cuba in general and Havana in particular.

When we visit a foreign city or country, it becomes fixed in our minds as it was at the time we saw it. And unless we have read extensively about it, the place has no history. I'm not talking here about the great, dramatic sweep of historic periods and movements. I'm talking about the particulars of streets and shops and neighborhoods and buildings and people who have preceded us in those very same places.

I first visited London, for example, in 1966. Barely twenty years after World War II, you could still see scars in London — pockmarked walls in the Strand, a ruined church near St. Paul's. Since then, for thirty years, I've been visiting the city for several weeks or months at a time. I think of a particular few streets in Bloomsbury as my own neighborhood, my own London. I remember the area before the horrid Centre Point was built. I remember when Brunswick Centre, a few streets from Russell Square, still looked new; the area it covered had been hit hard by bombs. I remember when the traffic at the top of Shaftesbury Avenue flowed in the opposite direction. I remember restaurants and shops that have come and gone. I remember when the trees in my street were newly planted. I remember friends I brought and friends I made. On the other hand, the pub that I think of as my own local hasn't changed a whit in thirty years, and I take special pleasure in knowing that.

The element of passing time — which only time itself, alas, can provide — is missing from most of our experience of travel.

These *Reader's Companion* volumes are meant to fill the gap. They are not meant to be histories, although they certainly reflect history. Rather, they are meant to provide close-up, firsthand, eyewitness reports of what the place looked and felt like to visitors who preceded us.

In these pages, for example, the oldest streets and buildings of Havana remain exactly the same, the Convent of Santa Clara and the National Cathedral remain the same, but the city spreads out. Horse-drawn vehicles are replaced by automobiles. And because this is Cuba, currently undergoing what the Cuban government has declared "a special period in a time of peace," the automobiles are replaced by Flying Dove bicycles made in China.

All the eyewitness reports in these books are those of visitors, not natives. Natives have their own prejudices and make their own assumptions. Visitors—ideally, at least—arrive with no prejudices and make no assumptions. They ask questions, they are surprised, they get lost, they make mistakes, but, if they are reasonably good travelers, they bring with them a broad curiosity and a large capacity for wonder. Which, of course, is what we hope to bring ourselves.

By the time Richard Henry Dana, Jr., and Anthony Trollope visited Havana in January and February of 1859, the city had been a bustling merchant center, funneling the wealth of the New World back to the Old, for three hundred years. Trollope, who did not have a good time, may still have been out of sorts from his visit to Jamaica, which he didn't much care for either, and from his protracted and uncomfortable journey from there to Cuba.

Dana, on the other hand, returned home and in a matter of weeks wrote *To Cuba and Back,* a book that would remain the principal English-language "guidebook" to the island into the second decade of the twentieth century.

Every traveler seeks and finds his own version of his destination. John Muir, in 1868, was gathering and studying botanical specimens on the eastern side of Havana harbor, probably just about where the highway curves and offers several exit options, one to Pinar del Río and western Cuba, another to Matanzas and the Playas del Este, the beautiful stretch of beaches east of Havana.

It was the escalating revolution, and William Randolph Hearst, that brought artist and newspaper correspondent Frederic Remington to Cuba several times in the 1890s. Much of the local color he sent back was tinged by yellow journalism.

The early-twentieth-century visitors in this book went to Cuba for more personal reasons, rather than business. Anaïs Nin had family in Havana. Langston Hughes and Thomas Merton went on vacation, though each called it something more substantial. Young Arnold Samuelson went to find his literary hero, Ernest Hemingway, and later wrote one of the most intimate portraits we have of the writer at what was certainly the best time in his life.

Patrick Leigh Fermor, one of the great travel writers of our century, visited Cuba as part of a slow progress he was making through the islands of the Caribbean. Norman Lewis went on a literary assignment. Graham Greene went to do research, and because he liked the place.

Frank Ragano went to Havana because he worked for the mob and the mob wanted to see him. Tommy Lasorda went to play baseball, and happened to meet two historic figures *and* happened to be in town for the most historic New Year's Eve in Havana's history.

Visitors after *la revolución* went for different reasons. Amiri Baraka (known as LeRoi Jones at the time) went in 1960 because he was a political activist himself and wanted to see the revolution and its leader up close. He got a ringside seat. Frank Mankiewicz and Kirby Jones went to do a television interview with Fidel. And photojournalist Fred Ward went in 1977 on assignment for *National Geographic*.

The reasons for visits in the eighties and nineties by the writers in this book are subtler, more marked by sheer curiosity. Journalist Hugh O'Shaughnessy had been covering Cuba for two decades when he made the trip reported here. Mark Kurlansky had a similar background. Canadian writer Graeme Gibson went to investigate an interesting business opportunity. Martha Gellhorn, of course, had lived at the Finca Vigía when she was married to Hemingway. Carlo Gébler, Tom Miller, and Pico Iyer all went, for extended periods, as writers who saw a fascinating subject to write about.

This might, of course, have been a very different book. It might have included pieces by other writers, Theodore Roosevelt, for example, or Winston Churchill, Jean-Paul Sartre, Jacobo Timerman, Jose Yglesias or Ernesto Cardenal, Robert Service or James Michener, or something by the charming Dane Chandos, or a more reflective 1963 piece by Graham Greene, or a selection from Thomas Barbour's *A Naturalist in Cuba,* or many others.

But it doesn't. Sometimes this is for mundane reasons, such as contractual difficulties or the unavoidable problem of length. Sometimes it's for other reasons: I wanted to cover a variety of periods and locales; I wanted accounts of specific aspects of Cuban life; in some cases, as with Carlo Gébler and Tom Miller, I could choose only one selection from a book of travels that covered the whole island of Cuba.

And there are some things missing that I would have liked to include. I especially would have liked a full report on the state of Cuban jazz. This gap seems all the worse because, just as I began typing this paragraph, my local jazz radio station, WBGO-FM, was, I swear it, playing Cuban trumpeter Arturo Sandoval's new recording of Dizzy Gillespie's "Dizzy Atmosphere."

This is not meant to be a political book, but I am not so naive as to think that it won't be seen as political, particularly by some readers in the United States. In the United States, anything anyone says about Cuba is heard as political, except maybe a simple statement of the island's latitude and longitude. And maybe even that. Since I started work on this project and began carrying around books on Cuba, some people I know have been watching me closely for signs of aberrant behavior and other possibly un-American activities.

So be it. Dame Rose Macaulay, in the Preface to her 1946 *They Went to Portugal,* wrote, "The selections in this volume may seem capricious, as selections always must." Yes, they may, as they must.

Three brief points remain to be made.

First, I have usually written "American" in referring to people and things of the United States, in the full knowledge that we are all Americans, all of us from Hudson's Bay to Tierra del Fuego. But language fails us here. "North American" and "*norteamericano*" are imprecise, and we don't have, and don't want, a word like "United-States-ian." Spanish has "*estadounidense*," but that's no better.

Second, I have sometimes referred to Cuba's leader as Castro and sometimes as Fidel. There's nothing in it, except perhaps an awareness that, in Cuba, Fidel is usually Fidel. Otherwise, I've been guided by the need of the moment, or the context, or sometimes, because the stresses in the two names are different, merely by the rhythm of the sentence.

Third, as I said in the Introduction to *The Reader's Companion to Mexico,* don't try to learn Spanish from this book. It won't work. The selections included here are reprinted exactly as they were first published, complete with errors. After all, this is the way readers of another time first encountered this material, and we can't go correcting the past. There's an error in the quote under Frank Ragano's name in the Contents. For another, as amusing as it is glaring, see the headnote for the selection by Tommy Lasorda.

Finally, for U.S. citizens only, two points need clarification. Please bear in mind that this information is correct at the time of writing but could well be very different even before this book is published.

The reason U.S. citizens can't go to Cuba does not emanate from Havana; it comes from Washington. And, as a matter of fact, *the U.S. government does not forbid travel to Cuba by U.S. citizens.*

The operative factor here is the Trading with the Enemy Act, which forbids the expenditure of U.S. dollars in—or dollars that end up in—Cuba. In order to spend money in Cuba, a U.S. citizen needs a special license, for which one applies to the Office of Foreign Assets Control of the Treasury Department. In order to apply, one needs a good reason, in accordance with Treasury Department guidelines. (These guidelines are subject to interpretation by the understaffed office that handles applications, and interpretation may depend, at times, on which way the wind is blowing.) Such licenses are granted—not routinely, but they are granted—if an applicant has a legitimate journalistic, professional, religious, or academic reason for traveling to Cuba, if one is Cuban-American and traveling to visit immediate family, or if one is invited by a Cuban organization and the trip will be "fully hosted."

Thousands of U.S. citizens travel legally to Cuba every year. Although it's possible to travel independently, many do so through U.S. organizations that have long professional experience arranging such travel. They include the Center for Cuban Studies in New York City and two organizations in San Francisco, Global Exchange and Caribbean Music and Dance.

Once again, I have a long list of people to thank for various expressions of help and kindness which, sometimes, they didn't even know they were providing. My warmest thanks go to Jill Bauman, Bob Booth, Diane Buchanan, John Coyne, Michael Dirda, Nancy Dunnan, Cathy Fauver, Beverly Fisher, Eleanor Garner, Leslie Hunt, Helen Kasimis, Chris Katechis, Dan Kelly, Deirdre Killen, Ellen Levine, Christa Malone, Juana Ponce de León, Sean Ryan, Dan Shapiro, Michael Skube, Wendy Viggiano, Carolyn Warmbold, Dori Weintraub, Dave Wood, and, as in the past, all my pals at the Chariot.

Special thanks go to Sandra Levinson and the Center for for Cuban Studies in New York; Ann Alexander, Larry Williams, and all the staff of the Mosholu Branch of the New York Public Library: and the Society of American Travel Writers.

One of these days, I'll see you all in C-U-B-A.

ALAN RYAN
New York City
August 1996

RICHARD HENRY DANA, JR.

Havana, 1859

"HAVE I EVER SEEN A CITY VIEW SO GRAND? THE VIEW OF
QUEBEC FROM THE FOOT OF THE MONTMORENCI FALLS MAY
RIVAL, BUT DOES NOT EXCEL IT. MY PREFERENCE IS FOR
THIS."

*Every schoolboy knows—or should know—that Richard Henry
Dana, Jr. (1815–1882), wrote the great classic of real-life
seafaring adventure,* Two Years Before the Mast. *Published in
1840, it chronicles the author's own experiences as a sailor on
a voyage from Boston, around Cape Horn, northward in the
Pacific, and then along the coast of California.*

*Dana was an attorney, and his early interest in the sea car-
ried over into his professional life. He specialized in maritime
law, and his 1841 handbook,* The Seaman's Friend, *became a
standard work in the field. His career was distinguished. In the
1840s, he was a founder of the Free-Soil Party. In the 1850s, he
assisted in revising the constitution of Massachusetts. During the
Civil War years, he served as U.S. Attorney for Massachusetts. In
the 1860s, he was co-counsel for the United States when Jeffer-
son Davis was tried for treason. His will to serve was great, and
he sought public office several times, failing in each attempt. In
1876, he had what was no doubt his greatest disappointment*

when he failed to win confirmation after President Grant named him as ambassador to the Court of St. James's.

In March of 1859, Dana took a short vacation trip to Cuba, spending about two weeks on the island. As soon as he returned, he began setting down his very detailed impressions of Cuba. He was finished in several weeks, and To Cuba and Back *was published in both Boston and London before the end of the year.*

From the time it first appeared, and for more than half a century after, To Cuba and Back *was the primary source of information on Cuba in the English language. It was widely read by American soldiers and adventurers going to Cuba in the time of the Spanish-American War, as well as by curious travelers, and it remained constantly in print until the second decade of the twentieth century.*

Although little read today, To Cuba and Back *enjoys a special place in the history of travel literature. Now and then a book of travel writing is so well written and so vividly descriptive of an exotic and enticing locale that it serves to focus new attention on the place. Two twentieth-century examples illustrate this. Charles Macomb Flandreau's 1908* Viva Mexico! *drew the attention of North Americans and others to the marvels and comforts of Mexico, and helped to make that country into the favorite travel destination of U.S. residents. (An excerpt from* Viva Mexico! *is included in* The Reader's Companion to Mexico.) *Likewise, Rose Macaulay's 1949* The Fabled Shore: From the Pyrenees to Portugal *focused travelers' attention for the first time on what would come to be called Spain's Costa del Sol and on Portugal's Algarve. And one day, perhaps, Tom Miller's 1992* Trading with the Enemy: A Yankee Travels Through Castro's Cuba *will come to be seen in the same way. In the nineteenth century, travel was a pastime for the wealthy, and the tourist industry as we know it did not exist, but Dana's* To Cuba and Back *focused attention on the riches and the possibilities of Cuba in a way that readers could never forget.*

It's worth noting here that ingrained habits of language do not always truly express a man's mind. Dana's references to blacks and slaves in Cuba, which sound condescending a century and a half later, are very much those of a man of his time.

But, in fact, Dana campaigned actively against slavery as a founder of the Free-Soil Party and often served as attorney in the trials of runaway slaves.

It's worth noting, too, that Dana was in Havana only weeks after the visit of Anthony Trollope, some of whose impressions follow those of Dana in this book. They both saw the same city at the same time, but they came away with very different reactions.

WE ARE TO GO IN AT SUNRISE, AND FEW, IF any, are the passengers that are not on deck at the first glow of dawn. Before us lie the novel and exciting objects of the night before. The Steep Morro, with its tall sentinel lighthouse, and its towers and signal staffs and teeth of guns, is coming out into clear daylight; the red and yellow striped flag of Spain—blood and gold—floats over it. Point after point in the city becomes visible; the blue and white and yellow houses, with their roofs of dull red tiles, the quaint old Cathedral towers, and the almost endless lines of fortifications. The masts of the immense shipping rise over the headland, the signal for leave to enter is run up, and we steer in under full head, the morning gun thundering from the Morro, the trumpets braying and drums beating from all the fortifications, the Morro, the Punta, the long Cabaña, the Casa Blanca, and the city walls, while the broad sun is fast rising over this magnificent spectacle.

What a world of shipping! The masts make a belt of dense forest along the edge of the city, all the ships lying head in to the street, like horses at their mangers; while the vessels at anchor nearly choke up the passage ways to the deeper bays beyond. There are the red and yellow stripes of decayed Spain; the blue, white and red—blood to the fingers' end—of La Grande Nation; the Union crosses of the Royal Commonwealth; the stars and stripes of the Great Republic, and a few flags of Holland and Portugal, of the states of northern Italy, of Brazil, and of the republics of the Spanish Main. We thread our slow and careful way among these, pass under the broadside of a ship-of-the-line, and under the stern of a screw frigate, both bearing the Spanish flag, and cast our anchor in the Regla Bay, by the side of the steamer *Karnac,* which sailed from New York a few days before us.

Instantly we are besieged by boats, some loaded with oranges and bananas, and others coming for passengers and their luggage, all with awnings spread over their sterns, rowed by sallow, attenuated men, in blue and white checks and straw hats, with here and there the familiar lips and teeth, and vacant, easily-pleased face of the Negro. Among these boats comes one, from the stern of which floats the red and yellow flag with the crown in its field, and under whose awning reclines a man in a full suit of white linen, with straw hat and red cockade and a cigar. This is the Health Officer. Until he is satisfied, no one can come on board, or leave the vessel. Capt. Bullock salutes, steps down the ladder to the boat, hands his papers, reports all well—and we are pronounced safe. Then comes another boat of similar style, another man reclining under the awning with a cigar, who comes on board, is closeted with the purser, compares the passenger list with the passports, and we are declared fully passed, and general leave is given to land with our luggage at the custom-house wharf.

Now comes the war of cries and gestures and grimaces among the boatmen, in their struggle for passengers, increased manifold by the fact that there is but little language in common between the parties to the bargains, and by the boatmen being required to remain in their boats. How thin these boatmen look! You cannot get it out of your mind that they must all have had the yellow fever last summer, and are not yet fully recovered. Not only their faces, but their hands and arms and legs are thin, and their low-quartered slippers only half cover their thin yellow feet.

In the hurry, I have to hunt after the passengers I am to take leave of who go on to New Orleans:—Mr. and Mrs. Benchley, on their way to their intended new home in western Texas, my two sea captains, and the little son of my friend, who is the guest, on this voyage, of our common friend the captain, and after all, I miss the hearty hand-shake of Bullock and Rodgers. Seated under an awning, in the stern of a boat, with my trunk and carpet-bag and an unseasonable bundle of Arctic overcoat and fur cap in the bow, I am pulled by a man with an oar in each hand and a cigar in mouth, to the custom-house pier. Here is a busy scene of trunks, carpet-bags, and bundles; and up and down the pier marches a military grandee of about the rank of a sergeant or sub-lieutenant, with a preposterous strut, so out of keeping with the depressed military character of his country, and not possible to be appreciated without seeing it. If he would give that strut on the boards, in New York, he would draw full houses nightly.

Our passports are kept, and we receive a license to remain and travel in the island, good for three months only, for which a large fee is paid. These officers of the customs are civil and reasonably rapid; and in a short time my luggage is on a dray driven by a Negro, and I am in a volante, managed by a Negro postilion, and am driving through the narrow streets of this surprising city.

The streets are so narrow and the houses built so close upon them, that they seem to be rather spaces between the walls of houses than highways for travel. It appears impossible that two vehicles should pass abreast; yet they do so. There are constant blockings of the way. In some places awnings are stretched over the entire street, from house to house, and we are riding under a long tent. What strange vehicles these volantes are!—A pair of very long, limber shafts, at one end of which is a pair of huge wheels, and the other end a horse with his tail braided and brought forward and tied to the saddle, an open chaise body resting on the shafts, about one third of the way from the axle to the horse; and on the horse is a Negro, in large postilion boots, long spurs, and a bright jacket. It is an easy vehicle to ride in; but it must be a sore burden to the beast. Here and there we pass a private volante, distinguished by rich silver mountings and postilions in livery. Some have two horses, and with the silver and the livery and the long dangling traces and a look of superfluity, have rather an air of high life. In most, a gentleman is reclining, cigar in mouth; while in others, is a great puff of blue or pink muslin or cambric, extending over the sides to the shafts, topped off by a fan, with signs of a face behind it. "Calle de los Oficios," "Calle del Obispo," "Calle de San Ignacio," "Calle de Mercaderes," are on the little corner boards. Every little shop and every big shop has its title; but nowhere does the name of a keeper appear. Almost every shop advertises "por mayor y menor," wholesale and retail. What a Gil Blas—Don Quixote feeling the names of "posada," "tienda," and "cantina" give you!

There are no women walking in the streets, except Negresses. Those suits of seersucker, with straw hats and red cockades, are soldiers. It is a sensible dress for the climate. Every third man, perhaps more, and not a few women, are smoking cigars or cigarritos. Here are things moving along, looking like cocks of new mown grass, under way. But presently you see the head of a horse or mule peering out from under the mass, and a tail is visible at the other end, and feet are picking their slow way over the stones. These are the carriers of green fodder, the fresh cut stalks and blades of corn; and my chance companion in the carriage, a fellow passenger by the "Cahawba," a Frenchman, who has been here before, tells me that they supply all the horses and mules in the city with their daily feed, as no hay is used. There are also mules, asses, and horses with bananas, plantains, oranges, and other fruits in panniers reaching almost to the ground.

Here is the Plaza de Armas, with its garden of rich, fragrant flowers in full bloom, in front of the Governor's Palace. At the corner is the chapel erected over the spot where, under the auspices of Columbus, mass was first celebrated on the island. We are driven past a gloomy convent, past innumerable shops, past drinking places, billiard rooms, and the thick, dead walls of houses, with large windows, grated like dungeons, and large gates, showing glimpses of interior court-yards, sometimes with trees and flowers. But horses and carriages and gentlemen and ladies and slaves, all seem to use the same entrance. The windows come to the ground, and, being flush with the street, and mostly without glass, nothing but the grating prevents a passenger from walking into the rooms. And there the ladies and children sit sewing, or lounging, or playing. This is all very strange. There is evidently enough for me to see in the ten or twelve days of my stay.

But there are no costumes among the men, no Spanish

hats, or Spanish cloaks, or bright jackets, or waistcoats, or open, slashed trousers, that are so picturesque in other Spanish countries. The men wear black dress coats, long pantaloons, black cravats, and many of them even submit, in this hot sun, to black French hats. The tyranny of systematic, scientific, capable, unpicturesque, unimaginative France evidently rules over the realm of man's dress. The houses, the vehicles, the vegetation, the animals, are picturesque; to the eye of taste

"Every prospect pleases, and only man is vile."

We drove through the Puerta de Monserrate, a heavy gateway of the prevailing yellow or tawny color, where soldiers are on guard, across the moat, out upon the "Paseo de Isabel Segunda," and are now "extramuros," without the walls. The Paseo is a grand avenue running across the city from sea to bay, with two carriage-drives abreast, and two malls for foot passengers, and all lined with trees in full foliage. Here you catch a glimpse of the Morro, and there of the Presidio. This is the Teatro de Tacón; and, in front of this line of tall houses, in contrast with the almost uniform one-story buildings of the city, the volante stops. This is Le Grand's hotel.

TO A PERSON UNACCUSTOMED TO THE TROP- ics or the south of Europe, I know of nothing more discouraging than the arrival at the inn or hotel. It is nobody's business to attend to you. The landlord is strangely indifferent, and if there is a way to get a thing done, you have not learned it, and there is no one to teach you. Le Grand is a Frenchman. His house is a restaurant, with rooms for lodgers. The restaurant is paramount. The lodging is secondary, and is left to servants. Monsieur does not condescend to show a room, even to families; and the servants, who are whites, but mere lads, have all the interior in their charge, and there are no women employed about the chambers. Antonio, a swarthy Spanish lad, in shirt sleeves, looking very much as if he never washed, has my part of the house in charge, and shows me my room. It has but one window, a door opening upon the veranda, and a brick floor, and is very bare of furniture, and the furniture has long ceased to be strong. A small stand barely holds up a basin and ewer which have not been washed since Antonio was washed, and the bedstead, covered by a canvas sacking, without mattress or bed, looks as if it would hardly bear the weight of a man. It is plain there is a good deal to be learned here. Antonio is communicative, on a suggestion of several days' stay and good pay. Things which we cannot do without, we must go out of the house to find, and those which we can do without, we must dispense with. This is odd, and strange, but not uninteresting, and affords scope for contrivance and the exercise of influence and other administrative powers. The Grand Seigneur does not mean to be troubled with anything; so there are no bells, and no office, and no clerks. He is the only source, and if he is approached, he shrugs his shoulders and gives you to understand that you have your chambers for your money and must look to the servants. Antonio starts off on an expedition for a pitcher of water and a towel, with a faint hope of two towels; for each demand involves an expedition to remote parts of the house. Then Antonio has so many rooms dependent on him that every door is a Scylla, and every window a Charybdis, as he passes. A shrill, female voice, from the next room but one, calls "Antonio! Antonio!" and that starts the parrot in the courtyard, who cries "Antonio! Antonio!" for several minutes. A deep, bass voice mutters "Antonio!" in a more confidential tone; and last of all, an unmistakably Northern voice attempts it, but ends in something between Antonio and Anthony. He is gone a good while, and has evidently had several episodes to his journey. But he is a good-natured fellow, speaks a little French, very little English, and seems anxious to do his best.

I see the faces of my New York fellow-passengers from the west gallery, and we come together and throw our acquisitions of information into a common stock, and help one another. Mr. Miller's servant, who has been here before, says there are baths and other conveniences round the corner of the street; and, sending our bundles of thin clothes there, we take advantage of the baths, with comfort. To be sure, we must go through a billiard-room, where the Creoles are playing at the tables, and the cockroaches playing under them, and through a drinking-room, and a bowling-alley; but the baths are built in the open yard, protected by blinds, well ventilated, and well supplied with water and toilet apparatus.

With the comfort of a bath, and clothed in linen, with straw hats, we walk back to Le Grand's, and enter the restaurant, for breakfast—the breakfast of the country, at ten o'clock. Here is a scene so pretty as quite to make up for the defects of the chambers. The restaurant with cool marble floor, walls twenty-four feet high, open rafters painted blue, great windows open to the floor and looking into the Paseo, and the floor nearly on a level with the street, a light breeze fanning the thin curtains, the little tables, for two or four, with clean, white cloths, each with its pyramid of great red oranges and its fragrant bouquet—the gentlemen in white pantaloons and jackets and white stockings, and the ladies in fly-away muslins, and hair in the sweet neglect of the morning toilet, taking their leisurely breakfasts of fruit and claret, and omelette and Spanish mixed dishes (ollas), and café noir. How airy and ethereal it seems! They are birds, not substantial men and women. They eat ambrosia and drink nectar. It must be that they fly, and live in nests, in the tamarind trees. Who can eat a hot, greasy breakfast of cakes and gravied meats, and in a close room, after this?

I can truly say that I ate, this morning, my first orange; for I had never before eaten one newly gathered, which had ripened in the sun, hanging on the tree. We call for the usual breakfast, leaving the selection to the waiter; and he brings us fruits, claret, omelette, fish fresh from the sea, rice excellently cooked, fried plantains, a mixed dish of meat and vegetables (olla), and coffee. The fish, I do not remember its name, is boiled, and has the colors of the rainbow, as it lies on the plate. Havana is a good fishmarket; for it is as open to the ocean as Nahant, or the beach at Newport; its streets running to the blue sea, outside the harbor, so that a man may almost throw his line from the curb-stone into the Gulf Stream.

After breakfast, I take a volante and ride into the town, to deliver my letters. Three merchants whom I call upon have palaces for their business. The entrances are wide, the staircases almost as stately as that of Stafford House, the floors of marble, the panels of porcelain tiles, the rails of iron, and the rooms over twenty feet high, with open rafters, the doors and windows colossal, the furniture rich and heavy; and there sits the merchant or banker, in white pantaloons and thin shoes and loose white coat and narrow necktie, smoking a succession of cigars, surrounded by tropical luxuries and tropical protections. In the lower story of one of these buildings is an exposition of silks, cotton, and linens, in a room so large that it looked like a part of the Great Exhibition in Hyde Park. At one of these counting-palaces, I met Mr. Theodore Parker and Dr. S. G. Howe, of Boston, who preceded me, in the *Karnac*. Mr. Parker is here for his health, which has caused anxiety to his friends lest his weakened frame should no longer support the strong intellectual machinery, as before. He finds Havana too hot, and will leave for Santa Cruz by the first opportunity. Dr. Howe likes the warm weather. It is a comfort to see him—a benefactor of his race, and one of the few heroes we have left to us, since Kane died.

The Bishop of Havana has been in delicate health, and is out of town, at Jesús del Monte, and Miss M—— is not at home, and the Señoras F—— I failed to see this morning; but I find a Boston young lady, whose friends were desirous I should see her, and who was glad enough to meet one so lately from her home. A clergyman to whom, also, I had letters is gone into the country, without much hope of improving his health. Stepping into a little shop to buy a plan of Havana, my name is called, and there is my hero's wife, the accomplished author and conversationist, whom it is an exhilaration to meet anywhere, much more in a land of strangers. Dr. and Mrs. Howe and Mr. Parker are at the Cerro, a pretty and cool place in the suburbs, but are coming in to Mrs. Almy's boarding-house, for the convenience of being in the city, and for nearness to friends, and the comforts of something like American or English housekeeping.

In the latter part of the afternoon, from three o'clock, our parties are taking dinner at Le Grand's. The little tables are again full, with a fair complement of ladies. The afternoon breeze is so strong that the draught of air, though it is hot air, is to be avoided. The passers-by almost put their faces into the room, and the women and children of the poorer order look wistfully in upon the luxurious guests, the colored glasses, the red wines, and the golden fruits. The Opera troupe is here, both the singers and the ballet; and we have Gazzaniga, Lamoureux, Max Maretzek and his sister, and others, in this house, and Adelaide Phillips at the next door, and the benefit of a rehearsal, at nearly all hours of the day, of operas that the Habaneros are to rave over at night.

I yield to no one in my admiration of the Spanish as a spoken language, whether in its rich, sonorous, musical, and lofty style, in the mouth of a man who knows its uses, or in the soft, indolent, languid tones of a woman, broken by an occasional birdlike trill—

"With wanton heed, and giddy cunning,
The melting voice through mazes running"—

but I do not like it as spoken by the common people of Cuba, in the streets. Their voices and intonations are thin and eager, very rapid, too much in the lips, and, withal, giving an impression of the passionate and the childish combined; and it strikes me that the tendency here is to enfeeble the language, and take from it the openness of the vowels and the strength of the harder consonants. This is the criticism of a few hours' observation, and may not be just; but I have heard the same from persons who have been longer acquainted with it. Among the well educated Cubans, the standard of Castilian is said to be kept high, and there is a good deal of ambition to reach it.

After dinner, walked along the Paseo de Isabel Segunda, to see the pleasure-driving, which begins at about five o'clock, and lasts until dark. The most common carriage is the volante, but there are some carriages in the English style, with servants in livery on the box. I have taken a fancy for the strange-looking two-horse volante. The postilion, the long, dangling traces, the superfluousness of a horse to be ridden by the man that guides the other, and the prodigality of silver, give the whole a look of style that eclipses the neat appropriate English equipage. The ladies ride in full dress, décolletées, without hats. The servants on the carriages are not all Negroes. Many of the drivers are white. The drives are along the Paseo de Isabel, across the

Campo del Marte, and then along the Paseo de Tacón, a beautiful double avenue, lined with trees, which leads two or three miles, in a straight line, into the country.

At eight o'clock, drove to the Plaza de Armas, a square in front of the governor's house, to hear the Retreta, at which a military band plays for an hour, every evening. There is a clear moon above, and a blue field of glittering stars; the air is pure and balmy; the band of fifty or sixty instruments discourses most eloquent music under the shade of palm trees and mangoes; the walks are filled with promenaders, and the streets around the square lined with carriages, in which the ladies recline, and receive the salutations and visits of the gentlemen. Very few ladies walk in the square, and those probably are strangers. It is against the etiquette for ladies to walk in public in Havana.

I walk leisurely home, in order to see Havana by night. The evening is the busiest season for the shops. Much of the business of shopping is done after gas lighting. Volantes and coaches are driving to and fro, and stopping at the shop doors, and attendants take their goods to the doors of the carriages. The watchmen stand at the corners of the streets, each carrying a long pike and a lantern. Billiard-rooms and cafés are filled, and all who can walk for pleasure will walk now. This is also the principal time for paying visits.

There is one strange custom observed here in all the houses. In the chief room, rows of chairs are placed, facing each other, three or four or five in each line, and always running at right angles with the street wall of the house. As you pass along the street, you look up this row of chairs. In these, the family and the visitors take their seats, in formal order. As the windows are open, deep, and large, with wide gratings and no glass, one has the inspection of the interior arrangement of all the front parlors of Havana, and can see what every lady wears, and who is visiting her.

IF MOSQUITO NETS WERE INVENTED FOR THE purpose of shutting mosquitoes in with you, they answer their purpose very well. The beds have no mattresses, and you lie on the hard sacking. This favors coolness and neatness. I should fear a mattress, in the economy of our hotel, at least. Where there is nothing but an iron frame, canvas stretched over it, and sheets and a blanket, you may know what you are dealing with.

The clocks of the churches and castles strike the quarter hours, and at each stroke the watchmen blow a kind of boatswain's whistle, and cry the time and the state of the weather, which, from their name (serenos), should be always pleasant.

I have been advised to close the shutters at night, whatever the heat, as the change of air that often takes place before dawn is injurious; and I notice that many of the bedrooms in the hotel are closed, both doors and shutters, at night. This is too much for my endurance, and I venture to leave the air to its course, not being in the draught. One is also cautioned not to step with bare feet on the floor, for fear of the nigua (or chigua), a very small insect, that is said to enter the skin and build tiny nests, and lay little eggs that can only be seen by the microscope, but are tormenting and sometimes dangerous. This may be excessive caution, but it is so easy to observe that it is not worth while to test the question.

There are streaks of a clear dawn; it is nearly six o'clock, the cocks are crowing, and the drums and trumpets sounding. We have been told of sea-baths, cut in the rock, near the Punta, at the foot of our Paseo. I walk down, under the trees, toward the Presidio. What is this clanking sound? Can it be cavalry, marching on foot, their sabres rattling on the pavement? No, it comes from that crowd of poor-looking creatures that are forming in files in front of the Presidio. It is the chain-gang! Poor wretches! I come nearer to them, and wait until they are formed and numbered and marched off. Each man has an iron band riveted round his ankle, and another round his waist, and the chain is fastened, one end into each of these bands, and dangles between them, clanking with every movement. This leaves the wearers free to use their arms, and, indeed, their whole body, it being only a weight and a badge and a note for discovery, from which they cannot rid themselves. It is kept on them day and night, working, eating, or sleeping. In some cases, two are chained together. They have passed their night in the Presidio (the great prison and garrison), and are marshalled for their day's toil in the public streets and on the public works, in the heat of the sun. They look thoroughly wretched. Can any of these be political offenders? It is said that Carlists, from Old Spain, worked in this gang. Sentence to the chaingang in summer, in the case of a foreigner, must be nearly certain death.

Farther on, between the Presidio and the Punta, the soldiers are drilling; and the drummers and trumpeters are practising on the rampart of the city walls.

A little to the left, in the Calzada de San Lázaro, are the Baños de Mar. These are boxes, each about twelve feet square and six or eight feet deep, cut directly into the rock which here forms the sea-line, with steps of rock, and each box having a couple of portholes through which the waves of this tideless shore wash in and out. This arrangement is necessary, as sharks are so abundant that bathing in the open sea is dangerous. The pure rock, and the flow and reflow, make these bathing-boxes very agreeable, and the water, which is that of the Gulf Stream, is at a temperature of 72 degrees. The baths are roofed over, and partially screened on the inside, but open for a view out, on the side towards the sea; and as you bathe, you see the big ships floating up the Gulf Stream, that great highway of the Equinoctial world. The water stands at depths of from three to five feet in the baths; and they are large enough for short swimming. The bottom is white with sand and shells. These baths are made at the public expense, and are free. Some are marked for women, some for men, and some "por la gente de color." A little further down the Calzada is another set of baths, and further out in the suburbs, opposite the Beneficencia, are still others.

After bath, took two or three fresh oranges, and a cup of coffee, without milk; for the little milk one uses with coffee must not be taken with fruit here, even in winter.

To the Cathedral, at eight o'clock, to hear mass. The Cathedral, in its exterior, is a plain and quaint old structure, with a tower at each angle of the front; but within, it is sumptuous. There is a floor of variegated marble, obstructed by no seats or screens, tall pillars and rich frescoed walls, and delicate masonry of various colored stone, the prevailing tint being yellow, and a high altar of porphyry. There is a look of the great days of Old Spain about it; and you think that knights and nobles worshipped here and enriched it from their spoils and conquests. Every new eye turns first to the place within the choir, under that alto-relief, behind that short inscription, where, in the wall of the chancel, rest the remains of Christopher Columbus. Borne from Valladolid to Seville, from Seville to San Domingo, and from San Domingo to Havana, they at last rest here, by the altar side, in the emporium of the Spanish Islands. "What is man that thou art mindful of him!" truly and humbly says the Psalmist; but what is man, indeed, if his fellow men are not mindful of such a man as this! The creator of a hemisphere! It is not often we feel that monuments are surely deserved, in their degree and to the extent of their utterance. But when, in the New World, on an island of that group which he gave to civilized man, you stand before this simple monumental slab, and know that all of him that man can gather up lies behind it, so overpowering is the sense of the greatness of his deeds, that you feel relieved that no attempt has been made to measure it by any work of man's hands. The little there is, is so inadequate, that you make no comparison. It is a mere fingerpoint, the *hic jacet,* the *sic itur.*

The priests in the chancel are numerous, perhaps twenty or more. The service is chanted with no aid of instruments, except once the accompaniment of a small and rather disordered organ, and chanted in very loud and often harsh and blatant tones, which reverberate from the marble walls, with a tiresome monotony of cadence. There is a degree of ceremony in the placing, replacing, and carrying to and fro of candles and crucifixes, and swinging of censers, which the Roman service as practised in the United States does not give. The priests seem duly attentive and reverent in their manner, but I cannot say as much for the boys, of whom there were three or four, gentlemen-like looking lads, from the college, doing service as altar boys. One of these, who seemed to have the lead, was strikingly careless and irreverent in his manner; and when he went about the chancel, to incense all who were there, and to give to each the small golden vessel to kiss (containing, I suppose a relic), he seemed as if he were counting his play-mates out for a game, and flinging the censer at them and snubbing their noses with the golden vessel.

There were only about half a dozen persons at mass, beside those in the chancel; and all but one of these were women, and of the women two were Negroes. The women walk in, veiled, drop down on the bare pavement, kneeling or sitting, as the service requires or permits. A Negro woman, with devout and even distressed countenance, knelt at the altar rail, and one pale-eyed priest, in cassock, who looked like an American or Englishman, knelt close by a pillar. A file of visitors, American or English women, with an escort of gentlemen, came in and sat on the only benches, next the columns; and when the Host was elevated, and a priest said to them, very civilly, in English, "Please to kneel down," they neither knelt nor stood, nor went away, but kept their seats.

After service, the old sacristan, in blue woollen dress, showed all the visitors the little chapel and the cloisters, and took us beyond the altar to the mural tomb of Columbus, and though he was liberally paid, haggled for two reals more.

In the rear of the Cathedral is the Seminario, or college for boys, where also men are trained for the priesthood. There are cloisters and a pleasant garden within them.

BREAKFAST, AND AGAIN THE COOL MARBLE floor, white-robed tables, the fruits and flowers, and curtains gently swaying, and women in morning toilets. Besides the openness to view, these rooms are strangely open to ingress. Lottery-ticket vendors go the rounds of the tables at every meal, and so do the girls with tambourines for alms for the music in the street. As there is no coin in Cuba less than the medio, $6\frac{1}{4}$ cents, the musicians get a good deal or nothing. The absence of any smaller coin must be an inconvenience to the poor, as they must often buy more than they want, or go without. I find silver very scarce here. It is difficult to get change for gold, and at public places notices are put up that gold will not be received for small payments. I find the only course is to go to one of the Cambios de Moneda, whose signs are frequent in the streets, and get a half doubloon changed into reals and pesetas, at four per cent discount, and fill my pockets with small silver.

Spent the morning, from eleven o'clock to dinner-time, in my room, writing and reading. It is too hot to be out with comfort. It is not such a morning as one would spend at the St. Nicholas, or the Tremont, or at Morley's or Meurice's. The rooms all open into the court-yard, and the doors and windows, if open at all, are open to the view of all passers-by. As there are no bells, every call is made from the veranda rail, down into the court-yard, and repeated until the servant answers, or the caller gives up in despair. Antonio has a compeer and rival in Domingo, and the sharp voice of the woman in the next room but one, who proves to be a subordinate of the opera troupe, is calling out, "Do-meen-go! Do-meen-go!" and the rogue is in full sight from our side, making significant faces, until she changes her tune to "Antonio! Antonio! Adónde está Domingo?" But as she speaks very little Spanish, and Antonio very little French, it is not difficult for him to get up a misapprehension, especially at the distance of two stories; and she is obliged to subside for a while, and her place is supplied by the parrot. She is usually unsuccessful, being either unreasonable, or bad pay. The opera troupe are rehearsing in the second flight, with doors and windows open. And throughout the hot middle day, we hear the singing, the piano, the parrot, and the calls and parleys with the servants below. But we can see the illimitable sea from the end of the piazza, blue as indigo; and the strange city is lying under our eye, with its strange blue and white and yellow houses, with their roofs of dull red tiles, its strange tropical shade-trees, and its strange vehicles and motley population, and the clangor of its bells, and the high-pitched cries of the vendors in its streets.

Going down stairs at about eleven o'clock, I find a table set in the front hall, at the foot of the great staircase, and there, in full view of all who come or go, the landlord and his entire establishment, except the slaves and coolies, are at breakfast. This is done every day. At the café round the corner, the family with their white, hired servants breakfast and dine in the hall, through which all the customers of the place must go to the baths, the billiard-rooms, and the bowling-alleys. Fancy the manager of the Astor or Revere, spreading a table for breakfast and dinner in the great entry, between the office and the front door, for himself and family and servants!

Yesterday and to-day I noticed in the streets and at work in houses men of an Indian complexion, with coarse black hair. I asked if they were native Indians, or of mixed blood. No, they are the coolies! Their hair, full grown, and the usual dress of the country which they wore, had not suggested to me the Chinese; but the shape and expression of the eye make it plain. These are the victims of the trade, of which we hear so much. I am told there are 200,000 of them in Cuba, or, that so many have been imported, and all within seven years. I have met them everywhere, the newly-arrived, in Chinese costume, with shaved heads, but the greater number in pantaloons and jackets and straw hats, with hair full grown. Two of the cooks at our hotel are coolies. I must inform myself on the subject of this strange development of the domination of capital over labor. I am told there is a mart of coolies in the Cerro. This I must see, if it is to be seen.

After dinner drove out to the Jesús del Monte, to deliver my letter of introduction to the Bishop. The drive, by way of the Calzada de Jesús del Monte, takes one through a wretched portion, I hope the most wretched portion, of Havana, by long lines of one-story wood and mud hovels, hardly habitable even for Negroes, and interspersed with an abundance of drinking shops. The horses, mules, asses, chickens, children, and grown people use the same door; and the back yards disclose heaps of rubbish. The looks of the men, the horses tied to the door-posts, the mules with their panniers of fruits and leaves reaching to the ground, all speak of Gil Blas, and of what we have read of humble life in Spain. The little Negro children go stark naked, as innocent of clothing as the puppies. But this is so all over the city. In the front hall of Le Grand's, this morning, a lady, standing in a full dress of spotless white, held by the hand a naked little Negro boy, of two or three years old, nestling in black relief against the folds of her dress.

Now we rise to the higher grounds of Jesús del Monte. The houses improve in character. They are still of one story, but high and of stone, with marble floors and tiled roofs, with court-yards of grass and trees, and through the gratings of the wide, long, open windows, I see the decent furniture, the double, formal row of chairs, prints on the walls, and well-dressed women maneuvering their fans.

As a carriage with a pair of cream-colored horses passed, having two men within, in the dress of ecclesiastics, my driver pulled up and said that was the Bishop's carriage, and that he was going out for an evening drive. Still, I must go on; and we drive to his house. As you go up the hill, a glorious view lies upon the left. Havana, both city and suburbs, the Morro with its batteries and lighthouse, the ridge of fortifications called the Cabaña and Casa Blanca, the Castle of Atares, near at hand, a perfect truncated cone, fortified at the top—the higher and most distant Castle of Principe,

> "And, poured round all,
> Old Ocean's gray and melancholy waste"—

No! Not so! Young Ocean, the Ocean of to-day! The blue, bright, healthful, glittering, gladdening, inspiring Ocean! Have I ever seen a city view so grand? The view of Quebec from the foot of the Montmorenci Falls may rival, but does not excel it. My preference is for this; for nothing, not even the St. Lawrence, broad and affluent as it is, will make up for the living sea, the boundless horizon, the dioramic vision of gliding, distant sails, and the open arms and motherly bosom of the harbor, "with handmaid lamp attending":—our Mother Earth, forgetting never the perils of that gay and treacherous world of waters, its change of moods, its "strumpet winds"—ready is she at all times, by day or by night, to fold back to her bosom her returning sons, knowing that the sea can give them no drink, no food, no path, no light, nor bear up their foot for an instant, if they are sinking in its depths.

The regular episcopal residence is in town. This is only a house which the Bishop occupies temporarily, for the sake of his health. It is a modest house of one story, standing very high, with a commanding view of city, harbor, sea, and suburbs. The floors are marble, and the roof is of open rafters, painted blue, and above twenty feet in height; the windows are as large as doors, and the doors as large as gates. The mayordomo shows me the parlor, in which are portraits in oil of distinguished scholars and missionaries and martyrs.

On my way back to the city, I direct the driver to avoid the disagreeable road by which we came out, and we drive by a cross road, and strike the Paseo de Tacón at its outer end, where is a fountain and statue, and a public garden of the most exquisite flowers, shrubs, and trees; and around them are standing, though it is nearly dark, files of carriages waiting for the promenaders, who are enjoying a walk in the garden. I am able to take the entire drive of the Paseo. It is straight, very wide, with two carriageways and two footways, with rows of trees between, and at three points has a statue and a fountain. One of these statues, if I recollect aright, is of Tacón; one of a Queen of Spain; and one is an allegorical figure. The Paseo is two or three miles in length; reaching from the Campo de Marte, just outside the walls, to the last statue and public garden, on gradually ascending ground, and lined with beautiful villas, and rich gardens full of tropical trees and plants. No city in America has such an avenue as the Paseo de Tacón. This, like most of the glories of Havana, they tell you they owe to the energy and genius of the man whose name it bears.—I must guard myself, by the way, while here, against using the words America and American, when I mean the United States and the people of our Republic; for this is America also; and they here use the word America as including the entire continent and islands, and distinguish between Spanish and English America, the islands and the main.

The Cubans have a taste for prodigality in grandiloquent or pretty names. Every shop, the most humble, has its name. They name the shops after the sun and moon and stars; after gods and goddesses, demi-gods and heroes; after fruits and flowers, gems and precious stones; after favorite names of women, with pretty, fanciful additions; and after all alluring qualities, all delights of the senses, and all pleasing affections of the mind. The wards of jails and hospitals are each known by some religious or patriotic designation; and twelve guns in the Morro are named for the Apostles. Every town has the name of an apostle or saint, or of some sacred subject. The full name of Havana, in honor of Columbus, is San Cristóbal de la Habana; and that of Matanzas is San Carlos Alcázar de Matanzas. It is strange that the island itself has defied all the Spanish attempts to name it. It has been solemnly named Juana, after the daughter of Ferdinand and Isabella; then Ferdinandina, after Ferdinand himself; then Santiago, and, lastly, Ave María; but it has always fallen back upon the original Indian name of Cuba. And the only compensation to the hyperbolical taste of the race is that they decorate it, on state and ceremonious occasions, with the musical prefix of "La siempre fidelísima Isla de Cuba."

At 7.30 P.M. went with my New York fellow-passengers to hear an opera, or, more correctly, to see the people of Havana at an opera. The Teatro de Tacón is closed for repairs. This is unfortunate, as it is said by some to be the finest theater, and by all to be one of the three finest theaters in the world. This, too, is attributed to Tacón; although it is said to have been a speculation of a clever pirate turned fish-dealer, who made a fortune by it. But I like well enough the Teatro de Villanueva. The stage is deep and wide, the pit high and comfortable, and the boxes light and airy and open in front, with only a light tracery of iron to support the rails, leaving you a full view of the costumes of the ladies, even to their slippers. The boxes are also separated from the passage-ways in the rear, only by wide lattice work; so that the promenaders between the acts can see the entire contents of the boxes at one view; and the ladies dress and sit and talk and use the fan with a full sense that they are under the inspection of a "committee of the whole house." They are all in full dress, décolletées, without hats. It seemed, to my fancy, that the mature women were divisible into two classes, distinctly marked and with few intermediates—the obese and the shrivelled. I suspect that the effect of time in this climate is to produce a decided result in the one direction or the other. But a single night's view at an opera is very imperfect material for an induction, I admit. The young ladies had, generally, full figures, with tapering fingers and well-rounded arms; yet there were some in the extreme contrast of sallow, bilious, sharp countenances, with glassy eyes. There is evidently great attention to manner, to the mode of sitting and moving, to the music of the voice in speaking, the use of the hands and arms, and, perhaps it may be ungallant to add, of the eyes.

The Governor-General, Concha (whose title is, strictly, Capitan-General), with his wife and two daughters, and two aides-de-camp, is in the Vice-regal box, hung with red curtains, and surmounted by the royal arms. I can form no opinion of him from his physiognomy, as that is rather heavy, and gives not much indication.

Between the acts, I make, as all the gentlemen do, the promenade of the house. All parts of it are respectable, and the regulations are good. I notice one curious custom, which I am told prevails in all Spanish theaters. As no women sit in the pit, and the boxes are often hired for the season, and are high-priced, a portion of an upper tier is set apart for those women and children who cannot or do not choose to get seats in the boxes. Their quarter is separated from the rest of the house by gates, and is attended by two or three old women, with a man to guard the entrance. No men are admitted among them, and their parents, brothers, cousins, and beaux are allowed only to come to the door, and must send in refreshments, and even a cup of water, by the hands of the dueñas.

Military, on duty, abound at the doors and in the passage-ways. The men to-night are of the regiment of Guards, dressed in white. There are enough of them to put down a small insurrection, on the spot. The singers screamed well enough, and the play was a poor one, *María de Rohan,* but the prima donna, Gazzaniga, is a favorite, and the excitable Cubans shout and scream, and throw bouquets, and jump on the benches, and, at last, present her with a crown, wreathed with flowers, and with jewels of value attached to it. Miss Adelaide Phillips is here, too, and a favorite, and has been crowned, they say; but she does not sing to-night.

TO-MORROW, I AM TO GO, AT EIGHT O'CLOCK, either to the church of San Domingo, to hear the military mass, or to the Jesuit church of Belén; for the service of my own church is not publicly celebrated, even at the British consulate, no service but the Roman Catholic being tolerated on the island.

To-night there is a public máscara (mask ball) at the great hall, next door to Le Grand's. My only window is by the side of the numerous windows of the great hall, and all these are wide open; and I should be stifled if I were to close mine. The music is loud and violent, from a very large band, with kettle drums and bass drums and trumpets; and because these do not make noise and uproar enough, leather bands are snapped, at the turns in the tunes. For sleeping, I might as well have been stretched on the bass drum. This tumult of noises, and the heat are wearing and oppressive beyond endurance, as it draws on past midnight, to the small hours; and the servants in the court of the hall seem to be tending at tables of quarrelling men, and to be interminably washing and breaking dishes. After several feverish hours, I light a match and look at my watch. It is nearly five o'clock in the morning. There is an hour to daylight—and will this noise stop before then? The city clocks struck five; the music ceased; and the bells of the convents and monasteries tolled their matins, to call the nuns and monks to their prayers and to the bedsides of the sick and dying in the hospitals, as the maskers go home from their revels at this hideous hour of Sunday morning. The servants ceased their noises, the cocks began to crow and the bells to chime, the trumpets began to bray, and the cries of the streets broke in before dawn, and I dropped asleep just as I was thinking sleep past hoping for; when I am awakened by a knocking at the door, and Antonio calling, "Usted! Usted! Un caballero quiere ver à Usted!" to find it half-past nine, the middle of the forenoon, and an ecclesiastic in black dress and shovel hat, waiting in the passage-way, with a message from the bishop.

His Excellency regrets not having seen me the day before, and invites me to dinner at three o'clock, to meet three or four gentlemen, an invitation which I accept with pleasure.

I am too late for the mass, or any other religious service, as all the churches close at ten o'clock. A tepid, soothing bath, at "Los baños públicos," round the corner, and I spend the morning in my chamber. As we are at breakfast, the troops pass by the Paseo, from the mass service. Their gait is quick and easy, with swinging arms, after the French fashion. Their dress is seersucker, with straw hats and red cockades: the regiments being distinguished by the color of the cloth on the cuffs of the coat, some being yellow, some green, and some blue.

Soon after two o'clock, I take a carriage for the bishop's. On my way out I see that the streets are full of Spanish sailors from the men-of-war, ashore for a holiday, dressed in the style of English sailors, with wide duck trousers, blue jackets, and straw hats, with the name of their ship on the front of the hat. All business is going on as usual, and laborers are at work in the streets and on the houses.

The company consists of the bishop himself, the Bishop of Puebla de los Ángeles in Mexico, Father Yuch, the rector of the Jesuit College, who has a high reputation as a man of intellect, and two young ecclesiastics. Our dinner is well cooked, and in the Spanish style, consisting of fish, vegetables, fruits, and of stewed light dishes, made up of vegetables, fowls and other meats, a style of cooking well adapted to a climate in which one is very willing to dispense with the solid, heavy cuts of an English dinner.

The Bishop of Puebla wore the purple, the Bishop of Havana a black robe with a broad cape, lined with red, and each wore the Episcopal cross and ring. The others were in simple black cassocks. The conversation was in French; for, to my surprise, none of the company could speak English; and being allowed my election between French and Spanish, I chose the former, as the lighter infliction on my associates.

I am surprised to see what an impression is made on all classes in this country by the pending "Thirty Millions Bill" of Mr. Slidell. It is known to be an Administration measure, and is thought to be the first step in a series which is to end in an attempt to seize the island. Our steamer brought oral intelligence that it had passed the Senate, and it was so announced in the *Diario* of the day after our arrival, although no newspaper that we brought so stated it. Not only with these clergymen, but with the merchants and others whom I have met since our arrival, foreigners as well as Cubans, this is the absorbing topic. Their future seems to be hanging in doubt, depending on the action of our government, which is thought to have a settled purpose to acquire the island. I suggested that it had not passed the Senate, and would not pass the House; and, at most, was only an authority to the President to make an offer that would certainly be refused. But they looked beyond the form of the act, and regarded it as the first move in a plan, of which, although they could not entirely know the details, they thought they understood the motive.

These clergymen were well informed as to the state of religion in the United States, the relative numbers and force of the various denominations, and their doctrinal differences; the reputations of Brownson, Parker, Beecher, and others; and most minutely acquainted with the condition of their own church in the United States, and with the chief of its clergy. This acquaintance is not attributable solely to their unity of organization, and to the consequent interchange of communication, but largely also to the tie of a common education at the Propaganda or St. Sulpice, the catalogues of whose alumni are familiar to the educated Catholic clergy throughout the world.

The subject of slavery, and the condition and prospects of the Negro race in Cuba, the probable results of the coolie system, and the relations between Church and State in Cuba, and the manner in which Sunday is treated in Havana, the public school system in America, the fate of Mormonism, and how our government will treat it, were freely discussed. It is not because I have any reason to suppose that these gentlemen would object to all they said being printed in these pages, and read by all who may choose to read it in Cuba, or the United States, that I do not report their interesting and instructive conversation; but because it would be, in my opinion, a violation of the universal understanding among gentlemen.

After dinner, we walked on the piazza, with the noble sunset view of the unsurpassed panorama lying before us; and I took my leave of my host, a kind and courteous gentleman of Old Spain, as well as a prelate, just as a few lights were beginning to sprinkle over the fading city, and the Morro Light to gleam on the untroubled air.

Made two visits in the city this evening. In each house, I found the double row of chairs, facing each other, always with about four or five feet of space between the rows. The etiquette is that the gentlemen sit on the row opposite to the ladies, if there be but two or three present. If a lady, on entering, goes to the side of a gentleman, when the other row is open to her, it indicates either familiar acquaintance or boldness. There is no people so observant of outguards, as the Spanish race.

I notice, and my observation is supported by what I am told by the residents here, that there is no street-walking, in the technical sense, in Havana. Whether this is from the fact that no ladies walk in the streets—which are too narrow for comfortable or even safe walking—or by reason of police regulations, I do not know. From what one meets with in the streets, if he does not look farther, one would not know that there was a vice in Havana, not even drunkenness.

ANTHONY TROLLOPE

Havana, 1859

"THERE IS NOTHING ATTRACTIVE ABOUT THE TOWN OF
HAVANA."

By the time Anthony Trollope saw Cuba, in 1859, he was forty-three years old and, following the unhappy poverty of his youth and several years of unrewarding work, had already achieved success in two fields of endeavor.

In 1841 he took a job with Great Britain's General Post Office, working as a surveyor's clerk in Ireland. He did well with the post office and advanced steadily, eventually rising to the level of inspector.

A few years after he went to work for the post office, he began writing novels, and his first books, though not successful commercially, won some positive critical notice. Then, in 1855, The Warden *brought him popular success, solidified in 1857 with the publication of* Barchester Towers, *which broadened the scope of his newly conceived Barsetshire chronicles.*

In 1858, the post office sent Trollope on a mission to inspect and secure postal service for Great Britain in Egypt. This trip was so successful that he was immediately ordered off to perform similar services in the Caribbean and Central America. He traveled first to Jamaica and then to Cuba, where he negotiated a postal treaty with the Spanish authorities. "From Cuba," he wrote in his 1883 Autobiography, "I made my way to St. Thomas, and through the island down to Demerara, then back to St. Thomas,—which is the starting-point for all places in that part of the globe,—to Santa Martha, Carthagena, Aspinwall, over the Isthmus to Panama, up the Pacific to a little harbour on the coast of Costa Rica, thence across Central America, through Costa Rica, and down the Nicaraguan rivers to the Musquito coast, and after that home by Bermuda and New York." He makes an extensive and difficult journey sound quite orderly and tidy.

Indeed, Trollope was famously orderly in his writing habits, applying himself to his work on trains and ships, wherever he might be, and always setting himself a certain number of pages before breakfast every day. He went at his work, he wrote, "just like a shoemaker on a shoe, only taking care to make honest stitches."

Before sailing for Jamaica, Trollope approached his publishers, Chapman and Hall, and proposed writing a book about his travels. They agreed to his demand for £250. Trollope began the book in January 1859, during an uncomfortably protracted voyage from Kingston, Jamaica, to Cienfuegos, Cuba. By the time he returned to Great Britain, the book was finished. The West Indies and the Spanish Main was published that same year, 1859. It was so successful that Trollope soon visited Messrs. Chapman and Hall again and demanded—and got—£600 for his next novel.

Readers of Trollope's wonderfully engaging novels know that he had a sharp and penetrating eye for the foibles of both individuals and society at large, and that his powers of description were nothing less than brilliant. These traits are all present in his travel writing, which later included volumes on North America, Australia and New Zealand, and South Africa.

Writing about The West Indies and the Spanish Main in 1883 in his Autobiography, Trollope declares, "The fact memorable to me now is that I never made a single note while writing or preparing it. Preparation, indeed, there was none. The descriptions and opinions came hot on to the paper from their causes. I will not say that this is the best way of writing a book intended to give accurate information. But it is the best way of producing to the eye of the reader, and to his ear, that which the eye of the writer has seen and his ear heard."

Trollope was a willing and curious traveler, but a stern one, whose opinions do come "hot on to the paper." When he finds fault, he can be politely scathing. And when the fault is his own, he is no less critical.

Departing Kingston for Cuba, he could have taken the standard route, through the Danish island of St. Thomas. "But I was ambitious," he writes, "of a quicker transit and a less beaten path, and here I am lying under the lee of the land, in a dirty, hot, motionless tub, expiating my folly. . . . Motionless, I said; I wish she were. Progressless should have been my word. She rolls about in a nauseous manner, disturbing the two sardines which I have economically eaten."

Before departing Kingston for Cuba, he had, of course, to obtain the proper permission from the local Spanish authority, and on this he writes with all the straight-faced humor of a Jane Austen. "I have before me the Spanish passport, for which I paid sixteen shillings in Kingston the day before I left it. It is simply signed Pedro Badan. But it is headed Don Pedro Badan Calderon de la Barca, which sounds to me very much as though I were to call myself Mr. Anthony Trollope Ben Jonson. To this will be answered that such might have been my name. But then I should not have signed myself Anthony Trollope. The gentleman, however, has doubtless been right according to his Spanish lights; and the name sounds very grand, especially as there is added to it two lines declaring how that Don Pedro Badan is a Caballero. He was as dignified a personage as a Spanish Don should be, and seemed somewhat particular about the sixteen shillings, as Spanish and other Dons generally are."

After his patience has been sorely tried in Jamaica and on the voyage from Jamaica, Trollope approaches at last the southern coast of Cuba.

In the pages that follow, it is especially interesting to note the space Trollope devotes to the volante, the stylish Cuban horse-drawn conveyance of the nineteenth century. He is absolutely right in noting its great importance in Cuban society.

Cubans have long been especially interested in such modes of transportation, which perhaps explains—along with dire necessity—the miracles of preservation performed today on pre-1960 American automobiles. In the nineteenth century, pictures of a broad variety of horse-drawn vehicles constituted a thriving and popular genre of Cuban painting, and at the turn of the century, any home with aspirations to dignity proudly displayed several on its walls.

CUBA IS THE LARGEST AND THE MOST westerly of the west Indian islands. It is in the shape of a half-moon, and with one of its horns nearly lies across the mouth of the Gulf of Mexico. It belongs to the Spanish crown, of which it is by far the most splendid appendage. So much for facts—geographical and historical.

The journey from Kingston to Cien Fuegos, of which I have said somewhat in my first chapter, was not completed under better auspices than those which witnessed its commencement. That perfidious bark, built in the eclipse, was bad to the last, and my voyage took nine days instead of three. My humble stock of provisions had long been all gone, and my patience was nearly at as low an ebb. Then, as a finale, the Cuban pilot who took us in hand as we entered the port ran us on shore just under the Spanish fort, and there left us. From this position it was impossible to escape, though the shore lay close to us, inasmuch as it is an offence of the gravest nature to land in those ports without the ceremony of a visit from the medical officer; and no medical officer would come to us there. And then two of our small crew had been taken sick, and we had before us in our mind's eye all the pleasures of quarantine.

A man, and especially an author, is thankful for calamities if they be of a tragic dye. It would be as good as a small fortune to be left for three days without food or water, or to run for one's life before a black storm on unknown seas in a small boat. But we had no such luck as this. There was plenty of food, though it was not very palatable; and the peril of our position cannot be insisted on, as we might have thrown a baby on shore from the vessel, let alone a biscuit. We did what we could to get up a catastrophe among the sharks, by bathing off the ship's sides. But even this was in vain. One small shark we did see. But in lieu of it eating us, we ate it. In spite of the popular prejudice, I have to declare that it was delicious.

But at last I did find myself in the hotel at Cien Fuegos. And here I must say a word in praise of the civility of the Spanish authorities of that town and, indeed, of those gentlemen generally wherever I chanced to meet them. They welcome you with easy courtesy; offer you coffee or beer; assure you at parting that their whole house is at your disposal; and then load you—at least they so loaded me—with cigars.

"My friend," said the captain of the port, holding in his hand a huge parcel of these articles, each about seven inches long—"I wish I could do you a service. It would make me happy for ever if I could truly serve you."

"Señor, the service you have done me is inestimable in allowing me to make the acquaintance of Don ———."

"But at least accept these few cigars;" and then he pressed the bundle into my hand, and pressed his own hand over mine. "Smoke one daily after dinner; and when you procure any that are better, do a fastidious old smoker the great kindness to inform him where they are to be found."

This treasure to which his fancy alluded, but in the existence of which he will never believe, I have not yet discovered.

Cien Fuegos is a small new town on the southern coast of Cuba, created by the sugar trade, and devoted, of course, to commerce. It is clean, prosperous, and quickly increasing. Its streets are lighted with gas, while those in the Havana still depend upon oil-lamps. It has its opera, its governor's house, its alaméda, its military and public hospital, its market-place, and railway station; and unless the engineers deceive themselves, it will in time have its well. It has also that institution which in the eyes of travellers ranks so much above all others, a good and clean inn.

My first object after landing was to see a slave sugar estate. I had been told in Jamaica that to effect this required some little management; that the owners of the slaves were not usually willing to allow strangers to see them at work; and that the manufacture of sugar in Cuba was as a rule kept sacred from profane eyes. But I found no such difficulty. I made my request to an English merchant at Cien Fuegos, and he gave me a letter of introduction to the proprietor of an estate some fifteen miles from the town; and by their joint courtesy I saw all that I wished.

On this property, which consisted altogether of eighteen hundred acres—the greater portion of which was not yet under cultivation—there were six hundred acres of cane pieces. The average year's produce was eighteen hundred hogsheads, or three hogsheads to the acre. The hogshead was intended to represent a ton of sugar when it reached the market, but judging from all that I could learn it usually fell short of it by more than a hundredweight. The value of such a hogshead at Cien Fuegos was about twenty-five pounds. There were one hundred and fifty negro men on the estate, the average cash value of each man being three hundred and fifty pounds; most of the men had their wives. In stating this it must not be supposed that either I or my informant insist much on the validity of their marriage ceremony; any such ceremony was probably of rare occurrence. During the crop time, at which period my visit was made, and which lasts generally from November till May, the negroes sleep during six hours out of the twenty-four, have two for their meals, and work for sixteen! No difference is made on Sunday. Their food is very plentiful, and of a good and strong description. They are sleek and fat and large, like well-preserved brewers' horses; and with reference to them, as also with reference to the brewers' horses, it has probably been ascertained what amount of work may be exacted so as to give the greatest profit. During the remainder of the year the labour of the negroes averages twelve hours a day, and one day of rest in the week is usually allowed to them.

I was of course anxious to see what was the nature of the coercive measures used with them. But in this respect my curiosity was not indulged. I can only say that I saw none, and saw the mark and signs of none. No doubt the whip is in use, but I did not see it. The gentleman whose estate I visited had no notice of our coming, and there was no appearance of anything being hidden from us. I could not, however, bring myself to inquire of him as to their punishment.

The slaves throughout the island are always as a rule baptized. Those who are employed in the town and as household servants appear to be educated in compliance with, at any rate the outward doctrines of, the Roman Catholic church. But with the great mass of the negroes—those who work on the sugarcanes—all attention to religion ends with their baptism. They have the advantage, whatever it may be, of that ceremony in infancy; and from that time forth they are treated as the beasts of the stall.

From all that I could hear, as well as from what I could see, I have reason to think that, regarding them as beasts, they are well treated. Their hours of labour are certainly very long—so long as to appear almost impossible to a European workman. But under the system, such as it is, the men do not apparently lose their health, though, no doubt, they become prematurely old, and as a rule die early. The property is too valuable to be neglected or ill used. The object of course is to make that property pay; and therefore a present healthy condition is cared for, but long life is not regarded. It is exactly the same with horses in this country.

When all has been said that can be said in favour of the slave-owner in Cuba, it comes to this—that he treats his slaves as beasts of burden, and so treating them, does it skilfully and with prudence. The point which most shocks an Englishman is the absence of all religion, the ignoring of the black man's soul. But this, perhaps, may be taken as an excuse, that the white men here ignore their own souls also. The Roman Catholic worship seems to be at a lower ebb in Cuba than almost any country in which I have seen it.

It is singular that no priest should even make any effort on the subject with regard to the negroes; but I am assured that such is the fact. They do not wish to do so; nor will they allow of any one asking them to make the experiment. One would think that had there been any truth or any courage in them, they would have declared the inutility of baptism, and have proclaimed that negroes have no souls. But there is no truth in them; neither is there any courage.

The works at the Cuban sugar estate were very different from those I had seen at Jamaica. They were on a much larger scale, in much better order, overlooked by a larger proportion of white men, with a greater amount of skilled labour. The evidences of capital were very plain in Cuba; whereas, the want of it was frequently equally plain in our own island.

Not that the planters in Cuba are as a rule themselves very rich men. The estates are deeply mortgaged to the different merchants at the different ports, as are those in Jamaica to the merchants of Kingston. These merchants in Cuba are generally Americans, Englishmen, Germans, Spaniards from the American republics—anything but Cubans; and the slave-owners are but the go-betweens, who secure the profits of the slave-trade for the merchants.

My friend at the estate invited us to a late breakfast after having shown me what I came to see. "You have taken me so unawares," said he, "that we cannot offer you much except a welcome." Well, it was not much—for Cuba perhaps. A delicious soup, made partly of eggs, a bottle of excellent claret, a paté de foie gras, some game deliciously dressed, and half a dozen kinds of vegetables; that was all. I had seen nothing among the slaves which in any way interfered with my appetite, or with the cup of coffee and cigar which came after the little nothings above mentioned.

We then went down to the railway station. It was a peculiar station I was told, and the tickets could not be paid for till we reached Cien Fuegos. But, lo! on arriving at Cien Fuegos there was nothing more to pay. "It has all been done," said someone to me.

If one was but convinced that those sleek, fat, smiling bipeds were but two legged beasts of burden, and nothing more, all would have been well at the estate which we visited.

All Cuba was of course full of the late message from the President of the United States, which at the time of my visit was some two months old there. The purport of what Mr. Buchanan said regarding Cuba may perhaps be expressed as follows:—"Circumstances and destiny absolutely require that the United States should be the masters of that island. That we should take it by filibustering or violence is not in accordance with our national genius. It will suit our character and honesty much better that we should obtain it by purchase. Let us therefore offer a fair price for it. If a fair price be refused, that of course will be a casus belli. Spain will then have injured us, and we may declare war. Under these circumstances we should probably obtain the place without purchase; but let us hope better things." This is what the President has said, either in plain words or by inference equally plain.

It may easily be conceived with what feeling such an announcement has been received by Spain and those who hold Spanish authority in Cuba. There is an outspoken insolence in the threat, which, by a first-class power, would itself have been considered a cause for war. But Spain is not a first-class power, and like the other weak ones of the earth must either perish or live by adhering to and obeying those who will protect her. Though too ignoble to be strong, she has been too proud to be obedient. And as a matter of course she will go to the wall.

A scrupulous man who feels that he would fain regulate his course in politics by the same line as that used for his ordinary life cannot but feel angry at the loud tone of America's audacious threat. But even such a one knows that that threat will sooner or later be carried out, and that humanity will benefit by its accomplishment. Perhaps it may be said that scrupulous men should have but little dealing in state policy.

The plea under which Mr. Buchanan proposes to quarrel with Spain, if she will not sell that which America wishes to buy, is the plea under which Ahab quarrelled with Naboth. A man is, individually, disgusted that a President of the United States should have made such an utterance. But looking at the question in a broader point of view, in one which regards future ages rather than the present time, one can hardly refrain from rejoicing at any event which will tend to bring about that which in itself is so desirable.

We reprobate the name of filibuster, and have a holy horror of the trade. And it is perhaps fortunate that with us the age of individual filibustering is well-nigh gone by. But it may be fair for us to consider whether we have not in our younger days done as much in this line as have the Americans—whether Clive, for instance, was not a filibuster—or Warren Hastings. Have we not annexed, and maintained, and encroached; protected, and assumed, and taken possession in the East—doing it all of course for the good of humanity? And why should we begrudge the same career to America?

That we do begrudge it is certain. That she purchased California and took Texas went at first against the grain with us; and Englishmen, as a rule, would wish to maintain Cuba in the possession of Spain. But what Englishman who thinks about it will doubt that California and Texas have thriven since they were annexed, as they never could have thriven while forming part of the Mexican empire—or can doubt that Cuba, if delivered up to the States, would gain infinitely by such a change of masters?

Filibustering, called by that or some other name, is the destiny of a great portion of that race to which we Englishmen and Americans belong. It would be a bad profession probably for a scrupulous man. With the unscrupulous man, what stumbling-blocks there may be between his deeds and his conscience is for his consideration and for God's judgment. But it will hardly suit us as a nation to be loud against it. By what other process have poor and weak races been compelled to give way to those who have power and energy? And who have displaced so many of the poor and weak, and spread abroad so vast an energy, such an extent of power as we of England?

The truth may perhaps be this:—that a filibuster needs expect no good word from his fellow-mortals till he has proved his claim to it by success.

From such information as I could obtain, I am of opinion that the Cubans themselves would be glad enough to see the transfer well effected. How, indeed, can it be otherwise? At present they have no national privilege except that of undergoing taxation. Every office is held by a Spaniard. Every soldier in the island—and they say that there are twenty-five thousand—must be a Spaniard. The ships of war are commanded and manned by Spaniards. All that is shown before their eyes of brilliancy and power and high place is purely Spanish. No Cuban has any voice in his own country. He can never have the consolation of thinking that his tyrant is his countryman, or reflect that under altered circumstances it might possibly have been his fortune to tyrannize. What love can he have for Spain?

He cannot even have the poor pride of being slave to a great lord. He is the lacquey of a reduced gentleman, and lives on the vails of those who despise his master. Of course the transfer would be grateful to him.

But no Cuban will himself do anything to bring it about. To wish is one thing; to act is another. A man standing behind his counter may feel that his hand is restricted on every side, and his taxes alone unrestricted; but he must have other than Hispano-Creole blood in his veins if he do more than stand and feel. Indeed, wishing is too strong a word to be fairly applicable to his state of mind. He would be glad that Cuba should be American; but he would prefer that he himself should lie in a dormant state while the dangerous transfer is going on.

I have ventured to say that humanity would certainly be benefited by such a transfer. We, when we think of Cuba, think of it almost entirely as a slave country. And, indeed, in this light, and in this light only, is it peculiar, being the solitary land into which slaves are now systematically imported out of Africa. Into that great question of guarding the slave coast it would be futile here to enter; but this I believe is acknowledged, that if the Cuban market be closed against the trade, the trade must perish of exhaustion. At present slaves are brought into Cuba in spite of us; and as we all know, can be brought in under the American stars and stripes. But no one accuses the American Government of systematically favouring an importation of Africans into their own States. When Cuba becomes one of them the trade will cease. The obstacle to that trade which is created by our vessels of war on the coast of Africa may, or may not, be worth the cost. But no man who looks into the subject will presume to say that we can be as efficacious there as the Americans would be if they were the owners of the present slave-market.

I do not know whether it be sufficiently understood in England, that though slavery is an institution of the United States, the slave-trade, as commonly understood under that denomination, is as illegal there as in England. That slavery itself would be continued in Cuba under the Americans—continued for a while—is of course certain. So is it in Louisiana and the

Carolinas. But the horrors of the middle passage, the kidnapping of negroes, the African wars which are waged for the sake of prisoners, would of necessity come to an end.

But this slave-trade is as opposed to the laws of Spain and its colonies as it is to those of the United States or of Great Britain. This is true; and were the law carried out in Cuba as well as it is in the United States, an Englishman would feel disinclined to look on with calmness at the violent dismemberment of the Spanish empire. But in Cuba the law is broken systematically. The Captain-General in Cuba will allow no African to be imported into the island—except for a consideration. It is said that the present Captain-General receives only a gold doubloon, or about three pounds twelve shillings, on every head of wool so brought in; and he has therefore the reputation of being a very moderate man. O'Donnel required twice as large a bribe. Valdez would take nothing, and he is spoken of as the foolish Governor. Even he, though he would take no bribe, was not allowed to throw obstacles in the way of the slave-trade. That such a bribe is usually demanded, and as a matter of course paid, is as well known—ay, much better known, than any other of the island port duties. The fact is so notorious to all men that it is almost as absurd to insist on it as it would be to urge that the income of the Queen of England is paid from the taxes. It is known to every one, and among others is known to the government of Spain. Under these circumstances, who can feel sympathy with her, or wish that she should retain her colony? Does she not daily show that she is unfit to hold it?

There must be some stage in misgovernment which will justify the interference of bystanding nations, in the name of humanity. That rule in life which forbids a man to come between a husband and his wife is a good rule. But nevertheless, who can stand by quiescent and see a brute half murder the poor woman whom he should protect?

And in other ways, and through causes also, humanity would be benefited by such a transfer. We in England are not very fond of a republic. We would hardly exchange our throne for a president's chair, or even dispense at present with our House of Peers or our Bench of Bishops. But we can see that men thrive under the stars and stripes; whereas they pine beneath the red and yellow flag of Spain. This, it may be said, is attributable to the race of the men rather than to the government. But the race will be improved by the infusion of new blood. Let the world say what chance there is of such improvement in the Spanish government.

The trade of the country is falling into the hands of foreigners—into those principally of Americans from the States. The Havana will soon become as much American as New Orleans. It requires but little of the spirit of prophecy to foretell that the Spanish rule will not be long obeyed by such people.

On the whole I cannot see how Englishmen can refrain from sympathizing with the desire of the United States to become possessed of this fertile island. As far as we ourselves are concerned, it would be infinitely for our benefit. We can trade with the United States when we can hardly do so with Spain. Moreover, if Jamaica, and the smaller British islands can ever again hold up their heads against Cuba as sugar-producing colonies, it will be when the slave-trade has been abolished. Till such time it can never be.

And then where are our professions for the amelioration, and especially for the Christianity of the human race? I have said what is the religious education of the slaves in Cuba. I may also say that in this island no place of Protestant worship exists, or is possible. The Roman Catholic religion is alone allowed, and that is at its very lowest point. "The old women of both sexes go to mass," a Spaniard told me; "and the girls when their clothes are new."

But above all things it behoves us to rid ourselves of the jealousy which I fear we too often feel towards American pretension. "Jonathan is getting bumptious," we are apt to say; "he ought to have—" this and that other punishment, according to the taste of the offended Englishman.

Jonathan is becoming bumptious, no doubt. Young men of genius, when they succeed in life at comparatively early years, are generally afflicted more or less with this disease. But one is not inclined to throw aside as useless the intellect, energy, and genius of youth because it is not accompanied by modesty, grace, and self-denial. Do we not, in regard to all our friends, take the good that we find in them, aware that in the very best there will be some deficiency to forgive? That young barrister who is so bright, so energetic, so useful, is perhaps *soi-disant* more than a little. One cannot deny it. But age will cure that. Have we a right to expect that he should be perfect?

And are the Americans the first bumptious people on record? Has no other nation assumed itself to be in advance of the world; to be the apostle of progress, the fountain of liberty, the rock-spring of manly work? If the Americans were not bumptious, how unlike would they be to the parent that bore them!

The world is wide enough for us and for our offspring, and we may be well content that we have it nearly all between us. Let them fulfil their destiny in the West, while we do so in the East. It may be that there also we may establish another child who in due time shall also run alone, shall also boast somewhat loudly of its own doings. It is a proud reflection that we alone, of all people, have such children; a proud reflection, and a joyous one; though the weaning of the baby will always be in some respects painful to the mother.

Nowhere have I met a kinder hospitality than I did at Cien Fuegos, whether from Spaniards, Frenchmen, Americans, or Englishmen; for at Cien Fuegos there are men of all these countries. But I must specify my friend Mr. M——. Why should such a man be shut up for life at such an outlandish place? Full of wit, singing an excellent song, telling a story better, I think, than any other man to whom I have ever listened, speaking four or five languages fluently, pleasant in manner, hospitable in heart, a thorough good fellow at all points, why should he bury himself at Cien Fuegos? "Auri sacra fames." It is the presumable reason for all such burials. English reader, shouldst thou find thyself in Cien Fuegos in thy travels, it will not take thee long to discover my friend M——. He is there known to every one. It will only concern thee to see that thou art worthy of his acquaintance.

From Cien Fuegos I went to the Havana, the metropolis, as all the world knows, of Cuba. Our route lay by steamer to Batavano, and thence by railway. The communication round Cuba—that is from port to port—is not ill arranged or ill conducted. The boats are American built, and engineered by

Englishmen or Americans. Breakfast and dinner are given on board, and the cost is included in the sum paid for the fare. The provisions are plentiful, and not bad, if oil can be avoided. As everything is done to foster Spain, Spanish wine is always used, and Spanish ware, and, above all things, Spanish oil. Now Spain does not send her best oil to her colonies. I heard great complaint made of the fares charged on board these boats. The fares when compared with those charged in America doubtless are high; but I do not know that any one has a right to expect that he shall travel as cheaply in Cuba as in the States.

I had heard much of the extravagant charges made for all kinds of accommodation in Cuba; at hotels, in the shops, for travelling, for chance work, and the general wants of a stranger. I found these statements to be much exaggerated. Railway travelling by the first class is about 3½d. a mile, which is about 1d. a mile more than in England. At hotels the charge is two and a half or three dollars a day. The former sum is the more general. This includes a cup of coffee in the morning, a very serious meal at nine o'clock together with fairly good Catalan wine, dinner at four with another cup of coffee and more wine *ad libitum*, bed, and attendance. Indeed, a man may go out of his hotel, without inconvenience, paying nothing beyond the regular daily charge. Extras are dear. I, for instance, having in my ignorance asked for a bottle of champagne, paid for it seventeen shillings. A friend dining with one also, or breakfasting, is an expensive affair. The two together cost considerably more than one's own total daily payment. Thus, as one pays at an hotel whether one's dinner be eaten or no, it becomes almost an insane expense for friends at different hotels to invite each other.

But let it not be supposed that I speak in praise of the hotels at the Havana. Far be it from me to do so. I only say that they are not dear. I found it impossible to command the luxury of a bedroom to myself. It was not the custom of the country they told me. If I chose to pay five dollars a day, just double the usual price, I could be indulged as soon—as circumstances would admit of it; which was intended to signify that they would be happy to charge me for the second bed as soon as the time should come that they had no one else on whom to levy the rate. And the dirt of that bedroom!

I had been unable to get into either of the hotels at the Havana to which I had been recommended, every corner in each having been appropriated. In my grief at the dirt of my abode, and at the too near vicinity of my Spanish neighbour—the fellow-occupant of my chamber was from Spain—I complained somewhat bitterly to an American acquaintance, who had as I thought been more lucky in his inn.

"One companion!" said he; "why, I have three; one walks about all night in a bed-gown, a second snores, and the other is dying!"

A friend of mine, an English officer, was at another house. He also was one of four; and it so occurred that he lost thirty pounds out of his sac de nuit. On the whole I may consider myself to have been lucky.

Labour generally is dear, a workman getting a dollar or four shillings and twopence, where in England a man might earn perhaps half a crown. A porter therefore for whom sixpence might suffice in England will require a shilling. A volante—I shall have a word to say about volantes by-and-by—for any distance within the walls costs eightpence. Outside the walls the price seems to be unconscionably higher. Omnibuses which run over two miles charge some fraction over sixpence for each journey. I find that a pair of boots cost me twenty-five shillings. In London they would cost about the same. Those procured in Cuba, however, were worth nothing, which certainly makes a difference. Meat is eightpence the English pound. Bread is somewhat dearer than in England, but not much.

House rent may be taken as being nearly four times as high as it is in any decent but not fashionable part of London, and the wages of house servants are twice as high as they are with us. The high prices in the Havana are such therefore as to affect the resident rather than the stranger. One article, however, is very costly; but as it concerns a luxury not much in general use among the inhabitants this is not surprising. If a man will have his linen washed he will be made to pay for it.

There is nothing attractive about the town of Havana; nothing whatever to my mind, if we except the harbour. The streets are narrow, dirty, and foul. In this respect there is certainly much difference between those within and without the wall. The latter are wider, more airy, and less vile. But even in them there is nothing to justify the praises with which the Havana is generally mentioned in the West Indies. It excels in population, size, and no doubt in wealth any other city there; but this does not imply a great eulogium. The three principal public buildings are the Opera House, the Cathedral, and the palace of the Captain-General. The former has been nearly knocked down by an explosion of gas, and is now closed. I believe it to be an admirable model for a second-rate house. The cathedral is as devoid of beauty, both externally and internally, as such an edifice can be made. To describe such a building would be an absurd waste of time and patience. We all know what is a large Roman Catholic church, built in the worst taste, and by a combination of the lowest attributes of Gothic and Latin architecture. The palace, having been built for a residence, does not appear so utterly vile, though it is the child of some similar father. It occupies one side of a public square or pláza, and from its position has a moderately-imposing effect. Of pictures in the Havana there are none of which mention should be made.

But the glory of the Havana is the Paseo—the glory so called. This is the public drive and fashionable lounge of the town—the Hyde Park, the Bois de Boulogne, the Cascine, the Corso, the Alaméda. It is for their hour on the Paseo that the ladies dress themselves, and the gentlemen prepare their jewelry. It consists of a road running outside a portion of the wall, of the extent perhaps of half a mile, and ornamented with seats and avenues of trees, as are the boulevards at Paris. If it is to be compared with any other resort of the kind in the West Indies, it certainly must be owned there is nothing like it; but a European on first seeing it cannot understand why it is so eulogized. Indeed, it is probable that if he first goes thither alone, as was the case with me, he will pass over it, seeking for some other Paseo.

But then the glory of the Paseo consists in its volantes. As one boasts that one has swum in a gondola, so will one boast of having sat in a volante. It is the pride of Cuban girls to appear on the Paseo in these carriages on the afternoons of holidays and Sundays; and there is certainly enough of the picturesque about the vehicle to make it worthy of some description. It is the most singular of carriages, and its construction is such as to give a flat contradiction to all an Englishman's preconceived notions respecting the power of horses.

The volante is made to hold two sitters, though there is sometimes a low middle seat which affords accommodation to a third lady. We will commence the description from behind. There are two very huge wheels, rough, strong, high, thick, and of considerable weight. The axles generally are not capped, but the nave shines with coarse polished metal. Supported on the axletree, and swinging forward from it on springs, is the body of a cabriolet, such as ordinary cabriolets used to be, with the seat, however, somewhat lower, and with much more room for the feet. The back of this is open, and generally a curtain hangs down over the open space. A metal bar, which is polished so as to look like silver, runs across the footboard and supports the feet. The body, it must be understood, swings forward from these high wheels, so that the whole of the weight, instead of being supported, hangs from it. Then there are a pair of shafts, which, counting from the back of the carriage to the front where they touch the horse at the saddle, are about fourteen feet in length. They do not go beyond the saddle, or the tug depending from the saddle in which they hang. From this immense length it comes to pass that there is a wide interval, exceeding six feet, between the carriage and the horse's tail; and it follows also, from the construction of the machine, that a large portion of the weight must rest on the horse's back.

In addition to this, the unfortunate horse has ordinarily to bear the weight of a rider. For with a volante your servant rides, and does not drive you. With the fashionable world on the Paseo a second horse is used—what we should call an outrider and the servant sits on this. But as regards those which ply in the town, there is but one horse. How animals can work beneath such a yoke was to me unintelligible.

The great point in the volante of fashion is the servant's dress. He is always a negro, and generally a large negro. He wears a huge pair—not of boots, for they have no feet to them—of galligaskins I may call them, made of thick stiff leather, but so as to fit the leg exactly. The top of them comes some nine inches above the knee, so that when one of these men is seen seated at his ease, the point of his boot nearly touches his chin. They are fastened down the sides with metal fastenings, and at the bottom there is a huge spur. The usual dress of these men, over and above their boots, consists of white breeches, red jackets ornamented with gold lace, and broad-brimmed straw hats. Nothing can be more awkward, and nothing more barbaric than the whole affair; but nevertheless there is about it a barbaric splendour, which has its effect. The great length of the equipage, and the distance of the horse from his work, is what chiefly strikes an Englishman.

The carriage usually holds, when on the Paseo, two or three ladies. The great object evidently has been to expand their dresses, so that they may group well together, and with a good result as regards colour. It must be confessed that in this respect they are generally successful. They wear no head-dress when in their carriages, and indeed may generally be seen out of doors with their hair uncovered. Though they are of Spanish descent, the mantilla is unknown here. Nor could I trace such similarity to Spanish manner in other particulars. The ladies do not walk like Spanish women—at least not like the women of Andalusia, with whom one would presume them to have had the nearest connection. The walk of the Andalusian women surpasses that of any other, while the Cuban lady is not graceful in her gait. Neither can they boast the brilliantly dangerous beauty of Seville. In Cuba they have good eyes, but rarely good faces. The forehead and the chin too generally recede, leaving the nose with a prominence that is not agreeable. But as my gallantry has not prevented me from speaking in this uncourteous manner of their appearance, my honesty bids me add, that what they lack in beauty they make up in morals, as compared with their cousins in Europe. For travelling *en garçon*, I should probably prefer the south of Spain. But were I doomed to look for domesticity in either clime—and God forbid that such a doom should be mine!—I might perhaps prefer a Cuban mother for my children.

But the volante is held as very precious by the Cuban ladies. The volante itself, I mean—the actual vehicle. It is not intrusted, as coaches are with us, to the dusty mercies of a coach-house. It is ordinarily kept in the hall, and you pass it by as you enter the house; but it is by no means uncommon to see it in the dining-room. As the rooms are large and usually not full of furniture, it does not look amiss there.

The amusements of the Cubans are not very varied, and are innocent in their nature; for the gambling as carried on there I regard rather as a business than an amusement. They greatly love dancing, and have dances of their own and music of their own, which are peculiar, and difficult to a stranger. Their tunes are striking, and very pretty. They are fond of music generally, and maintain a fairly good opera company at the Havana. In the pláza there—the square, namely, in front of the Captain-General's house—a military band plays from eight to nine every evening. The place is then thronged with people, but by far the majority of them are men.

It is the custom at all the towns in Cuba for the family, when at home, to pass their evening seated near the large low open window of their drawing-rooms; and as these windows almost always look into the streets, the whole internal arrangement is seen by every one who passes. These windows are always protected by iron bars, as though they were the windows of a prison; in other respects they are completely open.

Four chairs are to be seen ranged in a row, and four more opposite to them, running from the window into the room, and placed close together. Between these is generally laid a small piece of carpet. The majority of these chairs are made to rock; for the Creole lady always rocks herself. I have watched them going through the accustomed motion with their bodies, even when seated on chairs with stern immovable legs. This is the usual evening living-place of the family; and I never yet saw an occupant of one of these chairs with a book in her hand, or in his. I asked an Englishman, a resident in Havana, whether he had ever done so. "A book!" he answered; "why, the girls can't read, in your sense of the word reading."

The young men, and many of those who are no longer young, spend their evenings, and apparently a large portion of their days, in eating ices and playing billiards. The accommodation in the Havana for these amusements is on a very large scale.

The harbour at the Havana is an interesting sight. It is in the first place very picturesque, which to the ordinary visitor is the most important feature. But it is also commodious, large, and safe. It is approached between two forts. That to the westward, which is the principal defence, is called the Morro. Here also stands the lighthouse. No Englishman omits to hear, as he enters the harbour, that these forts were taken by the English in Albemarle's time. Now, it seems to me, they might very easily be taken by any one who chose to spend on them the necessary amount of gunpowder. But then I know nothing about forts.

This special one of the Morro I did take; not by gunpowder, but by strategem. I was informed that no one was allowed to see it since the open defiance of the island contained in the last message of the United States' President. But I was also informed—whisperingly, in the ear—that a request to see the lighthouse would be granted, and that as I was not an American the fort should follow. It resulted in a little black boy taking me over the whole edifice—an impudent little black boy, who filled his pockets with stones and pelted the sentries. The view of the harbour from the lighthouse is very good, quite worth the trouble of the visit. The fort itself I did not understand, but a young English officer, who was with me, pooh-poohed it as a thing of nothing. But then young English officers pooh-pooh everything. Here again I must add that nothing can exceed the courtesy of all Spanish officials. If they could only possess honesty and energy as well as courtesy!

By far the most interesting spot in the Havana is the Quay, to which the vessels are fastened end-ways, the bow usually lying against the Quay. In other places the side of the vessel is, I believe, brought to the wharf. Here there are signs of true life. One cannot but think how those quays would be extended, and that life increased, if the place were in the hands of other people.

I have said that I regarded gambling in Cuba, not as an amusement, but an occupation. The public lotteries offer the daily means to every one for gratifying this passion. They are maintained by the government, and afford a profit, I am told, of something over a million dollars per annum. In all public places tickets are hawked about. One may buy a whole ticket, half, a quarter, an eighth, or a sixteenth. It is done without any disguise or shame, and the institution seemed, I must say, to be as popular with the Europeans living there as with the natives. In the eyes of an Englishman new from Great Britain, with his prejudices still thick upon him, this great national feature loses some of its nobility and grandeur.

This, together with the bribery, which is so universal, shows what is the spirit of the country. For a government supported by the profits of a gambling-hell, and for a Governor enriched by bribes on slaves illegally imported, what Englishman can feel sympathy? I would fain hope that there is no such sympathy felt in England.

I have been answered, when expressing indignation at the system, by a request that I would first look at home; and have been so answered by Englishmen. "How can you blame the Captain-General," they have said, "when the same thing is done by the French and English consuls through the islands?" That the French and English consuls do take bribes to wink at the importation of slaves, I cannot and do not believe. But Cæsar's wife should not even be suspected.

I found it difficult to learn what is exactly the present population of Cuba. I believe it to be about 1,300,000, and of this number about 600,000 are slaves. There are many Chinese now in the island, employed as household servants, or on railways, or about the sugar-works. Many are also kept at work on the cane-pieces, though it seems that for this labour they have hardly sufficient strength. These unfortunate deluded creatures receive, I fear, very little better treatment than the slaves.

My best wish for the island is that it may speedily be reckoned among the annexations of the United States.

JOHN MUIR

Havana, 1868

"HAVANA ABOUNDS IN PUBLIC SQUARES, WHICH IN ALL MY
RANDOM STROLLS THROUGHOUT THE BIG TOWN I FOUND TO
BE WELL WATERED, WELL CARED FOR, WELL PLANTED, AND
FULL OF EXCEEDINGLY SHOWY AND INTERESTING PLANTS,
RARE EVEN AMID THE EXHAUSTLESS LUXURIANCE OF
CUBA."

John Muir was born in Scotland in 1838, and in 1849 his family emigrated to the United States, settling on a large farm near Portage, Wisconsin. He attended the University of Wisconsin, where his favorite subjects were chemistry and geology, but in 1863 he left without taking a degree, preferring to shape his studies himself. By the time he was thirty, his curiosity about the natural world could not be contained. He took to the road, eager to look everywhere, and in 1868, the year he visited Cuba, he also saw California and the Yosemite Valley, experiences that would shape the rest of his life. Muir went on to become a great naturalist, a spokesman for the conservation of natural resources, and, in 1892, the founder of the Sierra Club. (Another selection from Muir's writing, describing his first sight of Glacier Bay, is included in The Reader's Companion to Alaska.)*

Muir's 1868 travels took him through the states of Kentucky, Georgia, and Florida, then out to the Keys, whence he sailed for Havana.*

Muir's interests lay primarily with Cuba's flora. It's no sur-

prise, then, that he was a little put off by the considerable urban noise of this bustling city. Even so, he was favorably impressed. And though he seems not to have learned its name, he too, like visitors before him, took special note of the volante, Havana's unique horse-drawn carriage.

ONE DAY IN JANUARY I CLIMBED TO THE housetop to get a view of another of the fine sunsets of this land of flowers. The landscape was a strip of clear Gulf water, a strip of sylvan coast, a tranquil company of shell and coral keys, and a gloriously colored sky without a threatening cloud. All the winds were hushed and the calm of the heavens was as profound as that of the palmy islands and their encircling waters. As I gazed from one to another of the palm-crowned keys, enclosed by the sunset-colored dome, my eyes chanced to rest upon the fluttering sails of a Yankee schooner that was threading the tortuous channel in the coral reef leading to the harbor of Cedar Keys. "There," thought I, "perhaps I may sail in that pretty white moth." She proved to be the schooner *Island Belle*.

One day soon after her arrival I went over the key to the harbor, for I was now strong enough to walk. Some of her crew were ashore after water. I waited until their casks were filled, and went with them to the vessel in their boat. Ascertained that she was ready to sail with her cargo of lumber for Cuba. I engaged passage on her for twenty-five dollars, and asked her sharp-visaged captain when he would sail. "Just as soon," said he, "as we get a north wind. We have had northers enough when we did not want them, and now we have this dying breath from the south."

Hurrying back to the house, I gathered my plants, took leave of my kind friends, and went aboard, and soon, as if to calm the captain's complaints, Boreas came foaming loud and strong. The little craft was quickly trimmed and snugged, her inviting sails spread open, and away she dashed to her ocean home like an exulting war-horse to the battle. Islet after islet speedily grew dim and sank beneath the horizon. Deeper became the blue of the water, and in a few hours all of Florida vanished.

This excursion on the sea, the first one after twenty years in the woods, was of course exceedingly interesting, and I was full of hope, glad to be once more on my journey to the South. Boreas increased in power and the *Island Belle* appeared to glory in her speed and managed her full-spread wings as gracefully as a sea-bird. In less than a day our norther increased in strength to the storm point. Deeper and wider became the valleys, and yet higher the hills of the round plain of water. The flying jib and gaff topsails were lowered and mainsails closereefed, and our deck was white with broken wave-tops.

"You had better go below," said the captain. "The Gulf Stream, opposed by this wind, is raising a heavy sea and you will be sick. No landsman can stand this long." I replied that I hoped the storm would be as violent as his ship could bear, that I enjoyed the scenery of such a sea so much that it was impossible to be sick, that I had long waited in the woods for just such a storm, and that, now that the precious thing had come, I would remain on deck and enjoy it. "Well," said he, "if you can stand this, you are the first landsman I ever saw that could."

I remained on deck, holding on by a rope to keep from being washed overboard, and watched the behavior of the *Belle* as she dared nobly on; but my attention was mostly directed among the glorious fields of foam-topped waves. The wind had a mysterious voice and carried nothing now of the songs of birds or of the rustling of palms and fragrant vines. Its burden was gathered from a stormy expanse of crested waves and briny tangles. I could see no striving in those magnificent wave-motions, no raging; all the storm was apparently inspired with nature's beauty and harmony. Every wave was obedient and harmonious as the smoothest ripple of a forest lake, and after dark all the water was phosphorescent like silver fire, a glorious sight.

Our luminous storm was all too short for me. Cuba's rockwaves loomed above the white waters early in the morning. The sailors, accustomed to detect the faintest land line, pointed out well-known guiding harbor-marks back of the Morro Castle long before I could see them through the flying spray. We sailed landward for several hours, the misty shore becoming gradually more earthlike. A flock of white-plumaged ships was departing from the Havana harbor, or, like us, seeking to enter it. No sooner had our little schooner flapped her sails in the lee of the Castle than she was boarded by a swarm of daintily dressed officials who were good-naturedly and good-gesturedly making all sorts of inquiries, while our busy captain, paying little attention to them, was giving orders to his crew.

The neck of the harbor is narrow and it is seldom possible to sail in to appointed anchorage without the aid of a steam tug. Our captain wished to save his money, but after much profitless tacking was compelled to take the proffered aid of steam, when we soon reached our quiet mid-harbor quarters and dropped anchor among ships of every size from every sea.

I was still four or five hundred yards from land and could determine no plant in sight excepting the long arched leaf banners of the banana and the palm, which made a brave show on the Morro Hill. When we were approaching the land, I observed that in some places it was distinctly yellow, and I wondered while we were yet some miles distant whether the color belonged to the ground or to sheets of flowers. From our harbor home I could now see that the color was plant-gold. On one side of the harbor was a city of these yellow plants; on the other, a city of yellow stucco houses, narrowly and confusedly congregated.

"Do you want to go ashore?" said the captain to me. "Yes," I replied, "but I wish to go to the plant side of the harbor." "Oh, well," he said, "come with me now. There are some fine squares and gardens in the city, full of all sorts of trees and flowers. Enjoy these to-day, and some other day we will all go over the Morro Hill with you and gather shells. All kinds of shells are over there; but these yellow slopes that you see are covered only with weeds."

We jumped into the boat and a couple of sailors pulled us to the thronged, noisy wharf. It was Sunday afternoon, the noisiest day of a Havana week. Cathedral bells and prayers in the forenoon, theaters and bull-fight bells and bellowings in the afternoon! Lowly whispered prayers to the saints and the Virgin, followed by shouts of praise or reproach to bulls and matadors!

I made free with fine oranges and bananas and many other fruits. Pineapple I had never seen before. Wandered about the narrow streets, stunned with the babel of strange sounds and sights; went gazing, also, among the gorgeously flowered garden squares, and then waited among some boxed merchandise until our captain, detained by business, arrived. Was glad to escape to our little schooner *Belle* again, weary and heavy laden with excitement and tempting fruits.

As night came on, a thousand lights starred the great town. I was now in one of my happy dreamlands, the fairest of West India islands. But how, I wondered, shall I be able to escape from this great city confusion? How shall I reach nature in this delectable land? Consulting my map, I longed to climb the central mountain range of the island and trace it through all its forests and valleys and over its summit peaks, a distance of seven or eight hundred miles. But alas! though out of Florida swamps, fever was yet weighing me down, and a mile of city walking was quite exhausting. The weather too was oppressively warm and sultry.

January 16. During the few days since our arrival the sun usually has risen unclouded, pouring down pure gold, rich and dense, for one or two hours. Then islandlike masses of white-edged cumuli suddenly appeared, grew to storm size, and in a few minutes discharged rain in tepid plashing bucketfuls, accompanied with high wind. This was followed by a short space of calm, half-cloudy sky, delightfully fragrant with flowers, and again the air would become hot, thick, and sultry.

This weather, as may readily be perceived, was severe to one so weak and feverish, and after a dozen trials of strength over the Morro Hill and along the coast northward for shells and flowers, I was sadly compelled to see that no enthusiasm could enable me to walk to the interior. So I was obliged to limit my researches to within ten or twelve miles of Havana. Captain Parsons offered his ship as my headquarters, and my weakness prevented me from spending a single night ashore.

The daily programme for nearly all the month that I spent here was about as follows: After breakfast a sailor rowed me ashore on the north side of the harbor. A few minutes' walk took me past the Morro Castle and out of sight of the town on a broad cactus common, about as solitary and untrodden as the tangles of Florida. Here I zigzagged and gathered prizes among unnumbered plants and shells along the shore, stopping to press the plant specimens and to rest in the shade of vine-heaps and bushes until sundown. The happy hours stole away until I had to return to the schooner. Either I was seen by the sailors who usually came for me, or I hired a boat to take me back. Arrived, I reached up my press and a big handful of flowers, and with a little help climbed up the side of my floating home.

Refreshed with supper and rest, I recounted my adventures in the vine tangles, cactus thickets, sunflower swamps, and along the shore among the breakers. My flower specimens, also, and pocketfuls of shells and corals had to be reviewed. Next followed a cool, dreamy hour on deck amid the lights of the town and the various vessels coming and departing.

Many strange sounds were heard: the vociferous, unsmotherable bells, the heavy thundering of cannon from the Castle, and the shouts of the sentinels in measured time. Combined they made the most incessant sharp-angled mass of noise that I ever was doomed to hear. Nine or ten o'clock found me in a small bunk with the harbor wavelets tinkling outside close to my ear. The hours of sleep were filled with dreams of heavy heat, of fruitless efforts for the disentanglement of vines, or of running from curling breakers back to the Morro, etc. Thus my days and nights went on.

Occasionally I was persuaded by the captain to go ashore in the evening on his side of the harbor, accompanied perhaps by two or three other captains. After landing and telling the sailors when to call for us, we hired a carriage and drove to the upper end of the city, to a fine public square adorned with shady walks and magnificent plants. A brass band in imposing uniform played the characteristic lance-noted martial airs of the Spanish. Evening is the fashionable hour for aristocratic drives about the streets and squares, the only time that is delightfully cool. I never saw elsewhere people so neatly and becomingly dressed. The proud best-family Cubans may fairly be called beautiful, are under- rather than over-sized, with features exquisitely moulded, and set off with silks and broadcloth in excellent taste. Strange that their amusements should be so coarse. Bull-fighting, brain-splitting bell-ringing, and the most piercing artificial music appeal to their taste.

The rank and wealth of Havana nobility, when out driving, seems to be indicated by the distance of their horses from the body of the carriage. The higher the rank, the longer the shafts of the carriage, and the clumsier and more ponderous are the wheels, which are not unlike those of a cannon-cart. A few of these carriages have shafts twenty-five feet in length, and the brilliant-liveried negro driver on the lead horse, twenty or thirty feet in advance of the horse in the shafts, is beyond calling distance of his master.

Havana abounds in public squares, which in all my random strolls throughout the big town I found to be well watered, well cared for, well planted, and full of exceedingly showy and interesting plants, rare even amid the exhaustless luxuriance of Cuba. These squares also contained fine marble statuary and were furnished with seats in the shadiest places. Many of the walks were paved instead of graveled.

The streets of Havana are crooked, labyrinthic, and exceedingly narrow. The sidewalks are only about a foot wide. A traveler experiences delightful relief when, heated and wearied by raids through the breadth of the dingy yellow town, dodging a way through crowds of men and mules and lumbering carts and carriages, he at length finds shelter in the spacious, dustless, cool, flowery squares; still more when, emerging from all the din and darkness of these lanelike streets, he suddenly finds himself out in the middle of the harbor, inhaling full-drawn breaths of the sea breezes.

The interior of the better houses which came under my observation struck me with the profusion of dumpy, ill-proportioned pillars at the entrances and in the halls, and with the spacious open-fielded appearance of their enclosed square house-gardens or courts. Cubans in general appear to me superfinely polished, polite, and agreeable in society, but in their treatment of animals they are cruel. I saw more downright brutal cruelty to mules and horses during the few weeks I stayed there than in my whole life elsewhere. Live chickens and hogs are tied in bunches by the legs and carried to market thus, slung on a mule. In their general treatment of all sorts of animals they seem to have no thought for them beyond cold-blooded, selfish interest.

In tropical regions it is easy to build towns, but it is difficult to subdue their armed and united plant inhabitants, and to clear fields and make them blossom with breadstuff. The plant people of temperate regions, feeble, unarmed, unallied, disappear under the trampling feet of flocks, herds, and man, leaving their homes to enslavable plants which follow the will of man and furnish him with food. But the armed and united plants of the tropics hold their rightful kingdom plantfully, nor, since the first appearance of Lord Man, have they ever suffered defeat.

A large number of Cuba's wild plants circle closely about Havana. In five minutes' walk from the wharf I could reach the undisturbed settlements of Nature. The field of the greater portion of my rambling researches was a strip of rocky common, silent and unfrequented by anybody save an occasional beggar at Nature's door asking a few roots and seeds. This natural strip extended ten miles along the coast northward, with but few large-sized trees and bushes, but rich in magnificent vines, cacti-composites, leguminous plants, grasses, etc. The wild flowers of this seaside field are a happy band, closely joined in splendid array. The trees shine with blossoms and with light reflected from the leaves. The individuality of the vines is lost in trackless, interlacing, twisting, overheaping union.

Our American "South" is rich in flowery vines. In some districts almost every tree is crowned with them, aiding each other in grace and beauty. Indiana, Kentucky, and Tennessee have the grapevine in predominant numbers and development. Farther south dwell the greenbriers and countless leguminous vines. A vine common among the Florida islets, perhaps belonging to the dogbane family, overruns live-oaks and palmettos, with frequently more than a hundred stems twisted into one cable. Yet in no section of the South are there such complicated and such gorgeously flowered vine-tangles as flourish in armed safety in the hot and humid wild gardens of Cuba.

The longest and the shortest vine that I found in Cuba were both leguminous. I have said that the harbor side of the Morro Hill is clothed with tall yellow-flowered composites through which it is difficult to pass. But there are smooth, velvety, lawnlike patches in these *Compositæ* forests. Coming suddenly upon one of these open places, I stopped to admire its greenness and smoothness, when I observed a sprinkling of large papilionaceous blossoms among the short green grass. The long composites that bordered this little lawn were entwined and almost smothered with vines which bore similar corollas in tropic abundance.

I at once decided that these sprinkled flowers had been blown off the encompassing tangles and had been kept fresh by dew and by spray from the sea. But, on stooping to pick one of them up, I was surprised to find that it was attached to Mother Earth by a short, prostrate, slender hair of a vine stem, bearing, besides the one large blossom, a pair or two of linear leaves. The flower weighed more than stem, root, and leaves combined. Thus, in a land of creeping and twining giants, we find also this charming, diminutive simplicity—the vine reduced to its lowest terms.

The longest vine, prostrate and untwined like its little neighbor, covers patches of several hundred square yards with its countless branches and close growth of upright, trifoliate, smooth green leaves. The flowers are as plain and unshowy in size and color as those of the sweet peas of gardens. The seeds are large and satiny. The whole plant is noble in its motions and features, covering the ground with a depth of unconfused leafage which I have never seen equaled by any other plant. The extent of leaf-surface is greater, I think, than that of a large Kentucky oak. It grows, as far as my observation has reached, only upon shores, in a soil composed of broken shells and corals, and extends exactly to the water-line of the highest-reaching waves. The same plant is abundant in Florida.

The cacti form an important part of the plant population of my ramble ground. They are various as the vines, consisting now of a diminutive joint or two hid in the weeds, now rising into bushy trees, wide-topped, with trunks a foot in diameter, and with glossy, dark-green joints that reflect light like the silex-varnished palms. They are planted for fences, together with the Spanish bayonet and agave.

In one of my first walks I was laboriously scrambling among some low rocks gathering ferns and vines, when I was startled by finding my face close to a great snake, whose body was disposed carelessly like a castaway rope among the weeds and stones. After escaping and coming to my senses, I discovered that the snake was a member of the vegetable kingdom, capable of no dangerous amount of locomotion, but possessed of many a fang, and prostrate as though under the curse of Eden, "Upon thy belly shalt thou go and dust shalt thou eat."

One day, after luxuriating in the riches of my Morro pasture, and pressing many new specimens, I went down to the bank of brilliant wave-washed shells to rest awhile in their beauty, and to watch the breakers that a powerful norther was heaving in splendid rank along the coral boundary. I gathered pocketfuls of shells, mostly small but fine in color and form, and bits of rosy coral. Then I amused myself by noting the varying colors of the waves and the different forms of their curved and blossoming crests. While thus alone and free it was interesting to learn the richly varied songs, or what we mortals call the roar, of expiring breakers. I compared their variation with the different distances to which the broken wave-water reached landward in its farthest-flung foam-wreaths, and endeavored to form some idea of the one great song sounding forever all around the white-blooming shores of the world.

Rising from my shell seat, I watched a wave leaping from the deep and coming far up the beveled strand to bloom and die in a mass of white. Then I followed the spent waters in their return to the blue deep, wading in their spangled, decaying fragments until chased back up the bank by the coming of another wave. While thus playing half studiously, I discovered in the rough, beaten deathbed of the wave a little plant with closed flowers. It was crouching in a hollow of the brown wave-washed rock, and one by one the chanting, dying waves rolled over it. The tips of its delicate pink petals peered above the clasping green calyx. "Surely," said I, as I stooped over it for a moment, before the oncoming of another wave, "surely you cannot be living here! You must have been blown from some warm bank, and rolled into this little hollow crack like a dead shell." But, running back after every retiring wave, I found that its roots were wedged into a shallow wrinkle of the coral rock, and that this wave-beaten chink was indeed its dwelling-place.

I had oftentimes admired the adaptation displayed in the structure of the stately dulse and other seaweeds, but never thought to find a highbred flowering plant dwelling amid waves in the stormy, roaring domain of the sea. This little plant has smooth globular leaves, fleshy and translucent like beads, but green like those of other land plants. The flower is about five eighths of an inch in diameter, rose-purple, opening in calm weather, when deserted by the waves. In general appearance it is like a small portulaca. The strand, as far as I walked it, was luxuriantly fringed with woody *Compositæ,* two or three feet in height, their tops purple and golden with a profusion of flowers. Among these I discovered a small bush whose yellow flowers were ideal; all the parts were present regularly alternate and in fives, and all separate, a plain harmony.

When a page is written over but once it may be easily read; but if it be written over and over with characters of every size and style, it soon becomes unreadable, although not a single confused meaningless mark or thought may occur among all the written characters to mar its perfection. Our limited powers are similarly perplexed and overtaxed in reading the inexhaustible pages of nature, for they are written over and over uncountable times, written in characters of every size and color, sentences composed of sentences, every part of a character a sentence. There is not a fragment in all nature, for every relative fragment of one thing is a full harmonious unit in itself. All together form the one grand palimpsest of the world.

One of the most common plants of my pasture was the agave. It is sometimes used for fencing. One day, in looking back from the top of the Morro Hill, as I was returning to the *Island Belle,* I chanced to observe two poplarlike trees about twenty-five feet in height. They were growing in a dense patch of cactus and vine-knotted sunflowers. I was anxious to see anything so homelike as a poplar, and so made haste towards the two strange trees, making a way through the cactus and sunflower jungle that protected them. I was surprised to find that what I took to be poplars were agaves in flower, the first I had seen. They were almost out of flower, and fast becoming wilted at the approach of death. Bulbs were scattered about, and a good many still remained on the branches, which gave it a fruited appearance.

The stem of the agave seems enormous in size when one considers that it is the growth of a few weeks. This plant is said to make a mighty effort to flower and mature its seeds and then to die of exhaustion. Now there is not, so far as I have seen, a mighty effort or the need of one, in wild Nature. She accomplishes her ends without unquiet effort, and perhaps there is nothing more mighty in the development of the flower-stem of the agave than in the development of a grass panicle.

Havana has a fine botanical garden. I spent pleasant hours in its magnificent flowery arbors and around its shady fountains. There is a palm avenue which is considered wonderfully stately and beautiful, fifty palms in two straight lines, each rigidly perpendicular. The smooth round shafts, slightly thicker in the middle, appear to be productions of the lathe, rather than vegetable stems. The fifty arched crowns, inimitably balanced, blaze in the sunshine like heaps of stars that have fallen from the skies. The stems were about sixty or seventy feet in height, the crowns about fifteen feet in diameter.

Along a stream-bank were tall, waving bamboos, leafy as willows, and infinitely graceful in wind gestures. There was one species of palm, with immense bipinnate leaves and leaflets fringed, jagged, and one-sided, like those of *Adiantum*. Hundreds of the most gorgeous-flowered plants, some of them large trees, belonging to the *Leguminosæ*. Compared with what I have before seen in artificial flower-gardens, this is past comparison the grandest. It is a perfect metropolis of the brightest and most exuberant of garden plants, watered by handsome fountains, while graveled and finely bordered walks slant and curve in all directions, and in all kinds of fanciful playground styles, more like the fairy gardens of the Arabian Nights than any ordinary man-made pleasure-ground.

In Havana I saw the strongest and the ugliest negroes that I have met in my whole walk. The stevedores of the Havana wharf are muscled in true giant style, enabling them to tumble and toss ponderous casks and boxes of sugar weighing hundreds of pounds as if they were empty. I heard our own brawny sailors, after watching them at work a few minutes, express unbounded admiration of their strength, and wish that their hard outbulging muscles were for sale. The countenances of some of the negro orange-selling dames express a devout good-natured ugliness that I never could have conceived any arrangement of flesh and blood to be capable of. Besides oranges they sold pineapples, bananas, and lottery tickets.

AFTER PASSING A MONTH IN THIS MAGNIFI- cent island, and finding that my health was not improving, I made up my mind to push on to South America while my stock of strength, such as it was, lasted. But fortunately I could not find passage for any South American port. I had long wished to visit the Orinoco basin and in particular the basin of the Amazon. My plan was to get ashore anywhere on the north end of the continent, push on southward through the wilderness around the headwaters of the Orinoco, until I reached a tributary of the Amazon, and float down on a raft or skiff the whole length of the great river to its mouth. It seems strange that such a trip should ever have entered the dreams of any person, however enthusiastic and full of youthful daring, particularly under the disadvantages of poor health, of funds less than a hundred dollars, and of the insalubrity of the Amazon Valley.

Fortunately, as I said, after visiting all the shipping agencies, I could not find a vessel of any sort bound for South America, and so made up a plan to go North, to the longed-for cold weather of New York, and thence to the forests and mountains of California. There, I thought, I shall find health and new plants and mountains, and after a year spent in that interesting country I can carry out my Amazon plans.

It seemed hard to leave Cuba thus unseen and unwalked, but illness forbade my stay and I had to comfort myself with the hope of returning to its waiting treasures in full health. In the mean time I prepared for immediate departure. When I was resting in one of the Havana gardens, I noticed in a New York paper an advertisement of cheap fares to California. I consulted

Captain Parsons concerning a passage to New York, where I could find a ship for California. At this time none of the California ships touched at Cuba.

"Well," said he, pointing toward the middle of the harbor, "there is a trim little schooner loaded with oranges for New York, and these little fruiters are fast sailers. You had better see her captain about a passage, for she must be about ready to sail." So I jumped into the dinghy and a sailor rowed me over to the fruiter. Going aboard, I inquired for the captain, who appeared on deck and readily agreed to carry me to New York for twenty-five dollars. Inquiring when he would sail, "To-morrow morning at daylight," he replied, "if this norther slacks a little; but my papers are made out, and you will have to see the American consul to get permission to leave on my ship."

I immediately went to the city, but was unable to find the consul, whereupon I determined to sail for New York without any formal leave. Early next morning, after leaving the *Island Belle* and bidding Captain Parsons good-bye, I was rowed to the fruiter and got aboard. Notwithstanding the north wind was still as boisterous as ever, our Dutch captain was resolved to face it, confident in the strength of his all-oak little schooner.

Vessels leaving the harbor are stopped at the Morro Castle to have their clearance papers examined; in particular, to see that no runaway slaves were being carried away. The officials came alongside our little ship, but did not come aboard. They were satisfied by a glance at the consul's clearance paper, and with the declaration of the captain, when asked whether he had any negroes, that he had "not a d——d one." "All right, then," shouted the officials, "farewell! A pleasant voyage to you!" As my name was not on the ship's papers, I stayed below, out of sight, until I felt the heaving of the waves and knew that we were fairly out on the open sea. The Castle towers, the hills, the palms, and the wave-white strand, all faded in the distance, and our mimic sea-bird was at home in the open stormy gulf, curtsying to every wave and facing bravely to the wind.

FREDERIC REMINGTON

Havana, 1899

"IT IS HOT, DIRTY, STUCCOED, AND PICTURESQUE. IT HAS
FINE FRUITS, NEW BUGS, EXCELLENT MICROBES, AND
STONE FLOORS IN THE BEDROOMS. IT CERTAINLY HAS A
SENSATION IN STORE FOR THE AVERAGE AMERICAN."

*The muscular and melodramatic paintings and sculptures of
Frederic Remington (1861–1909) did much to shape the idea
of the West in the minds of Americans. His images—cowboys,
cavalry troops, Indians, charging soldiers, galloping horses,
heated battles—all portrayed on a heroic scale, gave flesh to the
lasting legend of the West in the American consciousness.*

*But while it is Remington's pictures that endure today, he
was also known in his lifetime as a vivid and popular correspondent for newspapers and magazines, reporting most often from
the American southwest but also writing from Mexico, Europe,
and Africa. Between 1887 and 1906, he contributed 111 articles and stories to periodicals. He also wrote two novels; John Er-
mine of the Yellowstone was published by Macmillan in 1902,
and The Way of an Indian was serialized in five issues of Cosmopolitan, beginning in November 1905.*

*His writing, in fact, was central to his artistic work, and
more than a fifth of his pictures were created specifically as illus-
trations for his journalism.*

*Over the years, Remington visited Cuba several times. The
first time was in 1891, when he sent back to Harper's Weekly
from Havana a short piece called "Coolies Coaling a Ward
Liner," accompanied by a wood engraving to illustrate it.*

*In 1898 he sent back two pieces from Cuba, and another
visit in 1899 provided material for four articles. Writing of the
far eastern end of the island in an 1899 piece called "Cuban
Bandits in Santiago Province," he vividly describes the mountainous region that has historically been the safest hideaway for bandits and revolutionaries, including Fidel Castro.*

*"It is a mountainous region," he writes, "covered with dense
jungle, and utterly wild. The predatory bands of negro soldiery
have roamed it for years. They know its trails, its fastnesses, and
its commissary resources. They will be in collusion with towns-
people who will renew their ammunition, and they will have perfect information of our troop movements. They will ambuscade
us in bands, and then disperse as individuals. The country is hot
and not healthy."*

*The following piece, datelined "Havana, March 10, 1899"
and originally titled "Under Which King?," was published in
Collier's for April 8 of that year.*

Havana, March 10, 1899   The rural districts of Cuba are
full of soldiers of the Army of Liberation. They rack along
the roads on their mice-like ponies—they stroll along with their
blankets and rifles. They do not seem to have any definite purpose, and doubtless have none beyond locating fruitful fields.

Our regulars have organized a patrol of certain districts,
and it only happened that I noticed a haughty reserve was
maintained between these two soldiery when they passed. They
lack a common language, and they hardly know what their official relations are to be.

Meanwhile the poor peasant of Cuba gives both the road.
He is the most ignorant being I ever saw; he has been harried
by soldiers until his soul shrinks at the sight of one. These two
men of my picture are friendly enough, but, like a wild animal
newly caught, it will take time for him to gather the fact. The

pathos of the spiritless people appeals to one's sympathies—makes him long to take them by the hand and reassure them. It would do little good; the crackers of the Relief Fund go further. He can understand that a warm heart only prompts the crackers, but man on horseback he cannot approve.

In proportion to the people the numbers who were in the Cuban army was small. The peasants, as it is the custom of the country to call them, were left helpless before the cruelty of the Spanish soldiers, and suffering also from the necessities of their own men in the field. Weyler concentrated them and intended to exterminate the race. Only the most vigorous, the most daring and enterprising, took to the *maniqua*—only those with force and cunning enough to provide themselves with arms. The men of small holdings and large families stayed on the plot of ground, and they did the suffering for both parties. Among these are many Spaniards—men who came out to labor on the land; and never having experienced the quality of mercy, they do not expect it from the victors now. But, so far as I could learn, the Cuban soldiers had not disturbed these people—quite contrary to all preconceived notions; and it is greatly to their credit. To be sure, this fellow-feeling does not extend to those who served as guerillas for Spain. These the Cubans regard as murderers, and yearn to kill. I regard their ideas on the subject as perfectly right. The guerillas were Spanish soldiers, and by the fortunes of war should leave the island which they were unable to keep.

To paraphrase: "If I were a Cuban, as I am an American, as long as there was a Spanish guerilla on the island, I would not lay down my arms—never—never—never."

When I ponder on Havana it is positively startling how little I know about it. No one can understand anything unless he lives with it. The modern facilities for going somewhere are so well adjusted that we go. Having gone to these places we come back to the quiet of our domesticity and then think about what we have seen. Our indefinite feeling is one of pity for people who are not as we are and things which are not like ours. There is no harm in this. It is typical. A Congo cannibal would not like asparagus *a la vinaigrette*.

Havana had a great call on winter-killed Americans before

the war, and will have yet. It presents a change to one who wants to leave the comforts of a Northern home. It is hot, dirty, stuccoed, and picturesque. It has fine fruits, new bugs, excellent microbes, and stone floors in the bedrooms. It certainly has a sensation in store for the average American. It will give you the same nice little shock that the cold water does in the morning bath, or losing your job, or having your best girl work back in the breeching on you. Still, no one leaves his settled ways and buys steamship tickets with any idea of approving of everything he is going to see or do. The critical instinct is involved immediately. To like everything is impossible—even ordinary hoboes have tastes.

It is far from my purpose to discourage passenger traffic or the Havana habit. I have only seen Havana four times, so as a collection my experiences are incomplete. My first offence was in company with American tourists from Vera Cruz bound to New York. I dismounted at Havana from a Ward liner with a Dr. Daly of Pittsburg—since notorious for his dislike of rotten beef. We found the city full of Americans who were wintering their jaded minds, their remaining lung, or their East-wind catarrhs, but all were dressed-up, bustling and happy. Bands played in the Plaza, the Prado was thronged with carriages, mounted gendarmes sat on their horses. The shops were full of gentle-minded idiots buying those absurdly-painted bull-fight fans. The Yankee dollar twinkled on every counter. The big cafe of the Inglaterre clattered its wares. It was all very Latin, very Spanish, very agreeable.

I drove out with my friend the doctor in a rattelty-bang cab, pulled by a puppy-pony, to see an object which the serious-minded scientist said would cheer my intellect. We arrived before a rather imposing building, with its entrance closed by iron bars. Behind these were pleasing figures in white.

"This, you see, is the regular leper hospital. I am investigating leprosy—a most interesting and difficult subject. Come in." So said the doctor.

I simply smote the cabby on the head with my umbrella, not once or twice, but as fast as my arm could work, saying softly, but with great guttural force, "Go on, you yellow ——! Get up! Underlay! Vamoose! Get to hades out of here!" and I prevailed. The doctor was torn violently away from his dear scientific cripples, but he only assured me that the streets were full of them, and there was no need to run away from them. He later showed me people walking freely about the streets who were lepers. Indeed, the Chinese coolies who coaled our ship were all lepers. I parted with Havana without a pang.

But time plays strange tricks on wayward mortals. The revolution against Spain came, and Havana became the centre of the earth. Things so arranged themselves that I was expected to go to Cuba to illuminate the genius of Mr. Richard Harding Davis. We tried to run the Spanish blockade with a very narrow-waisted yacht, but the sailors did not like their job, and finally our patience gave out. The Spanish consul at Key West kept Weyler fully informed of our designs.

Mr. Davis proposed that, since we could not get in the coal-cellar window, we had best go around and knock at the front door. I should never have dreamed of such a thing, but Davis has the true newspaper impudence, so we arranged passage on the regular line steamer *Olivette* for Havana.

Our passports were quaint little papers made out on some sort of custom-house blanks by a friend in Key West, but plastered with gold seals and draped with ribbons like May queens.

Upon our arrival, Consul-General Lee added us to his burden and escorted us up to the great Captain-General Weyler, who was at that time in the full glory of his "reconcentrado" and "forty-battalion" fame. To my simple democratic soul, the marble stairway of the palace which we entered looked like the Gates of Heaven. It recalled Gérôme's painting, *L'éminence Grise*. There were gold-laced officers, black-robed church dignitaries, sentries and couriers coming and going, or whispering by the way. They turned lupine eyes on us, but there was no resisting Lee. To be sure, his government was affording him no support. He represented no one but himself; but his doughty presence, and, I suppose, the foresight of the Spanish, as they thought of the American millions that were behind Lee when his day should come, made courtesy possible and imperative. After being introduced, General Lee sat on a sofa, which he filled with his impassive presence; Weyler teetered in a cane rocking-chair nervously; Davis squinted at the scene for future reference, and I made the only profile of Weyler on this side of the Atlantic on my cuff.

The interview was long, and we never flattered ourselves with having impressed Weyler with our innocence. No good ever came of the beautiful papers which he said would take us everywhere. We might as well have presented a last-year's calendar to the Spanish officers. I saw ill-clad, ill-fed Spanish soldiers bring their dead and wounded into the city, dragging slowly along in ragged columns. I saw scarred Cubans with their arms bound stiffly behind them being marched to the Cabañas. They were to face the black-line in the Laurel Ditch. I saw the "reconcentrados" being hurried in by mounted guerillas, and the country was a pall of smoke from their burning homes. Sailing out past the Morro, I shook my fist at the receding town, and thought, "I shall like the town better the next time I come, because I shall never come unless in company with about one hundred thousand American soldiers."

Man only proposes, for Fate had it that the next view I got of Havana was from the deck of the battleship *Iowa*, Captain Robley D. Evans. We were eight miles off shore, where we sailed and sailed and sailed, up and down. Captain Evans did not like the view we got—it was too far off; but Admiral Sampson said that eight miles was the best view he could give Evans for the present. By day we gazed on the long blue shore-line, with its yellow houses, and by night we sat in the dark, behind the after turret, smoking, while we watched the big searchlights flash from the Morro. I do not know that this view of Havana put me in possession of much information concerning it, but I am bound I liked Havana better this time than before.

And, lastly, I have just been there again. This time I did not go feeling like a thief in the night or an unbidden guest, and I lived at the American Club, and sat at a mess of good old American soldiers, and ate roast beef rare. I saw the free Cubans greet their great hero with cheers as he marched in. I saw the new police being prepared to guard the interests of their own native community, and I called on General Ludlow at his office. There were no gold-laced or black-robed ones; no sentries, no fuss; nothing but a quiet engineer officer sitting at a desk before stacks of official papers, and very busy officers hurrying in and running out, all doing something useful. Soldiers patrolled the streets with loaded rifles, and nothing happened. Business men were figuring and discussing the future commercial development of the town. Every one was hopeful, and the Cubans gradually adjusting themselves to their freedom. Too much cannot be expected at once of a people who have always lived under Spanish misrule and abuse. Cuba is not a new-born country, peopled by wood-cutting, bear-fighting, agricultural folks, who must be fresh and virtuous in order to exist. It is an old country, time worn, decayed, and debauched by thieving officials and fire and sword. The people are negroes or breeds, and they were sired by Spaniards who have never had social virtues since they were overrun by the Moors.

The Cubans have known no civic rectitude; they have had no examples of honest, plain-dealing, public men; they are, in the aggregate, the most ignorant people on earth, so far as letters go. But there are in the rural districts of Cuba an honest folk, whose only aim is to till the land in safety and to be allowed to reap what they shall sow. The Nanigoes, or bands of criminal negroes which infest the cities, are a mere incident, and should be shot on sight—gotten rid of in the shortest possible way, like wild beasts, which is what will happen in the natural order of events. The people will, in my judgment, follow Gomez, who begins to develop a sanity regarding reconstruction which is good to see. And now with good American soldier governors to sit quietly by and see that no throats are cut, things will slowly come right. I very much fear this furrow to which we have set our plow will be a long one. The end is not in sight.

Physically, one is immediately impressed with the undeveloped state of Havana and Cuba generally, and of the illimitable possibilities. The Spanish officials taxed thrift right out of the island; they took industry by the neck and throttled it. The Church charged a poor man so much to get married that they, for the most part, were compelled to forego that ceremony, and when they were dead they taxed their bones. This may seem strong, but we have all seen the photographs of the piles of bones in the cemeteries which were thrown out for arrears of taxes.

It is for no one to say how long a time it will take before

Cuba is a prosperous and well-mannered country, but if we hold her up to her work, and have no nonsense in dealing with the reactionary elements, it ought not to be long. The task is delicate—this bringing of order out of chaos. The Cubans are entitled to our greatest consideration, but with "new-caught" people the grandest of all errors is indecision. No sentimentalist should go from our ports to Cuba. It is my belief that, as between the avarice of politicians and business men, the sentimentalist, with his fussy little social recipes, can do most harm in dealing with such subjects. These last are all very well in their place. We Americans understand them, but a yellow islander could never make the combination. Therefore let us continue to send honest soldiers to lead these undisciplined people.

ANAÏS NIN
Havana, 1922

"I HAVE BEEN TRANSPORTED TO FAIRYLAND, I NOW LIVE
IN AN ENCHANTED PALACE! ALL MY SADNESS AND
APPREHENSION FLED THE MOMENT I CAUGHT SIGHT OF
HAVANA."

Anaïs Nin's reputation rests in part on such works of fiction as
The Four-Chambered Heart *and* A Spy in the House of Love,
*and in part on the subtle and beautifully composed erotica she
wrote for a private client, published as* Delta of Venus *in 1977,
the year of her death, and* Little Birds, *published in 1979. But
Nin's major literary work will probably always be her volumi-
nous* Diary.

*Nin was born in Paris in 1903. Her mother was a French-
Danish singer and her father a Cuban musician and composer.
When she visited Cuba for the first time, in 1922, Nin was nineteen years of age and she had already been writing her diaries
for eight years. "By beginning a diary," she declared in 1973, "I
was already conceding that life would be more bearable if I
looked at it as an adventure and a tale. I was telling myself the
story of a life, and this transmutes into an adventure the things
which can shatter you."*

*Nin's reactions to Havana are more than a little breathless,
but then, so were John Muir's.*

*The Convent of Santa Clara which Nin visited in 1922 is
one of the most precious of the nine hundred Spanish colonial
structures that still stand—some of them quite unsteadily—in
Habana Vieja. But Old Havana has been declared a World Heritage site by UNESCO (as has the city of Trinidad, on the southern coast), and so some money and much interest have since
been dedicated to preserving the treasured buildings of Havana's
colonial past.*

*Work on the Convent of Santa Clara began in the early
1980s, and Cuban architects, artisans, and historians have now
restored it to its former glory. Its yellow walls glow in the sunshine, its peaceful porticos offer welcome shade and opportunities for reflection, and the tropical plants in its Spanish
courtyard flourish. Similar work is currently being done on Havana's cathedral.*

*Havana was first settled in 1519, and the colonial buildings
of Habana Vieja are filled with treasures from the sixteenth century. All the wealth of the New World, from Mexico and Peru
and elsewhere, passed through Havana before crossing the Atlantic to Spain. The city's wealthy merchants and businessmen had
plenty of money to spend, and when they built homes, they
wanted only the best. So, amid today's crumbling plaster and
peeling paint, there are still many examples—delicately colored
marble and Spanish tiles and inlay and ironwork—of the best
materials and workmanship of sixteenth-century Europe.*

October 9.   Finca La Generala,* Luyanó, Havana.
     To Hugo:
     *I have been transported to Fairyland, I now live in an
     Enchanted Palace! All my sadness and apprehension fled the
     moment I caught sight of Havana, and as the ship neared
     the harbor, I was thrilled beyond words at the strangeness of
     all that was happening to me. You can hardly imagine what
     it is to see a new city, to hear a new language, to see the
     faces of an altogether different race and yet to recognize all
     this as belonging to part of you. Whatever is Spanish in me
     has now come to the surface, and in every glance from large*

---

* The ranch of Tía Antolina, who was the widow of General de Cárdenas.

dark eyes I read feelings to which I can respond and charac-
ters I understand as well as my own. The spell of the south
is upon me, and I feel the soft, caressing air and the warm,
vibrant touch of its twilight, and my thoughts are lulled into
dreamy indolence . . .

To Eduardo:

I had promised myself not to weave about my change of
home and my new adventure, and so I approached Havana
very soberly and with many misgivings, knowing too well the
penalty one pays for illusions and determined to live hence-
forward with as few as possible. And the gods, therefore,
showered their gifts upon me. I find myself living in the most
beautiful of houses on the outskirts of the city, one which
seems a palace to me, most exquisitely furnished and decor-
ated, surrounded by an enchanting garden. And all about us
are unfolded the sloping fields of Cuba, fertile and rich un-
der the ever shining sun.

And the air is soft and balmy and the tall, straight, infi-
nitely graceful palm trees are outlined everywhere against a
most brilliant and colorful sky. Everything seems penetrated
by some hidden warmth and softness and one feels the spell
of the south—languor and fire by turn steal upon you
through spirit and senses.

All these days I have been in appearance like one dazed
by the strangeness and novelty of my surroundings, because I
could not write as well or talk as much but I was simply
observing intently, absorbing all things, gathering experience
and impressions in order to understand and explain better
later on. You now know why, Eduardo, today I send you but
a short letter and one filled with the outward appearance of
things, description of the tangible and visible things only.
The thoughts will come later; they lurk in the background,
half-fearful of I know not what, but I am contented to see
and hear and feel meanwhile, and to write in the manner of
ordinary creatures.

Yes, I will give expression to the wrath your intended-to-
be poem kindled in me, but not now, for I am in the mood
for gentleness, and if you were here, you would be treated

*with extraordinary consideration. And the more so when you
are so far and I wish to coax you into writing a heart-satis-
fying letter to your "cuisine" whom the world has abandoned
on an island to perish in solitude. Mimi*

Still dazed, still unable to believe that it is true. First I
have known Cuba through the medium of nature, her fields,
her sky, her sea; every scene has filled me with mute wonder,
and a feeling akin to tenderness has crept into me when I have
looked about, seeing beauty in the things so many have passed
unnoticing—a beauty which has touched me and which I have
understood in a purely miraculous way.

And then I have seen the city from the lowest to the highest houses. I have become familiar with its strange little houses
painted white and yellow and pale blue and rose; have distinguished a quaint charm in a mass of bizarre coloring, in the
narrow streets. One passes over the dirt and the laziness and
the vivid, vulgar ornamentations and the primitive, barbaric
traits that cannot be denied, and finds much that appeals in its
inhabitants. The poor are desperately poor; the rich are ostentatiously rich, but one feels in sympathy with both. Whatever re-
pels is redeemed by much that is touching.

Havana strikes me as a city of extremes, of contrasts, or it
may only seem so because it is comparatively small. It seems
all to be condensed in a handful, so to speak, and can be so
easily observed.

Now I have begun to know Havana through its society. Nature I saw and felt; the city I saw and judged by its appearance.
But society I shall absorb and through it understand all of Havana in unity, for are not the people the most complete and
convincing proof of the character and temper of a city, of its
traits as a whole, its main faults and virtues?

November 8. Resting from sorrow! Free from pressure and
limitation, soaring above the oppressive phantoms of self-in-
flicted agony . . . And with this, the desire to write becomes
more intense, the joy of composition becomes ecstasy, and I
surrender to its delicious domination.

November 9. The one great privilege attending this state of rest from sorrow is the turn the mind takes once freed from its subjection to the one emotion, and how it branches out and embraces the entire situation, and can once more profit from experience and be enriched by it in general, universal terms.

It is in such a state that I have rediscovered Havana. Havana, en masse, vaguely stirs in one memories of pictures of ancient Moorish cities—cream-white stone houses, flat-roofed, with arched doorways, columns and balconies, all linked, following the fantastic curves of narrow, irregular streets. Or it rouses faint recollections of old Spain, and vestiges of Spanish dominion are distinguishable everywhere, in the homes of the middle class, with their plaster-walled, high-roofed, stone-floored rooms; in the Cubans' dress, taste, and customs.

Tradition hangs about the quaint furniture, and nothing within the commonplace home is either modern or even moderately up to date. And tradition walks about the streets, too, and one is strongly tempted to plead thus: for less tradition and more cleanliness!

Shops, cafés, etc. open out upon the streets. Misery is more apparent since one can see into the inmost heart of the houses through wide windows and doors flung open—across rooms to the very backyard. A habit of inordinate hospitality fostered by the climatical conditions and atmospheric pressure!

Poverty stands fully revealed, naked, a striking, repulsive sight to a stranger until all feeling of condemnation melts into an all-absorbing compassion.

In the walk of the people about the streets is reflected a peculiar indolence. It is a slow, dragging step, a deliberate, swinging movement, a gliding, serpentlike motion, something speaking indefinably of that characteristic laziness of the tropics and a something else which might be called a state of mental apathy, a universal malady of Havana, at least to my mind. Mental idleness, vacuity, are what I read in most passing faces. Eyes seeming to wander forever, alighting on everything but carrying no thoughts to the mind, eyes devoid of vision, gleaming alone when the senses are pleased . . . All this with a few exceptions, but it strikes one as universal in comparison with the expressions on the faces of any other crowd or mere passers-by of other cities.

Traces of religious bigotry—a deep-seated ignorance and superstitious slavery to custom—the total absence of individual will, intelligence, understanding, a faith of childish simplicity, all these are still found in some women here. And in most cases she does not even fulfill the demands of beauty, for she lacks grace and charm and culture. Vanity is her all-absorbing passion and only interest, and whatever else conforms with the character of the doll that she is. If she is sweet and submissive, it is the submission of unconscious inferiority. All this, with exceptions and taking into consideration that the younger girls, educated abroad, are returning with knowledge and ideals, so that for Havana, as for every city, one can count on the gradual influence of progress.

The Latin race, outspoken, expressive, generous, hospitable, exemplifying "largesse" in every sense, would be better appreciated and loved but for its sad deficiency in dignity and fastidiousness. One trained in English reserve and delicacy is bound to look with arrogance and disdain upon that unrestrained conduct, that carelessness in regard to propriety and reserve in individuals and family life, so strangely visible throughout the city. The frank, irresponsible, uneducated Cuban appears unintelligible to those who possess instinctively that quality, elusive and indescribable, which might be called culture (for lack of a better term) or innate refinement—all that includes personal appearance, manner of speech, manner of living, through which good taste or lack of it is irrevocably expressed. In these an unsubdued coarseness distinguishes the Cuban, a state of primitive vulgarity, man uncultivated, and unsuspecting of his failing, which silences reproach.

November 11. I have struggled to mark the distinctions between the thousand kinds and forms of happiness in the world, have gone so far as to term sorrow the most divine happiness and the one pursued by ordinary mortals and their material craving, commonplace, unworthy. And I have struggled to distinguish true from false joy, the valuable from the worthless, to separate the low from the high, the noble from the ignoble.

But I have gone no further than a thousand others who, each in turn, gave his own name to what he loved and placed his own value upon things he praised in the innocent sincerity of his soul, and in the end made things no more or less right than they were before, nor more or less believable, beautiful, or noble.

Can anyone efface the individual note that rings so through all such utterances? Can no one voice a universal, all-embracing teaching and be heard? Well, then, shall I be silent? I wonder at all this because my words struck me with their uselessness, their helpless bondage to the eternal "I," which renders them as lifeless to the others. My desire now is to gradually move away from the personal and individual. I wish to merge myself into the universal experience.

Shall I ever find the all-revealing light? By my desire I breathe so close to its own sacred existence that if it should ever shine, I would be the first to feel its warmth . . . I wait.

November [?].   Notes on a Visit to the Convent of Santa Clara.

Through a curious architecture, twisted to meet the need of aggrandizement, a whole world lay enclosed within the high, forbidding outer wall, a world of many houses linked to one another by passageways and little wooden bridges, forming spaces and courts in so immense and confused a plan that no clear conception of it could be gained in a short visit.

Quaint and unforgettable details could be gathered on the way, suggesting bygone centuries—old lanterns; arched colonnades; wide windows, heavily barred with iron, opening upon the street; heavy, imposing doors creaking on their ancient, rusty hinges or locked by ancient, rusty locks; and every stone, every step, old, worn, and yellow.

It was sad to have its historical sacredness thus violated by the intrusion of unfeeling strangers. To the poet or the dreamer the place was filled with traces that he could recognize and by which he could reconstruct the broken web of many human documents.

One could imagine the old garden in the tender sunlight, calm, serene, and nuns gliding about, softly murmuring their beads; or moving across the frail wooden bridges and bending over the wooden banister . . . shadows crowding in one's mind, fantastic characters of one's own making, moving, giving a semblance of life . . . praying, laboring, and then at night perhaps retiring into their bare, cold cells to sleep on their beds of board. And the candlelight perhaps trembling in the still night and throwing the shadows of their window bars upon the stone floor—the symbol of their voluntary exile and imprisonment.

Days later. Since then I have heard many stories about the old convent which have supplied the last touch of reality to my fantastic imaginings—stories of folded love notes found in the crevice of a door, of drawers in the kitchen wall through which the nuns did their marketing, of secret tunnels under the chapel leading out into the city for the escape of the nuns at the time when they lived in constant fear of the pirates and of pillages (to protect their treasures, the walls were built so high and so forbidding and the windows barred and the doors massive, strongly locked), of the well in the center of the court, dating back as far as 400 years, and of the "poseta," or kind of public bath.

Some are in possession of documents and diaries in the handwriting of the nuns themselves, strange, romantic stories of girls seeking refuge in religion, the seclusion of the cloister against the cruelty of parents forcing them to marry against their inclination; stories probably of unrequited love, of disappointments, of separations by violence or misunderstanding—of all the causes, in short, which can turn a creature against the world and move her to total renunciation of it. It is curious to notice how few are the people who have faith in the vocation—in a pure, religious spirit, in a truly pious inspiration. With their small minds they cannot conceive a disinterested and purely unworldly sacrifice. To them it must be a human reason, a lower incentive which can move a man or woman to retire within these austere walls and to seek forgetfulness and peace in religion. Not a love and devotion to God but an unhappy experience with the world.

And as I heard this I was struck by disgust—a disgust toward all things, toward life, human nature, toward myself for being human. I suddenly saw all action reduced to nothingness

where before it signified growth—all nobility shrunk to calculated, selfish motive. Alas, contact with Skepticism, a glimpse
of those ignoble depths of others' hearts, in which Doubt sits
enthroned, gave me a sense of absolute loneliness in my faith,
my conceptions, my aspirations . . .

LANGSTON HUGHES

Havana nights and Cuban color lines, 1930

"A GROUP OF YOUNG BUSINESS AND PROFESSIONAL MEN
OF HAVANA ONCE GAVE A RUMBA PARTY IN MY HONOR. IT
WAS NOT UNLIKE AN AMERICAN FRATERNITY OR LODGE
SMOKER—EXCEPT THAT WOMEN WERE PRESENT. THE WOMEN
WERE NOT, HOWEVER, WIVES OR SWEETHEARTS OF THE
GENTLEMEN GIVING THE RUMBA. FAR FROM IT."

By the time Langston Hughes visited Cuba in 1930, at the age
of twenty-eight, he was already an experienced traveler. He had
spent the summers of 1919 and 1920—the summers just before
and after his senior year of high school—with his father in To-
luca, Mexico, not far from the capital. In 1923 he had sailed
down the western coast of Africa, touching at thirty-two ports
from Dakar, Senegal, to Luanda, Angola. Later, he lived for a
while in Paris and also visited Italy.

And he had made two brief trips to Cuba before the longer
visit of 1930. The first time, while on a visit to New Orleans
and almost on a whim of the moment, he signed on as a steward
on a ship, the Nardo, making a round-trip journey to Havana.
On board, he became good friends with the Chinese cooks, and
when the ship reached Havana, he stayed with them to visit
their friends and to see the town.

"We bought red Chinese whiskey," he writes in the first volume of his autobiography, The Big Sea, "flavored with lichee
nuts, in brown clay jugs. Then we went to a house of pleasure

exclusively for Orientals, although the girls were Cuban. The house had a large, dusky patio and the rooms opened all around the patio. A girl sat in the doorway of each room, rocking or fanning, or doing fancy work or smoking, and the men moved silently from doorway to doorway, looking, as one would move from cage to cage in a zoo. It was very quiet, because the girls and the men did not speak the same language, so there was little verbal communication. . . . It was the most depressing brothel I have ever seen."

Hughes didn't penetrate very far into the city, seeing only the obvious places a sailor on a brief shore leave might see. *"The sailors' cafés on San Isidro Street did not seem very amusing either,"* he continues. *"The weather was terrifically hot that August and everybody sort of lifeless from the heat, and not much dancing. Bad little orchestras played rhumbas and sones, but nobody bothered to move from the tables. It was too hot even to get drunk."*

His second visit is described in a single paragraph of The Big Sea. At the suggestion of his patron, "the lady on Park Avenue," he went to Cuba "looking for a Negro composer to write an opera with me, using genuinely racial motifs." His search for a composer failed, but, he writes, "Miguel Covarrubias had given me a letter to José Antonio Fernandez de Castro, person extraordinary of this or any other world. And José Antonio saw to it that I had a rumba of a good time and met everybody, Negro, white, and mulatto, of any interest in Havana—from the drummers at Marianao to the society artist and editor of Social, Masaguer."

Hughes spent Christmas of 1929 with his mother in Cleveland, Ohio, intending to leave from there by bus to Key West, Florida, and then continue on to Cuba and Haiti. In Cleveland, however, he joined forces with a new friend, Zell Ingram, who was about to give up his studies at the Cleveland School of Art, and who wanted to travel too. Ingram borrowed his mother's car and three hundred dollars. Hughes had three hundred of his own; his novel, Not Without Laughter, had won an award and four hundred dollars, one hundred of which he had given to his mother. So, armed with car and cash, the two of them left the March snows of Cleveland and headed south.

Despite the jolly sound of it, this was a reflective time for Hughes, filled with questions about how he might shape his life and his work as "a Negro who wanted to make his living from poems and stories."

With a quarter century of hindsight, he carefully recalled his thoughts of that time. "I thought," he writes, "with the four hundred dollars my novel had given me, I had better go sit in the sun awhile and think, having just been through a tense and disheartening winter after a series of misunderstandings with the kind lady who had been my patron. She wanted me to be more African than Harlem—primitive in the simple, intuitive and noble sense of the word. I couldn't be, having grown up in Kansas City, Chicago and Cleveland. So that winter had left me ill in my soul. I could not put my mind on writing for months. But write I had to—or starve—so I went to sit in the sun and gather my wits."

In Africa, Hughes had had a new experience of color. When he described himself as "a Negro" in a conversation with Africans, they "only laughed," he writes, "and shook their heads and said: 'You, white man! You, white man!'

"It was the only place in the world where I've ever been called a white man. They looked at my copper-brown skin and straight black hair . . . and they said: You—white man."

This experience, too, is in his mind when he encounters an unexpected color bar in Cuba.

HAVANA NIGHTS

In Miami, Zell and I put the Ford in a garage. We went by rail to Key West, thence by boat to Cuba. It was suppertime when we got to El Moro with Havana rising white and Moorish-like out of the sea in the twilight. The evening was warm and the avenues were alive with people, among them many jet-black Negroes in white attire. Traffic filled the narrow streets, auto horns blew, cars' bells clanged, and from the wine-shops and fruit-juice stands radios throbbed with drumbeats and the wavelike sounds of maracas rustling endless rumbas. Life seemed fluid, intense, and warm in the busy streets of Havana.

Our hotel was patronized mostly by Cubans from the provinces, with huge families. Its inner balconies around an open courtyard were loud with the staccato chatter of stout mamas and vivacious children. Its restaurant on the first floor—with the entire front wall open to the street—was as noisy as only a Cuban restaurant can be, for, added to all the street noises, were the cries of waiters and the laughter of guests, the clatter of knives and forks, and the clinking of glasses at the bar.

I liked this hotel because, since tourists never came there, the prices were on the Cuban scale and low. None of the rooms had any windows, but they had enormous double doors opening onto the tiled balconies above the courtyard. Nobody troubled to give anyone a key. The management simply took for granted all the guests were honest.

I went the next day to look up José Antonio Fernandez de Castro to whom, on a previous trip to Cuba, I had been given a letter of introduction by Miguel Covarrubias. José Antonio was a human dynamo who at once set things in motion. A friend of many American artists and writers, he drank with, wined and dined them all; fished with Hemingway; and loved to go to Marianao—the then nontourist amusement center. He knew all the taxicab drivers in town—with whom he had accounts—and was, in general, about the best person in Cuba to know, if you'd never been there before.

José Antonio was a newspaperman on the *Diario De La Marina*. He later became an editor of *Orbe*, Cuba's weekly pictorial magazine. Then he went into the diplomatic service to become the first secretary of the Cuban Embassy in Mexico City, and from there to Europe. Painters, writers, newsboys, poets, fighters, politicians, and rumba dancers were all José's friends. And, best of all for me, he knew the Negro musicians at Marianao, those fabulous drum beaters who use their bare hands to beat out rhythm, those clave knockers and maraca shakers who somehow have saved—out of all the centuries of slavery and all the miles and miles from Guinea—the heartbeat and songbeat of Africa. This ancient heartbeat they pour out into the Cuban night from a little row of café hovels at Marianao. Or else they flood with song those smoky low-roofed dance halls where the poor of Havana go for entertainment after dark.

Most Cubans who lived in Vedado, Havana's fashionable section, had no idea where these dance halls were. That is why I liked José Antonio. He lived in Vedado, but he knew *all* Havana. Although he was a white Cuban of aristocratic background, he knew and loved Negro Cuba. That first night in town we went straight to Marianao.

This was my third trip to Cuba. Once I had been there as a sailor, and I had known the life of the water front and San Isidro Street. The winter preceeding my present trip, I had come in search of a Negro composer to do an opera with me at the behest of my New York patron. So I had by now many friends in Havana, including the then unknown Nicolás Guillén, who later became a famous poet. My own poems had been published in Spanish in a number of Cuban magazines and papers, and I had given readings of them previously for Havana cultural organizations. The Club Atenas, leading club of color, had entertained me.

The Club Atenas occupied a large building with a staircase of marble, beautiful reception rooms, a ballroom, a comfortable library, a fencing room, and a buffet. I had been astonished and delighted with its taste and luxury, for colored people in the United States had no such club. Diplomats, politicians, professional men and their families made up its membership—and a cultured and charming group they were. Then no rumbas were danced within the walls of the Atenas, for in Cuba in 1930 the rumba was not a respectable dance among persons of good breeding. Only the poor and declassé, the sporting elements, and gentlemen on a spree danced the rumba.

Rumbas and *sones* are essentially hip-shaking music—of Afro-Cuban folk derivation, which means a bit of Spain, therefore Arab-Moorish, mixed in. The tap of claves, the rattle of gourds, the dong of iron bells, the deep steady roll of drums speak of the earth, life bursting warm from the earth, and earth and sun moving in the steady rhythms of procreation and joy.

A group of young business and professional men of Havana once gave a rumba party in my honor. It was not unlike an

American fraternity or lodge smoker—except that women were present. The women were not, however, wives or sweethearts of the gentlemen giving the rumba. Far from it. They were, on the whole, so a companion whispered to me, younger and prettier than most of their wives. They were ladies of the demimonde, playgirls, friends and mistresses of the hosts, their most choice females invited especially for zest and decorativeness.

The party was held in a large old Spanish colonial house, presided over by a stout woman with bold ways. It began about four in the afternoon. At dusk dinner was served; then the fiesta went on far into the night. It was what the Cubans call a *cumbancha*. Spree, I suppose, would be our best word.

When I arrived a Negro rumba band was playing in the courtyard, beating it out gaily, with maracas beneath the melody like the soft undertow of sea waves. Several kegs of wine sat on stools in the open air, and a big keg of beer decorated one end of the patio. Hidden in a rear court was a bar from which waiters emerged with Bacardi or whatever else one wished to drink that was not already in sight.

A few lovely mulatto girls sat fanning in wicker chairs. One or two couples were dancing as I came in, but the sun still shone in the courtyard and it was not yet cool enough for much action. Gradually more and more people began to arrive, girls in groups, men in ones or twos, but no men and women together. These were the women men kept, but did not take out. I had become acquainted with this custom of the mistress in Mexico and other Latin lands, where every man who was anybody at all had both a wife and a pretty mistress.

As the sun went down beyond the skyline, life began to throb in the cool enclosure. The taps on the wine kegs flowed freely. Lights were lighted in the patio, more chairs brought, and I was given a seat of honor near the orchestra. Most of the dancing pairs sat down, or disappeared inside the house. But the music seemed to take a new lease on life. Now various couples, one or two at a time, essayed the rumba in the center of the court as the rest of the party gathered to watch. I could not make out whether it was a dance contest or not, and my hosts were slightly tipsy by then so not very coherent in their explanations. But when the dancing couples seemed to tire, others took the floor. Sometimes a short burst of applause would greet an especially adept pair as the man swept around the woman like a cock about a hen, or the woman without losing a beat of the rhythm went very slowly down to the floor on firm feet and undulated up again. Tirelessly the little Negro band played. Like a mighty dynamo deep in the bowels of the earth, the drums throbbed, beat, sobbed, grumbled, cried, and then laughed a staccato laugh. The dancing kept up until it was quite dark and the first stars came out.

Glass after glass was thrust into my hands as I sat looking and listening with various friends about me. Then after a while, a little tired of sitting still so long, I got up and moved to the other end of the courtyard. As soon as I rose, the music stopped. People began to drink and chatter, but there was no more exhibition dancing. Later I learned that I, as the guest of honor, controlled that part of the entertainment. By rising, I had indicated a lack of further interest, so the rumba stopped. Had I known, I might have not risen so soon.

After supper—delicious sea food served with boiled bananas and Spanish rice—the general dancing began again. Several pretty girls did their best to teach me to rumba. Cuban dancing is not as easy as it looks, but I had a good time trying to learn, and I was interested in trying to understand the verses the musicians sang as they played. Some of the men who spoke English translated for me. Most of the songs were risqué in an ingenious folk way. One thing that struck me was that almost all the love lyrics were about the charms of *mi negra,* my black girl, *mi morena,* my dark girl, my chocolate sweetie or my mulatto beauty, plainly described as such in racial terms. These dusky nuances, I notice, are quite lost in the translations that Broadway makes of Cuban songs for American consumption.

As the night laughed on and big stars sparkled lazily over the festive courtyard, some of the men of the party explained to me that within the house there were rooms with big old-fashioned beds to which one might retire. "And here are girls," they said. "You are the guest of honor. Take your choice from any. Our women are your women, tonight."

So it goes at a rumba party in Havana to which one does not invite one's wife, one's mother, or one's sweetheart.

CUBAN COLOR LINES

In spite of the fact that Cuba is distinctly a Negroid country, there exists there a sort of triple color line. This triple line, in varying degrees of application, is common to all the West Indies. At the bottom of the color scale are the pure-blooded Negroes, black or dark brown in color. In the middle are the mixed bloods, the light browns, mulattoes, golden yellows and near whites with varying textures of Indian-Spanish hair. Then come the nearer whites, the octoroons, and the pure white of skin. In Cuba, although these three distinct divisions exist, the lines are not so tightly drawn as in some of the other islands of the Caribbean. The British Islands are the worst in this respect. The Latin Islands are more careless concerning racial matters.

But in Cuba one quickly notices that almost all the clerks in the bigger shops are white or near white; that in the daily papers almost all the photographs of society leaders are white, or light enough to pass for white; that almost all the gentlemen who represent the people and sit on government commissions and staff the Cuban consulates and ministries abroad are white, or at least "meriney," as American Negroes term that reddish blond border line between colored and white. But this scale is not 100% true. Occasionally a very dark Negro occupies a very high position in Cuba. That is what misleads many visitors from the United States—particularly colored visitors who are looking anxiously for a country where they can say there is *no color line*—for Cuba's color line is much more flexible than that of the United States, and much more subtle. There are, of course, no Jim Crow cars in Cuba, and at official state gatherings and less official carnivals and celebrations, citizens of all colors meet and mingle. But there are definite social divisions based on color—and the darker a man is, the richer and more celebrated he has to be to crash those divisions.

The use of Havana as a winter playground by American tourists has, of course, brought its quota of Southern racial prejudice from the mainland. Hotels that formerly were lax in their application of the color line now discourage even mulatto Cubans, thus seeking the approval of their American clientele.

But the purely Cuban hotels, with no eye out for tourists, cater to guests of all shades of complexion and the service is most courteous.

My single unpleasant experience in Havana took place at the entrance to the Havana Beach. The Cubans later explained to me that the only wide clean stretch of bathing beach near the city had been leased by politicians to an American concern that built there handsome pavilions and bathing houses for the use of tourists, charged a dollar to go on to the beach—a prohibitive sum then to most Cubans—and proceeded to draw the color line, as well. But since, in Havana, it is very difficult for even North Americans to draw a *strict* color line, the beach often had mulatto politicians and plutocrats sporting thereon. But entrance to the beach then seemed to depend, if you were colored, largely on whether you had enough political pull or social prestige to *force* the management to sell you a season ticket. At the gate, I discovered to my discomfort that they would not sell colored people the customary dollar entrance tickets at all, although they were sold quite freely to whites for a single afternoon's bathing. If you were colored, the gatekeeper demanded a season ticket.

My friend, José Antonio Fernandez de Castro, and a group of journalists one Saturday had planned a beach party to which Zell Ingram and I were invited. Zell and I, since we had a lot of free time, decided to go to the beach early and spend the whole morning there in the sun until our friends arrived. We got off the street car in front of the tropical entrance pavilion and went to the window to purchase tickets. The young woman at the window said she was sorry there were no tickets. Zell and I stepped back and studied the tariff list posted beside the window. In both English and Spanish the rates for entrance tickets, season tickets, the renting of bathing suits, etc. were clearly printed. Since I speak Spanish I again approached the young lady.

"It says tickets are a dollar each. I'll take two."

She shoved the money back through the wicket. "You'll have to see the manager. I can't sell them to you."

The same sort of treatment had been meted out to me so

often in my own country from Kansas to New York, Boston to Birmingham, that I began to understand.

I went to the entrance gate and asked the attendant there to kindly call the manager for me. Instead the attendant called a bouncer. The bouncer was an old American boxer—white, of course—with cauliflower ears and a flat nose.

"What do you guys want? This place ain't run for you," he said. "You can't come in."

"Do you mean to tell me that you're drawing the color line on a *Cuban* beach against *American* citizens—and you're an American yourself?"

"Don't start no arguments," he growled, drawing back his fist.

By now Zell had doubled up his fists, too, and squared off for a fight. Zell was a big fellow, but it seemed better to me not to attempt to settle the matter by a brawl, so I said, "Don't hit him, Ingram." But the ex-pug had already backed up beyond reach.

"Get out," he yelled from within the enclosure, "or I'll send for the police."

"Go ahead," I said, "send for them."

The bouncer retired. A Cuban attendant permitted me to enter the lobby where there was a telephone. I called up José Antonio who asked us to wait there for him; he would be right out by taxi. As a newspaperman he no doubt scented a story. Zell and I sat down in the lobby to wait. Just then a policeman, at the instigation of the bouncer, came up to us. He was a pleasant young officer, a white Cuban, with apparently little relish for his task.

"*No pueden sentarse aquí*," he said. "You can't sit here."

"Why?" I asked.

"The manager says you can't."

Zell, who spoke no Spanish, kept asking, "Shall I hit him, man?"

"No," I said. "Let's not give them any cause to arrest us. Let José Antonio, who is a Cuban, get at the bottom of this."

"Please get the manager for me then," I requested of the officer.

He went away and shortly returned with the manager, a tall patronizing American white man. I began to explain to the manager why we had come to the beach, but he interrupted to say that we would not be allowed within and insisted that we leave the lobby at once. I said that since it was a public lobby, we would wait there for our friends. The manager declared he would have us ejected.

He went away. Zell and I sat in the big wicker chairs and waited, knowing that it would take perhaps an hour for José Antonio to arrive. Shortly a car sped rapidly up to the entrance, screeched to a halt, and four policemen with drawn sabres jumped out. They came running toward us as if they intended to slice us to mince meat.

"Out!" cried the cops, waving their swords in the air and descending upon us. "Get out!"

In the face of such ferocious weapons there was nothing to do but withdraw, so Zell and I went outside to the platform in front of the pavilion where the street cars stopped. Apparently satisfied the police got back into their car and sped away as we stood by the tracks to wait for our Cuban friends. But shortly the ex-pug appeared again and commanded us to leave the area at once. "Scram! Get going!"

"I'll report this to the American consulate," I said, stubborn and angry by now.

"Report it," cried the pug with a series of oaths. "Go ahead. They won't do nothing."

I knew American consulates had seldom been known to fight the battles of colored citizens abroad if Jim Crow were involved.

"I'll do something," said Zell as his fists doubled up again. This time the bouncer slammed the gate and retreated for good into the beach-house. He did not want to fight. Then, in a few moments, with a wail of sirens a large police van swept down the road, stopped in front of us, and a dozen cops leaped out armed to the teeth. This time we were surrounded, hustled into the patrol wagon, and carried off to the nearest station. It happened that the station was in charge of a Negro captain, an enormous, very dark, colored man who listened to the officers' charges against us, wrote them down in his book—and refused to lock us up.

"Wait here for your friends," he said gently. "This is outrageous, but it is what happens to colored people in Cuba where white Americans are in control! This is not the first time there has been trouble at the Havana beach."

Out of breath and quite red in the face after not finding us at the beach, José Antonio arrived shortly, and Zell and I were released from the police station to appear for a hearing on the morrow. To court the next morning the beach authorities sent several Cuban attendants whom we had never seen to present their side of the case to the judge. The attendants swore that Mr. Ingram and I had come into the beach café in our wet bathing suits, had put our feet upon the tables, had used profane language, and had otherwise misbehaved to the discomfort of all the more genteel tourists and bathers.

The judge, a kindly old mulatto gentleman—who might have been termed a Negro had he lived in the United States, but who was "white" in Havana—looked at the beach attendants sternly and said, "These gentlemen, I am sure, never set foot on your beach at all. They had no opportunity to change into their bathing suits. They had not been in the water. The police report indicates that they were arrested fully clothed on the street car platform outside. I believe their statement—that you refused to sell tickets to them—and I do *not* believe your fabrications. What you have done is against all the tenets of Cuban hospitality and against Cuban law, which recognizes no differences because of race or color. These guests on our shores have suffered enough at your hands and deserve an apology. Case dismissed!"

When Zell and I moved on that week to Haiti, our Cuban friends who had invited us to a beach party that never came off gave instead a farewell lobster supper with wine, music, and dancing—so we left Cuba with the rumba throbbing in our ears.

ARNOLD SAMUELSON

Havana, 1934: Summer with El Hemingway

"WE WALKED THE NARROW, SHADED STREETS LINED WITH
BUILDINGS CEMENTED TOGETHER IN A SOLID FRONT
AGAINST THE SIDEWALKS, WHICH WERE JUST WIDE ENOUGH
FOR US TO WALK IN SINGLE FILE, WITH E. H. IN THE LEAD
TAKING LONG STEPS, PAULINE TAKING SHORT STEPS BEHIND
HIM, AND ME IN THE REAR TAKING MEDIUM STEPS, WALKING
ON AIR."

*In the spring of 1934, a young man named Arnold Samuelson
hitchhiked and rode the rails from Minneapolis down to Key
West, Florida, to meet Ernest Hemingway. Born in a sod house
in North Dakota in 1912, Samuelson was twenty-two, a farm
boy, a graduate of the University of Minnesota, a cub reporter
for the* Minneapolis Tribune, *and an aspiring writer. Hemingway was by that time the author of* The Sun Also Rises, A Farewell to Arms, *and a good number of short stories. Samuelson
had read one of them, "One Trip Across" (which later became
the first part of* To Have and Have Not), *and it made him want
to meet the author.*

*That spring, Hemingway and his second wife, Pauline, were
living in Key West, and he was starting work on the book that
would be* Green Hills of Africa. *And he was about to take delivery, shortly after Samuelson's arrival, of a new fishing boat. Hemingway liked Samuelson, agreed to advise him on his writing,
and hired him to guard and work on the boat, at a rate of a dollar a day. Samuelson stayed for a year.*

After his death in 1981, Samuelson's daughter found the manuscript her father had worked on over the years, detailing his time with Hemingway in Key West and Cuba. Of all the memoirs about Hemingway, this one is especially interesting, capturing the writer up close when he was at the peak of his energies, both physical and literary.

Samuelson is a very appealing writer. Freely admitting that he had not, at the time, "been around much," he honestly records, for example, how impressed he was by Pauline's painted toenails, the first such he had ever seen.

And then, one day in May, Hemingway went to Miami to take delivery of the new boat, the Pilar, and bring her over to Key West. Samuelson was there.

"She was a beautiful thirty-eight-foot cabin cruiser, new and shiny, with a black hull, a green roof and varnished mahogany in the big cockpit and along the sides. . . . There were many people on the dock looking down at her and E. H. was on board answering questions and showing natives through his ship. . . . I took my shoes off in order not to scratch the varnished deck and went aboard my new home. The cockpit was twelve feet wide and sixteen feet long, with leather-cushioned bunks on each side; the cabins below, smelling of fresh paint and alcohol from the cook stove, had a washroom, a galley with an ice box, sink, cupboards and shelves, and a three-burner alcohol stove, and there were two compartments with bunks to sleep six people. E. H. said she had a stock Wheeler hull with alterations he had designed himself: a fish box built into the stern, cut down to within three feet of the water line to make it easier to gaff big fish and haul them on board; a live-bait well built under the deck; an auxiliary 40 h.p. Lycoming engine installed to run in on if the 80 h.p. marine Chrysler broke down. She was a fine boat, the most valuable property E. H. owned."

Indeed she was, having cost more than the Model A roadster Hemingway was driving at the time.

They spent the summer fishing. Hemingway entertained an ichthyologist from the Philadelphia Academy of Natural History who wanted to classify marlin. One day they sighted a school of sperm whales in the Gulf Stream, but no one in Havana believed they actually had seen whales where whales had never been seen before. *And now and then they ran in to Cojímar, a little fishing village three or four miles east of Havana, which would later figure in both* To Have and Have Not *and* The Old Man and the Sea.

And finally the season was over and it was time to return to Key West.

E. H. WAS LIKE A FATHER TO ME. HE treated me like one of the family and in return I tried to keep the boat in shape. Although that was what he was paying me for, he was grateful for everything I did. It was the first time in my life that I was completely happy when I had a job, and the only thing I worried about was losing it. He never said anything about not taking me along to Cuba and I assumed he would but was afraid he might change his mind. He had planned to leave in late May so as to be in Havana in time for the first of the marlin run and fish it through to the end of the season in the fall, but when the time came to go he received word that the marlin had not yet been sighted by Havana fishermen and he postponed the trip to wait for better reports, being well along in his story and going good, and he thought it would be more profitable to write in Key West than loaf in Havana until the fish came. We waited another month, fishing sailfish in the Gulf Stream, and in the middle of July, Carlos Gutiérrez, his Cuban boatman, wrote that the marlin had begun running and that Woodward, an American living in Havana, had hooked into a doubleheader, both big marlin and both getting away.

We began to get ready the day the news came. E. H. applied for clearance papers, signing himself on the crew list as captain and me as first engineer, as we were permitted to carry more guns and ammunition when we went as officers. We had already stowed half a truckload of canned food on board, and all there was left to do was to run the *Pilar* over to the Thompson dock and fill her gasoline tanks. In the evening, E. H. brought down his rumble seat full of heavy fishing tackle, eighteen-ounce Hardy rods; big 5° Hardy reels; thirty-two-thread line, 500 yards to the spool, and enough pfleuger hoods and heavy piano-wire leaders for several seasons. Then we were ready to leave, there was no doubt of my going along, and I stayed awake most of the night thinking of how it would be over there in Havana, having Cubans doing all the work and me a guest, fishing big fish with Hemingway in the daytime and seeing the sights of Havana at night.

E. H. had said "You haven't seen anything yet."

On the morning of July 18, I heard the cars come out on the dock before sunrise, when it was getting gray in the east over town and a cool breeze was coming off the reef after a hot night. The boat being tied to both piers, lying out of reach between them, I slacked a few yards off the bowline and pulled the stern into the pier, making her fast when the rudder touched. E. H. was on the dock with Pauline and several friends who had got up early to see us off. He handed me heavy fishing reels, marlin-size rods, tuna gut, guns in sheepskin cases, clothes, and boxes of hooks and leads.

"Well, Ernest, I hope you get that big marlin you're after," Sully, the boilermaker, said.

"Thanks, Sully."

"I hope he beats Zane Grey."*

"You want to watch out for those hot Spanish señoritas," old Captain Bra told me. "Three ways! *Tres veces.*" He held up three fingers.

"Tell them hello for me," he said. "There are some good-looking ones over there. I wish I was going along."

"You'll be over later on, won't you?"

"I'd like to, but my old woman wouldn't stand for it."

Captain Bra had had one hell of a time last year. E. H. doctored his penis every night. One woman kept coming down to the boat and had him convinced she was in love with him three ways and that she wanted to marry him. Mrs. Bra wanted no more of that.

---

* Zane Grey (1875–1939), known primarily for his Western stories, had recently authored two highly successful books on big-game fishing, *Tales of Fishing* and *Tales of Swordfish and Tuna.*

We had to wait a few minutes for Charles Lund, the navigator E. H. had hired to steer us across. He came at daybreak, slim and smiling and apologizing for being late. E. H. started both motors, and the people on the dock cast off the lines and stood waving at us until we were out of sight on the other side of the breakwater.

E. H. and Lund changed off at the wheel, steering a southward course to the left of Sand Key. The buildings of Key West disappeared behind our wake, in an hour we had dropped the radio towers and in another hour the Sand Key lighthouse, and all we could see was water. I opened three bottles of beer and E. H. and Lund threw the empties over for target practice with the .22 Colt automatic. It was too rough to hit a target tossing on the waves and the boat rolled so much I began to feel like not eating and lay on my back on the bunk opposite the wheel most of the time, listening to Lund and E. H. talk. E. H. was watching for flying fish and birds, and Lund, standing at the wheel with his feet far apart, said he was used to the slow motion of the Havana—Key West ferry. He was getting a kick out of taking the cruiser across. They were enjoying the trip, E. H. as a fisherman exploring untried fishing grounds, and Lund as a boatman. I was the seasick passenger waiting for land.

"Do you like the sea?" I asked Lund.

"Hell, yes," he said. "If I wasn't married I'd travel all over the damned world."

"How do you like it on the ferry?"

"Too much the same thing all the time. I wouldn't have taken the job if it wasn't for my wife."

"Have you ever tried to get a job as captain of a yacht?" E. H. asked him.

"No."

"Now that you're married, I think you'd like that. You get along well with people and the yacht owners would make a God of you. They always do. Their captain is the God they've made with their own money, they're proud of him and they treat him like a king. If you got in with a rich bastard, he might stay in one port six months at a time and you'd be home every night."

"I'd like to take a shot at it."

"If you met the right people, you'd be all set."

Flying fish sailed out of the water away from both sides of the boat and more kept shooting out in thick droves as we passed over their grounds.

"Look at them! Look at them!" E. H. said. "There must be fish out here. You know what? Sometime it would be fun to take the boat out to the middle of the stream. We could fish all day and drift all night. It would be fun just to see what we'd catch. It might be bloody marvelous fishing out here. What do you think?"

"It might," Lund answered, having crossed the stream almost every day for years. "Funny, I never thought of it before."

"In the morning when we wanted to go back we could take our bearings and run in. There must be fish here. Let's get a feather out."

E. H. trolled a feather for a while, but the boat was going too fast and he reeled in.

Lund knew when the mountains would appear early in the afternoon if the boat was averaging ten knots and the course was true, and when the time came, E. H., standing in the bow looking ahead through his field glasses, saw them first because he was up higher.

"Exactly where they should be," Lund said, proud of his navigation. "Havana is dead ahead."

"Are they near Havana?" I asked E. H.

"Thirty miles up the coast," he answered. "They're the mountains of Cabañas."

"Will we ever see them up close?"

"When Pauline comes over. We'll take a trip up the coast and stay overnight in Cabañas harbor."

"I'd like to see some mountains again."

"They're not very rough. Nothing like the Rockies."

By afternoon, the tiny round tops of the mountains had risen higher and wider, and spread out in a blue ridge above the sea, and then, toward sundown, the long flat line of the Cuban coast came into sight, turning from blue to a dark green as we approached at an angle, the grayish buildings of Havana looking like a small town.

"Think we'll make her in time to clear?" E. H. asked.

"Think we will," Lund replied, pushing the gasoline levers ahead and racing the motors.

"Better take her easy and be sure of getting in."

Lund left the motors racing because he wanted to spend the night ashore in Havana and he knew after six o'clock we would be too late to clear and nobody could leave the ship until morning. E. H. was afraid the motors were being pushed too hard, but he said nothing more about it.

"I smell something," I said, being seasick and sensitive to smells.

"Something's burning!" E. H. said. "Take a look in the galley."

The odor of burning grew stronger and stronger, but we could not locate the fire. We looked everywhere, with the growing, tense excitement known only to passengers on burning ships. E. H. opened the doors above the engine pit and found the big motor so hot the paint was frying off the cylinder head, causing the smell. The pump that circulated water to cool the motor had stopped pumping, and we had to turn the motor off and try to run in on the 40 h.p. Lycoming, which E. H. had had installed for such emergencies.

The Morro Castle was only three miles ahead and we would have arrived in twenty more minutes at the usual cruising speed, but with the small motor barely able to hold the boat against the current of the Gulf Stream, we crawled along slowly for two hours and entered the harbor between the stone wall of Morro Castle and the low Havana waterfront at twilight. A launch filled with soldiers in khaki came out to meet us, and ran alongside, a soldier standing with his rifle at parade dress in the bow asking E. H. questions in Spanish. The guards on the lookout tower of the Morro Castle had seen the *Pilar* approach at a good speed until within three miles of land at sundown and then it had stopped and approached slowly, acting as if she might be loaded with contraband ammunition for the revolutionaries, afraid to come in before dark. They had sent the soldiers to search the ship. E. H. told the soldiers he was an American yachtsman and fisherman and had come to Havana to fish marlin, and the soldiers replied it was a good story but they had to search the boat anyhow. They were ready to come on board and search when another launch approached and an excited voice shouted, "¡El Hemingway!"

"¡Qué tal, Carlos!" E. H. greeted his boatman.

The soldiers became polite and apologetic when they heard that name. They knew Hemingway as the American millionaire who the summer before had caught sixty-four marlin with rod and reel and had given away tons of marlin meat to the natives on the dock. They said they had not recognized him in his new yacht, they were sorry they had made the mistake, they hoped he would catch many marlin again this year, and they went away.

The water in the Havana harbor was calm and restful, and everything was new and interesting. We ran in through the channel, past the fishing smacks along the fortress and the ocean boulevard on the Havana side. The channel widened and E. H. stopped near the pier the fishing smacks used to unload their fish. Lund threw the big anchor off the bow and when it took a hold in the mud, he hitched the rope to the bitt. The incident with the soldiers was over and now when we lay at anchor and had to stay there all night we had time to think about the big motor having broken down. We did not know how long we would be delayed until it could be fixed, or whether E. H. would have to send to the factory for new parts or whether there were mechanics in Havana who could fix it or what the cost might be, and Lund was blaming himself for having run the motors too fast and E. H. might have been silently agreeing with him, although neither of them mentioned it while they talked of other things.

It would have cost $25 extra to clear after six o'clock. E. H. offered to clear if Lund wanted to go uptown to Havana, but he turned the offer down. They talked in the cabin until bedtime and then we all slept on board.

When the customs officers came on board in the morning, they seemed interested only in the way the boat was built, with sleeping accommodations for six people below and a galley and a john and everything, and they didn't try to find hidden ammunition. They opened a few locker drawers as they passed through the cabins without unpacking anything or finding the rifles concealed behind the bunks. E. H. could have had a ton of dynamite under the cockpit deck without it being discovered. The doctor glanced at us and we took down the yellow quarantine flag.

Carlos, the fifty-six-year-old Cuban, wearing a new white outfit with an officer's cap and the letters PILAR sewed across his chest, was standing by in a rowboat with the name *Bumby* painted on its side. When the yellow flag came down, he climbed on board, shook hands with E. H., his black eyes glistening with emotion, and talked excitedly in Spanish, finding the mop and mopping the deck as he talked. There had never been any deck-mopping in Key West. While I watched him mop the deck, I began to lose the comfortable feeling of being useful. I felt the uneasiness of a guest when he sees work being done and wonders whether he ought to help and feels in the way doing nothing. Carlos was getting the attention E. H. had given me when I was his boatman in Key West and E. H., besides being busy with other matters, seemed more reserved; he was now the captain of his ship, an army officer again, and our relationship was becoming less personal because we were on a long expedition together and he had to have discipline.

E. H. went ashore to send a telegram to Pauline, Carlos went along to help find a mechanic, and Charles Lund was in a hurry to get on the ferry, leaving me alone on board.

"Don't worry, you'll see plenty of Havana," E. H. said. "You're not in the navy and you won't be seeing the world through a porthole."

I didn't mind being alone. There was plenty to look at. There was the immense stone wall of the old fortress, running all the way along the narrow channel to the turret of Morro Castle at the point of the harbor entrance, old and gray-looking in the early morning sunlight. There were the passenger boats and freighters from all over the world occasionally coming in and going out of the harbor, seeming to move very slowly because they were so big and leaving a swell that rocked the *Pilar* violently for several minutes after they had passed, and there were many smaller boats—motor launches filled with Cubans, and small, slow-moving rowboats with canvas tops over the stern to shade passengers while the oarsman sat toward the bow, rowing backward in the hot sun. On the Havana side, there were the dark faces and white suits of Cubans riding past the gray apartment buildings in small street cars and open automobiles on the waterfront boulevard. There were other Cubans, whose clothes were not so white, standing on the dock nearby, watching men whirl baited handlines around their fingers without having a bite, then throwing the untouched bait far out again.

An old rowboat came toward me and the Cuban in it, wearing more patches than pieces of his original shirt, pointed at the pineapples, grapefruit, and bananas in the bow.

"No speak Spanish," I said.

"Ho Kay," he answered, waving his hands. "Me speak English. Want this? Want this? Want this?"

"How much pineapples?"

"How many want? One five cent. Two ten cent."

"Two," I said, handing him a dime.

"Want wine?" he asked, holding up a quart bottle.

"How much?"

"Forty cent."

"No, that's all."

"You have American cigarette, no?"

"Yes."

"Trade. Wine, one package American cigarette."

"Against the law."

"Me no speak," he said, shaking his head.

"Sorry."

"Two bottles wine, one package cigarette."

"No can do."

"One other day, more pineapple?"

"Sure, come back again."

When I told E. H. about it, he said, "Don't trust anybody. That fellow might have been a government spy trying to get you in bad. You can never tell who they are."

E. H. had returned with several Cubans, all gesturing freely with their arms and shoulders and speaking excitedly as if they were plotting a new revolution, and E. H., now that he was in Cuba where it was the custom of the country, talked as loudly and gestured as much as anybody. It was fun watching them talk, although I couldn't make anything out of it except that the water pump of the big motor was causing all the excitement and the rotund man named Cojo who walked on his heels was the mechanic who had come to find out why it did not work. Cojo took the pump apart and told E. H. the metal was burned out and the brass would have to be replaced. He knew metal workers in Havana who could do it, the motor would be as good as new the next morning and it would cost less than if E. H. were in the United States and had to send to the Chrysler factory for a new pump. That was wonderful news. It made everybody happy again, and from then on Cojo was our best friend and the most welcomed guest on board the ship. He was welcome to come along fishing every day and drink himself drunk on good whiskey every night if he wanted to.

In the evening, E. H. was preparing to meet Pauline on board the ferry. He had hired a young Spaniard named Juan who was recommended by the pilots as a good cook, and he left us with this admonition:

"We'll be staying at the Ambos Mundos, so I'll leave you and Juan to watch the ship tonight. Sleep light and if you hear anything get up and see what it is. You've heard us talk about the *Terribles Reglanos*. They're a gang of professional pirates living in Regla, that town over there, and they make their living stealing off American yachts anchored in the harbor. They come across the harbor in the night and they don't make any noise so you've got to be ready for them when they come. You sleep up forward with the pistol under your pillow. They might climb the anchor rope and try the forward hatch. Juan will sleep in the stern with the club. If they come aboard stern first, he'll yell and wake you up, then he'll start clubbing them over the heads till you can get out with the pistol. You'll be down below, so you'll be able to see them and they won't be able to see you. Don't shoot to kill unless you have to. Try to shoot them in the legs but be careful not to shoot any holes in the ship."

"I see. I'll shoot at their knees first, and if they keep coming, I'll raise."

"Chances are the first shot will scare them away because we're so close to the dock, but be sure you've got a full clip."

"It's loaded."

"The moon will be out so they probably won't come tonight, but it's always best not to take chances. How do you sleep?"

"Like a log."

"You can train yourself to sleep light. Even if you don't hear anything, make a practice of getting up a few times in the night anyway and look around to see that everything is all right."

"Okay."

"Is there anything you need on shore?"

"No."

"Then Juan will row me ashore and I'll see you in the morning. Good night."

"*Buenos notches.*"

"That's it. Pick up all the Spanish you can. Juan will make you a good tutor. He speaks pure Spanish."

Juan, hungry-looking, with high cheekbones, hollow cheeks, and shoes that were cracked open, was thirty years old. He was a fiery talker, proud because he was a Spaniard and talked like one and not like a Cuban. He had come over from Spain when he was eighteen, and cooked on Cuban fishing smacks several years, staying out weeks at a time with no protection against hurricanes. During his last bad storm, he made up his mind that if he ever got out of it alive he would starve to death on land before he would ever go to sea again. When E. H. hired him, he was almost starved, not having had any work for two years. Now he found himself suddenly prosperous, having a job that paid twenty dollars a month and his board, good wages in Cuba, and that night, as we sat together on the afterdeck, he tried to start a conversation.

"*Yo* Juan," he said, pointing at himself. Then he pointed at me, "*¿Usted?*"

"Arnold."

"*¿Cómo?*"

"Arnold."

"Arnold, Engleesh, *muy bien,*" he said, nodding his head. "*Pero en español*, Arnold, no. *Es Arnoldo!*"

"Juan, Spaneesh, very good," I replied. "But in English, Juan, no. It's applesauce."

"¿Cómo?"

"Applesauce." Juan had never known that his name could be changed so much when translated into good English, and he tried to learn to pronounce the word "applesauce" so he could remember it and tell his friends. He was an enthusiastic teacher and scholar, and traded English for Spanish, pointing at the water, the boats, streetcars, automobiles, the moon and the stars and everything else we could see, each giving the names for them as spoken in his own country, soon forgetting the words of the other language and having to point at them again, repeating the words until we could remember some of them, and when we decided to go to bed, Juan appeared well satisfied with our progress.

"*Pronto* Arnoldo speaka *español,* Juan speaka Engleesh," he said.

"Watch out for the *Terribles Reglanos.*"

Juan grinned and flourished the club. Hearing the word "*Terribles,*" he knew what I meant.

The *Terribles* did not come that night. At sunrise, I awoke hearing Carlos, barefooted on the cabin roof, mopping the dew off the painted canvas as I used to do in Key West every morning. I went to sleep again and slept until the sun was high enough to come down on me through the forward hatch and the heat made me feel like getting up. Juan was ashore buying food at the market and Carlos, having raised the American flag and cleaned up the ship, was sitting in the stern oiling the big fishing reels. At eight o'clock, E. H. showed up with Pauline to see how things were going, and Carlos, who had seen Cojo, told him the water pump could not be fixed till noon. E. H. said he and Pauline were going for a walk downtown and I was welcome to come along. Carlos rowed us ashore and we walked the narrow, shaded streets lined with buildings cemented together in a solid front against the sidewalks, which were just wide enough for us to walk in single file, with E. H. in the lead taking long steps, Pauline taking short steps behind him, and me in the rear taking medium steps, walking on air. I was having that exhilaration which only comes in full force during your first trip on foot in a foreign city, when everything you have seen before is forgotten, everything you see and hear then being so strange you feel it is the same thing as living again, as if you had died and come to life in a different world.

"I don't care if I ever see the United States again," I announced recklessly.

"Do you really like Havana?" Pauline asked.

"It's great! I'm having the time of my life."

"I'm so glad you are. Some people are disappointed. They don't seem able to appreciate it."

The Cubans stepped off the sidewalk to let us pass and stopped and stared at us as we went by. We passed many policemen and soldiers with rifles and they nodded their heads at us because we were Americans and they knew Americans never throw bombs or start revolutions but think only of having a good time spending American dollars. We came out of the cool narrow streets into the open, hot sun of the Prado and turned up the Prado on the marble walk in the center, under cover of shade trees, between the wide traffic lanes on both sides. An American beggar got up from one of the concrete benches along the walk and asked E. H. for a dime. I saw E. H. reach in his pocket for a large coin, which the fellow accepted ungratefully—as if he had more coming—and we went on to a café across the Prado from the Capitolio where they served beer on the sidewalk in the shade. While we sat there, resting after the walk and drinking the Hatuey Cerveza, a street photographer wanted to take our picture and E. H. let him do it. It was a very marvelous life, I thought, when you can make a business of living for the pleasure there is to be got out of it, and I was having a fine time.

E. H. hired a taxi to take us back, and when we stopped at the Ambos Mundos Hotel, a block from the waterfront, the driver demanded twice the usual fare, which E. H. paid in disgust, knowing he was overcharged because we were Americans.

THE CUBAN COAST LOOKED AS DARK GREEN and fresh as it had in the spring when we came over, but we could tell it was fall by the tang of autumn in the air, which had become cooler and windier. The offshore winds blew small rainclouds off the land in the afternoons, and the sudden squalls kept the hills fresh and green and we could smell the hills way out in the stream, but when the wind swung to the north it was a cool, dry wind with winter behind it and we were reminded that the season was almost over. The stream seemed to be emptier every day, and we did not have much to look forward to except the possibility of hooking into a big marlin and seeing it make the same kind of jumps, the difference being it might put up a stronger fight and would weigh more on the dock and look bigger in the pictures. Soon the northers would begin to blow, and before they came we would have to go back to Key West. It would not be long now and we were all thinking about it. The worthwhile part of the marlin season had been over a long time, all the other motor launches had given it up a month ago, there were not many market fishermen to be seen in their skiffs, and we were alone every day in the stream except for the big ships passing in and out of Havana. No guests came with us and we no longer went into the cove to swim and eat, but had our lunch out in the stream, drifting when it was calm and trolling through an empty sea when it was too rough to drift. There was no more of the spirited conversation there had been in the beginning with the Gattornos and Lopez Mendez. Now, alone, we talked less every day as we were coming to the close of a disastrous fishing season, having taken only twelve marlin in three months. E. H. knew it was not much use staying on, but he wanted to fish the season completely through to the finish and could not make up his mind to leave. Carlos and Bolo were very sorry the season was almost over and they would lose their jobs without having saved any money to eat on. Carlos, from his experience with E. H. in other years, told me he expected to get a $200 tip on top of his wages, but Bolo had only been with us a few weeks, he knew he had not been good for much and he could not expect more than he had coming. He wished he was me, he said, so he could go along and stay on the boat at Key West. I had been very eager to come over, I had had a wonderful time in Cuba, but now returning to Key West would be something different again, going back to that quiet, restful life of fishing half days. Although not as excited about it, I was almost as eager to go back.

We had fished in silence all day, drifting in the morning and trolling in the afternoon when the wind came up, and toward sunset, as we were coming in, E. H. hooked a 400-pound striped marlin that came out in a beautiful succession of long, greyhound leaps and Carlos, swinging the boat around with the motors wide open, raced alongside on a parallel course with the fish.

"Not so fast," E. H. said, working on the long U of the line.

Marlin meat being worth ten cents a pound in the market, Carlos was seeing forty dollars coming out of the sea with every jump, and he kept the motors at top speed, racing with the fish as if trying to head it off.

"*¡Córtelo! ¡No tanta máquina!*" E. H. yelled, with his bent rod pointing astern, while the fish was jumping ahead to the right.

"*Sin juventud* [without youth]," Carlos replied, too excited to take orders.

The fish broke off and E. H. reeled in the empty line. He told Carlos that too much speed in chasing a fish was the worst thing they could have, that it put so much strain on the belly of the line it was impossible to avoid breaking off the fish, chasing it that way, but Carlos answered that he had been fishing marlin forty years and he could not believe he had done wrong or lost the fish through lousy boat handling.

On October 15, E. H. cut his left index finger on the fin of a small blue runner he had caught drifting; it was only a surface scratch and he never noticed it until a few days later, when it started an infection and the finger swelled to twice its normal size. Then his whole fist swelled so that it was smooth across the knuckles with red streaks spreading up along the veins of his arm. E. H. had the finger lanced and bandaged and went fishing every day, even though the doctor was uncertain whether it would turn into blood poisoning and advised him to stay in bed and keep his hand in hot water and Epsom salts. E. H. was always the first to insist on having a doctor and following his orders if anything happened to any of us, but with himself it was different. He ignored the torture as if he never felt it. I could see the pain in the hardened expression of his face, but he never complained and something told me not to ask him how his finger was when he came on board in the mornings, although he had always asked me how I felt when I had a bad knee.

The swollen hand and the spreading red streaks on his arm looked more like blood poisoning every day, without being aggravated. I knew E. H. would fight anything that grabbed his hook and I was afraid he would kill himself on a big fish, but, fortunately, he did not have any strikes and one morning the first bad norther was kicking up such a big sea, blowing the white caps off the crests of the waves, there was danger of losing the ship and we had to turn back into the harbor. E. H., realizing there was no fishing weather left except between the northers, ran the *Pilar* over to Casa Blanca, had her put on the ways, her bottom scraped and painted, and when he slid her back into the water and filled the gasoline tanks a few days later we were ready to leave.

They were all down to see us off the last night. All the people in Havana who had fished with us during the summer came on board, and the cockpit was the fullest it had ever been and I could scarcely get through with the whiskies. They were all there, comic Lopez Mendez, still wanting to marry an American girl, Ginger Rogers preferred; his dark, silent cousin Enrique, the straw-hat eater; the great artist Gattorno with the weak voice and delicate face and his beautiful wife still keeping him broke smoking American cigarettes at eighty cents a pack in Cuba and believing she would become a movie star automatically when she arrived in Hollywood; there was Julio, the big, hoarse-voiced pilot, who swung his arms dangerously when he talked; Cojo, the goodhearted mechanic who loved to sit and listen; Dick Armstrong, the Havana newspaper correspondent who always came out to the dock at Casa Blanca and took pictures for us when E. H. had a big marlin strung up; Aliende, the half-starved purchasing agent, who was delivering a huge antique vase E. H. was taking over for Pauline to have in the yard in Key West; and the Gallego, the wine-drinking chauffeur, who always used to ask, "You have *vino para me?*" They were all talking, so there was no connected conversation, and they were all drinking just the right amount of whiskey to feel good, under the dome light of the cockpit roof.

We had to leave before midnight because the clearance papers were made out for that day, the eighteenth of October, but E. H. was waiting till late as the sea was smoothest between midnight and morning. At five minutes to twelve the guests said goodbye, shaking hands with E. H. and wishing him luck as they piled into the skiff that carried them over to the black pilot boat, and E. H., Carlos, and I were left alone.

I went forward to help Carlos lift the big anchor out of the mud and E. H. started the motors and headed the *Pilar* into the dark, open gap between the tower of the Morro Castle and the lights of the Havana waterfront. The black pilot boat, with Hemingway's friends still feeling the effects of the whiskies I had mixed, followed us out of the harbor, past the stone wall of the tower into the open, dark sea.

"Goodbye!" they yelled in a chorus and we could hear Lillian Gattorno's shrill voice above the others.

"Goodbye!" E. H. answered, Carlos and I listening.

"Farewell!"

"Farewell!"

There was an interval of silence while we watched the running lights of the black ship scarcely visible beside us and then they started up again with their goodbyes and farewells. They followed us about three miles out and then we saw the red running light turn around and change to a green one as we saw the other side of the boat headed back to Havana.

It still blew from the northeast and when our eyes got used to the dark we could see the whitecaps of the waves in the dim starlight. The *Pilar* headed north, cutting sidewise into the running waves, both motors hooked up, and sometimes she rolled so much we heard the side propeller thrump when it came out of the water. Only the binnacle light was on, and Carlos sat at the wheel steering and looking down into the compass. I knew he could not read and I did not believe he knew anything about steering a boat in the dark by a compass, but E. H. trusted him and I wasn't afraid. E. H. lay on the starboard bunk with a blanket over him and went to sleep, so that he would be fresh to take the wheel when Carlos became sleepy. I looked down over the stern with the flashlight every once in a while to see if the water pumps were pumping, and when I saw the water spurt out of both holes I sat back in the fishing chair and watched the row of lights of the Havana waterfront growing smaller and shorter, the lights coming closer and closer together. I sat watching and waiting for them to join into a solid white line, so that I could not distinguish any one of them, and they were almost but not quite touching when they dipped under the last wave.

THOMAS MERTON

Havana and beyond, 1940: Blinded by the Light

"I TOLD MYSELF THAT THE REASON WHY I HAD COME
TO CUBA WAS TO MAKE A PILGRIMAGE TO OUR LADY
OF COBRE. AND I DID, IN FACT, MAKE A KIND OF A
PILGRIMAGE. BUT IT WAS ONE OF THOSE MEDIEVAL
PILGRIMAGES THAT WAS NINE-TENTHS VACATION AND
ONE-TENTH PILGRIMAGE."

Thomas Merton's father was English, his mother American, and he was born, in 1915, in the south of France. He grew up in so-phisticated circles, where poetry and painting and ideas were common currency. He attended Columbia University in New York and, like many young intellectuals in the 1930s, flirted for a while with communism.

His life in New York included poetry readings, smoky jazz clubs in Greenwich Village, and late hours all the time. "One stayed up all night," he later wrote, "and finally went to sleep wherever there happened to be room for one man to put his tired carcass." He was doing graduate work at Columbia, head-ing toward a Ph.D. and, with luck, a position as instructor. Meanwhile, in 1938, he converted to Roman Catholicism.

Then there was, among many others, one particularly long night, in 1939, spent with friends at the bar of a jazz club called Nick's, on Sheridan Square. Around four A.M., he and his friends went back to his place on Perry Street, just around the corner. They talked more, slept for five or six hours, and by eleven were awake again, "sitting around dishevelled and half stupefied, talking and smoking and playing records." Around one, Merton went out to get cigarettes and bring back breakfast. He and his friends ate and talked and smoked some more and listened to Bix Beiderbecke on the record player. Then an odd thought took shape in Merton's mind, and he casually announced to his friends, "You know, I think I ought to go and enter a monastery and become a priest."

And that is what he did.

Thomas Merton's calling to the priesthood is almost certainly the most famous vocation of the twentieth century. An autobiography he wrote not many years later, The Seven Storey Mountain (1948), chronicles his early years, his path to the priesthood, and his life as a Trappist monk. It is among the great literary works of our time, moving in its humanity and chilling in its confrontation with the Deity. By the time it came out, Merton had already seen his first volume of poetry published, and he continued writing highly regarded devotional poetry all his life. The Seven Storey Mountain and a 1949 book of prose meditations, Seeds of Contemplation, remain the most widely read books by this uniquely talented and influential spiritual writer and mystic.

The most famous Trappist of the twentieth century did not, at first, intend to join that order devoted to silence and contemplation. In 1939, he applied to the Franciscans, an order dedicated to working in the world, and by the spring of 1940, his application process complete, he was accepted and ordered to report to begin his studies for the priesthood in August. As it turned out, he joined the Trappist order instead and in 1941 entered their monastery at Gethsemani in Kentucky.

But in the spring of 1940, Merton, though looking forward to his new life, was also counting his remaining months of freedom. And he was counting his funds. "Since I was entering the monastery in the summer," he writes in the autobiography, "I assured myself that I ought to take a last vacation, and I was already leafing through books about Mexico and Cuba, trying to decide where I would spend the money that I was no longer going to need to support myself in the world."

An emergency appendectomy delayed his travel plans, but

several weeks of recovery gave him a welcome opportunity to examine and evaluate his spiritual life. "Weak and without strength as I was," he says, "I was nevertheless walking in the way that was liberty and life. I had found my spiritual freedom. My eyes were beginning to open to the powerful and constant light of heaven and my will was at last learning to give in to the subtle and gentle and loving guidance of that love which is Life without end. . . . I was being fed not only with the rational milk of every possible spiritual consolation, but it seemed that there was no benefit, no comfort, no innocent happiness, even of the material order, that could be denied me."

In that buoyant frame of mind, just around Eastertime, Merton sailed for Havana.

THE LIFE OF GRACE HAD AT LAST, IT seemed, become constant, permanent. Weak and without strength as I was, I was nevertheless walking in the way that was liberty and life. I had found my spiritual freedom. My eyes were beginning to open to the powerful and constant light of heaven and my will was at last learning to give in to the subtle and gentle and loving guidance of that love which is Life without end. For once, for the first time in my life, I had been, not days, not weeks, but months, a stranger to sin. And so much health was so new to me, that it might have been too much for me.

And therefore I was being fed not only with the rational milk of every possible spiritual consolation, but it seemed that there was no benefit, no comfort, no innocent happiness, even of the material order, that could be denied me.

So I was all at once surrounded with everything that could protect me against trouble, against savagery, against suffering. Of course, while I was in the hospital, there were some physical pains, some very small inconveniences: but on the whole, everybody who has had an ordinary appendix operation knows that it is really only a picnic. And it was certainly that for me. I finished the whole *Paradiso*, in Italian, and read part of Maritain's *Preface to Metaphysics.*

After ten days I got out and went to Douglaston, to the house where my uncle and aunt still lived and where they invited me to rest until I was on my feet again. So that meant two more weeks of quiet, and undisturbed reading. I could shut myself up in the room that had once been Pop's "den," and make meditations, and pray, as I did, for instance, on the afternoon of Good Friday. And for the rest my aunt was willing to talk all day about the Redemptorists whose monastery had been just down the street when she had been a little girl in Brooklyn.

Finally, in the middle of Easter week, I went to my doctor and he ripped off the bandages and said it was all right for me to go to Cuba.

I think it was in that bright Island that the kindness and solicitude that surrounded me wherever I turned my weak steps reached their ultimate limit. It would be hard to believe that anyone was so well taken care of as I was: and no one has ever seen an earthly child guarded so closely and so efficiently and cherished and guided and watched and led with such attentive and prevenient care as surrounded me in those days. For I walked through fires and put my head into the mouths of such lions as would bring grey hairs even to the head of a moral theologian, and all the while I was walking in my new simplicity and hardly knew what it was all about, so solicitous were my surrounding angels to whisk the scandals out from the path of my feet, and to put pillows under my knees wherever I seemed about to stumble.

I don't believe that a saint who had been elevated to the state of mystical marriage could walk through the perilous streets and dives of Havana with notably less contamination than I seem to have contracted. And yet this absence of trouble, this apparent immunity from passion or from accident, was something that I calmly took for granted. God was giving me a taste of that sense of proprietorship to which grace gives a sort of a right in the hearts of all His children. For all things are theirs, and they are Christ's, and Christ is God's. They own the world, because they have renounced proprietorship of anything in the world, and of their own bodies, and have ceased to listen to the unjust claims of passion.

Of course, with me there was no question of any real

detachment. If I did not listen to my passions it was because, in the merciful dispensation of God, they had ceased to make any noise—for the time being. They did wake up, momentarily, but only when I was well out of harm's way in a very dull and sleepy city called Camagüey where practically everybody was in bed by nine o'clock at night, and where I tried to read St. Teresa's *Autobiography* in Spanish under the big royal palms in a huge garden which I had all to myself.

I told myself that the reason why I had come to Cuba was to make a pilgrimage to Our Lady of Cobre. And I did, in fact, make a kind of a pilgrimage. But it was one of those medieval pilgrimages that was nine-tenths vacation and one-tenth pilgrimage. God tolerated all this and accepted the pilgrimage on the best terms in which it could be interpreted, because He certainly beset me with graces all the way around Cuba: graces of the kind that even a person without deep spirituality can appreciate as graces: and that is the kind of person I was then and still am.

Every step I took opened up a new world of joys, spiritual joys, and joys of the mind and imagination and senses in the natural order, but on the plane of innocence, and under the direction of grace.

There was a partial natural explanation for this. I was learning a thing that could not be completely learned except in a culture that is at least outwardly Catholic. One needs the atmosphere of French or Spanish or Italian Catholicism before there is any possibility of a complete and total experience of all the natural and sensible joys that overflow from the Sacramental life.

But here, at every turn, I found my way into great, cool, dark churches, some of them with splendid altars shining with carven retables or rich with mahogany and silver: and wonderful red gardens of flame flowered before the saints or the Blessed Sacrament.

Here in niches were those lovely, dressed-up images, those little carved Virgins full of miracle and pathos and clad in silks and black velvet, throned above the high altars. Here, in side chapels, were those *pietàs* fraught with fierce, Spanish drama, with thorns and nails whose very sight pierced the mind and heart, and all around the church were many altars to white and black saints: and everywhere were Cubans in prayer, for it is not true that the Cubans neglect their religion—or not as true as Americans complacently think, basing their judgements on the lives of the rich, sallow young men who come north from the island and spend their days in arduous gambling in the dormitories of Jesuit colleges.

But I was living like a prince in that island, like a spiritual millionaire. Every morning, getting up about seven or half-past, and walking out into the warm sunny street, I could find my way quickly to any one of a dozen churches, new churches or as old as the seventeenth century. Almost as soon as I went in the door I could receive Communion, if I wished, for the priest came out with a ciborium loaded with Hosts before Mass and during it and after it—and every fifteen or twenty minutes a new Mass was starting at a different altar. These were the churches of the religious Orders—Carmelites, Franciscans, the American Augustinians at El Santo Cristo, or the Fathers of Mercy—everywhere I turned, there was someone ready to feed me with the infinite strength of the Christ Who loved me, and Who was beginning to show me with an immense and subtle and generous lavishness how much He loved me.

And there were a thousand things to do, a thousand ways of easily making a thanksgiving: everything lent itself to Communion: I could hear another Mass, I could say the Rosary, do the Stations of the Cross, or if I just knelt where I was, everywhere I turned my eyes I saw saints in wood or plaster or those who seemed to be saints in flesh and blood—and even those who were probably not saints, were new enough and picturesque enough to stimulate my mind with many meanings and my heart with prayers. And as I left the church there was no lack of beggars to give me the opportunity of almsgiving, which is an easy and simple way of wiping out sins.

Often I left one church and went to hear another Mass in another church, especially if the day happened to be Sunday, and I would listen to the harmonious sermons of the Spanish priests, the very grammar of which was full of dignity and mysticism and courtesy. After Latin, it seems to me there is no language so fitted for prayer and for talk about God as Spanish:

for it is a language at once strong and supple, it has its sharpness, it has the quality of steel in it, which gives it the accuracy that true mysticism needs, and yet it is soft, too, and gentle and pliant, which devotion needs, and it is courteous and suppliant and courtly, and it lends itself surprisingly little to sentimentality. It has some of the intellectuality of French but not the coldness that intellectuality gets in French: and it never overflows into the feminine melodies of Italian. Spanish is never a weak language, never sloppy, even on the lips of a woman.

The fact that while all this was going on in the pulpit, there would be Cubans ringing bells and yelling lottery numbers outside in the street seemed to make no difference. For a people that is supposed to be excitable, the Cubans have a phenomenal amount of patience with all the things that get on American nerves and drive people crazy, like persistent and strident noise. But for my own part, I did not mind any of that any more than the natives did.

When I was sated with prayers, I could go back into the streets, walking among the lights and shadows, stopping to drink huge glasses of iced fruit juices in the little bars, until I came home again and read Maritain or St. Teresa until it was time for lunch.

And so I made my way to Matanzas and Camagüey and Santiago—riding in a wild bus through the olive-grey Cuban countryside, full of sugar-cane fields. All the way I said rosaries and looked out into the great solitary ceiba trees, half expecting that the Mother of God would appear to me in one of them. There seemed to be no reason why she should not, for all things in heaven were just a little out of reach. So I kept looking, looking, and half expecting. But I did not see Our Lady appear, beautiful, in any of the ceiba trees.

At Matanzas I got mixed up in the *paseo* where the whole town walks around and around the square in the evening coolness, the men in one direction and the girls in the other direction, and immediately I made friends with about fifty-one different people of all ages. The evening ended up with me making a big speech in broken Spanish, surrounded by men and boys in a motley crowd that included the town Reds and the town intellectuals and the graduates of the Marist Fathers' school and some law students from the University of Havana. It was all about faith and morals and made a big impression and, in return, their acceptance of it made a big impression on me, too: for many of them were glad that someone, a foreigner, should come and talk about these things, and I heard someone who had just arrived in the crowd say:

"¿Es católico, ese Americano?"

"Man," said the other, "he is a Catholic and a very good Catholic," and the tone in which he said this made me so happy that, when I went to bed, I could not sleep. I lay in the bed and looked up through the mosquito netting at the bright stars that shone in upon me through the wide-open window that had no glass and no frame, but only a heavy wooden shutter against the rain.

In Camagüey I found a Church to La Soledad, Our Lady of Solitude, a little dressed-up image up in a shadowy niche: you could hardly see her. La Soledad! One of my big devotions, and you never find her, never hear anything about her in this country, except that one of the old California missions was dedicated to her.

Finally my bus went roaring across the dry plain towards the blue wall of mountains: Oriente, the end of my pilgrimage.

When we had crossed over the divide and were going down through the green valleys towards the Caribbean Sea, I saw the yellow Basilica of Our Lady of Cobre, standing on a rising above the tin roofs of the mining village in the depths of a deep bowl of green, backed by cliffs and sheer slopes robed in jungle.

"There you are, Caridad del Cobre! It is you that I have come to see; you will ask Christ to make me His priest, and I will give you my heart, Lady: and if you will obtain for me this priesthood, I will remember you at my first Mass in such a way that the Mass will be for you and offered through your hands in gratitude to the Holy Trinity, Who has used your love to win me this great grace."

The bus tore down the mountainside to Santiago. The mining engineer who had got on at the top of the divide was talking all the way down in English he had learned in New York, telling me of the graft that had enriched the politicians of Cuba and of Oriente.

In Santiago I ate dinner on the terrace of a big hotel in front of the cathedral. Across the square was the shell of a five-storey building that looked as if it had been gutted by a bomb: but the ruin had happened in an earthquake not so very long before. It was long enough ago so that the posters on the fence that had been put up in front of it had time to get tattered, and I was thinking: perhaps it is now getting to be time for another earthquake. And I looked up at the two towers of the cathedral, ready to sway and come booming down on my head.

The bus that took me to Cobre the next morning was the most dangerous of all the furious busses that are the terror of Cuba. I think it made most of the journey at eighty miles an hour on two wheels, and several times I thought it was going to explode. I said rosaries all the way up to the shrine, while the trees went by in a big greenish-yellow blur. If Our Lady had tried to appear to me, I probably would never even have got a glimpse of her.

I walked up the path that wound around the mound on which the Basilica stands. Entering the door, I was surprised that the floor was so shiny and the place was so clean. I was in the back of the church, up in the apse, in a kind of oratory behind the high altar, and there, facing me, in a little shrine, was La Caridad, the little, cheerful, black Virgin, crowned with a crown and dressed in royal robes, who is the Queen of Cuba.

There was nobody else in the place but a pious middle-aged lady attendant in a black dress who was eager to sell me a lot of medals and so I knelt before La Caridad and made my prayer and made my promise. I sneaked down into the Basilica after that, and knelt where I could see La Caridad and where I could really be alone and pray, but the pious lady, impatient to make her deal, or perhaps afraid that I might get up to some mischief in the Basilica, came down and peeked through the door.

So, disappointed and resigned, I got up and came out and bought a medal and got some change for the beggars and went away, without having a chance to say all that I wanted to say to La Caridad or to hear much from her.

Down in the village I bought a bottle of some kind of *gaseosa* and stood under the tin roof of the porch of the village store. Somewhere in one of the shacks, on a harmonium, was played: *"Kyrie Eleison, Kyrie Eleison, Kyrie Eleison."*

And I went back to Santiago.

But while I was sitting on the terrace of the hotel, eating lunch, La Caridad del Cobre had a word to say to me. She handed me an idea for a poem that formed so easily and smoothly and spontaneously in my mind that all I had to do was finish eating and go up to my room and type it out, almost without a correction.

So the poem turned out to be both what she had to say to me and what I had to say to her. It was a song for La Caridad del Cobre, and it was, as far as I was concerned, something new, and the first real poem I had ever written, or anyway the one I liked best. It pointed the way to many other poems; it opened the gate, and set me travelling on a certain and direct track that was to last me several years.

The poem said:

> *The white girls lift their heads like trees,*
> *The black girls go*
> *Reflected like flamingoes in the street.*
>
> *The white girls sing as shrill as water,*
> *The black girls talk as quiet as clay.*
>
> *The white girls open their arms like clouds,*
> *The black girls close their eyes like wings:*
> *Angels bow down like bells,*
> *Angels look up like toys,*
>
> *Because the heavenly stars*
> *Stand in a ring:*
> *And all the pieces of the mosaic, earth,*
> *Get up and fly away like birds.*

When I went back to Havana, I found out something else, too, and something vastly more important. It was something that made me realize, all of a sudden, not merely intellectually, but experimentally, the real uselessness of what I had been half deliberately looking for: the visions in the ceiba trees. And this experience opened another door, not a way to a kind of writing but a way into a world infinitely new, a world that was out of this world of ours entirely and which transcended it infinitely, and which was not a world, but which was God Himself.

I was in the Church of St. Francis at Havana. It was a Sunday. I had been to Communion at some other church, I think at El Cristo, and now I had come here to hear another Mass. The building was crowded. Up in front, before the altar, there were rows and rows of children, crowded together. I forget whether they were First Communicants or not: but they were children around that age. I was far in the back of the church, but I could see the heads of all those children.

It came time for the Consecration. The priest raised the Host, then he raised the chalice. When he put the chalice down on the altar, suddenly a Friar in his brown robe and white cord stood up in front of the children, and all at once the voices of the children burst out:

"Creo en Diós. . . ."

"I believe in God the Father Almighty, the creator of heaven and earth . . ."

The Creed. But that cry, *"Creo en Diós!"* It was loud, and bright, and sudden and glad and triumphant; it was a good big shout, that came from all those Cuban children, a joyous affirmation of faith.

Then, as sudden as the shout and as definite, and a thousand times more bright, there formed in my mind an awareness, an understanding, a realization of what had just taken place on the altar, at the Consecration: a realization of God made present by the words of Consecration in a way that made Him belong to me.

But what a thing it was, this awareness: it was so intangible, and yet it struck me like a thunderclap. It was a light that was so bright that it had no relation to any visible light and so profound and so intimate that it seemed like a neutralization of every lesser experience.

And yet the thing that struck me most of all was that this light was in a certain sense "ordinary"—it was a light (and this most of all was what took my breath away) that was offered to all, to everybody, and there was nothing fancy or strange about it. It was the light of faith deepened and reduced to an extreme and sudden obviousness.

It was as if I had been suddenly illuminated by being blinded by the manifestation of God's presence.

PATRICK LEIGH FERMOR

Havana, late 1940s: Carnival

"AS THE LAST TROOP PASSED THE CAPITOL, THE SPECTA-
TORS SURGED ROUND AND AMONG THEM . . . ALL, DAN-
CERS AND CROWD ALIKE, SWELLING AND SEETHING AND
SHUFFLING IN A DAZZLING CONFUSION, UNTIL THE TOWN
BECAME A UNIVERSAL *CONGA* UNDER A HEAVING ROOF OF
LANTERNS AND STREAMERS AND CONFETTI, AND STARS."

*Unlike the other countries of Latin America and other islands in
the Caribbean, where Carnival celebrations take place in the
spring, just before the start of the Lenten season, Cuba has for
many years held its Carnival, devoid of Christian significance, in
July. Thus the Cuban Carnival neatly coincides with the July 26
national holiday, the anniversary of Fidel Castro's attack on the
Moncada barracks in 1953.*

*Although Patrick Leigh Fermor's description of Carnival in
Havana is vivid, as we would expect from the author of* Mani,
Roumeli, *and other modern classics of travel literature, the Carnival in Santiago de Cuba is generally agreed to be the country's
best.*

*Floats, organized groups of dancers in colorful costumes,
and conga lines that may include hundreds of people fill the
streets of the city. Some of the dance clubs, called carabalís,
date back to the eighteenth century and continue to meet
throughout the year, preparing costumes and rehearsing dance
routines for the next Carnival. Music is everywhere, and—*

though traditional Cuban music is also played—the dominant style for parades and street parties is Afro-Cuban percussion. The closest parallel in the rest of Latin America is the Carnival in Bahia, in the northeastern region of Brazil, where the African influence is strongest.

THE NIGHT TRAIN FROM CAMAGÜEY TO Havana was hurrying us towards the end of our Caribbean journey.

In the south-eastern corner of the island, far beyond the shimmering cordilleras through which we were travelling, lay the city of Santiago, the first capital of Cuba. What a wonderful town it sounds, with its High Renaissance churches in the Florentine style, its Tuscan altars, and its castles, museums, and palaces. It epitomizes for Spaniards who have not crossed the Atlantic all that is most exotic and beautiful in the islands of their lost empire, and it has proved the theme for a poem by Lorca that is almost a metrical litany of nostalgia. Nothing is omitted: the sound of the Trade Winds in the palm trees, the click of the wooden instruments, the rhythm of the dried seeds, the tobacco flower, the alligators:

> *Cuando llegue la luna llena iré a Santiago de Cuba*
> *Iré a Santiago*
> *En un coche de agua negra.*
> *Cantaran los techos de palmera*
> *Iré a Santiago . . .* *

The moon that hung so low over the mountains was as full, as expanded as it is possible for the luminary to be; filled to the point of brimming over, as it were, with lunar substance, until only a circumference ten times her normal size could accommodate it; a lamp that drowned the lustre of every star and

---

* When the moon is full, I will go to Santiago de Cuba
  I will go to Santiago
  In a coach of black water.
  The roofs of the palm trees will sing
  I will go to Santiago.

quickened the wild surrounding mountain ranges and every tree of the unflurried woods that throve in the valleys; and, with the same impartiality, struck everything dead. The branches hung with a metallic and thunderstruck rigidity, and only the sleek elongated reflections of the moon in the railway lines were subject to movement or change.

A strange landscape rose from the mists of the dawn. It was a vista of symmetrical and juxtaposed hemispheres of pale green, and each mound was placed in relationship to its neighbours with the precision of a cell in a honeycomb. The white mist still lingered in the ravines, so that the country rolled away in an infinity of green discs floating on a pale and softly moving network. Across this vague landscape the Royal Palms wandered away in Indian file, each of them taller and more slender than any imaginable tree. This wonderful plant, the *Orodoxia Regia,* is indigenous to Cuba, and it has become the emblem of the Republic. It appears again and again in the embossed and gilded panoramas inside the lids of cigar-boxes; those landscapes that so faithfully capture, as truth is captured by a parable, the atmosphere of Cuba. The smooth trunk, grey-green and perfectly cylindrical, shoots into the air to a phenomenal height, and, on its journey, swells and diminishes with the most gentle curves like the pillar of an Egyptian temple with its girth melted to the exiguity of a pencil and its length drawn ever higher into the sky to explode there in a miraculous corolla of leaves. These dark masses of foliage hung like enormous birds flying parallel to the track of the train or migrated in long winding flights towards the primrose and scarlet daybreak. Isolated *haciendas* floated past with the columns of their verandahs lost in the mist, surrounded now and then by palm-thatched colonies of huts. The little stations were thronged with Negroes and Mulattoes waiting for a later train to Havana: white assemblies of sombreros that all slanted upwards and rotated together as the express rushed past and above them. Yards full of ox-carts appeared for a few seconds, and heavily-caparisoned horses up to their hocks in mist. Then the tobacco-fields or a sudden lake of sugar-cane swept them away, and the strange ballooning savannah returned once more. Grey cattle meditated on the convexities under the palms or moved along the misty labyrinth like ghosts of which only the great emerging horns were real.

The humble Perla de Cuba had infinitely more charm than the luxury palaces that abounded in the more fashionable quarters of Havana. My great wooden bed was more elaborate and unwieldy than a Spanish galleon, and there was something pleasingly austere and monkish about the bare white stone walls of the room and the high ceilings. A single metal spigot fed the washbasin with water. The basin itself was a shallow fluted scallop-shell of marble, destined, one would have said, more for some symbolic sacerdotal purpose than for any mundane ablutions. During the heat of the afternoons, this tall white cell was a priceless refuge. Safely immured here behind closed shutters from the glare and the dust, I would lie and read the history of the Spanish empire. A jug of ice-cold beer stood within easy reach and only a muted suggestion of the traffic penetrated the cool and watery dimness. A ship's siren was audible now and then and every quarter of an hour the bells of Havana sounded. The sweetness of their tone, the Cubans say, is due to the quantities of silver and gold that their ancestors poured into the molten bronze when the bells were cast three centuries ago.

What an astonishing race of men these early Spaniards were! As I turned the pages of the chronicles and histories that record their gestures, the shadowy bearded figures assumed reality and life: the entire Columbus family, Diego Velasquez, Panfilo de Narvaez, Ponce de Leon of Puerto Rico and Florida, Hernandez de Cordoba and Juan de Grijalva who explored the islands of the Mexican Gulf and the coasts of Yucatan; Hernandez de Soto, the discoverer of the mouth of the Mississippi, Vasco Nuñez de Balboa who penetrated the swamps and forests of Darien and first contemplated the waters of the Pacific; the great Cortes* himself, who conquered the empire of the Aztecs with a handful of soldiers and wandered speechless through the saloons and aviaries of Montezuma; Olid and Sandoval, the knights who accompanied him, and Bernal Diaz, the soldier

* Who never, except by poetic right, sat upon a peak in Darien.

who recounts their adventures; the Montejos, who reduced the city-states of the Mayas, and Alvarado, the lieutenant of Cortes and the conqueror of Guatemala; Pizarro, who scaled the Andes and defeated the Incas of Peru. Volume after volume is filled with the expeditions through the jungles in full plate-armour, the battles with the Indian hosts, the victories and disasters, the sudden astounding visions of Popocatepetl and Chimborazo. The mind winged forward to these new realms, to the caciques and emperors in their palanquins of parrots' feathers, the warriors armed with weapons of chalcedony and obsidian, the cathedrals and the grandees' palaces which sprang up in the jungle. Their adventures made it hard to restrict one's thoughts to the confines of this island from which so many of them had set forth; from which, in a couple of days, we were to follow them.

The end of carnival coincided with our last night in Cuba. We forced a passage through the mob which thronged the sides of the Prado, the great boulevard that runs into the central square under the dome of the Capitol, and sat on the kerb with a family of Cubans. Decorated grandstands receded behind us in tiers, and the small boy beside me pointed out the President and other prominent figures. Posses of police roared up and down the empty street on motor-cycles. It all seemed too organized and civic for a carnival. The first beauty-queens, floating at a snail's pace on edifices like huge wedding-cakes of tinsel through dutiful outbursts of clapping, augured badly. It looked as if the whole thing might turn out to be a bore. Hold-ups of three-quarters of an hour turned the effulgence of their smiles to cardboard, and the bare arms that waved in acknowledgement of the languishing plaudits lent to the triumphal cars the purposeless, fluttering motion of sea anemones. They shrank, as the clapping subsided, into immobility, to unfurl and wave again only when the cortège moved on.

At last the final chariotload of Venuses sailed by, and a fanfare of trumpets heralded the arrival of a far stranger procession organized by the Chinese community of Havana. Little men in the costumes of Buddhist priests swelled their cheeks over the mouthpieces of long wind instruments resting on the shoulders of the boys in front of them. A cohort of pikemen followed. They were dressed from head to foot in Chinese armour and they grasped in their hands long halberds with fantastically shaped blades. After them came standard-bearers with silk banners which were embroidered and tasselled and fringed and charged with gleaming stars and with dragons. Others bore aloft on poles enormous three-dimensional dragons made of paper, lit from inside and spiked along their backs, with beams of light blazing from their eye-sockets; resplendent pterodactyls whose tails uncoiled for many yards overhead.

Other light-bearers accompanied them, supporting, in the slots of their baldricks, poles ten or fifteen yards high that poised on their summits many-coloured parchment globes. Some of them were several yards in circumference, the upper parts tapering into the air like pagodas. The curling gables of the superstructure were strung with coloured lights and tassels and bells and Chinese ideograms were painted on their illuminated parchment panels. As they moved along, the light-bearers twirled the staves in their sockets, and the airy palaces and temples, glowing with a soft lustre against the stars, swung and gyrated high over our heads to the sound of bells and trumpets and far-oriental music.

There was something unspeakably charming and almost magical about this flimsy flying architecture. Chinese girls in gold litters came after them, and then, trotting among pikemen, little piebald horses splendidly caparisoned, and miraculously emerging, one would say, from the T'ang dynasty. They bore upon their backs fairy-tale Manchu princesses whose heavy silk and gold-embroidered robes, sweeping to the ground with the stiffness of metal, entirely enveloped them. Under winged and pinnacled head-dresses, ivory Chinese faces of extreme beauty gazed into the night, as motionless and grave under their gleaming accoutrements as those saints on ikons of the Eastern Church whose faces and hands alone the silverwork reveals.

Like a length of Chinese embroidery the procession coiled away. The sound of the bugles and bells grew fainter, and the shining edifices receded; a diminishing Chinese Venice floating into the distance on a lagoon of stars.

An African sound now struck our ears: the clatter and

boom of tom-toms, the sneezing jerk of the shack-shack and the scraping of plectrums over slotted gourds; and, again in the wake of a forest of lights and escorted by the flames of torches, an interminable but orderly horde of Negroes came dancing down the street. They heaved backwards and forwards with the advance and the recoil of the authentic Negro dance of Cuba: the *Conga*. On they came in hundreds, each dancer evolving alone; surging three paces to the left, stopping with a sort of abrupt choreographic hiccup on a half beat, then three paces to the right (crash!), and then to the left again as all the barbaric instruments underlined the beat. As the impact of the music grew, the approaching dancers themselves increased every second in size, until they were dancing past like an invasion of giants.

They were tall, jet black Negroes and handsome Negro women in the slave costume of the plantations. The latter were dressed in white blouses and red billowing skirts with three rows of frills. Red scarves were tied round their heads and tartan shawls about their shoulders. The men were barefoot and sashed with scarlet. Their trousers ended in a fringe half-way down their calves, and a length of tartan stuff was bound about their loins. At their waists hung a tin cup and a plate and red handkerchiefs were tied round their foreheads under broad-rimmed wicker hats of which the front of the brim was fastened back with a large black scorpion. Enormous scorpions were also painted on the drums and banners, and below them were hung scarecrow figures of eighteenth-century plantation owners in powdered wigs. Each of the dancers held in one hand a length of green sugar-cane and in the other a cutlass which he flourished in rhythm with his steps. They were singing a deep repetitive African chant that rose and fell and abruptly ceased and then began all over again in the mode of a Voodoo incantation or one of the Koromantee songs of the Maroons.

In the middle of the throng danced the drummers, some with toms-toms slung from their shoulders and others moving along locust-fashion with their instruments between their bent knees. Troops of Negroes carried drums on their shoulders that were seven yards long; cylinders, like the Assotor drums of the Haitian forests, hollowed from the boles of large trees. Held high above the heads of the dancers, the drummers crouched forward astride these great instruments like demoniac jockeys, the palms of their hands beating the drumheads of membrane with a frenzy that sent each blow booming down the cavern of the drum and out into the air like a shot from a cannon. In this stupendous *Conga*, there was nothing frivolous or carnivalesque. The combination of dance and symbol and song was in the nature of a summing-up of the history and the revolts of the Negroes and of the lament for Africa. It was an apocalyptic intimation, too, of Voodoo, Obeah, Cambois, Schango, Ñañigo, Los Santos, Batonga-Naroca, Candomble, Caboclo, Ubanda, Macumba, and Wanga and all the secret Negro cults of the Americas, and the admiration evoked by the precision and the abandon of the dancing and the magnificent volume of the singing and of the music of the drums was closely allied to awe.

Gradually the Scorpion dancers moved on. They were succeeded, as the hours passed, by armies, each of them over a hundred strong, of Negroes and Mulattoes. First came a party of mock Spaniards in Andalusian dress. Then a Harlem group. The men sported top-hats and tail-coats and gold-knobbed canes and danced gravely along with cigars between the white gloved fingers of their right hands. On the sleeve of their gallantly crooked left elbows rested the gloved arms of their partners: tubes of silver or scarlet or lilac attached to sinuous figures in superbly exaggerated evening dresses that might have been designed by Balenciaga. From the naked shoulder to the knee, they clung as tightly as snakeskin and then flared out behind the stilt-heeled golden shoes in peacock's tails of coloured feathers and sequins. Panaches of ostrich-plumes rose from hip and shoulder and the towering Carmen Miranda headdresses, ascending from their sleek coiffures and climbing and branching and expanding in the air like multi-coloured pineapple foliage, tossed and coruscated with each advancing step.

Then came the Dark Town Strutters; the blazered and straw-hatted, banjo-strumming minstrels; *Charros* and *Vaqueros* with big spurs and sombreros; conquistadores in full armour, musketeers, courtiers in silk and brocade, animals, tumbling dwarfs, and a hunchback with his head flung back who, for mile after mile, balanced a glass of water on his forehead. As the last troop passed the Capitol, the spectators surged round and among them, and the procession simultaneously fanned out and disintegrated among the crowd in many brilliant islets of colour; all, dancers and crowd alike, swelling and seething and shuffling in a dazzling confusion, until the town became a universal *Conga* under a heaving roof of lanterns and streamers and confetti, and stars.

Holding hands lest the human currents should carry us off into different maelstroms, we headed back to the *Perla de Cuba* to collect our luggage. Breaking free from the main tide of dancers, we raced along the back streets, for our plane was leaving in half an hour. The rum-shops in the colonnaded lanes were packed to capacity with disguised Negroes. A party of Scorpions, with their cutlasses scattered about the tables, were drinking straight out of the bottle. One of their number still hammered away at a drum while a Minotaur span round and round, slowly clapping his hands. Confetti was scattered everywhere and tangled balls of streamers had collected in the gutters. Under a street lamp at the corner six amazing figures stood in colloquy. They were horses' heads ten feet high, like gigantic chessmen with bared teeth and staring eyes, their lower lips, articulated to mimic the action of speech, hanging inanely loose. Little portholes in their breasts revealed the faces of six Negroes smoking cigars. Intrigued by our three running figures, the great heads swung ponderously round and followed us out of sight with their great fatuous eyes.

The lights of Havana grew smaller and finally merged into a luminous smear. The only distinguishable object was the revolving beam of the lighthouse on the Morro, and in a little while we were flying over a bare tract of the Caribbean. The aeroplane was almost empty. Joan and Costa, exhausted like me by the doings of the last few hours, had turned off the lights over their seats and settled down to sleep. I felt I should soon do the same. The water was scarcely visible by the light of the stars, but in a little while the remains of a moon began to appear and a faint radiance was spread over the eastern rim of the sea.

Well, I thought, as I gazed out of the throbbing cocoon at

the emptiness, that was the last of the Antilles. The Negroes had come to an end, and, except for the narrow red quadrilateral of British Honduras towards which we were flying—which is little more, really, than a landing-stage on the shores of Latin America—so had the colonial world of the British, the French, the Americans, and the Dutch. All that lay ahead was Spanish, of which I knew very little, and Indian of which I knew nothing at all; a region of great rivers and swamps and steaming forests inhabited by baboons and jaguars and the quetzal, the semi-divine bird with the two long green tail feathers; waterless sierras and the pyramids and the ruined cities of the Mayas, baroque cathedrals and ruined cities of the Spaniards. The tapering sequence of the central American Republics, through which our travels for the next few months were about to begin, waited the other side of the night; dwindling southwards from the bulk of the Mexican mountains to the narrow filament of Darien in a long-drawn-out plague of volcanoes whose smouldering cones stood like a barrier between us and the Pacific Ocean. These tenebrous regions approached through the darkness while the curving line of our past itinerary streamed away behind us into memory. There lay the islands in the night, suspended between the stars and the sea's bottom with the abstraction of thoughts: the stages of a thesis that was still to be unravelled. Guadeloupe was the exordium. The Lesser and then the Greater Antilles and Haiti swelled into a ponderous exegesis waiting to be clinched and driven home at last with the triumphant peroration of Cuba. And what was the conclusion to be?

The day that was about to begin happened, by a coincidence that is no literary device, to be my birthday. Rilke mentions an old superstition, in one of his letters, that a microscopic chink exists between the ending of one year of a lifetime and the beginning of the next. For a split second, he says, one can peer through this fissure in the joinery of time and behold the Truth. This moment was now approaching, and no place surely could be more propitious for taking full advantage of it than this undetermined point two or three thousand feet above an empty sheet of water. Making my mind a blank, I watched the minute hand of my wrist-watch move forward.

But the moment of revelation failed to occur. Nothing happened. Nothing, that is, except a smell of garlic that ensnared me like a noose and the sound of a voice asking me the time. I opened my eyes again and saw that the fourth passenger, who had appeared till then to be asleep, was leaning across the alleyway. It was an ugly, cheerful, intelligent, and rather charming face made raffish by several days' growth of beard. He seemed inclined for conversation, and questioned me about my provenance and my destination. When he was duly informed, I asked him the same questions; where was he from—Cuba, Guatemala, Mexico? No, no, he said, he was a Greek from Sparta returning from a family visit in the Peloponnese to his grocery business in Nicaragua. Things were pretty bad in Greece, he continued. Prices were rising, the cost of olive oil was enormous, the drachma was falling every day; there were scarcely any caiques sailing between Crete and the Aegean islands—all sunk in the war; the civil war was wrecking the country's economy, and there were bandits even in the mountains of the Morea. No stability anywhere. "But still," he concluded, "the wine is cheap and the people don't change." His gold teeth appeared for a moment in a rather melancholy smile. "It was bad to leave just as spring was coming on." We talked of such matters for an hour or two, and then fell asleep.

NORMAN LEWIS

Havana and the Finca Vigia, 1957: Visiting Hemingway and one-fourth of James Bond

"THE SEVILLA BILTMORE WAS ON THE PRADO, HAVANA'S
PRINCIPAL STREET, WHICH EVEN NOW, AT HALF-PAST EIGHT
IN THE MORNING, WAS FULL OF STROLLING, LOUDLY
CHATTERING CROWDS, THE MEN SMOKING TREMENDOUS
CIGARS. THERE WERE MANY AMERICAN TOURISTS, SOME OF
THEM BEHAVING RATHER ERRATICALLY."

British author Norman Lewis instantly became one of my favor-
ite writers when I reviewed Voices of the Old Sea *for Smithson-*
ian in 1985. That movingly detailed book chronicles the
transformation of a traditional Catalonian fishing village into yet
another little vacation spot on Spain's Costa del Sol.

Lewis's interests have always been international. Among his
early books were The Honored Society: A Searching Look at
the Mafia *(1964) and* Naples '44 *(1978), a memoir about*
World War II. More recently, he has written Jackdaw Cake
(1987), an autobiography; The Missionaries *(1988), about the*
cultural destruction wrought in Latin America in the name of
Christianity; A Goddess in the Stones: Travels in India *(1992),*
one of the best books ever written about that complex country;
and An Empire of the East: Travels in Indonesia *(1993).*
Among his novels is Cuban Passage, *published in 1982.*

The Sevilla Biltmore Hotel where Lewis stayed in Havana
is once again just the Sevilla, as it was when it opened in 1908,

*catering to, as it advertised, "the diplomatic life and the most ex-
clusive society of Cuba's brilliant capital." On Calle Trocadero,
near the Prado, in Old Havana, the Moorish-style building has
188 rooms. It was closed for renovations for some years. Restored
to its 1920s glory, with its patios and Spanish fountains, it re-
opened for guests in 1993 and became home to Havana's tourism training school, giving students on-the-job experience. For
decades a centerpiece in Havana's social life, the Sevilla played
a role in Graham Greene's* Our Man in Havana.

I MET IAN FLEMING AT CAPE'S ANNUAL
party. Jonathan Cape made no secret of disliking Fleming,
had read only the first chapter of *Casino Royale* and nothing
whatever of his subsequent books, but reluctantly accepted that
he was likely to become the firm's best-selling author since
T. E. Lawrence.

When I arrived at the party, I was shunted off into a side
room of which Ian was the only occupant. He was prone to fits
of paranoia, and at that moment was in a foul mood, having
taken it into his head, quite wrongly, that the party was for
Cape's less prestigious authors. He soon recovered, and asked
me if I wrote poetry. When I replied that I did not, he seemed
disappointed. He admitted to being bored with thrillers of the
kind he wrote, and enjoyed the company of those who had dedicated their lives to higher literary ideals.

He then began to quiz me on the Caribbean. It was generally known that during the war he had been assistant to the
Director of Naval Intelligence, and from the way his questioning went, it seemed clear that although he was now foreign
editor of the *Sunday Times*, his link with intelligence had not
been severed, and that his field of operation was Latin America.

He wanted to talk to me about Cuba, and I told him that
I had visited the island twice, had travelled from one end of it
to the other, and still had friends there with whom I exchanged
occasional letters.

During the war, I had also been engaged in intelligence
duties at a fairly low level, and it was clear that Fleming was

aware of this. He asked me if I would consider visiting Cuba on behalf of the *Sunday Times*. This sounded to me like an interesting temporary escape, and I said that I would. He explained that an uprising had taken place on the island, and he was convinced that the reports passed to him through official sources tended to play down the importance of what was happening. He believed I might be able to get nearer the truth.

At this point, a strange convergence of interests became evident. Fleming believed that Ernest Hemingway was in contact with the revolutionaries, and that he was the man I should see. The trouble was that Hemingway had taken himself off to live in isolation on a farm somewhere outside Havana, and Jonathan Cape, his publisher, was the only man in England in touch with him. Jonathan was anxious to hear news of what was expected to be Hemingway's final masterpiece, and Fleming was convinced that if Cape could be induced to write a letter to him on my behalf, he would see me. This Jonathan Cape agreed to do, and the arrangements for the journey went ahead.

It was a Sunday in late December 1957 when I arrived in Havana. I was carrying a letter of introduction to a New Zealander named Edward Scott who edited the *Havana Post* and lived in the Sevilla Biltmore Hotel—rather splendidly, Ian told me, in the penthouse flat. At Ian's request, Scott had reserved a room there for me, but had since been called away to Pinar Del Rio, leaving me a note saying that he might be held up there for two or three days. I unpacked, took a quick bath, and decided to take a short tour of the neighbourhood.

The Sevilla Biltmore was on the Prado, Havana's principal street, which even now, at half-past eight in the morning, was full of strolling, loudly chattering crowds, the men smoking tremendous cigars. There were many American tourists, some of them behaving rather erratically, and I was told by the man at the kiosk from whom I bought the morning edition of Scott's newspaper that most of them were drunk and would probably remain so over the whole of their weekend in Havana. His words were confirmed by the number of bars advertising, in English, HANGOVER BREAKFASTS.

I carried on down to the port, where at this hour the Galician shark fishermen were bringing in their blood-lacquered boats, and then went on to the Malecón, the greatest sea promenade in the world. Nothing had changed in the nineteen years since my last visit. Once again, I was overwhelmed by the flowering, scented spaces, the grey, time-scoured walls with their granite facets glistening, the thrusting femininity of the women, the playful arrogance of the men, the soft growl of negro voices through the spray spattering over the sea wall, the rust-choked barrels of cannons that had last been fired at the English pirates, the millionaires' seaside houses like wedding cakes turned to stone and painted red, blue, or yellow according to the owner's political allegiance.

Despite these outward appearances, profound changes had taken place. Batista—formerly known as "the handsome mulatto"—had taken on and defeated the ferocious colonels of the old regime, but now Batista too was old, and had himself been defeated by success and time. Instead of laughing at his opponents, he shot them, and the city was filled with unmarked graves.

One of the old reactionary officers, Enrique Loynaz, had actually survived and, not only that, had risen to the rank of general. By the greatest of good luck, I had a letter of introduction to him, and the next day I paid him a call. He took me to see General García Velez, the other surviving hero of Cuba's war of independence against Spain.

Velez was an anglophile and for twelve years had been ambassador to Great Britain. Since his return to Cuba, he had done his best, against considerable odds, to create for himself a West End of London environment, filling his flat with heavy Victorian furniture imported from England. The room in which he received us was overflowing with fringed lampshades, antimacassars, and aspidistras. He was ninety-four and believed the fairly sedate surroundings in which he lived might help him to last out to a hundred.

The horrors of war had left Velez a pacifist, whereas Loynaz, despite a variety of wounds, was as bellicose as ever. The story of his most dramatic escape from death was held ready for such occasions, and as soon as the pretty mulatta in lace cap, apron, and gloves had brought the Earl Grey tea, he launched into it.

It happened at Babinay in 1898, as the war was drawing to a close. The Cubans could already taste victory, and the Spanish were preparing to sell their lives dearly behind a seven-foot stockade. Loynaz, a poor horseman at the best of times, as he readily admitted, was now compelled by custom to mount a white horse and lead the final charge.

"I was never a good jumper," he said. "I fell, landing on the horse's neck, and one of the Spaniards brought down his machete on the top of my head."

Both Velez and I were ordered to examine the result. There was a trough about six inches long on his skull, and its edges could still be felt through the skin.

"Three American presidents have felt that wound," Loynaz said, "Harding, Teddy Roosevelt, and—I forget the third. Anyway, I managed to scramble back into the saddle, holding my brain in with my fingers. They got me to the nearest house. There was a couple staying there on their honeymoon, and we commandeered their bed. It was a month before I was on my feet again, and I noticed a remarkable thing. Up until then, I had suffered from headaches all my life. Now they were gone. My doctor said that opening up the skull had made more space for the brains."

It was now García Velez's turn. "Do you think he'd like to see the album, Enrique?" he asked.

"I'm quite sure he would," Loynaz replied.

Velez found a bunch of keys on a shelf and took them into the next room. He returned with his album and, displacing an aspidistra, made room for it on a low table.

He opened it carefully, explaining that he had inherited it from an ancestor named Francisco Miranda. Loynaz released a preliminary cackle as I found myself looking down at a wisp of hair as dry as hay stuck to the centre of a yellowed page over an illegible scrawl of faded ink.

"What you see there is pubic hair, one of fifty-one examples donated by the great ladies of Miranda's acquaintance," said Loynaz.

"What on earth made them agree?" I asked.

"It was a passing craze," Velez said. "It did a woman's reputation no harm to have had an association with a man of the

standing of Francisco Miranda. All the women were after him."
He stroked the filaments of hair with a fingertip. "This is La
Perechola La Segunda," he said. "She was the greatest actress
ever to appear on the South American stage. Pay no attention
to the message. It's a fake. She couldn't write. Nine out of ten
of them couldn't."

"May we see the greatest of the conquests?" Loynaz asked.

"You may," Velez said. He leafed cautiously through the
pages, then stopped.

"This one should be in a museum," Loynaz said.

"It should. Where it could be properly looked after, before
it's lost altogether. I've offered it to the National Museum, but
they seem to be toffee-nosed these days."

This time, the writing was legible under the ragged little
tuft: a splendid, arrogant K, half-smothered in entwining curli-
cues. "Catherine," Loynaz murmured reverently.

Velez nodded. "The Great Queen."

"Apart from the remains in the Kremlin vault, this is all
that has survived of the body of Catherine the Great of all
Russias."

I expressed all the wonder expected of me, yet a lurking
doubt remained. Later, after Loynaz and I had left, I asked him
whether he thought the Catherine part were true.

Loynaz patted at the cavity in his skull as if to confirm that
the brains were still in position. It was a gesture that suggested
he might not be sure of the facts.

"No reason why it shouldn't be," he said. "Miranda was
forty-odd at the time, an absolute ram. Catherine put up money
for his adventures and invited him to stay in Moscow. She was
very lustful. And besides, she was fifty-eight."

On my next visit to Velez, I asked him about the political
situation. People, I said, were talking of the Castro revolt and
its chances of success. What was it all about? My question gave
Velez the chance to ride his favourite hobby-horse: the scandal-
ous treatment Cuba, and he himself, had received at American
hands after the War of Independence. This, he believed, had
sown the seeds of almost all the nation's subsequent troubles.

"The war was over before they arrived," Velez said. "They
dropped like vultures out of the sky to pick up the spoils. For

six years, the Yankees ran the country and snapped up every-thing worth having. Hence Castro."

"What do you mean?" I asked.

"A lot of middle-class boys see Castro as their only chance of getting anywhere. Don't ever believe Karl Marx has anything to do with it. We're talking about high-school boys who can't find nice white-collar jobs. Fidel started out as a lawyer. He went in for revolutions because he only had ten clients, and they were too poor to pay. Do you know how the present bother started? It was over an increase in bus fares. That's the cause of the trouble: university drop-outs who refuse to walk."

The next morning, Scott returned, and we met in the hotel coffee shop. His appearance came as such a surprise that for a moment I thought that I had picked out the wrong man. Ian had told me that James Bond was an amalgam of four actual persons, one of whom was Scott. But the man before me was short and somewhat plump, with rosy cheeks, small blue eyes, and the expression of a confiding child. He had once been a champion boxer, but had put on weight since then.

As this one-quarter of James Bond read my letter of intro-duction very slowly, folded it with great care, and put it into the breast pocket of his shirt. I took in further details of his appear-ance: the small feet encased in brilliantly polished shoes, the gold fountain-pen, and the small, dimpled hands. In moments of concentration, as while reading the letter, his expression be-came wary and stern.

"Let's go and talk things over," he suggested. He guided me to the lift, and we went up to his flat which was at the end of a long passage scented with wax polish and fine cigars. We passed first of all into a small anteroom, in which stood, ele-gantly posed, a quite naked negress. At first, I took her to be a statue, but in passing I could not help noticing the goose-pim-ples produced by the chill of the air-conditioning. Scott glanced at her as we passed into his office.

I later learned that Scott believed frequent intercourse to increase mental creativity, and I wondered if he had simply for-gotten that the girl was there. He kept a register in which he entered the details of several thousand encounters over the years. It was a compulsion he shared with John F. Kennedy, who occasionally popped over to Havana for random excitements of this kind, and Scott had had the pleasure of showing him round.

"Why do you want to see Hemingway?" he asked.

"Because Ian thinks that he and Castro may be working together."

Scott gave a bellowing laugh. "Hemingway, of all people!"

"There's some story that he met Castro when he was hunting in the mountains."

"The only mountain Hemingway hunts in is the Montana Bar. He's a burnt-out case. Any time you want, you can see him in there. His friends bring him king-sized prawns. He chews them up and swallows the lot, shells and all."

Scott's dislike of the great man stemmed from an incident that happened at a party to celebrate the Queen's birthday given by the British Ambassador, at which Ava Gardner had appeared on Hemingway's arm. In a moment of high spirits, the actress had taken off her pants and waved them at the crowd. Scott, who considered himself an ultra-patriot, objected to this insult to the Crown. In the wrangle that followed, Hemingway, known for his aggression, threatened to thrash Scott to "within an inch of his life."

"Next day," Scott said, "I sent him a formal challenge to a duel. Don't laugh. This is a serious matter."

"Do people still fight duels in Cuba?" I asked.

"They do. Frequently. Right now, they have a couple of victims in the city morgue, mixed up with the student revolutionaries."

"Do you think he'll accept?"

"No, I think he'll back down. Anyway, in case he doesn't, how about being my second?"

"Sorry," I said. "It would make a good story, but nobody would ever believe it."

Scott seemed to want to impress on me that his talk of duels was not to be taken lightly, and took me off to a private shooting gallery in the offices of the *Havana Post*. The far end of the room had been fixed up with an arrangement of the kind that might have been used in a fairground; playing cards were clipped to moving wires in a way that allowed them to move laterally at varying speeds, jerking up and down simultaneously.

He then produced two sinister-looking pistols. He set the cards in motion, bobbing and ducking on their wires, and we took aim. I failed to hit anything, and so did he.

"Pst . . . missed it again. Pst . . . this isn't my day. Pst . . . not again! I don't believe it. Pst . . . I'm not altogether happy with the way these fit into the hand. May have something to do with it. Hang on while I slow the thing down."

I expected no better of myself, but for someone who was a quarter of James Bond, it was not good enough, and it occurred to me that it might be as well for him if Hemingway did turn his challenge down.

Back at my hotel, a call came through from Ian Fleming.

"How's it all going?" he asked.

"Fairly well," I said.

"Have you talked to the writing man?"

"Not so far," I said.

"Do your best to see him."

I assured him that I would. Fleming had just re-read *The Old Man and the Sea,* and was more convinced than ever that it was a masterpiece. He had the book open by the telephone and read me a favourite passage. I agreed with him that it was superb but could not see that this literary skill had any bearing upon the author's judgment of a political situation. "People say he keeps out of politics these days," I said, "but I'll go on trying to have a word with him."

Some days later, a letter arrived from the great man saying that he had heard from Jonathan and would be pleased to see me. It was written in a small, neat hand, with a certain formality of tone. He would be sending a car to pick me up the next day.

The car duly arrived, and I was driven to Hemingway's converted farmhouse in the hilly outer suburbs of the city. The retreat was protected by a high fence over which hardly more than the roof was to be seen. There was a gate on the approach road, secured by a heavy padlock and chain. When we stopped, the driver got out, thrust a huge key into the padlock, and let us through. I wandered a short way up a drive to the house, little realizing that each step was taking me closer to an experience which would change my outlook on life, not instantly, but in a most fundamental way.

I was about to enter the presence of a being of a heroic, almost legendary kind, who had reconstructed the literary architecture of the twentieth century and had now, with his recent book, been awarded its highest prize. In addition to these achievements, Hemingway had had the courage and the vision to speak out on the side of the Spanish Republican government when it was under attack not only from Spanish rebels but from the troops sent to Spain by Mussolini and from Hitler's Luftwaffe, which first practised on Spanish territory its techniques of mass destruction. He had pleaded with the English, the inventors of non-intervention, to realize that they would be next, and even then he was a big enough man for his warnings to be listened to, even if they were subsequently ignored.

The driver pushed open the door and shoved me through it into a narrow passage with another door at the end. I tapped on this, and a growl came from the other side which I took to be an invitation to enter. I did so, and found myself in some kind of bedroom lined with bookshelves. Bottles were stacked within reach of the bed on which Hemingway was sitting. He hauled himself to his feet and turned to face me. He was in his pyjamas, and I was shocked and bewildered by what I saw. He had remained forever young in my imagination, boisterous and vigorous in the never-ending fiesta of life. But here was an old man, slow-moving, burdened with flesh.

He mumbled a welcome and, moving slowly under the great weight of his body to find the drinks, poured himself, to my astonishment, a tumbler of Dubonnet, half of which he immediately gulped down. Above all, it was his expression that shocked me, for there was an exhaustion and emptiness in his face: the corners of his mouth were dragged down by what might have been despair, and his eyes gave the impression that he was trying to weep.

Two objectives of this visit were to be kept in mind, the first being Jonathan Cape's hope for the imminent delivery of the book Hemingway had been reported as working on for several years. A cautious reference to this subject provoked something close to an outburst of fury. Wasted and watery eyes swivelled around to focus on me with suspicion. What did I want? What had I come for? "Is this an interview?" he asked coldly.

There was something about him which reminded me of Massart in *For Whom the Bell Tolls*—"one of France's great modern revolutionary figures," Chief Commissar of the International Brigade, a "symbol man" who cannot be touched. With infallible discernment, Hemingway had described this great old man's descent into pettiness, and now I was amazed that a writer who had understood how greatness could be pulled down by the wolves of weakness and old age should—as it appeared to me—have been unable to prevent himself from falling into the same trap. How grotesque, but how sad, must have been his appearance at the embassy party with Ava Gardner on his arm.

I hastily assured him that I was no more than a messenger from a very old and devoted friend, his enthusiastic publisher, who had hoped that I would be able to convey his heartfelt congratulations on the success of *The Old Man and the Sea*.

Humble pie produced the reverse of the desired effect. Hemingway embarked on a tirade over what he saw as Cape's parsimonious handling of the publication. "They didn't want to spend money on it," he said. To make sure the American edition had a good dust-jacket, he had hired a first-class artist himself, but the English version had been done on the cheap, and sales had suffered. At this point, someone rattled at the back door, and Hemingway lurched towards it with a cry of irritation to suppress the female twitterings that came through.

The subject of Scott's challenge now came up. "Do you know this guy? I hear you've been seen around with him. Is he a friend of yours?"

"I had an introduction from London. I've seen him a few times."

"He's been built up as some sort of dead-eye Dick. You think that's true?"

"I've no way of knowing," I said, "but I doubt it."

"Take a look at this," he said. He handed me a copy of a letter he had written to the *Havana Post*. I read it. He had taken note, he said, of a challenge to a duel made by Edward Scott, the newspaper's editor. This he had decided not to take up in the belief that he owed it to his readers not to jeopardize his life by its acceptance.

"Dignified?" he asked.

"Very," I said.

"Give me your frank opinion. What do you feel about this business yourself?"

"I wholly agree with you. The thing's absurd. Even if this is Cuba, it is the twentieth century."

"Right," he said. He nodded vigorously, smiling for the first time in the course of our meeting. "That's the way it is."

I was astonished, in view of the macho posturing for which he had become famous, that he was prepared to give this publicity to what many of the paper's readers would see as a loss of nerve and of face.

As there was nothing more to be done for Jonathan Cape, only Ian Fleming's interest remained to be served. I took the plunge.

"How do you see all this ending?" I asked. "Can Castro pull it off?"

Comrade Massart's cautious, watery, doubting eye was on me again. "My answer to such questions is bound to be that I live here," Hemingway said.

In my letter to Fleming, in which I reported on my meeting with Hemingway, I wrote:

> There was something biblical about it, like having the old sermon about the vanities shoved down your throat in the middle of whatever you happen to be doing with your life in the workaday world. They give funny names to the buses in this town, and there's one that runs past the hotel that says WE JUST RAN SHORT OF GREATNESS, which just about sums him up, although perhaps understating the case. This man has had about everything any man can ever have wanted, and to meet him was a shattering experience of the kind

likely to sabotage ambition—which may or may not be a good thing. You wanted to know his opinion on the possible outcome of what is happening here. The answer unfortunately is that he no longer cares to hold opinions, because his life has lost its taste. He told me nothing, but he taught me more than I wanted to know.

GRAHAM GREENE

Havana and Santiago de Cuba, 1957

"I ENJOYED THE *LOUCHE* ATMOSPHERE OF BATISTA'S CITY
AND I NEVER STAYED LONG ENOUGH TO BE AWARE OF
THE SAD POLITICAL BACKGROUND OF ARBITRARY
IMPRISONMENT AND TORTURE."

*In the years since his death, in 1991, we have come to learn
that Graham Greene's two volumes of autobiography,* Ways of
Escape *and* A Sort of Life, *were something less than forthright
and complete. In the first volume, he briefly describes visits to
Havana in 1954 and to Havana and Santiago de Cuba in 1957.
His breezy confession that he enjoyed the "louche atmosphere" of
Havana in the fifties, combined with an equally breezy avowal
that he had no opportunity to notice that this "sin city," this
"Pearl of the Antilles," filled as it was with gambling, liquor,
drugs, and prostitution, was rotten to the core, just doesn't ring
true.*

*But Greene knew what he was dealing with, as is perfectly
clear from his wonderful satire of international skulduggery,* Our
Man in Havana, *published in 1958. Wormold, the vacuum-
cleaner salesman at the center of that novel, becomes trapped
not only by his own web of deceit but by the inner workings of a
hopelessly corrupt city and society. This is a comic novel that includes some very bloody violence, and all readers are likely to*

remember Milly's friend, Captain Segura, who is the head police officer in the fashionable Vedado district of Havana, in charge of torturing prisoners, and who is reputed to carry a cigarette case made of human skin.

It's interesting to keep in mind that much of the novel turns on the presence of rebels who are building up their forces while hiding in the mountains of Oriente province at the far eastern end of the island. Those forces, of course, were led by Fidel Castro, who had become a heroic and revolutionary figure to many ordinary Cubans by his attack on the military's Moncada barracks on July 26, 1953. By the end of 1958, the year Greene's novel was published, Castro's revolutionary force had advanced westward nearly the length of the island and into Havana itself, ironically arriving in the streets of the capital in the midst of New Year's Eve celebrations. And by dawn on the morning of January 1, 1959, it was already a very new year indeed in the history of Cuba.

The following excerpt provides some background on the origins of the novel and hints at some of Greene's own adventures among the fleshpots of the Caribbean's hottest city.

The film of Our Man in Havana includes some brief but intriguing glimpses of city sights known to all visitors at the time.

SOON AFTER THE WAR ENDED, MY FRIEND Alberto Cavalcanti, the Brazilian director, had asked me to write a film for him. I thought I would write a Secret Service comedy based on what I had learned from my work in 1943–4 of German Abwehr* activity in Portugal. I had returned from Freetown—and my futile efforts to run agents into the Vichy colonies—and been appointed to Kim Philby's subsection of our Secret Service, which dealt with counterespionage in the Iberian peninsula. My responsibility was Portugal. There those Abwehr officers who had not been suborned already by our own Service spent much of their time sending home completely er-

---

* The Abwehr, with Admiral Canaris at the head, was the official German Secret Service.

roneous reports based on information received from imaginary agents. It was a paying game, especially when expenses and bonuses were added to the cypher's salary, and a safe one. The fortunes of the German Government were now in decline, and it is wonderful how the conception of honor alters in the atmosphere of defeat.

I had sometimes thought, in dealing with Portugal, of how easily in West Africa I could have played a similar game, if I had not been content with my modest salary. I had learned that nothing pleased the Service at home more than the addition of a card to their Intelligence files. For example there was a report on a Vichy airfield in French Guinea—the agent was illiterate and could not count over ten (the number of his fingers and thumbs); nor did he know any of the points of the compass except the east (he was Mohammedan). A building on the airfield which he said housed an army tank was, I believed from other evidence, a store for old boots. I had emphasized the agent's disqualifications, so I was surprised when I earned a rating for his report of "most valuable." There was no rival organization in the field, except S.O.E., with whose reports mine could be compared, and I had no more belief in S.O.E. reports than in my own—they probably came from the same source. Somebody in an office in London had been enabled to add a line or two to an otherwise blank card—that seemed the only explanation.

So it was that experiences in my little shack in Freetown, recalled in a more comfortable room off St. James's, gave me the idea of what twelve years later, in 1958, became *Our Man in Havana.*

The first version, written in the forties, was an outline on a single sheet of paper. The story was laid in 1938, in Tallinn, the capital of Estonia, a reasonable enough setting for espionage. The English agent had nothing at this stage in the story to do with vacuum cleaners, and it was the extravagance of his wife and not his daughter which led him to cheat his service. He was a more besotted character than Wormold in *Our Man in Havana* and less innocent. As the 1939 war approached, his enemies, like Wormold's, began to treat him seriously—the local police too. The incident of the misused microphotographs was already in this draft. Cavalcanti, before we started work, thought it necessary to get clearance from the censor, and he was told that no certificate could be issued to a film that made fun of the Secret Service. At least that was the story he told me. Perhaps he invented an excuse because he was not enamored of the subject.

The story remained at the back of my mind, submitting itself to the wise criticism of the preconscious. In the meanwhile I had visited Havana several times in the early fifties. I enjoyed the *louche* atmosphere of Batista's city and I never stayed long enough to be aware of the sad political background of arbitrary imprisonment and torture. I came there ("in search of pleasure for my punishment," Wilfred Scawen Blunt wrote) for the sake of the Floridita restaurant (famous for daiquiris and Morro crabs), for the brothel life, the roulette in every hotel, the fruit machines spilling out jackpots of silver dollars, the Shanghai Theatre, where for one dollar and twenty-five cents one could see a nude cabaret of extreme obscenity with the bluest of blue films in the intervals. (There was a pornographic bookshop in the foyer for young Cubans who were bored by the cabaret.) Suddenly it struck me that here in this extraordinary city, where every vice was permissible and every trade possible, lay the true background for my comedy. I realized I had been planning the wrong situation and placing it at the wrong period. The shadows in 1938 of the war to come had been too dark for comedy; the reader could feel no sympathy for a man who was cheating his country in Hitler's day for the sake of an extravagant wife. But in fantastic Havana, among the absurdities of the Cold War (for who can accept the survival of Western capitalism as a great cause?) there was a situation allowably comic, all the more if I changed the wife into a daughter.

Strangely enough, as I planned my fantastic comedy I learned for the first time some of the realities of Batista's Cuba. I had hitherto met no Cubans. I had never traveled into the interior. Now, while the story was emerging, I set about curing a little of my ignorance. I made Cuban friends, I took a car and traveled with a driver around the country. He was a superstitious man and my education began on the first day, when he ran over and killed a chicken. It was then he initiated me into the symbols of the lottery—we had killed a chicken, we must buy such and such a number. This was the substitute for hope in hopeless Cuba.

Destiny had produced this driver in a typically Cuban manner. I had employed him some two or three years before for a few days in Havana. I was with a friend and on our last afternoon we thought of trying out a novelty—we had been to the Shanghai, we had watched without much interest Superman's performance with a mulatto girl (as uninspiring as a dutiful husband's), we had lost a little at roulette, we had fed at the Floridita, smoked marijuana, and seen a lesbian performance at the Blue Moon. So now we asked our driver if he could provide us with a little cocaine. Nothing apparently was easier. He stopped at a newsagent's and came back with a screw of paper containing some white powder—the price was the equivalent of five shillings, which struck me as suspiciously cheap.

We lay on our bed and sniffed and sniffed. Once or twice we sneezed.

"Do you feel anything?"

"Nothing at all."

We sniffed again.

"No lift?"

"No lift."

I was of a more suspicious nature than my companion and I was soon convinced that we had been sold—at what now appeared an exorbitant price—a little boracic powder. Next morning I told the driver so. He denied it. The years passed.

When I came back to Havana in 1957 I looked for him in all the quarters where drivers congregated; I left messages for him without effect; I turned down many volunteers, for Castro's nocturnal bombs were frightening away the tourists and there was much unemployment. The man I remembered might be a swindler, but he had been a good guide to the shadier parts of Havana, and I had no desire for a dull and honest man to be my daily companion on this long trip. One night, when I had decided to wait no longer, I went to the Shanghai Theatre. When I came out into the dingy street I saw a number of taxis drawn up. A driver advanced towards me. "I have to apologize humbly, señor. You had reason. It *was* boracic powder. Three years ago I was deceived, too. The accursed newspaper seller. A swindler, señor. I trusted him. I give you back the five shillings. . . ." In the course of the tour which followed he made a better profit than he had lost. Every hotel, every restaurant, every cantina paid him his commission. I never saw him on my next two visits to the island. Perhaps he was able to retire on his gains.

There was one place in Cuba to which we were unable to drive—Santiago, the second city of the island. This was now the military headquarters in the operations against Fidel Castro, who made periodic sorties from the mountains with his handful of men. It was the beginning of the heroic period. The Oriente Province, almost to the last man, woman, and child (I say child advisedly), was on the side of Fidel. There were military roadblocks all round the capital of Oriente and every foreigner arriving by private car was suspect. An unofficial curfew began at nine P.M., dangerous to ignore; there were arbitrary arrests, and often when day broke a man's body would be found hanging from a lamp post. That was a lucky victim. One building had an unsavory reputation because of the screams which could be heard in the street outside, and after Santiago had fallen to Fidel a cache of mutilated bodies was found in the country outside the city bounds.

Not long before, the United States Ambassador, who had the disagreeable task of supporting Batista, had visited Santiago to be received by the Mayor. An impromptu demonstration by the women of Santiago was organized with the lightning speed that a regime of terror induces. There was no class differentiation. This was still the period of national revolt. Middle-class women and peasants joined in singing Cuban patriotic songs to the American Ambassador, who watched from the balcony of the town hall. The military ordered the women to disperse. They refused. The officer in command had fire hoses turned on them, and the Ambassador, to his honor, broke up the party. He was not going to stand there, he said, and watch women assaulted. For this he was later rebuked by John Foster Dulles: he had committed a breach of neutrality. There was to be no Bay of Pigs during Batista's reign of terror. In the eyes of the United States Government terror was not terror unless it came from the left. Later, at a diplomatic cocktail party in Havana, I referred to the American Ambassador's protest while I was talking to the Spanish Ambassador. "It was most undiplomatic," he said.

"What would you have done?"

"I would have turned my back."

The only way to go to Santiago was by plane. The night before I left I was at a late party with some Cuban friends. They were all of the middle class and all supporters of Fidel (though at least one of them has now left Cuba). One young woman there had been arrested by Batista's notorious police chief, Captain Ventura, and beaten. Another girl claimed that she was a courier for Fidel. She was going by the same plane as myself and she asked me to take in my suitcase a lot of sweaters and heavy socks badly needed by the men in the mountains. In Santiago the heat was tropical. There was a Customs' examination at the airport, and it was easier for a foreigner to explain away the winter clothes. She was anxious for me to meet Fidel's representatives in Santiago—the genuine ones, she said, for the place was full of Batista's spies, especially the hotel where I would be staying.

Thus began a comedy of errors as absurd as anything I described later in *Our Man in Havana*. The next morning the correspondent of *Time* called on me. His paper had instructed him to accompany me to Santiago to give me any aid I wanted. I wanted no aid, but his paper obviously thought that I might supply a paragraph of news in one way or another. I had to get hold of the girl to warn her that I would not be alone. Unfortunately I did not know her name or her address, nor was my host of the previous night better informed. However, he drove me to the airport and while I waited in the bar he watched by the entrance. Eventually he came back with the instruction that I was not to recognize her—she would telephone me in the morning at my hotel.

The hotel stood at the corner of the little main square of Santiago: on one side was the cathedral, its wall lined by shops. A couple of taxis and a horse cab looked as if they had given up all hope of custom. Nobody came to Santiago now, except presumably the spies against whom I had been warned. The night was hot and humid; it was nearly the hour of the unofficial curfew, and the hotel clerk made no pretense of welcoming strangers. The taxis soon packed up and went, the square cleared of people, a squad of soldiers went by, a man in a dirty white drill suit rocked himself backwards and forwards in a chair in the hall, making a small draft in the mosquitoey evening. I was reminded of Villahermosa during the persecution in Tabasco. The smell of a police station lay over the city. I was back in what my critics imagine to be Greeneland.

While I was having breakfast next morning there was a knock on my door—it was the *Time* correspondent accompanied by a middle-aged man in a smart gabardine suit with a businessman's smile. He was introduced as Castro's public-relations man in Santiago—he seemed a world away from the guerrillas in the mountains outside. I was embarrassed, for at any moment I expected the telephone to ring. I tried to persuade him to call a little later, when I was dressed. He went on talking. Then the telephone rang.

By this time I was so convinced of the danger of "spies" that I asked Mr. X and the correspondent of *Time* to leave my room while I answered the telephone. They went reluctantly. My caller was the girl, who asked me to come to a certain number in Calle San Francisco. Mr. X returned to the room. He told me he was convinced I had been contacted by a Batista agent. None of his organization would have been so reckless. . . . He demanded to know what had been said to me on the telephone.

I was irritated. I had never asked to be involved. I indicated that so far as I was concerned he might himself be a Batista agent. It was an impasse, and he left.

Now my problem was to find the street. I felt afraid even to consult the hotel clerk. I went into the square and sat down in one of the two forlorn taxis. Before I had time to speak to the driver a Negro, flashily dressed, took the seat beside him. "I speak British. I show you where you want to go." If any man was a Batista informer, I thought, this was the one.

"Oh," I said vaguely, "I want to see the city, the points of interest"—and off we went, down the hill to the port, up the hill to the memorial to the American Marines killed in the Spanish-American war, the town hall . . . I could see myself landed back at the hotel again, unless I found an excuse.

"You have an old church, San Francisco?" I asked. If such a church existed, surely it would be in the street of that name.

The guess proved correct: there was an old church and it was in the street I wanted. I told my guide that I would find my own way back to the hotel—I wanted to pray. Soon my stroll in the cloisters was interrupted by a priest, unfriendly and suspicious: I could hardly explain to him that all I wanted was a little time for my taxi and my Negro to disappear from sight.

After that began a walk up Calle San Francisco in the hot noon sun. The street was as long as Oxford Street and the number I wanted was at the farther end. I had only covered half the distance when a car drew up at my side. It was Mr. X and the *Time* correspondent.

"We have been searching for you everywhere," Mr. X said reproachfully.

I tried to think of an explanation of why I should be walking up this interminable street in the hot sun.

"It is O.K.," Mr. X said. "Completely O.K. I find my own organization has contacted you," so I finished the journey in comfort, in the car.

At the house, which was owned by a wealthy bourgeois family of Santiago, were the courier from Havana, her mother, a priest, and a young man who was having his hair dyed by a barber. The young man was a lawyer called Armando Hart, who later became Minister of Education in Castro's Government and then the second secretary of the Communist Party in Cuba. A few days before, he had made his escape from the law courts in Havana while he was being taken under military escort to trial. There was a long line of the accused—a soldier at each end. Hart knew the exact point beside the lavatory where the corridor turned and where momentarily he would be out of sight of the soldier in front and the soldier behind. He slipped into the lavatory and out the window; his friends were waiting in the street outside. His absence was not noted until his name was read out in court.

His wife, now known to all Latin America as Haidée Santamaria, was with him in the house, a young haggard woman who looked in those days as if she had been battered into fanaticism by events outside her control. Before she married Hart she had been affianced to another young Fidelista. He was captured after the unsuccessful attack on the Moncada barracks in Santiago in 1953 and she was taken to the prison to be shown his blinded and castrated corpse. (I remembered that story when the wife of the Spanish Ambassador spoke to me of Batista's social charm.)

That was past history. All they were concerned with now were the jet planes which the British were preparing to sell to Batista—they were better informed than the British Government in this house in Calle San Francisco, for when, after my return to England, a Labour M.P. at my request asked a question on the subject, he was assured by the Foreign Secretary, Selwyn Lloyd, that no arms at all were being sold to Batista. Yet some months later, a week or two before Castro entered Havana, the Foreign Secretary admitted that an export license for some out-of-date planes had been granted. At the time he had granted the license he had no information—so he said—that a civil war was in progress in Cuba.

For one observer there was already in Santiago plenty of evidence of civil war. The night after my arrival three sisters, aged between eight and ten, were seized from their home by soldiers in the middle of the night. Their father had fled from Santiago and joined Castro in the mountains, so they were taken in their nightclothes to the military barracks as hostages.

Next morning I saw the revolution of the children. The news had reached the schools. In the secondary schools the children made their own decision—they left their schools and went on the streets. The news spread. To the infants' schools the parents came and took away their children. The streets were full of them. The shops began to put up their shutters in expectation of the worst. The army gave way and released the three little girls. They could not turn fire hoses on the children in the streets as they had turned them on their mothers, or hang them from lamp posts as they would have hanged their fathers. What seemed strange to me was that no report of the children's revolt ever appeared in *Time*—yet their correspondent was there in the city with me. But perhaps Henry Luce had not yet made up his mind between Castro and Batista.

And the British Government? The civil war was still invisible as far as the Foreign Office was concerned. But by the time of my next visit to Havana—the very time when the export license for planes was granted—the civil war was sufficiently in evidence to confine me to Havana. Not even by plane could I visit Santiago. Indeed I was unable to travel more than a hundred kilometers from Havana—no taxi driver would accept the risk of ambush, for not even the main roads were secure. By that time I had finished *Our Man in Havana*. I had no regrets. It seemed to me that either the Foreign Office or the Intelligence Service had amply merited a little ridicule.

Alas, the book did me little good with the new rulers in Havana. In poking fun at the British Secret Service, I had minimized the terror of Batista's rule. I had not wanted too black a background for a light-hearted comedy, but those who had suffered during the years of dictatorship could hardly be expected to appreciate that my real subject was the absurdity of the British agent and not the justice of a revolution, nor did my aesthetic reasons for changing a savage Captain Ventura into a cynical Captain Segura appeal to them.

A postscript to history: Captain Ventura escaped from Cuba to the Dominican Republic by holding up his own President at the point of a gun. Batista intended to leave him behind like the last drop in a glass, a sacrifice to the gods. But Ventura arrived on the airfield at Havana and forced Batista to disgorge some of his baggage to make room for him. They must have made an uneasy couple, those two, in the hotel in Ciudad Trujillo, where Ventura spent long hours playing the fruit machines.

FRANK RAGANO and SELWYN RAAB

Havana, 1958: Out on the town with the mob

"HAVANA WAS FAMOUS FOR *LOS EXHIBICIONES*—SEX SHOWS—
AND SANTO THOUGHT I SHOULD SEE ONE. . . . 'THE FIRST
THING EVERY SECRETARY, SCHOOLTEACHER, AND NURSE
WANTS TO SEE WHEN THEY COME HERE IS *LA EXHIBICION.*' "

Batista and the mob were made for each other.

*During the 1930s, when Fulgencio Batista was first in
power in Cuba, the gangster Meyer Lansky described him to Mafia boss Lucky Luciano as "the best thing that ever happened to
us. I've got him in my pocket, whether he's president or whether
he puts somebody else in, no matter what happens. He belongs
to us. I handle all his money—every dollar, every peso he takes,
I'm handling the transfer to his account in Switzerland."*

The Last Testament of Lucky Luciano, *by Martin A.
Gosch and Richard Hammer, published in 1975, provides a colorful story of Luciano's historic visit to Havana.*

*In the fall of 1946, Luciano, who had been deported from
the United States, was living in the Excelsior Hotel on the Via
Veneto in Rome, keeping himself occupied with some local
black-market business but waiting all the time for word from
Meyer Lansky about bigger things, including a meeting to solid-
ify his position in the mob. Finally the message arrived, hand*

delivered by a new deportee. It was three words long. "December," it said, "Hotel Nacional."

In late October, Luciano arrived in Havana by air. Lansky met his private plane at the airport and swept him through customs without so much as a raised head. Luciano checked into the Nacional under the name on his passport, Salvatore Lucania, and moved into the suite reserved for him by Lansky, whose interests and influence in Havana permitted him to reserve anything or anyone he wanted.

The suite was at the east end of the building and offered a sweeping view of the whole city and what Luciano thought was the Caribbean Sea. It was, of course, the Atlantic Ocean, but Luciano thought the blue water was just as pretty as the Bay of Naples.

The conference of mob bosses was scheduled to begin on December 22. With two months ahead of him, Luciano moved out of the Nacional after a week and into a Spanish-style mansion, fully staffed with servants, on Quinta Avenida in the attractive Miramar section, which was filled with the estates of rich Americans. Lansky arranged for a new American car to be delivered to Luciano, without the usual annoying import duties. "It was," Luciano would declare years later, "one helluva change from Dannemora."

As a cover to legitimize Luciano's lengthy stay in Cuba, Lansky suggested that he buy an interest in the casino in the Hotel Nacional, which was easily arranged because the casino was jointly owned by Lansky and Batista. Batista at this time was living in Miami, counting his money and pulling the strings of the Cuban president, Ramón Grau San Martín.

The conference was going to last nearly a week at the Nacional, where meeting rooms and the top four floors of the building had been reserved for the exclusive use of delegates. The first to arrive was Vito Genovese, who settled into a penthouse suite. The next day the others began arriving, coming from all over the United States and including such people as Joe Adonis, Albert Anastasia, "Joe Bananas" Bonanno, Frank Costello, Tommy Lucchese, Joe Profaci, Tony Accardo from Chicago, Carlo Marcello from New Orleans, and Santo Trafficante from Tampa, plus Lansky and "Dandy Phil" Kastel, neither of whom would have a vote in the proceedings but whose influence was great.

If anyone had asked, the cover story for this historic Mafia conference—the biggest since Chicago in 1932 and the last of its kind until the ill-fated Apalachin meeting in 1957—was that it was meant to honor a nice Italian boy from Hoboken named Frank Sinatra.

By late 1946, Sinatra had long since graduated from the Rustic Cabin, a roadside bar in New Jersey, had put in a brief stint with Harry James, and was now the featured singer with Tommy Dorsey. How much help Sinatra needed with his career at this point is open to debate, but Luciano thought he needed a hand and the conference needed a cover story. "He needed publicity, clothes, different kinds of special music things," Luciano later told Gosch, "and they all cost quite a bit of money—I think it was about fifty or sixty grand." Under the circumstances, Sinatra went down to Havana to say thanks.

The conference began with a lavish evening dinner on the twenty-second, then formally opened the next morning in a conference room on the mezzanine level, which had been closed off to other hotel guests for the entire week. Luciano sat at the head of the table, with Lansky, Costello, Genovese, and Adonis closest to him. Beyond that, the other delegates could sit anywhere.

The first order of business clearly established the organization's loyalty to Luciano as Boss of Bosses. Luciano declared his already well-known opposition to dealing in drugs, but the group felt otherwise. And then they discussed the horrendous cost overruns Bugsy Siegel had amassed in building his Flamingo Hotel in sleazy little Las Vegas, when all the action was in Reno. Siegel, it was decided, had to be eliminated, but at Lansky's urging the hit was postponed until after the Flamingo's opening three days hence.

Wives and girlfriends—and Frank Sinatra—arrived on Christmas Eve, and everyone attended a gala party in the hotel that lasted until morning. Havana at that time had nearly two dozen newspapers, but despite all the holiday hoopla at the Nacional, not a word about it appeared in any of them.

At an evening meeting on the twenty-sixth, the group waited for word from Las Vegas about the opening of the Flamingo. Word finally came; the opening had been a disaster.

Still, the group agreed to Lansky's plan for reorganizing the Flamingo, and Siegel, unknowingly, got another lease on life.

At four in the morning, just as Luciano, exhausted and depressed, was leaving the conference room, Vito Genovese came up to him and said quietly that he wanted to talk. Luciano hated and distrusted Genovese, and they rode up in the elevator to Genovese's penthouse suite in silence.

As soon as the door was closed, Genovese declared rudely that he deserved and wanted "half of Italy," and hinted that he was in a position with the U.S. authorities to make things warm for Luciano if he didn't agree. At that, Luciano saw red. "I pushed him up against the wall," Luciano told his biographer, "and I beat the livin' daylights out of him. . . . I started to knock him around the room like he was a rubber ball. I didn't hit him in the face—I didn't want to mark him up. I just belted him in the guts and in the kidneys, and when he fell down I just started to kick him in the belly, and every shot I took with my fists and my foot I told him he was only a shit and a son of a bitch and a dirty rotten Neapolitan louse."

Besides the body bruises, Genovese had three broken ribs and a fractured left arm. A cooperative doctor was found, Genovese remained in his room for three days, word went out that he'd had a sudden attack of the flu, and the penthouse suite rapidly filled up with flowers, baskets of fruit, and get-well messages from his colleagues at the conference.

For three decades, attorney Frank Ragano provided legal guidance and defense for such Mafia bosses as Santo Trafficante (son of the Santo Trafficante who attended the 1946 meeting in Havana), who worked mostly in Florida and Cuba, and Carlos Marcello, in New Orleans, and for fifteen years he was one of the lawyers who worked for Teamsters boss Jimmy Hoffa.

Ragano's autobiography, Mob Lawyer, written with New York Times crime reporter Selwyn Raab, was published in 1994, violating omertà, the code of silence that protects the mob. In his Foreword to that book, Nicholas Pileggi writes that Ragano "loved what he was doing. He had been intoxicated by the men and the power that surrounded them. He was the envy, he was sure, of every hustling, non-trust-fund lawyer in America.

"When he and Hoffa and Trafficante and Marcello were rid-ing high, there were very few businessmen, and even fewer politicians, who wouldn't take his calls and beg to be included on his heady ride. He was a player, a participant in some of the nation's biggest games. The godfathers came to him. He knew nothing but secrets."

In 1952, at the age of twenty-nine, Ragano opened his first law office, in Tampa, Florida. Two years later he was doing busi-ness with Santo Trafficante.

At that time, using money from an illegal numbers game op-erated in Florida (as was thought by the Kefauver committee in-vestigating organized crime in the United States), Trafficante either owned outright or had a large interest in five Havana ho-tels and gambling casinos, which were legal there. While main-taining a modest home in a blue-collar section of Tampa, Trafficante spent a great deal of time in Havana, supervising his investments and living the good life.

The other big casino operator in Havana was Meyer Lansky, who had had business interests there since the 1930s. Because he was Jewish, Lansky could never be a full-fledged member of the Mafia, but Mafia bosses, including "Charlie Lucky" Luciano, trusted him and relied on his business acumen. Lansky had great skill in operating businesses, especially nightclubs and casi-nos, at a profit, and he had equal skill in making those profits disappear, even from legitimate enterprises. By 1957, he was the major partner in three Havana casino hotels, including the large Riviera.

After the murder of mob boss Albert Anastasia on October 25, 1957 (while he was getting a shave in the barbershop of the Park Sheraton Hotel, on New York's Fifth Avenue), law enforce-ment officials were eager to talk with Trafficante about a possi-ble connection between the murder and mob activities in Cuba. Trafficante had been in New York at the time, staying at the Warwick Hotel, where Anastasia maintained space; it just so happened that Trafficante had checked out that same morning and was boarding a direct flight to Havana at the very time that Anastasia was being blown away. Interest in Trafficante height-ened when, three weeks later, on November 14, he was among more than sixty mob bosses who were arrested at a summit meet-

*ing in Apalachin, New York. Unperturbed, Trafficante was back
in Tampa in December, making his usual rounds.*

*Trafficante told Ragano that he'd had dinner with Anastasia
the night before the murder and had outlined a deal they were
working on. The Hilton hotel chain was building a thirty-story
hotel in Havana, bigger even than Meyer Lansky's Riviera. Since
the Hilton people never operated casinos themselves, they were
prepared to offer a franchise, demanding a million dollars a
year, with two million up front (the equivalent of more than
thirty million in the mid-1990s). The plan, as Trafficante outlined it to Ragano, had been for Anastasia to put up one million
to match Trafficante's own million. The casino in the Hilton
was going to be a gold mine.*

*Early in January 1958, Trafficante went back to Havana.
Shortly after, Manhattan District Attorney Frank Hogan issued a
nationwide alarm for him, enabling law officers anywhere in the
country to detain him for questioning. Trafficante found it convenient to remain in Cuba for an extended period. And when Trafficante wanted to see Frank Ragano, Ragano had to go to
Havana.*

*Foresighted and businesslike as they were, neither antici-
pated that in a matter of months the party would be over, or
that in less than two years the new Havana Hilton would be renamed the Habana Libre.*

I KNEW THAT LIVING IN CUBA WAS
hardly an adversity for Santo. It had been his favorite place
before the troubles in New York in late 1957, and he had frequently rhapsodized about Havana as a near paradise.

My first trip to Havana had nothing to do with Santo. In
1956 I spent a brief vacation there with my wife, Betty, and
another couple, and the experience was startling. As a soldier, I
had seen decadence in postwar Japan, but Havana was wilder.
Prostitution was wide open and casino gambling went on almost twenty-four hours a day. There was nothing comparable
to it in the straitlaced United States. I had old-fashioned conservative notions about taking respectable women to places of

debauchery, and I decided never to return to Havana with my wife.

Santo, however, persistently urged me to visit him in his semi-exile, and to maintain our relationship, in 1958 I became a frequent passenger on the ninety-minute flight from Tampa to Havana.

On my first trip alone, Santo met me at the airport with a Cuban friend and casino partner, Evaristo Garcia. Santo and Garcia were the principal owners of the Commodoro Hotel and casino, one of the places into which the Trafficante family had put money in the late 1940s. On the drive into Havana, they talked about the best place for me to stay.

Garcia turned to Santo and said, "Why don't we put Frank up in the special suite at the Commodoro?"

The two of them burst into laughter.

"It's obviously a private joke," I said. "What's the special suite?"

Santo, the expression on his face now serious, remarked that in the previous year, 1957, he had met Senator John F. Kennedy of Massachusetts while the senator was visiting Havana. His instinct told him Kennedy had a yen for the ladies and he and Garcia offered to arrange a private sex party for him, a favor Santo thought might put the prominent Kennedy in his debt.

They set up the senator with three gorgeous prostitutes in the "special suite" at the Commodoro. It was special because a two-way mirror allowed Santo and Garcia to secretly watch the proceedings from an adjoining room.

Recounting the story, Garcia's face crinkled in smiles while Santo remained deadpan. Observing a respected U.S. senator cavorting in bed with three call girls was one of the funniest sights they had ever witnessed. Because Kennedy had accepted their offer, Santo and Garcia had lost all respect for him. From their point of view, an official like Kennedy, who publicly preached law, order, and decency and secretly took bribes or slept with prostitutes was a rank hypocrite who deserved no esteem.

Santo was no Peeping Tom, and from the way Garcia

laughed, I considered him to be the chief culprit in arranging the orgy.

Santo enjoyed a royal lifestyle in Havana. His wife, Josephine, whom he always referred to as Josie, and their two daughters, both of whom were schoolteachers, lived in Tampa and rarely visited him. He luxuriated in a vast apartment he owned in a chic twenty-five-story building with a panoramic view of Havana and the Malecón, the broad boulevard along the city's scenic harborfront.

For female companionship Santo, who was in his mid-forties, kept a Cuban mistress, Rita, a former showgirl at one of his nightclubs, who was some twenty years his junior.

"I've got a wonderful wife," he said matter-of-factly, "but everybody in Cuba has a mistress, even Batista. You've got to have fun in this world."

Santo and his father had been operating casinos in Havana since 1946, and their investments multiplied enormously after Fulgencio Batista seized power in a 1952 coup d'état. Everyone knew that Batista's government was thoroughly corrupt. Although he exacted a heavy price from the casino and hotel operators, Batista rewarded them richly. Tourism and gambling were priorities for Batista and he encouraged their growth. Visa requirements were waived to make it easy for Americans to spend time in Cuba, and with the expansion of the airline industry, Havana became a favorite playground for Americans. Batista unintentionally led the boom in tourism and gambling that later transformed the Caribbean.

More tourists meant more action in the casinos, and to help the Havana casinos compete with Las Vegas, the government permitted twenty-four-hour gambling and no limits on wagers. Government controls and supervision of the gaming rooms were minimal. Of course, all casino operators had to kick back sizable sums in return for the unrestricted privilege of providing blackjack, dice, roulette, and slot machines to players.

The cost of a government gambling license was nominally $25,000, but Santo explained that $250,000 was the expected amount to be paid under the table for a lucrative concession.

Each casino was visited almost nightly by bagmen who collected a percentage of the take for Batista and his cronies.

One of the first casino entrepreneurs in Cuba, Santo by 1958 had established the largest gambling network in Havana. It was all legal. He either owned or was the head of syndicates that controlled five casinos. One was in a nightclub, the Sans Souci, and the remainder in the Capri, Commodoro, Deauville, and Sevilla Biltmore hotels. (The mob had a penchant for continental names.) Except for the Commodoro, all were relatively new and had opened in the last decade.

At the Capri, George Raft, the movie tough guy of the thirties and forties, worked as a "greeter" who glad-handed and joked with the customers. Santo said Raft's charm and his reputation as a movie star were good for business, drawing customers who came to see him and stayed to gamble.

It was Santo's heavy investments in these five places, he said, that left him short of cash and compelled him to seek Anastasia as a partner in his unsuccessful bid to raise $2 million for the Havana Hilton casino concession. The Hilton lease was eventually given to a group led by a Cuban millionaire and business partner of Batista.

I never gambled and neither did Santo, although sometimes when asked for his occupation he described himself as a gambler.

"Bartenders don't drink because they see the consequences," he told me. "I know how the odds are stacked against the players. You can't beat the casinos."

On my first night in Havana, Santo took me on the rounds of several of his casinos. His favorite was the Sans Souci because it had a nightclub and floor show that was one of the most popular draws for Cubans and tourists.

We visited the nightclub shortly before the first show was to start and Santo gave me a backstage tour. He strolled into the chorus girls' dressing room where many of the dancers and singers were half nude and barebreasted. While I was uncertain about what to do with my eyes, Santo casually chatted with the girls in Spanish, which he spoke fluently. When he introduced me to some of his favorite performers, none exhibited any embarrassment.

In the men's dressing room, all the dancers and singers in a state of undress immediately covered their genitals.

Outside, I asked Santo, "Why are these guys running for cover? The girls didn't."

"You don't know? They're queers," he said, grinning at my naiveté. The men, who never performed in the nude, did not want to expose themselves to heterosexual men.

The next stop was the casino's counting room. A uniformed guard stood outside as Santo pulled out a key and unlocked the door to a small room, about twelve feet square, containing a wide table and a huge safe. The casino was air-conditioned but the room was stuffy, a floor fan providing only a warm breeze.

Two men, one wearing a green head visor and the other making entries in a ledger, were at a table covered with stacks of U.S. money.

"This is Henry," Santo said, introducing me to the man working on the ledger with an adding machine. "This is the most important room in any casino. We deal in cash and either you make it or lose it by what goes on in this room. Henry here is from Tampa and he watches that the count is right and that nothing gets lost. These people will steal you blind," he added, referring to the Cuban employees. "So I bring people from Tampa to watch the counting room."

On that first trip, I also accompanied Santo as he made his late rounds of the casinos. One night, close to dawn, he pointed out a visitor as the bagman for Batista's wife. She got 10 percent of the profits from the slot machines in all of Santo's places. "You pay for everything in Havana," he said without rancor.

Impressed by his holdings in Havana, I asked him why, since he was so successful legitimately in Cuba, he did not turn an honest dollar at home.

"Frank, a man who is blind in one eye has a great deal of vision among the blind," he said with a wide smile. In other words, corruption and loose standards made it easy for him to prosper in Cuba.

The other major gambling impresario in Havana was Meyer Lansky, the partner and close friend of Lucky Luciano. Lansky organized the syndicate that built the Riviera Hotel, one of Havana's largest, and the lavish new Gold Leaf Casino at the hotel. With his brother Jake, Lansky controlled another major casino, the Internacional, at the Hotel Nacional de Cuba, and the Montmartre Club, a casino with a reputation for attracting serious high rollers who cared little for gaudy floor shows.

Santo paid all my expenses in Havana and on one trip put me up at the Riviera instead of one of his hotels. I thought he had done so because he was friendly with Lansky, but it turned out that he just wanted me to get a look at one of Havana's poshest places.

At dinner that night I brought up Lansky's name and asked if he lived in the Riviera. Santo turned frosty. "That dirty Jew bastard, if he tries to talk to you, don't have anything to do with him. My father had some experiences with him and you can't trust him."

Santo never mentioned Lansky's name to me again. Back in Tampa, when I inquired discreetly among Santo's lieutenants, they said Santo's father had considered Lansky a dangerous potential rival in Cuba and that Santo despised him. I could only wonder how these two men, the most important overseers of mob investments in Havana, could function without getting along smoothly with each other and having mutual interests.

After several visits I had to agree that Havana was the most fantastic city in the world. It had everything—glamour, a great climate, excellent food, and an incredible nightlife.

An essential ingredient of Havana's ambience was its spectacular nightclub shows. Santo's Sans Souci had both an indoor club for rainy days and an outdoor club where, in good weather, shows were staged for audiences of five hundred. As in all the clubs the show at the Sans Souci continued without intermission from 8:00 P.M. to 4:00 A.M. Extra musicians were always ready to relieve the performers so that the music never stopped. Platforms were built on the palm trees surrounding the stage and forty to fifty dancers in elaborate, revealing costumes were illuminated as they performed dazzling routines there.

Sex was a big drawing card for the tourists and some motels in Havana rented rooms for fifteen minutes or a half hour—a practice that would come to America two decades later. The Cubans knew that some couples did not need an entire night to enjoy themselves. To ensure privacy, high walls were built around the motels so cars could park unseen.

Santo got a kick out of showing me around, introducing me to the eroticism that was unavailable in the States. He thought I was a bit innocent, not a man of the world. I became a different man in Cuba. In Havana, my traditional values seemed less important, and Santo's became more honest and less hypocritical than those of most people. He extracted all the pleasure he could out of life without the slightest twinge of moral guilt and he was absolutely uncritical of himself. I wanted to fit into his life, emulate him, gain his respect. Had he made a conspicuous effort to remodel my character I might have resisted him, but his influence was subtle. By remaining true to his own nature, he changed the course of my life.

I am Sicilian enough to acknowledge that, to me, respect is the most significant factor in a relationship between two men. So long as I respected Santo, he was the chief role model in my life.

I sometimes wondered if I had discarded all my ethical standards in Havana. Then I would reflect on Santo's theme that Havana's lifestyle was created to be enjoyed, and since everyone else was savoring its delights, why should I be the exception?

Havana was famous for *los exhibiciones*—sex shows—and Santo thought I should see one, assuring me that I would see the most select one available, offered only to the privileged cognoscenti.

"We don't want to go to the tourist traps," he said. "The first thing every secretary, schoolteacher, and nurse wants to see when they come here is *la exhibicion*."

Santo drove to a house in one of Havana's better neighborhoods and the woman who opened the door was obviously expecting him. A Cuban who spoke good English, she wore a low-cut evening gown. She escorted us to a room that had been converted into a cocktail lounge with a bar and tables. "When you gentlemen are ready to see a show, let me know," she said.

While we waited for drinks, Santo gave me another lesson on Havana's demimonde. Normally, he said, the shows were presented to groups of six to eight people, either a single party or couples who had arrived separately.

"There is a room across the hall where they present three men and three women and you select a pair who will be the performers. The charge is $25 per person—pretty cheap considering what kind of show they put on."

Santo had arranged a private performance for the two of us, and after our second drinks arrived, we said we were ready and carried the drinks with us into another room. The hostess silently introduced three men and three women wearing thin robes. In unison, they opened their garments, presenting their bodies for our inspection.

"We want El Toro and that girl over there," Santo told the hostess, pointing to a curvaceous woman with well-rounded and firm breasts.

Nodding, the hostess asked us to follow her into an adjoining room furnished with couches and settees for about a dozen people. A crescent-shaped platform surrounded by wall mirrors served as a stage. The other walls were hung with paintings of nude men and nude women, all of them amply endowed.

The hostess clapped her hands and El Toro and the woman entered in the nude and began the performance on quilts spread out on the platform, which was lighted like a real stage. They engaged each other for thirty minutes in every conceivable and contorted position possible and concluded with oral sex.

I was shocked to the core but tried to appear blasé to impress Santo. When it was over, Santo and I went back to the cocktail room for another round of drinks.

"What did you think of that show?" he asked.

"It was incredible. How can people do that for a living?"

"Frank, you've got to remember, over here there's something for everybody. You want opera, they have opera. You want baseball, they have baseball. You want ballroom dancing, they have ballroom dancing. And if you want sex shows, they have live sex shows. That's what makes this place so great."

El Toro was a man in his mid-thirties, about six feet tall and average-looking except for his genitalia. "Yeah," Santo said. "His cock is supposed to be about fourteen inches long. He's quite a guy. They also call him 'Superman.'"

Home movies was a hobby of mine and I thought Superman's performance would make a terrific erotic film. Santo obtained permission for me to privately film the great man in action; I still have the footage, probably the only movie made of Superman. After witnessing the second performance, I chatted with Superman, who had a fairly good command of English. He told me he earned about $25 a night.

"You come to Miami," I said jestingly. "I'll get you a pair of those loose, short shorts. We'll walk up and down the beach in front of the hotels. I guarantee you that you'll end up owning one of the big hotels." Superman laughed but he stayed in Havana where, according to a popular joke, he was better known than President Batista. Two decades later, he was immortalized in America's popular culture, although it failed to enrich him. In a scene in the film *Godfather II,* the mobsters are in Cuba, watching a sex exhibition, and there is a reference to a phenomenon known as "Superman." That scene was more accurate than the audience realized.

Every time I came to Havana I was given another lesson in the city's supply of sexual diversions. Martine Fox, the owner of the Tropicana nightclub, who produced the most popular shows in Havana, was Santo's friend. Through Santo's influence I was seated at a choice table with Martine one night at the Tropicana. The show's theme was "Miss Universe," and Martine offered me any girl in the show. "Take your pick," he said. "You want two girls? Three girls? Anything you want." Logically, the most beautiful woman in that show had to be the "entry" from Cuba, so I told Martine I wanted "Miss Cuba," sight unseen. After the show he escorted a stunningly beautiful woman to my table. She was Miss Cuba, my date for the remainder of the evening.

Martine then suggested that we see an unusual show that he set up for me at the Commodoro. The entertainers were all women, and they performed lesbian acts and offered to make love to men in the audience. Martine told me that many men found watching lesbian sex more stimulating than the heterosexual shows.

I was working hard in Tampa, with cases going all the time, and no pause for relaxation. My compensation was Cuba. I had an open invitation to be Santo's guest there whenever the mood struck me.

Although rumors abounded in Cuba that Santo was a drug kingpin, I never saw him use or sell drugs. He told me that the Cubans thought he was involved with drugs because his family name meant "trafficker" in Spanish. He made a joke out of it, dismissing the Cubans as gullible.

One of Santo's socialite friends, Alfredo, came from a prominent Cuban family and Santo took me to several of his lavish parties for Havana's social elite.

Alfredo had dozens of mistresses, each one living in a large villa he provided. A joke circulating in Havana was about Alfredo and his collection of love nests. Someone would ask what business he was in. The reply was, "Oh, he's in real estate."

Most of the voluptuous and statuesque beauties in the nightclub productions were only fourteen or fifteen years old. Alfredo and I were in a supper club watching the floor show one evening when a middle-aged woman approached him, introduced herself, and pointed out a young girl in the audience. "That's my daughter. Can you take care of her? She'll be glad to be your mistress." Alfredo refused; he told her he had all the mistresses he needed. "Please," the woman pleaded, "can't you just meet her?" She was again rebuffed. I was amazed that a mother would so brazenly offer him her daughter, but Alfredo shrugged; this was a common occurrence for him.

I watched my drinking carefully when I was around Santo, recalling his distaste for Pat Whitaker's escapades with alcohol. I knew he was measuring what he considered my "control" in Havana and I almost failed the test.

One night Santo, tied up with business, suggested I spend the evening with Alfredo at the Sans Souci. Trying to show my manliness, I kept pace with Alfredo's enormous capacity for drink. Although he was in his fifties, at least ten years older than I, I was no match for him. He frequently went to the men's room, returned, danced the cha-cha, and ordered a fresh round.

I was on the verge of passing out when Santo appeared. "You're drunk," he said.

I told him I had tried to keep up with Alfredo and failed. Laughing, Santo said, "Come with me, I want to show you something." He led me to the men's rest room and unlocked a door at the back of the room to reveal a wall filled with safety deposit boxes. Inside the boxes the rich Cubans kept their private stashes of cocaine, effective as pep pills when they were nightclubbing. Alfredo had dosed himself whenever he visited the men's room.

"That guy will be partying for the next two or three days," Santo said. "Don't bother trying to keep up with him."

Later I had second thoughts about the implications of those boxes filled with cocaine in Santo's club. They lent fuel to the rumors that dogged him at home and in Cuba that he and his family were drug dealers, but I never saw any other evidence that Santo was involved in narcotics.

Despite the seductive excitement and decadence surrounding him, Santo seemed to be placid and untroubled in Havana. He drank moderately and kept himself in reasonably good shape. Life was delicious for him in Havana and he was the living fulfillment of an adolescent boy's dreams.

Santo had lawyers in Cuba and Pat Whitaker still represented him as chief counsel in Florida, but he established a pattern of asking my opinion on legal and business matters in Cuba and in Florida. And he continued to refer clients to me at home.

One afternoon late in 1958 I was at the Columbia restaurant in Tampa and overheard Santo's brother Sam talking about Santo. "I hope to hell my brother knows what he is doing," Sam said. "All the money we're making is going down there, to Cuba."

In Cuba, Santo informed me about hotel business deals he was working on and several times suggested I invest in them. A new casino was being planned by his friends in 1958, with shares being sold privately at $25,000 for each one percent or point of the total investment.

"Buy a few points, you'll get rich," Santo advised, adding that Cuba was a better place than the United States to invest money for fast and large profits.

I discussed the proposals with my wife, Betty, but she said, "Hasn't Santo heard about that revolutionary, Castro? He's trying to take over Cuba."

When I mentioned Fidel Castro and his insurrection to Santo, he sneered. Castro, he assured me, was a joke, but just in case the unexpected happened, he and his friends were secretly contributing to the rebels as well as to Batista. Santo figured that no matter who won the war, he would emerge safe and sound. All his bets were covered.

"I'm sure Fidel Castro will never amount to anything," Santo said. "But even if he does, they'll never close the casinos. There is so much damned money here for everybody."

Late in December 1958, Santo telephoned me at my office from Havana, inviting my wife and me to come down as his guests for the New Year's Eve celebration. American newspapers were full of accounts of Castro's military victories and of bombings in Havana.

"Santo, I don't think it's a good idea to go now," I replied. "The newspapers say Castro is about to take over."

"Nonsense! He's got the mountains. He's a guy making noises up in the hills. He's going nowhere. Don't worry about it. We'll have a good time."

TOMMY LASORDA

Havana, 1950–1959: Baseball, Batista, and the Bearded Ones

"WHEN WE GOT TO THE STATION, THE INTERVIEWER TOOK US INTO THE STUDIO AND TOLD US WHERE TO SIT. THEN HE SAT WITH HIS BACK TO THE WALL, TOOK A LARGE GUN OUT OF HIS POCKET, AND LAID IT ON THE TABLE. I JUST STARED AT THAT GUN. . . . FINALLY, DICK WILLIAMS ASKED, 'WHAT'S THAT FOR?' 'WELL,' THE INTERVIEWER SAID, SMILING, 'YOU NEVER KNOW.' "

Baseball came to Cuba, according to one source, in 1866. In that year, a young man named Nemesio Guillot, who had been sent to school in the United States, returned to Cuba, bringing with him a burning interest in the new game he'd played at school, along with the rules of the game and samples of the necessary equipment.

Better documented is the story of another young Cuban, named Esteban Bellán, who was born in Havana in 1850. His family sent him to study at a recently opened Jesuit school, Fordham College, located on the grassy fields of the former Rose Hill farm near the village of Fordham in what is now the Bronx in New York City. Records show that in 1869 Bellán was playing for an upstate New York team called the Troy Haymakers, and when Troy joined the newly formed National Association, "Steve" Bellán became the first Cuban major leaguer. In 1874, Bellán returned home to Cuba and helped organize the first baseball game known to have been played there. For the record,

Bellán played third base, and his Havana team, perhaps because it had Bellán on its side, once walloped a team from the city of Matanzas 51–2.

Four years later, Havana, Matanzas, and a team formed in Almendares joined together into a professional league. Before the end of the century, there were more than seventy-five baseball teams in the small country.

The escalation of Cuba's fight for independence from Spain between 1868 and 1898 drove many Cubans to seek a more peaceful life in two other Spanish colonies, the Dominican Republic and Puerto Rico, and in the beautiful Mexican city of Mérida, on the Yucatan peninsula. And they took baseball with them wherever they went. A Cuban player named Emilio Cramer introduced baseball to Venezuela in 1895.

Early in the twentieth century, Cuban teams began visiting and playing in the United States. Because the Cubans came in a wide variety of skin colors, from black to white, many of them had to endure the bad treatment routinely accorded blacks in the United States. But there were fascinating opportunities in the U.S., and many black Cubans found positions in the Negro leagues. In fact, the first Negro league, organized by a group of black businessmen in 1920, had as one of its nine teams the Cuban Stars. And when Cuba's Baseball Hall of Fame was established in 1939, pitcher José Méndez and outfielder Cristóbal Torriente, both of whom had made their careers with teams in Chicago, Detroit, and Kansas City while playing during the winters in Cuba, were among the first players inducted. Another Cuban, Martín Dihigo, who played in the Negro leagues in the United States and later served as minister of sports in the Castro government, is the only player admitted to the Halls of Fame in four countries: Cuba, the United States, Mexico, and Venezuela.

Michael M. Oleksak and Mary Adams Oleksak, authors of Béisbol: Latin Americans and the Grand Old Game, *published in 1991, make the sad but necessary point that it was segregation in the United States that kept players like Méndez, Torriente, Dihigo, Luís "Lefty" Tiant (father of Luís Tiant, Jr.), "and countless others out of the majors [and] makes comparisons with the performances of other greats virtually impossible. . . . In a sport like baseball, where part of the joy of the game is in the* 'hot stove league' where fans argue and compare, that is a great loss indeed. And the loss was even greater to the talented players who couldn't play in the major leagues because their skin was too dark."

Havana's Gran Stadium, seating thirty-five thousand people, was built in 1946 and was state of the art for its time. But in the early 1950s, as Americans began pouring into Havana and as the city's nightlife blossomed, there were so many games being played that restaurant and nightclub owners begged Cuban President Carlos Prío Socarras to order the winter-league night games cut from six per week to three. Their petition was unsuccessful. The winter 1953 season, for example, saw one million paid admissions at the stadium.

In the fifties, too, U.S. teams began drawing on Cuban players for new strength, and also began visiting Cuba to play games there. Attendance dropped somewhat in 1959, immediately after the revolution, but there was a high spot in July of that year when Fidel himself pitched for the Barbudos ("bearded ones") in both innings of an exhibition match before a game between the Havana Sugar Kings and a team from Rochester, New York. (As a young player, Fidel had been unsuccessfully scouted by the Washington Senators as a pitching prospect.) Political relations with the U.S., however, were rapidly deteriorating, and in 1960 the International League moved its Havana franchise to Jersey City, New Jersey. One phase of Cuban baseball, like one phase of Cuban history, came to an end.

When the U.S. officially stopped doing business with Cuba, under the Trading with the Enemy Act, this meant, among many other things, that no more baseball equipment manufactured in the U.S. could reach the country. Castro quickly retaliated, developing the local manufacture of equipment under the government-owned brand name Batos.

Ironically, as the Oleksaks point out, the lack of trade between Cuba and the U.S. has been good for Cuban baseball because, since the 1960s, the best players have remained at home rather than being lured away to the States. And the Castro government has itself been a strong supporter of baseball. In 1971, Gran Stadium was renamed Estadio Latinoamericano and twenty thousand seats were added, giving it a total of fifty-five

*thousand about the same as Yankee Stadium. A new stadium,
the Estadio Victoria de Girón (a name that celebrates the Cuban victory at the Bay of Pigs, known in Cuba as Playa Girón),
seating thirty thousand, was built in Matanzas. In all, Cuba has
nine baseball stadiums, the smallest of which seats twenty thousand. Through the seventies and eighties, plans had been made
several times to organize a Cuba-U.S. match, but political differences intervened each time and the meeting still has not taken
place.*

*Describing the state of Cuban baseball in 1991, the Olek-
saks make it clear that the scene is lively, with passionate fans re-
acting loudly to the sound of an aluminum Batos bat striking a
ball. The fourteen provincial-champion teams play a thirty-nine-
game season, with the top seven teams going on to a fifty-four-
game National Series. Economic conditions mean that fans
throw foul balls back onto the field so they can be used again.
And the umpire, the Oleksaks write, "almost as an extension of
Castro himself, enjoys total control over the game and the
crowd. The umpire's raised hand now silences a stadium full of
fans." So great, in fact, is the umpire's authority that he can do
something that seems impossible in North America: he can keep
the length of a game to "under two hours."*

*Tommy Lasorda began his baseball career when he reported
for spring training with the Philadelphia Phillies in March
1945. The time was propitious for him, he says in his autobiography,* The Artful Dodger, *adding candidly, "If it weren't for
World War II I might never have played professional baseball."
At the end of the 1948 season, the young pitcher was drafted by
the Brooklyn Dodgers, then owned by Branch Rickey. In February 1949, he reported for spring training to the former Naval
Air Force Base at Vero Beach, Florida, beginning an association
with the Dodgers that would last, with only a few interruptions,
for more than half a century. In the summer of 1996, Lasorda
retired after twenty years as manager but continues as a vice
president of the organization.*

*Lasorda was twenty-three when he visited Cuba for the first
time in 1950.*

*In the selection from his autobiography that follows, note
that the name of the Cuban team is given incorrectly in the fem-*

inine form, barbudas, *instead of the correct masculine form,* barbudos. *The Cubans most certainly did not field a team of
bearded women baseball players.*

*On the other hand, it's easy to think that in 1960, if Fidel
had really* wanted *a team of bearded women baseball players,
the Cubans would have found a way.*

DURING THE 1970S SPORTSWRITERS BE-
gan referring to me as Baseball's Goodwill Ambassador.
Many people assumed that this was because I was always
preaching the gospel of baseball, that I was willing to talk to a
crowd of one about the great game, a game of thrills and chills
that brings so much enjoyment to so many young people and
old people, a game for the fans as well as the players, a game
of complex strategy and simple luck, a game of character and
heroics, a game which allowed the son of an Italian immigrant,
a runny-nosed little left-handed pitcher with a decent
curveball . . .

Maybe. But I suspect the real reason I've been called Baseball's Ambassador is that I've spent much of my baseball career
outside the country. Baseball may well be America's national
pastime, but you certainly couldn't prove that by looking at my
passport. Besides the eight seasons I spent playing in Montreal,
Canada, I've played, coached, or managed in Panama, Cuba,
the Dominican Republic, Venezuela, and Puerto Rico. I've par-
ticipated in exhibitions in Mexico and Japan, and brought the
good word, "baseball," to the great nation of Italy. During those
travels I've seen two governments overthrown, I've met dictators
and presidents, I've been a hero and I've been arrested, I've
started riots and run from riots, I've pitched with soldiers in the
dugout and umpires carrying six-shooters. Now, that's baseball.

In South America, they play the game with the same baseball we use in the States. In fact, they make the baseball
in South America. The pitcher's mound is the same sixty feet
six inches from home plate as it is in Denver, the team that
scores the most runs in nine innings wins, and the fans still
come out to the ball park to root, root, root for the home team.

But baseball in South America is very different than it is here. Instead of players wearing their last names on the backs of their uniforms, for example, they carry advertising. One year in Cuba I played for Bubbly Bubbly bubblegum. Another year I represented a tobacco company. And the fans have their own way of showing displeasure. Once I played in Cuba with Red Sox shortstop Eddie Pellagrini. He had a tough day, striking out three times. As he was walking back to the dugout after the third strikeout, the fans started whistling. Eddie sat down next to me shaking his head in admiration. "Aren't these fans great?" he said. "Here I strike out three times and they're still rooting for me."

"I think you got it wrong, Eddie," I explained. "Down here, whistling is the way they boo you." They were whistling very loudly. But I cheered him up when I added, "Just remember, as long as they're whistling, they won't be shooting."

"Shooting?" he said.

Actually, fans rarely shoot at ballplayers, but they do have subtle ways of showing their displeasure. Before a game in the Dominican one year, I saw six men parading through the stands carrying a wooden coffin. On top of the coffin was a sign in Spanish reading "Lasorda Is Dead." What bothered me most is that one of these pallbearers was my barber, and I had given him the tickets for the game.

My introduction to baseball in South America came in 1948, when Al Campanis arranged for me to play in Panama's Winter League. As I later learned, baseball in Panama is about as representative of baseball throughout South America as Devil Dogs are representative of good pasta. We played in the Canal Zone, which was mostly American. Everybody spoke English there, the fans generally remained in the stands during games, and few people carried guns. It was almost as much a paid vacation as a learning experience. I thought winter baseball was the best job in the world. While everybody I knew was freezing in Pennsylvania, I was being paid $1,000 a month to pitch in the sunshine. The only pressure on me was trying to sample every South American food in a short season.

Then, in 1950, I played in Cuba. This was pre-pre-revolutionary Cuba. There were three restaurants and one casino on every block in Havana, the Cuban people liked Americans, and they took their baseball very seriously. Very, very seriously. I thought Cuba was going to be just like Panama, but I quickly learned differently. Soon after I arrived, Dick Williams, Hank Workman, and I were asked to do a radio interview. When we got to the station, the interviewer took us into the studio and told us where to sit. Then he sat with his back to the wall, took a large gun out of his pocket, and laid it on the table.

I just stared at that gun. I couldn't believe the questions were going to be that difficult. Finally, Dick Williams asked, "What's that for?"

"Well," the interviewer said, smiling, "you never know."

You never know what? What did we never know? I was sitting there with my back to the door, I wanted to know. I was scared to death. I've done a lot of interviews since then, but none kept my attention the way that one did.

Baseball was the most important thing in many Cubans' lives. It was their escape from hard work and little money. There were four teams in the Cuban League, and all four played in the same ball park in Havana. Each team was represented by a different color. Havana was red, for example, so all Havana fans wore red clothing at the games. Cienfuegos was green, Marianao fans wore orange, and Almandaries was blue. Each team was allowed to have nine Americans, so there were thirty-six jobs for American ballplayers down there. Because baseball was a betting sport, the fans really got involved. One run could cost a man a week's wages, so you really didn't want to be responsible for that one run scoring. Cuban baseball was not a place to learn how to play; those fans expected you to win. If a player didn't do the job right away, his club simply shipped him back to the States and brought in someone to replace him.

My manager that first season was Adolfo "The Pride of Havana" Luque, who had pitched in the American big leagues for twenty years. Luque was the worst human being I have ever known. He made Bryant look like a saint. I argued with him practically every day. Once I remember telling him, "Luque, I'm a Catholic. I love Christmas. Christmas is a day when everybody is supposed to like each other, it's a time to forget bad feelings. But I'll tell you this, the way you act, if you walked down the main street of my hometown, Norristown, Pennsylvania, on Christmas Day, they'd punch your lights out."

He would do anything to win. We had a pitcher named Terry McDuffy, whose locker was right next to mine. One night, about a half hour before game time, Luque came over to Terry and said, "McDuffy, you are going to pitch tonight."

McDuffy shook his head. "No way," he said. "I pitched two nights ago. I'm not gonna pitch with two days' rest for nobody. I'll ruin my arm."

"I tell you you are going to pitch," Luque repeated, loudly.

"And I'm telling you I am not going to pitch," McDuffy shouted. They stood there screaming at each other, with Luque warning McDuffy he'd better pitch, and McDuffy insisting he was not going to pitch. Finally, Terry said, "That's it, that's enough. You feel that way about it, I quit. I'm going home right now. Tonight." He pulled his duffel bag from the top of his locker and started throwing his equipment into it. Luque disappeared into his office.

Less than a minute later, Luque came back carrying a pistol with a barrel that looked approximately a quarter-mile long. He put it against McDuffy's forehead. "You're pitching tonight," he said.

McDuffy started taking his equipment out of his duffel bag. "Gimme the ball," he said, "I'm ready to go." Terry pitched a two-hit shutout, proving the value of positive persuasion and a gun.

In my entire career, I never had a manager pull a gun on me. No way, not a manager. An umpire or an owner . . . that's a different story.

Usually, two American umpires worked Cuban games with two local umpires. One night I was pitching against Almandaries and Tom Gorman was going to work second base. We had been together in the Canadian-American League and the International League, so he knew I had an explosive temper and often screamed at the home plate umpire. The home plate umpire that night was Cuban Amando Maestri.

Before the game Gorman took me aside and said, "Tommy,

listen, do yourself a favor, don't get on this guy behind the plate tonight."

I thought that was a strange thing to say, so I asked him why.

He simply repeated, "Just believe me, don't get on this guy."

And I didn't get on him until the first inning. I threw a pitch that I thought was a strike, and he screamed, "Ball-a."

Ball-a? "Hey," I shouted at him, "what the   you   talking about? You blind? That was a   good pitch . . ." He stood there staring at me, not saying a word, so I figured he must not understand English.

I threw my second pitch. Again I thought it was a strike and again he called, "Ball-a."

Now I was really getting aggravated. The fans were screaming at me and I knew it was his fault. "Maestri," I yelled, "what the   is wrong with you? Don't you know a   good pitch when you see one? You gotta bear down back there . . ."

My next pitch split the plate in half. I think. Maestri did not. "Ball-a."

That was it. I walked halfway to the plate and really let him have it. "Why you   , no-good   ! How the   can you   miss that   pitch that badly, you   ?"

Maestri listened, then slowly walked about ten feet in front of home plate and started unbuttoning the jacket he was wearing over his chest protector. "Lasorda," he said, the only word I ever heard him speak in English. Of course, it was all he needed to say. He pulled open his jacket to show me the biggest pistol I have ever seen, tucked into his belt.

That convinced me. "Maestri," I shouted, "you are the greatest umpire I have ever seen in my life." As I turned around, slowly, the first thing I saw was Gorman standing behind second base, his arms crossed, laughing.

And once, when I was managing in the Dominican, the owner of the San Pedro team came hunting me with his gun because I'd called a game on account of rain after he'd given his team their meal money for the trip. The fact that I was very short of healthy pitchers had little to do with my decision, despite his claims, and there had been a persistent drizzle all day. Everything worked out fine, Manny Mota spoke to him, and he couldn't find me. It was that day that I learned the value of a good lock and a large hiding place.

I've always tried to learn at least a little of the local language wherever I've been. When I went to Japan, for example, I picked up a few words of Japanese. In Norristown, I learned Italian. And in South America, I gradually became fluent in Spanish. I spent considerable time sitting on the beach with jai-alai players my first year in Cuba, and they spoke about as much English as I did Spanish. So when a dog trotted by I'd point and say "dog," and they would respond "*perro.*"

When I knew enough to make myself understood, I started exploring the city. I learned that Cuba was a great country, with a rich, historic past, and many wonderful restaurants. Because I learned their language, enjoyed their hospitality, and played good baseball, I became very popular with the Cuban fans. I even became the subject of a famous joke.

Because my name is Lasorda I was known as "El Sorda," which translates to mean "the deaf woman." Garrio and Piñero were the Abbott and Costello of Cuba. They did a movie short, which was shown in all the theaters, telling the story of a farmer who lived high in the mountains with his wife and their deaf and dumb daughter. The daughter is never permitted to leave the village, but somehow she becomes interested in baseball. She begs her father to allow her to go to Havana to see a game, but he forbids it, telling her that the sophisticated people in the city would take advantage of her. But she persists, and eventually the farmer's wife persuades him to let their daughter go to one game.

On the day of the game the farmer sits by his radio. His wife continues to assure him that their daughter will be all right. But the very first words the farmer hears the announcer say are, "And El Sorda is heating up in the bullpen."

El Sorda? The deaf woman? With bulls? At a baseball game? The farmer screams at his wife, "And you said she would be all right!"

I played five seasons in Cuba, pitching for two pennant-winning teams, and in 1959 I pitched Cuba into the Caribbean World Series. I pitched a one-hitter, losing my no-hitter and the $1,000 bonus that went with it in the eighth inning when an outfielder lost a routine fly ball in the lights. I pitched a fourteen-inning shutout to beat Bob Shaw, 1–0. I pitched a number of low-hit games, but all people who know about Cuban baseball remember is the night I picked Chiquitin Cabrera over my head and swung him around.

I was pitching for Almandaries and Cabrera was Marianao's first baseman. He was about 6′1″, 220 pounds, and very strong. He was a very good hitter, with some power and great speed, similar to Pete Rose. The last time I had pitched against Marianao he had gotten three really cheap hits off me, three bleeders, and I told reporters that he was very lucky, and he would not get one hit off me the next time I faced him.

He responded by warning me that the next time he faced me he would "cut my legs off."

I assumed that meant he was going to bunt down the first-base line, which he often did, then barrel into me as I fielded the ball. When I heard that, I warned him that the next time he batted against me I was going to put him in the hospital and the first word he was going to hear from the surgeon was "scalpel" because that was what the surgeon would need to cut the baseball out of his ear.

The next time I pitched against Marianao was a Saturday night, a Ladies' Night, and it was a complete sellout, with 30,000 people in the ball park. Jo had not planned to go to the game, but changed her mind when I told her, "I'm gonna get him tonight. I guarantee you I'm going to get him."

Usually, when a baseball player leaves for the ball park his wife wishes him good luck. Jo never did that. Instead, whenever I was pitching, she'd kiss me good-bye and ask, "Please, Tommy, don't start any fights."

I retired the first two batters in the first inning, and Cabrera came to bat. Our catcher, Mike Guerra, signaled for a curveball. I shook him off. I couldn't hit Cabrera with a curveball. Guerra finally put down one finger—fastball.

I threw it right at Cabrera's neck. He went down, his bat

flying one way, his hat the other. He didn't say a word, just picked up his bat and his hat, and got set to hit again.

I threw another fastball at him. He stepped back and swung as hard as he could, sailing his bat at my legs. I hopped over it as it came spinning past me. This was now getting serious. When the batboy came out to retrieve it, I said, "Tell him it's now, now's the time to be ready."

I drilled him in the ribs with the next pitch. I mean, it was my fastball, it wasn't going to really hurt him. This is when I made my mistake. I assumed he was going to go to first base and I took my eyes off him. Suddenly, the ball park erupted. I looked up just in time to see all 220 pounds of Cabrera, carrying a 38-ounce bat, coming directly toward all 175 pounds of me.

It's amazing how quickly your mind functions in a life-threatening situation. Run, I thought, because this guy has a bat and he's going to try to kill you. But before I took that first step, I thought, No way, either he kills me or I kill him, but I've never seen an Italian from Norristown run and I'm not going to be the first one. If I had a baseball I would have fired that at him, and maybe even hit him, but I didn't. So I did the next best thing. Just as he started swinging the bat at my head, I threw my glove in his face and ducked.

I heard the bat *swizz*ing over my head. I acted on instinct. I grabbed his shirt with one hand and the inside of his leg with the other. Then, and how I did this I will never know, I lifted him up and held him over my head. I swung him around and then threw him down. The crowd was roaring, this had to be one of the best baseball games they'd ever seen.

As soon as he hit the ground I leaped on top of him and squeezed his head in an armlock. I grabbed the wrist of the arm cradling his head with my free hand and held tight. He started turning purple. Other players were trying to rip us apart, but I wouldn't let him go. I screamed, "The only way he's getting loose is for his head to go through my elbow." I believe in another ten seconds he would have been in serious physical trouble, like dead. I was enraged, the man had tried to kill me with a baseball bat. Finally, they managed to break my hands apart and got him free. There had to be fifteen players standing between us. I wanted more of him. This is not how I got to be known as Baseball's Goodwill Ambassador, however.

There was a law in Cuba prohibiting assault with a deadly weapon, even on a baseball field, so the police took both of us, still in uniform, to night court. After the judge heard the facts he asked me if I wanted to press charges against Cabrera. "No," I said, "I don't want to press charges, all I want to do is pitch against him again."

The following morning, Cabrera, me, and the directors of our ball clubs met with the league president. Cabrera was suspended for the remainder of the season. I was not penalized for my part in the fight. When we left the league office I figured that was the end of it. Actually, it was just starting to get exciting.

I was lying on the beach that afternoon when four men wearing sunglasses approached me. The sunglasses didn't bother me, most people wear sunglasses on the beach, it was the ties and jackets, shoes and hats they were wearing that made me suspect they were not trying to get a tan. They stopped in my sunlight and commanded, "Get your clothes on, you come with us."

They looked like they had just walked out of a B-movie. They were the kind of people who, when they said "Get your clothes on, you come with us," you didn't argue, you got your clothes on and went with them. "Where we going?" I asked.

"Please, get your clothes on," they repeated.

I put on my pants and shirt and told Jo not to worry, that I would worry for both of us. Naturally, they were driving a black stretch limousine. I got in the backseat and we started going wherever we were going. Wherever it was, it wasn't close, because we drove for a long time. Or maybe it just seemed like a long time. No one in the car said a word to me and, since I hadn't learned to speak Spanish yet, I couldn't talk to them. I couldn't guess where we were going, but I was pretty nervous. I knew that a lot of Cubans were not happy that a Cuban star had been suspended for the season while the American who started it was not punished.

Finally, we stopped in front of a large iron gate, guarded by soldiers with machine guns. Suspension for the rest of the season began to look very good to me. We drove up a long winding driveway to a farmhouse. There was a large veranda in front and perhaps forty men there, sipping drinks. My driver ordered me out of the car. I followed them up the steps of the veranda and suddenly saw standing in front of me President Fulgencio Batista, the Cuban dictator. I had met presidents of the Elks Lodge in Norristown, presidents of teams and presidents of leagues, but this was the first dictator I had ever met.

He offered me his hand, which I shook, gently. "Mr. Lasorda," he began, "I heard the game last night and I have invited you to come here because I want to apologize to you." The Cuban dictator apologizing to me because I tried to hit a batter? This had to be a pitcher's fantasy. "I'm very disappointed with Cabrera for coming after you with a bat," he continued. "That's not right. If he wanted to fight you, that's part of baseball, but no, not with a bat."

I agreed. I was feeling pretty good right about then, now that I was breathing again, so I said, "Mr. President, he will never come after me again, because he knows he came very close to being buried last night . . ."

Batista invited me to stay and have lunch with him. Since I had no plans for the afternoon, I accepted. So we spent the afternoon sitting on the veranda, watching armed guards patrolling the lawn, talking baseball.

I received numerous threatening letters the next few weeks. I couldn't read too much Spanish, but I recognized certain words, like "gun," "shoot," and "kill," and I assumed these were not requests for autographs. Jo wanted me to tell my new friends in the government about the threats, but I refused. I didn't need anybody's help. I believed I was tough enough to take on anybody who challenged me. I would've fought King Kong back then, believe me. They might get me, I thought, but if they try, I'm gonna take at least ten of them with me.

Cuba was really not very much like Panama at all.

Cabrera was reinstated with two weeks to go in the season. Coincidentally, I was scheduled to pitch against Marianao the day he returned to action. There was not an available ticket to that game anywhere on this island. "Please, Tommy," Jo said as she kissed me good-bye that day, "don't start any fights."

The first time Cabrera came to bat I aimed at his neck and fired at him. He went down. As he was lying on the ground, I took four steps toward the plate and shouted, "You don't like it, come on out again." He didn't make a move. I struck him out four times that night, four times.

I was in Cuba in 1952 when Batista overthrew Prio, and I was there in 1959 when Fidel Castro overthrew Batista. None of the American ballplayers had paid too much attention to Castro because he seemed hopelessly outnumbered and Batista seemed to be so strong. But on New Year's Eve, 1959, Jo and I, the Art Fowlers, and the Bob Allisons were leaving a party about 3 A.M. when three large planes flew low overhead. I wondered who would be flying that late at night. It turned out to have been Batista and his cabinet fleeing the country.

A general strike was called and baseball was suspended. That was fine with me; everywhere I looked people were walking around with guns. We were living at the Club Nautico, a fenced-in luxury compound, with seven or eight other American ballplayers and their families. At first we weren't worried, we figured that after a cooling-off period we would resume the season. Then we started hearing rumors that Club Nautico had been owned by one of Batista's ministers and Castro's soldiers were going to burn it down. *That's* when we started worrying.

We quickly organized a defense force to protect the compound. Since I'd spent my army career playing baseball and making sure basketballs were sufficiently inflated, I didn't know too much about being a soldier. The only combat experience I'd had was on the baseball field. Eventually, Cuban soldiers arrived to protect us from the rumors.

After nine days Castro permitted the baseball season to resume. We were scheduled to play the second game of a doubleheader. The ball park was jammed with Castro's *barbudas,* the "bearded men" who had been with him in the mountains. All of them still carried their weapons with them. Castro, we found out, was an outstanding baseball fan. Before becoming a revolutionary, he had been a pitcher. He'd even had a tryout with the Washington Senators, which he failed. So instead of becoming a Senator, he became a dictator.

In the fourth inning of the first game the *barbudas*

suddenly cleared out of the ball park. Minutes later we heard machine guns firing, a sound that made it particularly hard to concentrate on the game. The firing went on for about twenty minutes, then the soldiers returned to the stadium. We found out later that about thirty of Batista's men had been hiding in a nearby building, and the *barbudas* had killed them all.

I was pitching the second game. There were *barbudas* in the clubhouse, in the dugout, and on the field. Most of them looked to be fifteen or sixteen years old, all of them armed with carbines or submachine guns. When I went out to warm up, a *barbuda* was behind home plate wearing a catcher's glove. I didn't know where Dick Brown, our regular catcher, was, but I knew where I was: in a ball park in Havana, Cuba, nine days after the Castro revolution. I warmed up with that catcher.

During the game, I remember, Art Fowler and I were sitting next to each other in the dugout. A young soldier was directly in front of us. He carried his machine gun on his shoulder, and every time he cheered, he jumped up and down. Every time he went up, Art and I went down, because we didn't know if he had his machine gun safety on or off. Finally, Art said in his deep Southern accent, "Tommy, you speak Spanish. Would you please tell that young man to move out of the way?"

I looked at him and laughed. Who was he kidding? Then I told him, "I've got some news for you, buddy. I am not telling him to move. In fact, I'm going to move." I spent the rest of the game sitting against the wall outside the dugout.

I had been friends with some members of the revolution, particularly General Camilo Cienfueges. So soon after Castro marched into Havana, Pittsburgh Pirate scout Howie Haak and I were invited to Castro's suite in the Caribbean Hilton Hotel to meet him. This was before anyone knew he was a Communist, although we had heard stories that he was long before he took over. It would not have made any difference if we had known. In Latin America you never argue with a dictator.

Castro was wearing his jungle fatigues when we entered, and smoking a cigar. We stayed about an hour talking baseball. I kept thinking, Isn't it incredible, here I am, the son of an Italian immigrant, a runny-nosed little left-handed pitcher with a decent curveball, a player good enough only to be the third-string pitcher on his high school baseball team, sitting here talking to the leader of the entire revolution. Baseball had helped me find a wife, it enabled me to afford to have a family and build a home, it provided many thrills, and now it had allowed me to meet two Cuban dictators. However, during our conversation I did not tell Castro that I'd met Batista.

AMIRI BARAKA

Train to Oriente, July 26, 1960: A la Sierra con Fidel!

"FIDEL TOUCHED HIS HAND TO THE WIDE *CAMPESINO* HAT HE WAS WEARING. . . . ONE OF THE LATIN-AMERICAN GIRLS LEANED FORWARD SUDDENLY AND KISSED HIM ON THE CHEEK. EVERYONE MILLED AROUND THE TALL YOUNG CUBAN, ASKING QUESTIONS, SHAKING HIS HAND, TAKING PICTURES, GETTING AUTOGRAPHS."

Imamu Amiri Baraka was born as LeRoi Jones in Newark, New Jersey, in 1934. His Muslim name, which he took in the late sixties, is a Swahili version of an Arab name that means "blessed prince."

Although he was already an outspoken social critic while still in his twenties, he burst onto the public consciousness, and the public conscience, when his play Dutchman, *which treated the subject of race relations with brutal honesty, opened on March 24, 1964, at the off-Broadway Cherry Lane Theatre in New York. Other plays followed—more than a dozen of them in the remainder of the sixties alone—and Jones's reputation was secure. He had already published, in 1963,* Blues People: Negro Music in White America. *In 1967, he followed this with* Black Music, *and both books remain essential for anyone interested in music in America.*

Baraka's 1960 visit to Cuba gave him a close-up view of the country's new idealism and its charismatic young leader. It's important to remember that in 1960 Cuba was freshly rescued from a monumentally corrupt and murderous dictatorship, and to most of Cuba's poor, and also to many North American idealists and social observers, Fidel Castro was nothing less than a hero.

In The Autobiography of LeRoi Jones/Amiri Baraka, published in 1984, Baraka looked back with nearly a quarter century of perspective and wrote that in 1959 "the civil rights movement was rising with every headline, and for the last few months I had been fascinated by the headlines from Cuba. I had been raised on Errol Flynn's Robin Hood and the endless hero-actors fighting against injustice and leading the people to victory over tyrants. The Cuban thing seemed a case of classic Hollywood proportions."

But the Cuban revolution was real, and in 1984 Baraka could still write, "The Cuba trip was a turning point in my life. . . . I carried so much back with me that I was never the same again. The dynamic of the revolution had touched me. . . . When I returned I was shaken more deeply than even I realized."

The account he wrote of his trip first appeared in Evergreen Review, under the title "Cuba Libre."

It's interesting to note that the attitude of the North American press that Baraka illustrates at the end of the piece has changed little in nearly four decades. In the spring of 1996, the CBS television program Sunday Morning did a ten-minute feature on efforts to preserve the crumbling colonial buildings of Habana Vieja. In an otherwise well-informed and sympathetic report, correspondent Terence Smith included among the causes of decay "thirty-seven years of political isolation." Never mind the questionable logic. From whom, exactly, has Cuba been isolated? Not from Canada or Mexico or Brazil or Great Britain or France or Spain or Japan (all of whom are investing heavily in Cuba's future) or anyone except the United States. The notion that Cuba has wantonly and willfully parted ways with civilized society simply is not true.

IT WAS LATE AT NIGHT, AND STILL HA-bana had not settled down to its usual quiet. Crowds of people were squatting around bus stops, walking down the streets in groups headed for bus stops. Truckloads of militia were headed out of the city. Young men and women with rucksacks and canteens were piling into buses, trucks, and private cars all over the city. There were huge signs all over Habana reading "A La Sierra Con Fidel . . . Julio 26." Thousands of people were leaving Habana for the July 26th celebration at Sierra Maestra all the way at the other end of the island in Oriente province. The celebration was in honor of Fidel Castro's first onslaught against Moncada barracks, July 26, 1953, which marked the beginning of his drive against the Batista government. Whole families were packing up, trying to get to Oriente the best way they could. It was still three days before the celebration and people clogged the roads from Habana all the way to the Eastern province.

The night of our departure for Oriente we arrived at the train station in Habana about 6 P.M. It was almost impossible to move around in the station. *Campesinos,* businessmen, soldiers, *milicianas,* tourists—all were thrashing around trying to make sure they had seats in the various trains. As we came into the station, most of the delegates of a Latin-American Youth Congress were coming in also. There were about nine hundred of them, representing students from almost every country in Latin America. Mexicans, Colombians, Argentines, Venezuelans, Puerto Ricans (with signs reading "For the Liberation of Puerto Rico"), all carrying flags, banners, and wearing the large, ragged straw hat of the *campesino.* We were to go in the same train as the delegates.

As we moved through the crowds toward our train, the students began chanting: "Cuba Si, Yanqui No . . . Cuba Si, Yanqui No . . . Cuba Si, Yanqui No." The crowds in the terminal joined in, soon there was a deafening crazy scream that seemed to burst the roof off the terminal. Cuba Si, Yanqui No! We raced for the trains.

Once inside the train, a long modern semi-air-conditioned "Silver Meteor," we quickly settled down and I began scribbling illegibly in my notebook. But the Latin Americans came scrambling into the train still chanting furiously and someone handed me a drink of rum. They were yelling "Venceremos, Venceremos, Venceremos, Venceremos." Crowds of soldiers and militia on the platform outside joined in. Everyone was screaming as the train began to pull away.

The young militia people soon came trotting through the coaches asking everyone to sit down for a few seconds so they could be counted. The delegates got to their seats and in my coach everyone began to sing a song like "two, four, six, eight, who do we appreciate . . . Fidel, Fidel, Fidel!!" Then they did Ché (Guevara), Raul, President Dorticos, etc. It was about 1,000 kilometers to Oriente and we had just started.

Young soldiers passed out ham sandwiches and Maltina, a thick syrupy sweet beverage that only made me thirstier. Everyone in the train seemed to be talking excitedly and having a wild time. We were about an hour outside Habana and I was alternating between taking notes and reading about ancient Mexican religion when Olga Finlay came up to my seat accompanied by a young woman. "I told her you were an American poet," Olga said, "and she wanted to meet you." I rose quickly and extended my hand, for some reason embarrassed as hell. Olga said, "Señora Betancourt, Señor LeRoi Jones." She was very short, very blonde, and very pretty, and had a weird accent that never ceased to fascinate me. For about thirty minutes we stood in the middle aisle talking to each other. She was a Mexican delegate to the Youth Congress, a graduate student in Economics at one of the universities, the wife of an economist, and a mother. Finally, I offered her the seat next to mine at the window. She sat, and we talked almost continuously throughout the fourteen-hour ride.

She questioned me endlessly about American life, American politics, American youth—although I was jokingly cautioned against using the word *American* to mean the U.S. or North America. "Everyone in this car is American," she said. "You from the North, we from the South." I explained as best I could about the Eisenhowers, the Nixons, the DuPonts, but she made even my condemnations seem mild. "Everyone in the world," she said, with her finger, "has to be communist or anti-communist. And if they're anti-communist, no matter what kind of foul person they are, you people accept them as your allies. Do you really think that hopeless little island in the middle of the sea is China? That is irrational. You people are irrational!"

I tried to defend myself. "Look, why jump on me? I understand what you're saying. I'm in complete agreement with you. I'm a poet . . . what can I do? I write, that's all, I'm not even interested in politics."

She jumped on me with both feet as did a group of Mexican poets later in Habana. She called me a "cowardly bourgeois individualist." The poets, or at least one young wild-eyed Mexican poet, Jaime Shelley, almost left me in tears, stomping his foot on the floor, screaming: "You want to cultivate your soul? In that ugliness you live in, you want to cultivate your soul? Well, we've got millions of starving people to feed, and that moves me enough to make poems out of."

Around 10 P.M. the train pulled into the town of Matanzas. We had our blinds drawn, but the militia came running through the car telling us to raise them. When I raised the blind I was almost startled out of my wits. There were about 1,500 people in the train station and surrounding it, yelling their lungs out. We pulled up the windows. People were all over. They ran back and forth along the train screaming at us. The Mexicans in the train had a big sign painted on a bedspread that read "Mexico is with Fidel. Venceremos." When they raised it to the windows young men leaped in the air, and women blew kisses. There was a uniformed marching band trying to be heard above the crowd, but I could barely hear them. When I poked my head out of the window to wave at the crowds, two young Negro women giggled violently at first, then one of them ran over to the train and kissed me as hard as she could manage. The only thing to do I could think of was to say "Thank you." She danced up and down and clapped her hands and shouted to her friend, "Un americano, un americano." I bowed my head graciously.

What was it, a circus? That wild mad crowd. Social ideas? Could there be that much excitement generated through all the people? Damn, that people still *can* move. Not us, but people.

It's gone out of us forever. "Cuba Si, Yanqui No," I called at the girls as the train edged away.

We stopped later in the town of Colon. There again the same mobs of cheering people. Camaguey. Santa Clara. At each town, the chanting crowds. The unbelievable joy and excitement. The same idea, and people made beautiful because of it. People moving, being moved. I was ecstatic and frightened. Something I had never seen before, exploding all around me.

The train rocked wildly across and into the interior. The delegates were singing a "cha cha" with words changed to something like "Fidel, Fidel, cha cha cha, Ché Ché, cha cha cha, Abajo Imperialismo Yanqui, cha cha cha." Some American students whom I hadn't seen earlier ran back and forth in the coaches singing "We cannot be moved." The young folk-song politicians in blue jeans and pigtails.

About two o'clock in the morning they shut the lights off in most of the coaches, and everybody went to sleep. I slept for only an hour or so and woke up just in time to see the red sun come up and the first early people come out of their small grass-roofed shacks beside the railroad tracks, and wave sleepily at the speeding train. I pressed my face against the window and waved back.

The folk singing and war cries had just begun again in earnest when we reached the town of Yara, a small town in Oriente province, the last stop on the line. At once we unloaded from the train, leaving most luggage and whatever was considered superfluous. The dirt streets of the town were jammed with people. Probably everyone in town had come to meet the train. The entire town was decorated with some kind of silver Christmas tree tinsel and streamers. Trees, bushes, houses, children, all draped in the same silver holiday tinsel. Tiny girls in brown uniforms and red berets greeted us with armfuls of flowers. Photographers were running amok through the crowd, including an American newsreel cameraman who kept following

Robert Williams. I told Robert that he ought to put his big straw hat in front of his face American ganster style.

From the high hill of the train station it was possible to see a road running right through Yara. Every conceivable kind of bus, truck, car, and scooter was being pushed toward the Sierra, which was now plainly visible in the distance. Some of the *campesinos* were on horses, dodging in and out of the sluggish traffic, screaming at the top of their lungs.

The sun had already gotten straight up over our heads and was burning down viciously. The big straw *campesino* hats helped a little but I could tell that it was going to be an obscenely hot day. We stood around for a while until everyone had gotten off our train, and then some of the militia people waved at us to follow them. We walked completely out of the town of Yara in about two minutes. We walked until we came to more railroad tracks; a short spur leading off in the direction of Sierra Maestra. Sitting on the tracks were about ten empty open cattle cars. There were audible groans from the American contingent. The cars themselves looked like movable jails. Huge thick bars around the sides. We joked about the American cameraman taking a picture of them with us behind the bars and using it as a *Life* magazine cover. They would caption it "Americans in Cuba."

At a word from the militia we scrambled up through the bars, into the scalding cars. The metal parts of the car were burning hot, probably from sitting out in the sun all day. It was weird seeing hundreds of people up and down the tracks climbing up into the cattle cars by whatever method they could manage. We had been told in Habana that this was going to be a rough trip and that we ought to dress accordingly. Heavy shoes, old clothes, a minimum of equipment. The women were told specifically to wear slacks and flat shoes because it would be difficult to walk up a mountain in a sheath dress and heels. However, one of the American women, the pretty young middle-class lady from Philadelphia, showed up in a flare skirt and "Cuban" heels. Two of the Cubans had to pull and tug to get her into the car, which still definitely had the smell of cows. She slumped in a corner and began furiously mopping her brow.

I sat down on the floor and tried to scribble in my notebook, but it was difficult because everyone was jammed in very tight. Finally, the train jerked to a start, and everyone in all the cars let out a wild yell. The delegates began chanting again. Waving at all the people along the road, and all the dark bare-foot families standing in front of their grass-topped huts calling to us. The road which ran along parallel to the train was packed full of traffic, barely moving. Men sat on the running boards of their cars when the traffic came to a complete halt, and drank water from their canteens. The train was going about five miles an hour and the *campesinos* raced by on their plow horses jeering, swinging their big hats. The sun and the hot metal car were almost unbearable. The delegates shouted at the trucks, "Cuba Si, Yanqui No," and then began their "Viva" shouts. After one of the "Vivas," I yelled, "Viva Calle Cuaranta y dos" (42nd Street), "Viva Symphony Sid," "Viva Cinco Punto" (Five Spot), "Viva Turhan Bey." I guess it was the heat. It was a long slow ride in the boiling cars.

The cattle cars stopped after an hour or so at some kind of junction. All kinds of other coaches were pulled up and resting on various spurs. People milled about everywhere. But it was the end of any tracks going further toward Sierra. We stood around and drank warm water too fast.

Now we got into trucks. Some with nailed-in bus seats, some with straw roofs, others with just plain truck floors. It was a wild scramble for seats. The militia people and the soldiers did their best to indicate which trucks were for whom, but people staggered into the closest vehicle at hand. Ed Clarke and I ran and leaped up into a truck with leather bus seats in the back. The leather was too hot to sit on for a while so I put my handkerchief on the seat and sat forward. A woman was trying to get up into the truck, but not very successfully, so I leaned over the rail and pulled her up and in. The face was recogniz-able immediately, but I had to sit back on the hot seat before I remembered it was Françoise Sagan. I turned to say something to her, but some men were already helping her back down to the ground. She rode up front in the truck's cab with a young lady companion, and her manager on the running board, cling-ing to the door.

The trucks reared out onto the already heavily traveled road. It was an unbelievable scene. Not only all the weird trucks and buses but thousands of people walking along the road. Some had walked from places as far away as Matanzas. Whole detachments of militia were marching, route step, but carrying rifles or .45's. Women carrying children on their shoulders. One group of militia with blue shirts, green pants, pistols, and knives was carrying paper fans, which they ripped back and forth almost in unison with their step. There were huge trucks full of oranges parked along the road with lines of people circling them. People were sitting along the edge of the road eating their lunches. Everyone going *a la* Sierra.

Our trucks sped along on the outside of the main body of traffic, still having to stop occasionally when there was some hopeless roadblock. The sun, for all our hats, was baking our heads. Sweat poured in my dry mouth. None of us Americans had brought canteens and there was no water to be had while we were racing along the road. I tried several times to get some oranges, but never managed. The truck would always start up again when we came close to an orange vendor.

There was a sign on one of the wood shack "stores" we passed that read "Niños No Gustan Los Chicle Ni Los Cigarros Americanos Ni El Rocan Rool." It was signed "Fondin." The traffic bogged down right in front of the store so several French photographers leaped off the truck and raced for the orange stand. Only one fellow managed to make it back to our truck with a hat full of oranges. The others had to turn and run back empty handed as the truck pulled away. Sagan's manager, who had strapped himself on the running board with a leather belt, almost broke his head when the truck hit a bump and the belt snapped and sent him sprawling into the road. Another one of the correspondents suddenly became violently ill and tried to shove his head between the rough wooden slats at the side of the truck; he didn't quite make it, and everyone in the truck suffered.

After two hours we reached a wide, slow, muddy river. There was only one narrow cement bridge crossing it, so the trucks had to wait until they could ease back into the regular line of traffic. There were hundreds of people wading across the river. A woman splashed in with her child on her shoulders, hanging around her neck, her lunch pail in one hand, a pair of blue canvas sneakers in the other. One group of militia marched right into the brown water, holding their rifles high above their heads. When our truck got on the bridge directly over the water, one of the Cuban newspapermen leaped out of the truck down ten feet into the water. People in the trucks would jump right over the side, sometimes pausing to take off their shoes. Most went in shoes and all.

Now we began to wind up the narrow mountain road for the first time. All our progress since Yara had been upgrade, but this was the first time it was clearly discernible that we were going up a mountain. It took another hour to reach the top. It was afternoon now and already long lines of people were headed back down the mountain. But it was a narrow line compared to the thousands of people who were scrambling up just behind us. From one point where we stopped just before reaching the top it was possible to look down the side of the long hill and see swarms of people all the way down past the river seeming now to inch along in effortless pantomime.

The trucks stopped among a jumble of rocks and sand not quite at the top of the last grade. (For the last twenty minutes of our climb we actually had to wind in and out among groups of people. The only people who seemed to race along without any thought of the traffic were the *campesinos* on their broken-down mounts.) Now everyone began jumping down off the trucks and trying to re-form into their respective groups. It seemed almost impossible. Detachments of *campesino* militia (work shirts, blue jeans, straw hats, and machetes) marched up behind us. *Milicianas* of about twelve and thirteen separated our contingent, then herds of uniformed, trotting boys of about seven. "Hup, hup, hup, hup," one little boy was calling in vain as he ran behind the rest of his group. One of the girls called out "Hup, hup, hup, hup," keeping her group more orderly. Rebel soldiers wandered around everywhere, some with long, full beards, others with long, wavy black hair pulled under their blue berets or square-topped khaki caps, most of them young men in their twenties or teen-agers. An old man with a full gray beard covering most of his face, except his sparkling blue eyes and the heavy black cigar stuck out of the side of his mouth, directed the comings and goings up and down this side of the mountain. He wore a huge red- and black-handled revolver and had a hunting knife sewn to his boot. Suddenly it seemed that I was lost in a sea of uniforms, and I couldn't see anyone I had come up the mountain with. I sat down on a rock until most of the uniforms passed. Then I could see Olga about fifty yards away waving her arms at her lost charges.

There was a public address system booming full blast from what seemed the top of the hill. The voice (Celia Sanchez, Fidel's secretary) was announcing various groups that were passing in review. When we got to the top of the rise, we could see a large, austere platform covered with all kinds of people, and at the front of the platform a raised section with a dais where the speakers were. Señora Sanchez was announcing one corps of militia and they marched out of the crowd and stopped before the platform. The crowd cheered and cheered. The militia was commended from the platform and then they marched off into the crowd at the other side. Other groups marched past. Young women, teen-age girls, elderly *campesinos,* each with their own militia detachment, each to be commended. This had been going on since morning. Hundreds of commendations, thousands of people to be commended. Also, since morning, the officials had been reading off lists of names of *campesinos* who were to receive land under the Agrarian Reform Law. When they read the name of some farmer close enough to the mountain to hear it, he would leap straight up in the air and, no matter how far away from the platform he was, would go barreling and leaping toward the speaker. The crowd delighted in this and would begin chanting "Viva Fidel, Viva Fidel, Viva Reforma Agraria." All this had been going on since morning and it was now late afternoon.

After we walked past the dais, introduced to the screaming crowd as "intellectual North American visitors," we doubled back and went up onto the platform itself. It was even hotter up there. By now all I could think about was the sun; it was burning straight down and had been since early morning. I tugged the straw hat down over my eyes and trudged up onto the platform. The platform itself in back of the dais was almost overflowing, mostly with rebel soldiers and young militia troops. But there were all kinds of visitors also, the Latin American delegates, newsmen, European writers, American intellectuals, as well as Cuban officials. When we got up on the platform, Olga led us immediately over to the speakers' dais and the little group of seats around it. We were going to be introduced to all the major speakers.

The first person to turn around and greet us was a tall, thin, bearded Negro in a rebel uniform bearing the shoulder markings of a *Commandante*. I recognized his face from the papers as that of Juan Almeida, chief of the rebel army, a man almost unknown in the United States. He grinned and shook our hands and talked in a swift combination of Spanish and English, joking constantly about conditions in the United States. In the middle of one of his jokes he leaned backward, leaning over one man to tap another taller man on the shoulder. Fidel Castro leaned back in his seat, then got up smiling and came over to where we were standing. He began shaking hands with everybody in the group, as well as the many other visitors who moved in at the opportunity. There were so many people on the platform in what seemed like complete disorder that I wondered how wise it was as far as security was concerned. It seemed awfully dangerous for the Prime Minister to be walking around so casually, almost having to thread his way through the surging crowd. Almost immediately, I shoved my hand toward his face and then grasped his hand. He greeted me warmly, asking through the interpreter where I was from and what I did. When I told him I was a New York poet, he seemed extremely amused and asked me what the government thought about my trip. I shrugged my shoulders and asked him what did he intend to do with this revolution.

We both laughed at the question because it was almost like a reflex action on my part: something that came out so quick that I was almost unaware of it. He twisted the cigar in his mouth and grinned, smoothing the strangely grown beard on his cheeks. "That *is* a poet's question," he said, "and the only poet's answer I can give you is that I will do what I think is right, what I think the people want. That's the best I can hope for, don't you think?"

I nodded, already about to shoot out another question, I didn't know how long I'd have. Certainly this was the most animated I'd been during the entire trip. "Uh—" I tried to smile— "what do you think the United States will do about Cuba ultimately?" The question seemed weird and out of place because everyone else was just trying to shake his hand.

"Ha, well, that's extremely difficult to say, your government is getting famous for its improvisation in foreign affairs. I suppose it depends on who is running the government. If the Democrats win it may get better. More Republicans . . . I suppose more trouble. I cannot say, except that I really do not care what they do as long as they do not try to interfere with the running of this country."

Suddenly the idea of a security lapse didn't seem so pressing. I had turned my head at a weird angle and looked up at the top of the platform. There was a soldier at each side of the back wall of the platform, about ten feet off the ground, each one with a machine gun on a tripod. I asked another question. "What about communism? How big a part does that play in the government?"

"I've said a hundred times that I'm not a communist. But I am certainly not an anti-communist. The United States likes anti-communists, especially so close to their mainland. I said also a hundred times that I consider myself a humanist. A radical humanist. The only way that anything can ever be accomplished in a country like Cuba is radically. The old has been here so long that the new must make radical changes in order to function at all."

So many people had crowded around us now that it became almost impossible to hear what Fidel was saying. I had shouted the last question. The young fashion model brushed by me and said how much she had enjoyed her stay in Cuba. Fidel touched his hand to the wide *campesino* hat he was wearing, then pumped her hand up and down. One of the Latin-American girls leaned forward suddenly and kissed him on the cheek. Everyone milled around the tall young Cuban, asking questions, shaking his hand, taking pictures, getting autographs (an American girl with pigtails and blue jeans) and, I suppose, committing everything he said to memory. The crowd was getting too large, I touched his arm, waved, and walked toward the back of the platform.

I hadn't had any water since early morning, and the heat and the excitement made my mouth dry and hard. There were no water fountains in sight. Most of the masses of Cubans had canteens or vacuum bottles, but someone had forgotten to tell the Americans (North and South) that there'd be no water. Also, there was no shade at all on the platform. I walked around behind it and squatted in a small booth with a tiny tin roof. It had formerly been a soda stand, but because the soda was free, the supply had given out rapidly and the stand had closed. I sat in the few inches of shade with my head in my hands, trying to cool off. Some Venezuelans came by and asked to sit in the shade next to me. I said it was all right and they offered me the first cup of water I'd had in about five hours. They had a whole chicken also, but I didn't think I'd be able to stand the luxury.

There were more speakers, including a little boy from one of the youngest militia units, but I heard them all over the public address system. I was too beat and thirsty to move. Later Ed Clarke and I went around hunting for water and finally managed to find a small brown stream where the soldiers were filling up their canteens. I drank two Coca-Cola bottles full, and when I got back to Habana came down with a fearful case of dysentery.

Suddenly there was an insane, deafening roar from the crowd. I met the girl economist as I dragged out of the booth and she tried to get me to go back on the front platform. Fidel was about to speak. I left her and jumped off the platform and trotted up a small rise to the left. The roar lasted about ten minutes, and as I got settled on the side of the hill Fidel began to speak.

He is an amazing speaker, knowing probably instinctively all the laws of dynamics and elocution. The speech began slowly and haltingly, each syllable being pronounced with equal stress, as if he were reading a poem. He was standing with the *campesino* hat pushed back slightly off his forehead, both hands on the lectern. As he made his points, one of the hands would slide off the lectern and drop to his side, his voice becoming tighter and less warm. When the speech was really on its way, he dropped both hands from the lectern, putting one behind his back like a church usher, gesturing with the other. By now he would be rocking from side to side, pointing his finger at the crowd, at the sky, at his own chest. Sometimes he seemed to lean to the side and talk to his own ministers there on the platform with him and then wheel toward the crowd calling for them to support him. At one point in the speech the crowd interrupted for about twenty minutes, crying, "Venceremos, venceremos, venceremos, venceremos, venceremos, venceremos, venceremos, venceremos." The entire crowd, 60 or 70,000 people all chanting in unison. Fidel stepped away from the lectern grinning, talking to his aides. He quieted the crowd with a wave of his arms and began again. At first softly, with the syllables drawn out and precisely enunciated, then tightening his voice and going into an almost musical rearrangement of his speech. He condemned Eisenhower, Nixon, the South, the Monroe Doctrine, the Platt Amendment, and Fulgencio Batista in one long, unbelievable sentence. The crowd interrupted again, "Fidel, Fidel, Fidel, Fidel, Fidel, Fidel, Fidel, Fidel, Fidel, Fidel, Fidel, Fidel." He leaned away from the lectern, grinning at the chief of the army. The speech lasted almost two and a half hours, being interrupted time and again by the exultant crowd and once by five minutes of rain. When it began to rain, Almeida draped a rain jacket around Fidel's shoulders, and he re-lit his cigar. When the speech ended, the crowd went out of its head, roaring for almost forty-five minutes.

When the speech was over, I made a fast move for the platform. Almost a thousand other people had the same idea. I managed to shout something to Castro as he was being whizzed to the back of the platform and into a car. I shouted, "A fine speech, a tremendous speech."

He shouted back, "I hope you take it home with you," and disappeared in a host of bearded uniforms.

We were told at first that we would be able to leave the mountain in about three hours. But it had gotten dark already, and I didn't really fancy shooting down that mountain road with the same exuberance with which we came . . . not in the dark. Clarke and I went out looking for more water and walked almost a mile before we came to a big pavilion where soft drinks and sandwiches were being served. The soft drinks were hot and the sandwiches took too long to get. We came back and lay down at the top of a hill in back of the speakers' platform. It drizzled a little bit and the ground was patently uncomfortable. I tried to go to sleep but was awakened in a few minutes by explosions. The whole sky was lit up. Green, red, bright orange: the soldiers were shooting off fireworks. The platform was bathed in the light from the explosions and, suddenly, flood-lights from the rear. The public address system announced that we were going to have a show.

The show was a strange mixture of pop culture and main-stream highbrow *haute culture*. There was a choral group sing-ing a mildly atonal tone poem, a Jerome Robbinsesque ballet about Hollywood, Calypso dancers, and Mexican singers and dancers. The last act was the best, a Mardi Gras scene involv-ing about a hundred West Indian singers and dancers, complete with floats, huge papier-mâché figures, drummers, and masks. The West Indians walked through the audience shouting and dancing, their many torches shooting shadows against the mountains. When they danced off and out of the amphitheatre area up toward a group of unfinished school buildings, except for the huge floodlights on stage, the whole area was dark.

Now there was great confusion in the audience. Most Cu-bans were still going to try to get home that night, so they were getting themselves together, rounding up wives and children, trying to find some kind of transportation off the mountain. There were still whole units of militia piling into trucks or walking off down the hill in the dark. The delegates, our group, and a cou-ple more thousand people who didn't feel like charging off into the dark were left. Olga got all the Americans together and we lined up for what was really our first meal of the day: beans, rice, pork, and a small can of fruit juice. At that time, we still had some hopes of leaving that night, but soon word was passed around that we weren't leaving, and it was best that we slept where we were. "Sleep wherever you want," was what Olga said. That meant the ground, or maybe cement sidewalks around the unfinished school buildings and dormitories of the new "school city." Some of the

Americans started grumbling, but there was nothing that could be done. Two of our number were missing because of the day's festivities: the young lady from Philadelphia had to be driven back to Habana in a station wagon because she had come down with diarrhea and a fever, and the model had walked around without her hat too often and had gotten a slight case of sunstroke. She was resting up in the medical shack now, and I began to envy her her small canvas cot.

It was a very strange scene, about three or four thousand people wandering around in semi-darkness among a group of unfinished buildings, looking for places to sleep. The whole top of the mountain alive with flashlights, cigarette lighters, and small torches. Little groups of people huddled together against the sides of buildings or stretched out under new "street lamps" in temporary plazas. Some people managed to climb through the windows of the new buildings and sleep on dirt floors, some slept under long aluminum trucks used for hauling stage equipment, and some, like myself and the young female economist, sat up all night under dim lights, finally talking ourselves excitedly to sleep in the cool gray of early morning. I lay straight back on the cement "sidewalk" and slept without moving, until the sun began to burn my face.

We had been told the night before to be ready by 6 A.M. to pull out, but when morning came we loitered around again till about eight o'clock, when we had to line up for a breakfast of hot milk and French bread. It was served by young militia women, one of whom wore a big sidearm in a shoulder holster. By now, the dysentery was beginning to play havoc with my stomach, and the only toilet was a heavy thicket out behind the amphitheatre. I made it once, having to destroy a copy of a newspaper with my picture in it.

By nine no trucks had arrived, and with the sun now beginning to move heavily over us, the crowds shifted into the few shady areas remaining. It looked almost as if there were as many people still up on the mountain as there had been when we first arrived. Most of the Cubans, aside from the soldiers, stood in front of the pavilion and drank luke-warm Maltina or pineapple soda. The delegates and the other visitors squatted against buildings, talking and smoking. A French correspondent made a bad joke about Mussolini keeping the trains running on time, and a young Chinese student asked him why he wasn't in Algeria killing rebels.

The trucks did arrive, but there were only enough of them to take the women out. In a few minutes the sides of the trucks were almost bursting, so many females had stuffed inside. And they looked terribly uncomfortable, especially the ones stuck in the center who couldn't move an inch either way. An American newspaperman with our group who was just about to overstay his company-sanctioned leave began to panic, saying that the trucks wouldn't be back until the next day. But only a half-hour after the ladies pulled out, more trucks came and began taking the men out. Clarke, Williams, another member of our group, and I sat under the tin roof of an unfinished school building drinking warm soda, waiting until the last truck came, hoping it would be the least crowded. When we did climb up into one of the trucks it was jammed anyway, but we felt it was time to move.

This time we all had to stand up, except for a young *miliciano* who was squatting on a case of warm soda. I was in the center of the crowd and had nothing to hold on to but my companions. Every time the truck would stop short, which it did every few yards we traveled, everyone in the truck was slung against everyone else. When the truck did move, however, it literally zoomed down the side of the mountain. But then we would stop again, and all of us felt we would suffocate being mashed so tightly together, and from all the dust the trucks in front of us kicked up. The road now seemed like The Exodus. Exactly the same as the day before, only headed the opposite way. The trucks, the people on foot, the families, the militias, the *campesinos,* all headed down the mountain.

The truck sat one place twenty minutes without moving, and then when it did move it only edged up a few yards. Finally the driver pulled out of the main body of traffic and, honking his horn continuously, drove down the opposite side of the road. When the soldiers directing traffic managed to flag him down, he told them that we were important visitors who had to make a train in Yara. The truck zoomed off again, rocking back and forth and up and down, throwing its riders at times almost out the back gate.

After a couple of miles, about five Mexicans got off the truck and got into another truck headed for Santiago. This made the rest of the ride easier. The *miliciano* began opening the soda and passing it around. We were really living it up. The delegates' spirits came back and they started their chanting and waving. When we got to the train junction, the cattle cars were sitting, but completely filled with soldiers and farmers. We didn't even stop, the driver gunned the thing as fast as it would go, and we sailed by the shouting soldiers. We had only a few more stops before we got to Yara, jumped down in the soft sand, and ran for the big silver train marked "CUBA" that had been waiting for us since we left. When we got inside the train we discovered that the women still hadn't gotten back, so we sat quietly in the luxurious leather seats slowly sipping rum. The women arrived an hour later.

While we were waiting in Yara, soldiers and units of militia began to arrive in the small town and squat all around the four or five sets of tracks waiting for their own trains. Most of them went back in boxcars, while we visitors had the luxury of the semi-air-conditioned coach.

The ride back was even longer than the fourteen hours it took us before. Once when we stopped for water, we sat about two hours. Later, we stopped to pick up lunches. The atmosphere in the train was much the same as before, especially the Mexican delegates who whooped it up constantly. They even made a conga line up and down the whole length of the train. The young Mexican woman and I did a repeat performance also and talked most of the fifteen or sixteen hours it took us to get back to Habana. She was gentler with me this time, calling me "Yanqui imperialist" only a few times.

Everyone in the train was dirty, thirsty, and tired when it arrived in Habana. I had been wearing the same clothes for three days and hadn't even once taken off my shoes. The women were in misery. I hadn't seen a pocket mirror since the cattle cars.

The terminal looked like a rear outpost of some battlefield. So many people in filthy wrinkled clothes scrambling wearily out of trains. But even as tired as I was I felt excited at the prospect of being back in the big city for five more days. I was even more excited by the amount of thinking the trip to the Sierra was forcing me to. The "new" ideas that were being shoved at me, some of which I knew would be painful when I eventually got to New York.

The idea of "a revolution" had been foreign to me. It was one of those inconceivably "romantic" and/or hopeless ideas that we Norteamericanos have been taught since public school to hold up to the cold light of "reason." That reason being whatever repugnant lie our usurious "ruling class" had paid their journalists to disseminate. The reason that allows that voting, in a country where the parties are exactly the same, can be made to assume the gravity of actual moral engagement. The reason that permits a young intellectual to believe he has said something profound when he says, "I don't trust men in uniforms." The *residue* had settled on all our lives, and no one can function comfortably in this country without it. That thin crust of lie we cannot even detect in our own thinking. That rotting of the mind which had enabled us to think about Hiroshima as if someone else had done it, or to believe vaguely that the "counter-revolution" in Guatemala was an "internal" affair.

The rebels among us have become merely people like myself who grow beards and will not participate in politics. Drugs, juvenile deliquency, complete isolation from the vapid mores of the country, a few current ways out. But name an alternative here. Something not inextricably bound up in a lie. Something not part of liberal stupidity or the actual filth of vested interest. There is none. It's much too late. We are an *old* people already. Even the vitality of our art is like bright flowers growing up through a rotting carcass.

But the Cubans, and the other *new* peoples (in Asia, Africa, South America) don't need us, and we had better stay out of their way.

I came out of the terminal into the street and stopped at a newsstand to buy a paper. The headlines of one Miami paper read, "CUBAN CELEBRATION RAINED OUT." I walked away from the stand as fast as I could.

FRANK MANKIEWICZ and KIRBY JONES

Havana, 1974: Around town with Fidel

"THEN PEPÍN NOTICED THAT THERE WAS NOT ENOUGH ROOM
FOR BOTH FIDEL AND THE DRIVER. 'I'LL DRIVE,' FIDEL
SAID. HE CLIMBED BEHIND THE WHEEL AND OFF WE WENT."

*In 1974, television producers Frank Mankiewicz and Kirby
Jones formed a company whose purpose was to produce exclusive
television interviews with world leaders and personalities seldom
seen in the U.S. One of the first leaders they sought, fifteen years
after the Cuban Revolution, was Fidel Castro.*

*Mankiewicz and Jones, plus their film crew, made three
trips to Cuba between June 1974 and February 1975. They
spent a total of six weeks there. Four days and nights were spent
with Castro, doing the lengthy interviews he had agreed to. Most
of the rest of the time was spent traveling and filming throughout the island. The government placed no restrictions on them
and, indeed, aided them in every possible way.*

*Portions of their long interview with Castro were included
in a* CBS Reports *television special called "Castro, Cuba and
the USA," which aired on October 22, 1974. Excerpts of the
interview material were published in* Oui *magazine and in foreign editions of* Playboy. *The full interview, with photos, was*

published as With Fidel: A Portrait of Castro and Cuba, *in* 1975.

The account that follows is a fascinating portrait of Havana, kitchen and all, and an equally lively portrait of a very affable Fidel. The "maximum leader" makes an excellent tour guide.

GETTING TO CUBA

In early 1974, we formed a small company to produce exclusive television interviews with world leaders and personalities who hadn't appeared on U.S. television—or had not appeared for a long time. Fidel Castro was certainly one of them. We first contacted Saul Landau, a film maker and writer, who had been to Cuba many times and who we had heard had become a friend of Castro after producing a film, *Fidel,* for educational television in 1968. We met with Saul, outlined our project, and asked him to produce and direct the film and the interview. Saul agreed to help.

We then wrote a long proposal to Castro describing our idea. We told him we felt that 1974 might be an appropriate time for the American people to hear not only what he had to say about international events, but also what was going on in Cuba today. We said we shared with many Americans a feeling that news about Castro and Cuba had been minimal and that what news appeared was based too often on ignorance and possibly even bias. We offered to conduct an interview in which the final product would be unaltered, so that Castro could be measured and judged by his own words.

After submitting this document, we received a request from Havana for additional information, chiefly about our own backgrounds, plus an expanded list of the possible areas to be covered in the interview. This second document was prepared and sent. By this time six weeks had passed.

About three weeks later, we were told that Castro had received literally dozens of requests from all three U.S. television networks, several U.S. newspapers, and many foreign countries—all asking for an interview. Castro had rejected them all, but we were also told he had decided that if he were to accept any interview for U.S. consumption, it would be ours. The last word was that we could only wait and "that it might be two days, two weeks, two years, or never."

Much to our surprise, in the early part of May we received a message inviting us to come to Cuba at the end of June to do the interview.

The most convenient way to get to Cuba at that time was through Mexico City. (Now, a trip through Jamaica is cheaper and quicker.) We arranged for a crew, wrote the State Department for permission to travel to Cuba (it is almost always granted to journalists, and in this instance the State Department was quite helpful).

From Mexico City, Cuban Airlines flies a prop-jet Russian-built Ilyushin 18 to Havana. The night we flew, the plane was jammed, mainly with an Argentine volleyball team, diplomatic couriers, and some returning Cuban film makers. The service on the plane was good. We were served a club sandwich; a choice of Cuban beer or pineapple juice; and deep, sweet Cuban coffee that shot through the body as though it had been injected directly into the veins. (On Cuban menus, coffee is listed under *Infusiones*—it is an accurate classification.) And, of course, we had our first Cuban cigars.

We landed at José Martí International Airport at 4:30 A.M., Havana time. Stepping out of the plane, we felt the hot muggy air of the Caribbean, and as we walked into the terminal, we came face to face with three wall-sized posters of Che Guevara. It was then that it really hit us where we were. For the only place one sees Che posters in the United States is likely to be on the dormitory walls of students who often pretend at their brand of relatively safe "revolution." But there in Havana it was no different from a foreigner's visiting the United States and seeing a picture of Abraham Lincoln or George Washington. In Cuba, Che Guevara is indeed a national hero, not a "camp" sign of protest.

We immediately encountered Cuban technology when we discovered that we had both forgotten our yellow International Health Certificates. Our first inclination was to try to bluff our way through. But we were quickly escorted into a small room at the back of the airport where we were met by a female Cuban medical technician who could not have been more than fifteen years old. It was our first exposure to the new Cuba, a Cuba run largely by people under thirty-five, building houses, teaching in schools, managing ports—and inoculating visitors.

Greeting us were the three people who were to be our companions for the next three and a half weeks. There was Daniel Rodriguez of the Cuban Foreign Ministry, thirty-three years old, married and the father of a small baby. He had rejected the life of his wealthy parents—the life of the "*burgesa*," as he called it—and had completely committed himself to the revolution of Fidel Castro. Having seen so much of the U.S. protest of the sixties led by the sons and daughters of the rich, it was not hard for us to understand Daniel.

Alina Alayo, also thirty-three, is an official of the Ministry of Foreign Relations. Alina speaks almost perfect English and is, in fact, often used as one of Fidel's translators. She is a militant Marxist who understands Marxism-Leninism well, but whose ideology is tempered by a sense of humor. Alina was pregnant, her third pregnancy after two miscarriages. A strong advocate of women's rights, she told us she wanted a baby girl so she could "educate her child in the ways of men."

Maria Elena Vallejera, twenty-two, works with ICAP (Cultural Institute of Friendship with People)—sort of a national Welcome Wagon agency. A more bubbly, chubby, enthusiastic tour guide would be hard to find. Maria Elena has the voice of Tallulah Bankhead and the spirit of a college cheerleader.

After waiting for our thirty-five pieces of luggage and equipment to be processed, we finally boarded a Russian bus at 5:30 A.M. and headed for downtown Havana. As we left José Martí Airport, we saw the first of hundreds of political signs—this one a picture of Ho Chi Minh calling for friendship with the North Vietnamese people.

At six o'clock on a Saturday morning, the Hotel Riviera seemed deserted except for a small night crew. Walking in, one thought of the Doral or the Americana hotels in Miami Beach. It was an appropriate comparison. The Hotel Riviera was built by Meyer Lansky and completed a few months before Fidel took power. Daniel proudly pointed to a closed door on the right. "The casino used to be in there in 1958, but Fidel closed them all."

MEETING FIDEL

We first met Fidel Castro almost three weeks later. Although we had been expecting to begin the interview well before, we now waited patiently—and with little knowledge whether our filmed interview would last one hour or several—in front of the hotel.

As we stood at the curb, someone exclaimed, "Here comes Fidel." We looked left and there appeared, driving slowly up the half-circle driveway, one lonely jeep with a bearded man in the front passenger seat.

The Cubans who were at the entrance just watched from a distance; some came out from inside, but there was no commotion. It was almost as if a taxi had delivered just another passenger.

Castro looked just the way he was supposed to look, but neater and more dapper. He wore the traditional olive-green fatigues, but they were well tailored and pressed and appeared to be made from an extremely lightweight material. His black boots were brilliantly shined and he wore a pistol belt—complete with pistol—around his middle. On each shoulder was the diamond of red and black with a white star in the middle signifying his military rank as *commandante* (major). His insignia was partially encircled by a gold braid, which meant *commandante en jefe* (commander-in-chief). There is only one of those.

There are some surprising things about Castro physically. He is taller than expected, and, for a forty-seven-year-old man who has been the leader of his country for fifteen years, he looks surprisingly youthful. At about six-foot-two and 190 pounds, he has the build of a cornerback, or maybe an Ivy League tackle. Considering the hours Castro keeps, his face is remarkably unlined, his eyes unpouched. The hairline is receding a trifle, and the beard is flecked with gray, but the midriff is flat, the eyes are clear, and he is remarkably unchanged from the young man whose last appearance in the United States was at the famous heads-of-state United Nations General Assembly in 1962.

Castro chatted briefly and then suggested that we all go for a drive. We were ushered into the backseat with Pepín Naranjo, Fidel's aide-de-camp and government minister without portfolio. Pepín has been a friend since Fidel's university days. Saul Landau climbed in front. Then Pepín noticed that there was not enough room for both Fidel and the driver. "I'll drive," Fidel said. He climbed behind the wheel and off we went.

The following entourage was a small Alfa Romeo sedan with one ministry official and one bodyguard. The jeep was Russian-made and equipped with a two-way radio placed between the front seats. On the floor was a box of six-inch cigars and a blue metal tin containing candy mints. Across the front dashboard, securely mounted, was a Russian-made AK-47 automatic rifle.

It is questionable whether Fidel Castro could pass a high-school drivers' education course. He has the habit—admirable under normal circumstances—of wanting to look a person in the eye when he is talking. But we were in the backseat.

There was no apparent itinerary. In spite of our wariness of his driving, Fidel stopped at red lights and obeyed traffic signs just as if we were out for a Sunday drive. People along the road waved and called out "Fidel, Fidel." Castro waved back most times. He was very busy talking and explaining everything.

As he drove he described the botanical gardens that were being developed outside Havana, pointed out a school, drove through Lenin Park and explained the facilities, and asked about our trip through Cuba. He seemed to know everything about everything we saw—and after subsequent trips with him we realized that he *did* know everything.

We stopped alongside a factory that was being built to produce radios, batteries, and minicalculators. He chatted a bit with the manager, asking him what the building was made of, about construction schedules, the number of workers to be employed, what the projected production schedule was, and if any problems existed. The manager replied that they were on schedule but would be able to move faster if they had more trucks.

They talked as if they already knew each other, had talked before, and would again. We soon learned that this was the way most people talked to Fidel. They had seen him before, and they did expect to see him again. He was interested in everything about the factory, and it was something that he was not to forget. The manager knew that, too.

We soon arrived at Las Ruinas, a restaurant in Lenin Park which was built in and around the shell of an old hacienda. It was a fine building of whitewashed brick and stained glass, with plants growing in old stone pillars with holes drilled in them to permit watering pipes for the plants.

As we walked into the restaurant, Fidel stopped at a room in which several of the restaurant employees were seated in rows, as if in a class. "What are you doing?" he asked. "We are studying," they replied. He turned to us and explained, "Here in Cuba everyone attends some classes, everyone has the opportunity to learn."

Inside, the maître d' escorted us to a table as if we were ordinary customers. Daiquiris were served all around and for the next few hours Fidel quizzed us on Watergate and American politics with the same interest that he had demonstrated about the factory. This was July: John Ehrlichman had just gone to trial, the Supreme Court was considering the tape decision, and the Judiciary Committee was getting ready for public debate. "You Americans," Castro said after a while, "talk a lot about stability and the need to deal with stable governments. I think my government is the most stable in the western hemisphere." Then he paused and added with a slight smile, "Including, it would seem, your own."

He asked questions about the upcoming conspiracy trial, impeachment, who the Judiciary Committee members were and what they were like, what we thought Nixon's chances were of surviving. We answered all these questions with the easy wisdom that living in Washington seemed to require—wisdom built upon not much more than reading the *Washington Post* and being around some Democratic political campaigns. We never pretended to be experts, only observant amateurs. We told him we thought Richard Nixon was not going to survive and that indeed he might resign before the actual impeachment debate began in the House. "You might be right," Fidel commented, "but I think you overstate the case. In any event, Cuba must maintain a conservative policy and operate as if Richard Nixon is to complete his term."

After one and a half hours, he finally turned to the main purpose of our visit.

"What about this interview?" he asked. "A lot of the subjects that you want to discuss will require careful preparation and planning. I want it to be a good interview. Can we start on Saturday? That will give me a few days to prepare."

We gulped silently; we really did not particularly want to wait another three days. Landau finally asked whether we could begin that night and see how it went.

Fidel crinkled his forehead and finally said, "OK, why not? Where would you like to do it?"

"Anywhere convenient for you," we answered.

Fidel then turned to Pepín and suggested a room just outside his office in the Palacio de la Revolución.

"You people no doubt want to wash up and get everything ready, so why don't we begin around eleven tonight? Let's do the interview just as we have been talking here—informal, a conversation. Isn't that better than a formal question-and-answer session?

"One more thing," he added. "I'd like to invite you on an extended tour of some areas around Havana before you leave. Would you like to take a jeep tour on Saturday?"

So it was decided we would spend three nights filming, and follow that with a day's informal tour. Things were looking up.

Comparing notes later, it seemed clear we had been with one of the most charming and entertaining men either of us had ever met. Whether one agrees with him or not, Castro is personally overpowering. U.S. political writers would call it a simple case of charisma, but it is more than that. Political leaders often can be and are charismatic in a public sense, but rather normal in more private moments. Such is not the case with Fidel Castro. He remains one of the few truly electric personalities in a world in which his peers seem dull and pedestrian.

Such personal feelings should not be confused with

ideological or political agreement on our own part, for there was much on which we were to differ. But from the moment he looked you straight in the eye and spoke directly to every question, from the moment he first leaned eagerly forward to stress a point, his beard no more than six inches away, each of us knew we were in for a fascinating interview and an exciting experience. We were not let down.

THE INTERVIEW

The crew—Saul Landau, Dick Pearce, and Mark Berger—left the hotel early Wednesday evening to set up. We ate a leisurely dinner, showered, changed clothes, and waited to be picked up by Daniel and Alina at 9:00 P.M. We had dressed informally. Even a sit-down interview with Fidel Castro does not require a coat and tie in Cuba. At exactly 9:00 P.M., we piled into Daniel's Alfa Romeo and headed for the Palacio.

The Palacio is a well-cared-for structure with high ceilings, polished marble floors, and indoor plants. It was completed just before Castro took power, and had been destined to be the new headquarters for the national police. It now houses the highest government offices and the headquarters of the Cuban Communist Party.

Castro's study is a simple room with several couches, chairs, and potted plants spread throughout. Along one entire side is a bookcase filled with colorfully bound books in Spanish, a gift to him from the President of Mexico. Castro has no room for them in his office proper so he built a bookcase in this room for their display.

From this study, one door leads to the cabinet room, which contains a long chrome table for about forty people—complete, curiously enough, with simultaneous translation equipment—and another door leads to Fidel's office.

Inside the office, just to the left of the door, is a desk, uncluttered, but with several telephones. Behind the desk is a bookcase filled with the writings of Che, various books on Cuba, and a variety of highly technical works on agriculture, farming, and economics. At the far end is a small conference table for eight and on the right, a sofa, two large chairs, and a coffee table.

Three chairs were arranged in the center of the study for the interview: Cameras were placed, lights tested, all under the watchful eye of Fidel's staff. Everything we did was watched and checked out, not unlike the way in which the Secret Service watches over an interview with the President of the United States.

At exactly 10:45 P.M., Fidel walked in with Pepín. Gone was the pistol belt—and the pistol—around his middle, and his hair had been carefully combed. He greeted us warmly, surveyed the scene, and seemed to approve.

We sat down. Microphones were tested, and we began the first of what would be three nights of interview. The interview is included in other sections of this book. But a conversation with Fidel at close range should be described.

The interview was conducted totally in Spanish. No questions were submitted in advance, and Fidel answered everything put to him.

Castro speaks very softly. Contrary to the public image built up over the years in the United States, he converses in a relaxed, but serious, manner. He is the head of his country, and what he says is carefully thought out and logically presented. He knows what he is doing and saying all the time. He was completely aware of the camera, and demonstrated all the professionalism of a seasoned political candidate in the United States.

Our interview was really a conversation. Generally, Fidel sat easily in his chair, leaning back, legs crossed, and smoking on his ever-present small cigars. But when he wanted to place special emphasis on a remark, he would lean forward to within a few inches of his questioner, tap him on the knee, and look directly into his eyes. It bothered him when he was misunderstood. He did not at all demand agreement, but he would not leave a point until he was satisfied that there was at least a basic understanding of what he was saying.

It was so easy to become engrossed in his style and logic that we often found ourselves starting from point A and within

ten minutes agreeing with point B. Fidel is a former trial lawyer and he shows it. All his arguments follow a carefully struc-
tured presentation. By the time he has built his case, if you
do not watch out, he has you convinced of things you do not
believe.

(During our October visit, we were standing with Dan
Rather of CBS, talking with Fidel. In the middle of a heated
discussion between Rather and Fidel, Jones turned to Mankiewicz and whispered, "Frank, I'll bet within five minutes, Dan's
head will begin nodding agreement."

Right on cue, as Fidel continued making his case, Dan's
head began to move, and soon the words, "Yes, yes," were being
uttered.)

Castro is not a passive talker. His whole body seems to
become involved in what he says. His fingers stroke his beard,
his arms and hands punctuate his points in a fluid manner. He
often raises one finger against his face or in the air as he thinks
and talks. Even as he sat quietly talking in his chair there was
a magnetic energy and motion to him.

After ninety minutes we called a break. Immediately, frozen Daiquiris were brought in and served to everyone—guards,
aides, and camera crew.

Fidel offered us all cigars from his leather carrying case.
We emptied the case right away, whereupon from over Fidel's
shoulder appeared the hand of an efficient aide who took the
case and quickly returned it full. Fidel joked and tried to speak
with the rest of our crew. He was interested in all of us and
asked questions about our work and how we thought the interview was going.

As we sat down for the second session that first night, an
aide interrupted with an urgent cable for Fidel. After reading
quickly, he said, "Here, look at this. The Greeks have just overthrown the government of Cyprus." An update was handed to
him.

"What do you think about this? It is a very serious situation
now in Cyprus. . . . You know what I think," he said as he sat
back in his chair, thoughtfully analyzing what he had just read.
"I think that the action of the Greeks will result in an invasion
by the Turks, the expulsion of the Greek troops from Cyprus,

and will have serious repercussions in Athens—perhaps the end of the military junta."

After only a few minutes of reading and thinking about a situation many thousands of miles away, Fidel's apparent instinct about a distant crisis turned out to be right on the mark.

At about 3 in the morning, an aide signaled to Saul Landau that the time had come to stop.

"I don't think that we have nearly finished," commented Fidel. "Why don't we continue again tomorrow night and start a bit earlier—let's say about ten?"

Fidel offered us all a nightcap and, as we were about to leave, we presented him with a few gifts. We had heard that he liked mechanical objects and was fascinated with how things work, so we gave him one of the new Polaroid SX-70 cameras. He immediately wanted to try it out. We showed him quickly how it was supposed to work, but he was a bit impatient and it was not clear that he fully understood. He backed up, put it to his eyes, and clicked away. Out shot the picture, and everyone gathered around. The picture was miserably out of focus. Never one to be discouraged, he tried again. All of us assembled in a group, with Fidel Castro as the most unlikely photographer we had ever faced. Out came a second picture, somewhat out of focus but better than the first. He was like a small boy at Christmas, totally enthusiastic. After a third try and much laughter at what terrible subjects we were, he thanked us for the camera and left quickly by his office door.

To this day, we don't know if that camera ever produced a good picture.

Late Thursday, July 18, we picked up where we had left off. We had decided that the second night would include all the tough questions—those things that bothered North Americans the most.

At 10:00 P.M. sharp, Fidel entered the room. He was never late at any of our agreed-upon hours. Indeed, promptness—a most un-Latin characteristic—seems a Cuban habit.

At the conclusion of the first interview segment, we asked him how he got his news about the United States and the world.

"I have a daily news digest," he answered. "Every morning

at eight, there is a digest on my desk. Sometimes I don't get to read the entire thing until late at night when I do most of my reading, but if something important is happening, I will of course study the material."

"Might we see it?" we asked.

"Of course."

He motioned to an aide, who quickly brought in a one-and-a-half-inch-thick notebook containing cabled news stories from all over the world, all the news services from AP to Tass. Clearly indexed and summarized, it was broken down into various sections—Cuba, United States, Latin America, Europe, Third World. Each section was subindexed.

"Most of the time," Fidel explained, "I do not have the time to read the entire digest. But if an article seems particularly interesting or important, I do."

"When do you find time to do all this reading?" Mankie-wicz asked.

"Mostly at night, usually after midnight. That's when I do most of my reading."

"Have you read any American books lately?"

"I've just finished *Jaws* and I liked it because of its splendid Marxist message."

We were surprised at this remark, as *Jaws* had seemed to us to be simply a first-rate adventure story. But Castro went on to discuss that part of the book where the local chief of police was urging the town officials to close their beaches while the great white shark, which had eaten a few bathers, was tracked down. The officials refused, on the ground that the Fourth of July weekend was coming up and the bad publicity would ruin the season's business.

"Thus," Castro said, "the book makes the point that capitalism will risk even human life in order to keep the markets open." It was not a point made by many U.S. reviewers.

As we sat down after the break, Fidel again brought up the subject of Watergate.

"Yesterday, I mentioned that we in Cuba could not count on the impeachment of Nixon, but today something happened that seems very important. There was a Republican member of the Judiciary Committee who held what appears to me to be a significant press conference."

"Do you mean Congressman McClory?" we asked.

"Yes, exactly. He said today that he will vote for the impeachment of President Nixon. I think I now agree with you. For the first time I believe that Richard Nixon will not survive."

We ended at one in the morning, and Castro invited us to continue for a third session the following night. The final session, Friday night, was shorter than the previous two. At its conclusion, Fidel repeated his invitation to take us on a jeep tour the following day throughout the countryside surrounding Havana. Then, just as we were taking our leave, Fidel asked when we were planning to return to the United States. We said we would probably leave on Sunday, on the flight to Madrid.

"Do you *want* to go to Europe?" he asked.

"No, not at all," we answered, "but that is the only flight until next Wednesday."

"But, it seems a terrible inconvenience for you. Would you like to fly on my plane to Nassau instead? Would that be better?"

A four-hour flight to Washington via Nassau was infinitely preferable to a twenty-four-hour trip via Madrid. Fidel turned to Pepín and instructed him to call Foreign Minister Raul Roa and ask him to contact the English ambassador for permission for the official plane to land in Nassau.

He then turned back to us. "Well, done. Until tomorrow, then." He departed quickly through his office door.

ON THE ROAD

Saturday, July 20, was one of those heavy tropical days, so hot and muggy that by 9:45 A.M. our eyeglasses steamed over upon leaving the air-conditioned comfort of the hotel.

Shortly after ten, three jeeps swung up to the Hotel Riviera, with Fidel in the front passenger seat of the first one. Fidel slid out to greet us, and the crew loaded their gear into the second jeep.

We had no idea where we were going until Pepín mentioned that we were off to visit Alamar, a large new housing development—actually a "new town" of some thirty thousand—outside of Havana. We had, in fact, visited Alamar before; it is a favorite showcase of the new Cuba.

Riding through Havana's streets in a Fidel Castro caravan did not really evoke the wild response that we had come to expect with some American leaders and politicians. Often we passed so rapidly that people alongside the road barely had a chance to grasp exactly who had driven by. But when we did stop for red lights or were forced to slow down, people waved at Fidel, called out his name, and smiled warmly.

At Alamar a crowd had assembled—but, as it turned out, not for us or for Castro. A delegation of South Vietnamese from the PRG (Provisional Revolutionary Government) on a state visit was due to arrive within a half hour.

The streets were filled with people waving PRG flags, and when they realized that our caravan included Fidel, they swarmed around him. Children brought him flowers and fathers hoisted the smaller ones onto their shoulders for a better view. Fidel was gentle with the people as he shook hands, patted heads, and chatted informally. He asked the kids about the swimming pool, how often they swam, what hours it was open, and why there was no one swimming on such a hot day. The pool was due to open within the next few hours.

Disengaging himself from the crowd, Fidel walked with us toward a small ice cream stand. A woman—obviously a resident of Alamar he had met before—ran up and gave him a big *abrazo*; they warmly held hands for a minute. As they headed for the ice cream stand, Fidel's arm around the woman's shoulder, families began to appear on the balconies of their homes. There was no ecstatic shouting, but smiles were everywhere.

Fidel then suggested that we go visiting, and led us up the stairs of a five-story building. He knocked on the door of a third-floor apartment. The lady of the house opened the door and shouted, "Fidel, Fidel, come on in."

The apartment was like most in the Alamar complex—two bedrooms, living room, kitchen, bathroom, balcony, complete with electricity and running water. There were several chairs, a coffee table, a Russian television set, and a dining room table set for six.

Fidel's path was filled in by all of us, his aides, and an ever-increasing number of neighbors. Word had traveled quickly. Fidel took off his cap (but not his gun) and sat down. An old man in a straw hat squatted next to him, two small children sat down on the floor alongside, and the man and woman of the house seated themselves across from him.

"Quick," someone yelled, "get a fan; it's hot in here."

Immediately a light-blue table fan was placed on the small coffee table so that it blew in Fidel's direction.

"Does anyone have any rum?" asked Fidel.

A bottle and several shot glasses were brought in and we all toasted. And then Fidel and the family began chatting as if Uncle Harry had just blown in from Toledo after six years.

APARTMENT

CASTRO: How many people now live here?

#1: Seven hundred and seventy, with one hundred and seventy-five apartments completed.

c: How are you? How are you? Listen here, how many frozen custards are eaten daily?

#1: Three or four per person.

c: How many do you sell?

#1: Two hundred or so pesos worth.

c: You mean that you sell more than a thousand ice creams per day?

#1: Sure, a large amount.

c: Well, they're very good.

#1: We're located right next door to the dairy. The peasants like this housing complex. One hundred and seventy-five families have moved in already. We have a medical clinic, a pharmacy. . . .

c: And you're going to build a barbershop, a beauty parlor, and a movie house?

#1: But don't tell me that it's big, it's just right. It just grows and grows and grows.

c: You're soon going to start competing with Havana? Eh?

#1:	No, Havana's bigger. Are you kidding?
c:	How is the television reception here?
#1:	Very good. They're trying a new antenna, *Commandante*.
c:	You mean one central one?
#1:	No, individual ones . . . one per each eight apartments for eight sets. In one building they're testing it.
c:	Here's a toast to the success of your town, that it doesn't grow too large.
CRIES:	No—here's to the change that's been made from before until now.
#1:	And here's to the development of those countries that still haven't developed like we have—those still backward like we used to be.
c:	He's in the political cadre here?
#2:	Who couldn't be a political militant after undergoing the changes we've been through? Isn't that right, *Commandante*?
c:	I think it is.
#3:	Look, we've got more than a tableful of postcards. They say that all these big things we've done are making the Revolution.
c:	From where did you receive those cards?
#2:	From Mexico, from the Mayor of Morelia in Mexico, and all of the visitors that came here and then sent postcards about their impressions. We're going to answer them.
c:	It's going to cost you a lot of money.
#1:	Ah, no. The young French Communists who are in Jibacoa visited here three times. And now they have an impression of the community.
c:	And who is going to fill these apartments?
#1:	We are going to fill them up with peasants, but some are still on the ranch.
c:	Grandmother, come here. I almost called you Grandpa.

#3: Go on, go on.

c: How big are the fields of the school?

#1: Imagine this, we have nine hectares of corn.

c: And what do you produce in all?

#1: Well, we had nine thousand last year, and this year thirty-six hundred and sixty-three worth, fifty thousand pesos.

c: And the vegetables that are consumed—tomatoes, peppers, onions—I'm not talking only about corn.

#4: We've loaded some trucks with our corn.

c: Have you sent it to other places?

#5: Yes, to the Mezorra Mental Hospital, to the workers' dining rooms.

c: Do you have all that you want here?

#1: Ah, yes. Plenty of corn given out every week.

c: Any complaints?

#1: No, things are going well with the Provincial Party people.

c: How many hectares do you have in the eastern part?

#1: Eighteen now. But we are going to develop more. A peasant lives on the land now, but he'll be moving to the apartments and we'll be able to work the land better.

c: How many students are there in the school?

#1: *Commandante,* do you want to eat a snack?

c: No, no, thank you. . . . What are those things?

#1: *Commandante,* they're sweet—corn with peanuts and eggs.

c: Yes, but I shouldn't eat many eggs.

#1: But it has only one egg, no more.

c: I like fried bananas better. . . . How many students are there again?

#2: We have one hundred and eighty-nine at this time who live in the community in this area, but this year we will have five hundred or a little more because of the peripheral residents.

The preschool program will take kids from the outlying areas. This way these children also will have the opportunity to participate in the community.

c: And in the day-care center, how many children are there?

#1: One hundred and twenty.

c: How many women are working now?

#1: At this time one hundred and eleven women.

c: And what percent of the work force are women?

#1: We have more than eighty-five percent of the women working. Almost ninety percent. And we are building a new day-care center. It's very pretty in nice colors.

c: When will it be finished?

#1: In September it will open.

c: Very good. You really have everything here—day-care center, school, and now stores are being built.

#1: Yes, we have everything—and a medical clinic as well. We have a doctor four days here and one in Santo Cruz. He helps there, too.

c: And that doctor, how much do you pay for his services?

#1: We're going to pay him, *Commandante*. With our work, with milk. Ah, *Commandante,* don't talk to me like that. We'll pay for everything.

c: You're going to have to produce milk like crazy if you're going to pay for all that.

#1: Ah, *Commandante,* don't kid us like that. Nooooo.

c: One has to sell rum at very high prices to support the milk of all of you.

#1: No, it's not that way.

c: If you—your whole area—produces one half a million liters of milk, Havana'll be drinking a million. But we have a lot of dairy plants going. At least, you're not the only producers.

Do you only have one child?

#2: Yes.

c: And you're not thinking of having more than one?

#2: That's right.

c: Good. If we keep producing kids the way we have been, they won't fit in this country.

(LOUD CRIES)

As we left the apartment we saw that a crowd had gathered from all over the huge housing complex. Alamar was being built to house over 125,000 people. It already contained 30,000, and it seemed as if most of them were in the street. We inched toward the jeeps. Fidel stopped to shake hands and to talk to as many as possible. But there were no requests for autographs and, unlike the case with popular American politicians, the people always seemed to leave a pocket of space around Fidel— not because of security guards, for there was only one directly with him. It was evident that he evoked a combination of feelings. Part of it was his own attitude of a visiting relative that allowed people the informality and openness. But there was also demonstrated a feeling that people were in the presence of their liberator—the man who, they clearly felt, had led them from the miseries of the past into a new day. For that reason, they seemed to keep a step away as if afraid to puncture the bubble. Women would greet Fidel with a friendly touch or pat and then take a step back. The scene was warm and friendly, Fidel obviously was enjoying himself, and the Alamar residents were having the time of their life.

Fidel slowly climbed into the front seat of his jeep, the rest of us took our places, and off we went. As we drove down the road, a line of people thought we were the Vietnamese delegates. Amidst the Vietnamese flags, suddenly there were cries of "It's Fidel! It's Fidel!" Fidel acknowledged their greetings with a slight wave and joked, "They think we are the Vietnamese."

As with our car ride with Fidel the previous Wednesday, there did not seem to be any predetermined pattern or schedule to our journey. We just went where his whim took him. After a drive of about twenty minutes, we started to chug up a steep hill, on top of which was a beautiful modern house of wood and glass.

"Where are we going?" Jones asked Pepín.

"That is a government protocol house. It is where foreign dignitaries stay. The last visitor that was here was President Boumédienne of Algeria."

As we stopped at the foot of some wide stone steps, Fidel turned to us and mentioned that he thought we "would like to see this new house we have built."

"But," he continued, "the Vietnamese delegation is expected here for lunch in a few minutes. I didn't know that, but maybe I can show it to you before they arrive. I certainly do not want to interrupt their schedule."

Fidel led us up the stairs and through a long corridor leading onto a veranda that overlooked a wide green valley. We passed the kitchen in which chefs were preparing a meal that, at least at a quick glance, included charcoal-broiled steaks. At the end of the corridor was a banquet table set for about thirty with stemware from eastern Europe, china and silver, and trays of different cheeses and fresh tropical fruits. Just as we walked out onto the terrace, cars appeared at the entrance and out stepped the Vietnamese delegation.

"Oh, oh," said Fidel, "now what are we going to do? I hope we haven't messed up their itinerary."

He immediately walked to the front door and greeted Madame Nguyen Thi Dinh, the deputy commander of the military forces of the PRG in South Vietnam. Accompanying her were two decorated soldiers from the PRG army. Both had been imprisoned from three to four years; both wore at least thirty medals of commendation; both were less than five feet tall; both were twenty years old and looked twelve; both were women. They were all escorted by Fidel's older brother, Ramon—as tall as Fidel, a bit thinner, his beard much grayer. "With his beard whiter than mine," says Fidel, "you can tell he is older." Ramon is director of one of four large animal husbandry programs.

Abrazos were given and received, and as Fidel and the guests came out onto the terrace, white-jacketed waiters passed trays of frozen Daiquiris, fresh fruit juices, and other cold drinks.

CASTRO: I came with a delegation of journalists and we were just passing by. How are you? Ah, here come the Daiquiris. Don't you drink?

MADAME
DINH: A little bit.

C: Nor the others in your group? Well, a toast to the Vietnamese. We were at Alamar. We were there a little while before you.

D: How long have you been here?

C: Only five minutes. I'm with a delegation of journalists. They are North Americans, but good people.

D: Of the North Americans, there are many that are good.

C: I explained that in my interview—that there are many North Americans who fought against the war in Vietnam.

D: The bad ones are the rich ones and Nixon.

C: Where are the journalists? . . . Here they are. . . .

D: We hate Nixon, but have a great sympathy toward the American people, and the American people have helped a lot to end the U.S. involvement in the war in Vietnam.

C: Look at all those medals on those two girls!

D: These two girls were in jail for several years and they do have a lot of medals. How long have the two of you been here in Cuba?

C: They have been here about twenty days. It's my fault they've been here so long—they've been waiting for me.

JONES: We're doing a television program for the United States. How long have you been in Cuba?

D: Three days.

C: We did not know that we were going to meet you and we just came from a place where there were a lot of people waiting for you. But I explained that the crowd was for you and not for me.

D: Have any of you ever visited South Vietnam?

MANKIEWICZ: Once in 1972 with Senator George McGovern—both Kirby and I were aides to him in his presidential campaign of 1972.

D: We wish you could come to the liberated parts of Vietnam to see the crimes committed by the Yankees.

J: We would like to go to Vietnam whenever it would be convenient for you.

M: When I was in South Vietnam, we were attacked in a church by people from Thieu's government, during a meeting with some anti-Thieu leaders.

D: The majority of the people in South Vietnam are against the current regime.

C: Look, Frank and Kirby, how many medals these two fighters have.

J: What are the medals for?

D: They wear these medals because for five years they fought bravely and helped to shoot down helicopters, planes, and to destroy tanks. One killed three soldiers before she was captured and spent two years in jail, but she maintained her spirits until she was freed.

C: Well, we should continue our trip. We have enjoyed our visit here, and the film they are making will be seen on American television by about ten to eleven million people.

D: When you return to the United States, please transmit our feeling of solidarity with all those Americans who have helped. Although the government of the United States continues to support the Thieu regime, we are sure we will be victorious over the Americans under Nixon's leadership.

C: Until later then.

(While walking out . . .)

D: It has been a surprise for us to see you today.

C: I had hoped to meet up with you, and we were lucky because those who were waiting to greet you at Alamar also greeted me. Have a good meal. Thank you all. I hope you will have a chance to rest. Are you returning to Havana now?

D: No, first we are going to the province of Oriente.

C: No chance for rest. It is very hot there—like in South Vietnam.

D: Yes, but we know the heat. Good-bye.

It was quickly back into the jeeps and on to the next stop, wherever that might be. Onto the highway, up more hills, and along some unpaved, dusty roads which led eventually to a rum factory in the final stages of completion—rows of warehouses holding thousands of kegs of aging rum. We entered the dark, hangarlike buildings where Fidel talked with the manager and the workers.

RUM FACTORY

WORKER: Fidel, Fidel, hello.

CASTRO: Good afternoon. How are you all? Do you have youth brigades working here?

W: Yes.

C: Are you accomplishing much here?

W: Yes.

C: Have they decided to build the building? All set with it?

W: Yes, already they have begun discussing it with Manolo.

C: It is coordinated. They are in agreement, right?

W: There is coordination between Levi and Raciel.

C: Prefabricated?

W: Yes.

c: For the people that are going to live here to work here? Are you going to produce liquors, too?

w: Yes.

c: And you haven't gotten that far yet?

w: That's going to be firmed up in August.

c: With the same capacity that we talked about, right?

w: Yes, with a hundred thousand tons, and it is possible that by next week the engineer will make the final analysis with Cointreau. They have many flavors—all kinds, including mandarin—and they're very tasty.

c: What I like about this is the smell. (laughter) One can almost get high on the smell, huh? I imagine that all of you who work here must always be a little tipsy. (laughter) And don't they ever give you a small bottle of *aguardiente*?

w: Sometimes.

c: But it makes much stronger Daiquiris, right? What a celebration the inauguration of this factory will be. What an odor—so pleasant here. And how many workers are there in the microbrigade [special voluntary force]?

　　And this little girl—where is she from? Ah, you must be from right next to the house of your little friend, right? We're making here some propaganda about your rum.

w: That's very good . . . excellent.

c: It's for television.

w: Someone should have a bottle in their hand to show it off.

c: How much does this barrel weigh?

w: Fifty. It has a capacity of fifty kilos, one hundred and eighty liters, and weighs two hundred and fifty kilos.

c: You'll be the heavyweight lifting champ.

After we left the rum factory, back onto the main highway, Pepín mentioned that Fidel wanted to visit some vacationers on a beach. As we neared the coast, we drove along a road bordered by tall, skinny pine trees through which we could see the clear turquoise water of the Caribbean. We made several false stops as we looked for a place with lots of people. Finally, Fidel's jeep came to a halt and he led us through the shaded trees and back into the hot sun.

"What a beautiful place," he commented as the first bather cried out, "Fidel, Fidel. Look everyone, Fidel is here."

A rather portly woman was even more friendly, yelling, "Ah, Chico, how good to see you," as she engulfed Fidel in a warm, wet embrace.

The swimmers began to turn toward the shore to see what was happening. As each saw who was there, he or she swam in to join the crowd.

Fidel began to chat and joke with the people.

BEACH

CASTRO: How nice, how nice it is here. Good day, good day.

CRIES: *Commandante.* Fidel! Fidel!

C: How are you? How are you? Aren't you going to swim in the sea?

#1: Yes, I already went.

C: Are you on vacation?

#2: Yes, we are the workers from nearby.

CRIES: Fidel! Fidel! Fidel!

C: Hello, hello, hello. I feel envious of all of you that have the chance to swim today. The water looks good today.

#3: Yes, yes, it is very nice.

C: How old is your child there?

#4: Five. His name is Ernesto, the same as Che.

C: More people come to the beach on Sunday, right?

#4: Yes.

C: And is the sea big enough for them all?

#4: Yes. (laughter)

C: How old are you?

#5: Twelve years old.

C: Which of you all swims the best?

#5: He does.

C: Your snow cone will melt. You better eat it. Eat it. (laughter) The water's very quiet now. Go in the water. It's no sin. You are not bored?

#6: No, no. We're so proud that you're here.

C: What grade are you in?

#7: Ninth.

C: That is a good grade. What do you want to study?

#7: Engineering.

C: And you?

#8: (A WOMAN): Engineering also.

C: With so many engineers, we're going to have a problem. (laughter) Every once in a while, I stop by the engineering school. In what do you work?

#9: I work in an office.

C: Yes? Well, I just came to make a short visit with some journalists who are going to shoot some scenes of all of you. It's going to be on television.

CROWD: Yeah, yeah.

C: I just said that I can't go swimming here. (laughter) Are you a student?

#10: Yes.

C: What are you studying?

#10: Ballet.

C: Well, I'm going to leave so that you all can return to your swimming.

CRIES: No, no, no.

C: Until later, have a good time. Hearty appetite. Study hard all of you.

CROWD: See you—Fidel! Fidel!

As we left, Mankiewicz said to Fidel, "You know, you remind me of an American politician during a campaign, shaking hands with the voters at the beach."

"Yes," answered Fidel, "but American politicians only go to the beach on the eve of the election—never afterward.

"It's too hot and muggy today for the jeeps," continued Castro. "We really should be riding around in our cars. It's too bad they're not here."

A few miles from the beach, the jeeps came to a sudden halt. There—from nowhere—was a whole line of automobiles. Fidel motioned Landau and us into his car, and the rest of the crew got into Alfa Romeos.

"We're lucky," Fidel said. "This car is air-conditioned; it should be a lot more comfortable."

It may have been comfortable, but hardly cool. The car was a large black Russian limousine with tan leather seats. The AK-47 rifle was secured to the floor under Fidel's feet. The small box of cigars and the tin of mints had been transferred from the jeep. The windows were closed and we waited for the cool air. But it never arrived.

As Fidel described the scenery, the car got hotter and hotter. The air conditioning was noisy but broken, and on top of that we were all smoking cigars. The heat and stuffiness were unbearable, but hardly mentionable because Fidel had made such a point about the new air conditioning. Finally, Jones tentatively pressed a button to lower the rear window half an inch. Nobody noticed, and Fidel kept right on talking. What made it even worse, Fidel seemed to be the only one in the car who didn't perspire. Over the next few miles, that rear window got lower and lower with each "invisible" touch of Jones's finger. In the front seat, Saul had begun to do the same with his window. Fidel kept talking. Finally he said, "Why don't we open the windows a bit and let the fresh air come in?" All the windows immediately came down the rest of the way and Fidel never missed a beat.

"You know," he said, "it's close to four o'clock. If we went back to Havana now, all of you could take a swim at the hotel and rest up for your trip home tomorrow. Or, if you wanted, we could perhaps have some lunch."

We really did not know what to say. Was the invitation real, or was Fidel only being polite? Did he want to go back? Who knew?

"Well, either way is OK with us," Jones answered.

"I think there might be a new Arab restaurant around here somewhere, if you did want to eat something."

"If you'd like to eat," Jones replied, "it would be fine with us."

"Well, I'm not sure where the restaurant is; I've never been there. Are you sure you want to eat instead of a swim?"

"Sure, we are a bit hungry."

"Fine, then. Let's eat."

Fidel turned to the driver and told him exactly where to go and what turns to make. All along, it appeared, he had known where we were and how to get to this Arab restaurant out in the middle of nowhere.

The limousine, followed by the cars and jeeps, pulled up in front of the restaurant, and Fidel jumped out. At the top of a curved stone stairway two waiters were taking a break at the front door.

"Are there many people inside?" Fidel shouted.

One of the waiters answered casually that there were indeed a lot of people. Then he saw who was to be his guest and changed his answer.

"No," he said, "nobody's here."—A pause, then, "I mean, yes . . . or no," all with the implication that by the time Fidel climbed the stairs, he could have his choice. Both waiters ran back into the restaurant.

Fidel turned back to us. "Come on, let's go inside. Do you want to visit the kitchen?"

Did we have a choice?

He quickly led us into the small kitchen, filled with steaming pots and frying pans cooking on the stove. He met the chefs and began to remove the tops of the pots and look at the food.

"It all looks pretty good here. Do you have room for all of us?"

"Why, of course," answered the maître d', who had just joined us.

"Well, if you don't serve us, we'll lower your prices," he

joked. With that, we were led to a large round center table. Fidel table-hopped, greeting all the patrons, and then joined us at our table.

The Arab meal was delicious—houmous, salad, shish kebab, 1971 (pre-coup) Chilean wines, dessert, and a large mild Cuban cigar.

But as good as the food was, it didn't compare with the conversation. We had just completed a fascinating day; the pressures of the formal interview were over; we all knew each other better and were more relaxed. As we finished our meal and lit up those long Cuban cigars, we launched into what was to become a three-hour discourse on revolution.

It began with a comment of Fidel's concerning the case of Lieutenant William Calley. "I just do not understand," he said, "why some men seem to like to kill just for the sake of killing. Why are men like that?"

Jones then asked Fidel about the system of justice during the revolutions. "Che wrote," Jones said, "that during a revolutionary war, traitors must be shot on the spot, without trial, to preserve the safety and integrity of the entire group. He called this the revolutionary system of justice. Did you face this situation in the Sierra Maestra?"

"Yes, we did. It was always a problem for us. Several times we found traitors or informers in our midst and they had to be executed. Some of those times, those fighters who were of the Calley kind were given those assignments. We never liked to do this, but it was forced upon us."

"Was the problem of traitors and informers a serious one?" followed Jones. "How did you know, for example, whether a new recruit was really on your side?"

"Well, it was a problem that we had to watch continually. I personally interviewed every person that came to the mountains to fight. I could tell after just a half hour's discussion whether that person was real or not. Not necessarily by asking him about his feelings and thoughts of the revolutionary struggle, but more by conversation about his background, his family, his past life. My intuition was very good and I just felt in the pit of my stomach whether a certain individual was on the level.

"I remember on various occasions the CIA tried to

infiltrate our ranks with people who posed as journalists. And we always knew right away who they really were. You see, journalists are particular kinds of people. They always ask hundreds of different questions. They are very inquisitive. That is their job. A few of them did come to the Sierra Maestra. But a phony journalist—a CIA agent posing as a journalist—never asked questions the way an authentic reporter would. They couldn't play the role. A real journalist could be a CIA agent, but a CIA agent can never realistically appear to be a journalist."

"Was there ever a time during the early days after the *Granma** landed that you thought you would not succeed?" Jones asked.

"No, never."

"Even after the Battle of Alegria del Pio?"†

"No, not even after that battle. You have to understand that we were right in what we were doing. Not only right in our cause, but correct in our overall method. Our basic tactic of beginning the revolutionary struggle in the mountains, at the time that we did, was correct. And we all knew that. Looking at events from a tactical point of view, we might have changed some things."

"Like what, for example?"

"Well, I might not have chosen to attack El Uvero."‡

"But wasn't that a great success?"

"Yes, we did win that battle. But in a revolutionary war, you must look at what you gained for what price. The winning of the battle for El Uvero cost us lives and equipment. You must always measure the possible loss against the possible gain. A rule of waging revolutionary warfare is to engage in only those battles in which there is the highest certainty that if you lose the battle the overall loss is minimal, but if the enemy loses the battle, their overall loss is great."

As Fidel talked on about the old days in the mountains, his

---

* *Granma* is the name of the boat in which Castro and his initial guerrilla force traveled to Cuba from Mexico in December 1956 to begin the revolution.
† The first real battle of the revolution on December 5, 1956, in which a Batista surprise attack nearly decimated the embryonic guerrilla force.
‡ The first major success of the guerrilla war, during which an army post had been defeated but at a cost of fifteen dead or wounded—or a little less than twenty percent of the entire guerrilla force at that time.

mind began to wander, and a hazy look came over his face as he remembered what must be for him the most romantic days of his life and his struggle—"the good old days." He seemed to enjoy talking about the time in the Sierra Maestra. But it was time to leave. We never saw anyone pay the check; someone must have.

Back in the limousine, Jones continued to probe Fidel's memory and thoughts on revolution.

"You're very interested in this subject, aren't you?" Fidel asked Jones.

"Yes, I am. Ever since Santo Domingo in 1965."

"You were there during the Dominican Revolution, weren't you?"

"Yes, I was," confirmed Jones.

"Then let me tell you some things in more detail. You know there is a lot of strategy in waging a guerrilla war. For example, let me tell you about fighting in the mountains in difficult terrain against far better equipped forces than your own. There is a definite technique in attacking a column of approaching soldiers. You have to position your men well and know which part of the column to attack in what order. Almost the worst thing that can happen to a band of guerrilla fighters is to sustain a lot of wounded. That is really one of the greatest problems, because they have to be carried and cared for. It has a great effect on the mobility of the force and it is a serious factor."

By this time, Fidel's cigar was working overtime and he was oblivious to the passing scenery. His left hand was spread out to form an imaginary battlefield, and with the fingers of the right he began to diagram how to attack a column of enemy soldiers. It was a detailed lesson in guerrilla warfare, enthusiastically explained not by an army war college colonel reading from a textbook, but by one of the few men in the world who had successfully accomplished what he himself was describing.

The complicated explanation continued for the next half hour. Fidel then launched into an analysis of other revolutions—in Vietnam, China, Venezuela, Guatemala, and the Dominican Republic.

"Francisco Caamaño [leader of the 1965 Dominican Revolution]," he said, "was very much like Che. Both were valiant fighters, very courageous, with a lot of energy. Caamaño went back to the Dominican Republic because he believed in the people, he had confidence in the people.

"Some revolutionary fighters, though, let their enthusiasm for the cause overwhelm their tactical decision-making. A reckless fighter, even a brave and valiant one, can cause serious problems for the entire force.

"Let me give you an example. On several occasions when we would receive word that a column of Batista's troops was approaching, some of the guerrilla fighters would immediately propose an attack without really thinking about the possible outcome of that attack. That is what I was saying before about always judging the impact of any battle. There exist occasions when it may be wisest to let the column go through without attacking because the time, place, and tactical considerations are not the best. When everything is not just right, the possibilities for unforeseen events and for damage are greatly increased."

Back at the hotel, it was time to say good-bye; after all—although for nearly four days it had hardly seemed so—Fidel Castro did have other things to do than chat with a few Americans about guerrilla warfare and the state of the world.

FRED WARD

Havana, 1977: Welcome, tourists!

"BECAUSE CUBA HAS BEEN OFF LIMITS TO AMERICANS,
THERE IS A PREVALENT IMPRESSION THAT IT HAS BEEN
CLOSED TO EVERYONE ALL THESE YEARS. THIS IS A
SOURCE OF GREAT AMUSEMENT TO THE CUBANS."

*In the late 1970s, photojournalist Fred Ward made seven sepa-
rate trips to Cuba, staying on the island for a total of six
months, while he prepared a report for* National Geographic
magazine. Ward, whose previous books included The Golden Islands of the Caribbean, *traveled freely and interviewed countless people, including Fidel Castro, in all parts of the island.*

Following his articles in National Geographic, *Ward's
book-length report,* Inside Cuba Today, *was published in 1978.*

*In that book, Ward covers, with an observant eye and lively
writing, every aspect of life in this contradictory country: home
and family life, jobs, the economy, education, public health, the
arts, agriculture and industry, the presence of U.S. forces at
Guantánamo Bay, the role of Fidel Castro and the Communist
Party in the life of the country, and Cuba's always troubled relationship with the U.S. Very little escaped him.*

*The chapter on tourism follows. Ward's survey of the lead-
ing hotels and restaurants and attractions offers a visitor's-eye
view of Havana in 1977, eighteen years after the revolution.*

Havana has changed a great deal since then, and so have official Cuban attitudes. Now, in the 1990s, Cuba recognizes that tourism is not merely a sideline but that it offers the best hope for the country's economic future.

Note that other visitors to Havana included in this book saw many of the same places Ward describes. Frank Mankiewicz and Kirby Jones, for example, had lunch with Fidel Castro at Las Ruinas in 1974.

> *We have always been ready for the United States. We see all tourists as one, whether they come from Canada, the United States, or Mexico. We do not expect any problems. The Americans will come out of curiosity, for the sun and surf, and will be well behaved. I am not worried about their coming. Who knows, they may be our biggest market in a year or two.*
>
> —JESÚS JIMÉNEZ, DIRECTOR, CUBATUR

IT WAS AFTER MIDNIGHT AND STILL quiet inside the cave. Shadowy figures lingered by the overhanging rock entrance, whispering and nudging before the solitary guard motioned them in. Like Noah's creatures, they entered by pairs to join a waiting group already assembled in the darkened interlocking chambers. Candles flickered and then died back, briefly illuminating the huddled couples sharing their secrets. A few colored lights played across the rough stone ceiling, its reverberant dome gradually filling with more and louder nervous chatter. Word came from the five silhouettes in the room's center that the time had come.

An explosion of sound from the electric guitars signaled the beginning of the midnight show in Pirate's Cave, a natural oceanside cavern and popular weekend nightclub in Varadero Beach, Cuba's best-known tourist site. Spotlights illuminated the musicians, whose sounds soon had the mixed Cuban and Canadian audience on its feet, filling the small dance floor. Interchanging dancing partners and language in a style to make the United Nations envious, the revelers continued their fun until almost time to have a good-morning swim in the crystal clear waters before breakfast. It was a night to relive in memories when the snow is two feet deep back in Toronto, and the kind of evening that Americans are once again planning.

President Carter's decision in March, 1977, made it possible and legal for Americans to vacation in Cuba for the first time since relations were broken between the two countries in January, 1961. (Between those years, only a few journalists, scholars, medical and technical experts, and government officials were allowed to visit with State Department approval. Leftist U.S. student groups organized as the Vencerémos Brigade made the trip illegally through Mexico without proper authority.) Although the economic embargo, called a "blockade" in Cuba, is still in effect to prohibit trade, Carter's order lifted any restriction for U.S. citizens to travel to the island and allows them to bring back the same customs-free purchases permitted from other countries: $100 total value of goods including 100 cigars and a quart of an alcoholic beverage. Formerly, any U.S. citizen desiring to travel to Cuba had to join a Canadian or Mexican tour. Now, with a summer 1977 Treasury Department ruling related to the embargo, which is still in effect, U.S. travel agencies can organize tours within the United States, and the 1977–78 winter season will likely be the first that substantial numbers of Americans will enjoy in Havana and Varadero.

Because Cuba has been off limits to Americans, there is a prevalent impression that it has been closed to everyone all these years. This is a source of great amusement to the Cubans, who have enjoyed an absolute tourist boom by the Canadians during the Americans' absence. In 1976, 60 percent of the total number of tourists in Cuba, almost 40,000, flew in from Canada. Russia and the other socialist countries provided 7,500, Latin America sent about the same number, and 6,000 came from Europe, for a total of 60,000 guests. On a typical day at Havana hotels, tour groups can be seen from Canada, Italy, France, and perhaps Holland, while businessmen check in from Tokyo, London, Mexico City, and now New York and Minneapolis.

Two kinds of package tours are currently available to

foreigners, both organized by Cubatur, the country's government-operated tourist agency. Most popular are the flights directly to Varadero Beach, about sixty-five miles east of Havana. Long recognized as one of the world's most beautiful beaches, Varadero is a winter dream with over a dozen miles of pure white sand, and incredibly clear, blue water. A vacation favorite for decades, Varadero is now the center for Canadian tourists on holiday and is expected to be equally popular with Americans soon. International flights arrive at the airport only a few minutes away by bus and most guests are in the water within an hour after landing. A variety of accommodations are offered by Cubatur and are reflected in the package price now paid in Canada or Mexico. Charter air fares are added onto the Cuba fee by the travel agent, depending on distance flown. At the Internacional Hotel on the beach, a recently renovated prerevolutionary facility, one week costs about $320 per person including three meals daily, bus transfers to and from the airport, a "Cuba Night" party with entertainment, a seafood party, and some sightseeing. The air charter fare is additional. The Hotel Kawama is available for a similar rate. Much more common are the many motel-type accommodations along the beach for about $250 per week plus air fare, with the above features included.

More expensive and private are beach-front villas for larger groups. Meals can be catered for a family or several couples, providing a home rather than a hotel atmosphere. Of course, the main attraction is the beach, the center of Varadero's appeal. Boats and fishing equipment may be rented, but most people find lying in the sand activity enough. Generally, the surf contains an international mélange, with several tourists from Europe, the Soviet Union, and Latin America sharing the same wave. The Soviets will be the most difficult for gregarious Americans to decipher, since they seldom show any interest in conversation and almost universally hide their faces or turn away when a camera is present, a legacy of a lifetime of fear and distrust.

Entertainment ranges from the packed Pirate's Cave, where weekend reservations are a must, to the large variety show at the Internacional, usually good, but not as good as in

Havana's nightclubs. Each hotel has one or more bars and there are numerous other well-marked clubs and bars along Varadero's streets. All payment must be in pesos when a registered guest is outside his own hotel. Bills are straightforward, with seldom a cover charge, and domestic drinks are reasonably priced. Beer is usually eighty centavos to a peso, and rum drinks anywhere from one to two pesos, depending on the drink's complexity. Daiquiris, old Cuban favorites, are always served frozen, whipped with ice in a blender. Cubans prefer *mojitos,* which include rum, lime, sugar, soda, ice, and the refreshing aroma and taste of mint sprigs. Imported drinks like Scotch and bourbon are ridiculously expensive. Occasionally on menus a listing will include a bottle of Scotch for $150 and cordials for $75. Be forewarned so there are no surprises.

Not to be missed is the old DuPont estate toward the eastern end of Varadero's peninsula. Now used as the Las Américas Restaurant, it shows some of Cuba's former luxury that the present government propagandizes as one of the reasons for the Revolution. The breezy, open-air dining rooms and quiet elegance provide a marvelous atmosphere for a memorable meal. Prices are above average, with lunch and wine running over $10 and dinner $15 to $20.

Since more Americans will likely be visiting Varadero than any other location, a word about Cuban attitudes toward tourists might be useful. In general, the Cuban people harbor a great admiration for Americans and a genuine curiosity built on years of isolation following the decades in which hundreds of thousands of U.S. citizens visited and worked in Cuba. The government has taken a stance of continuing to isolate tourists. Part of it is due to the currency problems and part of it is political. Since there is so much trafficking in black market goods, tourists are a prime source for new products. Cubans will ask to buy visitors' shoes for $50 or more, blue jeans for $30 to $60, etc. To limit this, officials try to keep tourists and Cubans apart. They realize the hopelessness of it, but they continue to try. The government does not want individuals wandering around Cuba, because of a long ingrained fear that subversion comes from the outside, that terrorists may come in as tourists, that Cubans will get overly curious about wages, availability of goods, and general working and living conditions, and because a guest might simply get into trouble. It is easier for the government to maintain control if such contacts are kept to a minimum.

Finally, the question of safety can be put aside. Tourists can walk around at will and have no fears about personal welfare. Street crime as we know it is virtually nonexistent. There is only one area of concern. Petty thefts are increasing and Varadero is one of the centers, almost entirely as a result of international tourism. Bathing suits, towels, sunglasses, cameras, and personal items left unattended are disappearing with alarming frequency. Stealing is due to the lack of these products in the tightly rationed economy. So far, thefts are confined to small things and are nowhere as serious or pervasive as in other vacation centers, but one would do well to be cautious.

In addition to the more popular Varadero vacation, there is a second package tour offered by Cuba, which begins in Havana. In the better Canadian tours, and the ones most likely to be offered to Americans, four nights of the week will be spent in one of the capital's three renovated hotels, the Riviera, Capri, or Havana Libre (formerly the Hilton), or at the nearby beach resort, the Marazul. The additional three nights of the one-week package can be either at the Colony Hotel on the Isle of Pines or at three separate locations during a bus tour of areas outside Havana. Currently, the Riviera choice and either alternative for the additional three nights costs about $350 plus air charter, while the nearby Marazul, located about fifteen miles east of Havana on the beach at Santa Maria del Mar, is $270 plus air fare. The average Canadian package cost is approximately $415 for a week at the Marazul, including three meals daily, bus transfers, two party nights, and air charter.

Obviously, winter is going to be the popular season for Americans, as it is elsewhere in the Caribbean and is now in Cuba for Canadians. The climate is ideal, warm and dry, in the months when the northern United States is most unpleasant. Since the Cubans are interested only in group tours, there is little chance of organizing an itinerary outside the approved schedule. Taxis are available and some roaming is being permitted, but changing hotels or cities is not done. Within the confines of the tour, travel is safe. Some Canadians have been surprised on the beach at night by machine-gun-carrying guards out patrolling for invaders, but no real problems have developed. Walking is safe day or night. Some Spanish is very useful in asking for assistance, since English is dependable only around the hotels. Even though every high school graduate has studied English, few speak it. Few logistical details will bother Americans, since airport formalities, porters, and buses will all be prearranged.

Choosing a hotel should be no problem for tourists since the travel agencies are aware of the status of existing accommodations. Havana has had no new hotels since the Revolution, but renovations have been made on the three previously mentioned hotels to conform to accepted international standards. Sadly, the formerly elegant Nacional, an old pink palace on the Malecón, is scheduled for renovation in 1978 and for the present should be avoided. Rooms there are usually not air-conditioned, salty water runs in the faucets, and the general appearance is rather shabby. The Riviera, Cuba's best, is remembered as a Mafia haven before Castro. The casino is gone, but the other features are just as good as many Americans will remember them. A gigantic saltwater pool, cabanas, two restaurants, spa, and the Copa nightclub help make the days enjoyable. Without the package tours, rooms cost almost $40 a night. More central is the Capri, also with former Mafia ties, a smaller but very agreeable hotel. A rooftop swimming pool offers fine views of the city and ocean. Slightly less expensive than the Riviera, the Capri is often first choice among business travelers because of its location. Only three blocks away is the Havana Libre, a favorite for delegations in Cuba on official business. Its Hilton heritage is evident in the lobby and room decor, and its mezzanine-level swimming pool is a popular meeting place for drinks. The beach-front Marazul at Santa Maria del Mar, completed in 1976, provides a tropical atmosphere close enough to Havana to visit several times during a week's stay. Palms and ferns decorate the large, open lobby area, while a saltwater pool on the lower level, surrounded by the hotel but open to the sky, provides secluded swimming. The atmosphere is casual and the beach deserted throughout the week. For additional sightseeing or entertainment, taxis to downtown Havana run about six pesos and are readily available. As with the old Nacional, salty water runs in the faucets and should be avoided except for baths. One small problem is that the hotel leaks in heavy rains, fortunately usually only in the summer rainy season. When the problem was recently pointed out to Fidel, he mused, "I think perhaps our architects are becoming more concerned with beauty than function."

Generally, living in first-class Cuban hotels is convenient and pleasant. Tourists are spared almost all the everyday problems plaguing citizens. The hotels mentioned have their own water supplies and seldom experience the electrical blackouts that routinely darken homes and domestic hotels throughout the country. Although salty showers are manageable, the provided bottle water should be used for tooth brushing and drinking. Hot water may be unavailable or cooler than at home, but the climate is usually warm enough to make this only a mild inconvenience. Toilet paper and paper towels are common in the better hotels but in short supply elsewhere. Even though tipping is officially prohibited everywhere as a holdover from capitalistic days, it is the rare bellboy, chambermaid, or taxi driver who will refuse a gratuity of either cash or token gift. Laundry can be a real inconvenience except in the three discussed downtown hotels. Outside Havana, including the Hotel Marazul, it is extremely rare to find any laundries, and in-town operations can take several days when they are working. For short trips, it is best to plan for no washing. Even when laundries are available, they are expensive.

For the nostalgic tourist who is returning to Havana looking for some of the "good ole days," suffice it to report that they are mainly gone. No longer do pretty young prostitutes surround the hotels and parade on the main streets. The sexual exhibitions are only a faded memory to some of the elder residents, the "stars" having long departed for Mexico and south Florida. Gambling, one of the first casualties of the new Revolution, is unavailable to tourists, although playing the numbers is still a popular pastime for local residents, who use the Venezuelan winners for payoffs. Begging, practically a downtown staple in most Latin American cities, was prohibited years ago, its practitioners put to work.

There are two amateur exceptions to the above generalities. Recently, particularly in Havana, a few girls have been appearing once again in the evenings, looking for dates, and willing to trade their favors for goods rather than money. It is almost more a comment on rationing than on morals. The police occasionally pick up a few, but the problem is so small no one is overly concerned yet. Also, young boys, on their way to or from school, are developing the habit of lingering near tourist hotels asking for pens, cigarettes, or souvenirs. Hardly begging in the traditional sense, it still comes as a surprise to government officials who thought the children more socialistically indoctrinated than that. Still, when a youngster gets only one pen a year, it is extremely tempting to simply ask for another.

Of all the pleasures that visiting Cuba can bring, eating out can be one of the most enjoyable. This seems paradoxical since it is so widely known that food is rationed in the country. Obviously, both statements are true. Restaurant meals are one of the principal relief valves in the oppressive rationing system. A quick glance around any restaurant dispels any notion that the food is only for foreigners. Often over half the patrons will be Cubans.

Lunch at one of the new buffet tables can be a culinary treat, such as at the one provided by the Riviera Hotel. It is the most elaborate "Swedish Table" in Cuba; some of its overwhelming choices include three juices, milk, yogurt, three fresh fruits (such as bananas, pineapples, papaya, oranges, grapefruit, watermelon), two or three salads, two kinds of fish appetizers, tomatoes, cucumbers, potatoes, fried bananas, soup, bread, three main dishes (pork, fish, chicken, or beef), cheeses, French tarts, cakes, pies, custards, guava paste, and coffee. The spread costs eight pesos for either lunch or dinner, with beer an additional eighty centavos. For menu ordering, the Riviera also has the L'Aiglon Restaurant and a downstairs coffee shop.

Most of the other hotels have similar tables, although not as well stocked. And all the hotels have restaurants where meals on the package tours are served. For the first-time visitor, it is fascinating to observe how communism handles the problem of service. In a society ideologically striving for equality, the concept of one person waiting on another does not fit the ideal. Since the people who knew English and were used to working with tourists before the Revolution typically fled to Florida, creating a new industry of hotel and restaurant help has been a problem. The tourism ministry, INIT, has several schools struggling with training, but the results are spotty. Certainly the establishments have plenty of personnel. Two black-suited maîtres d'hôtel meet arriving guests at many restaurants, and separate people bring water, bread, take the order, and deliver the food. One morning in the Riviera's coffee shop, twenty-one people milled around in dowdy black uniforms, and it still took twenty minutes to get eggs. One could only wish the help would read INIT's carefully printed slogan on every placemat: "Your right is to enjoy; our duty is to serve."

Havana provides many eating possibilities outside the hotels. Easily the most spectacular view in town is at La Torre, a first-class restaurant atop the thirty-five-story Focsa, a prerevolutionary apartment building now used to house East European and Soviet technicians. Have drinks in the bar, located on the west side of the penthouse and overlooking the Malecón, the ocean, and much of the better residential areas of Havana. A move to the main dining room provides a panorama of the central city, El Morro fort, and bustling Havana Harbor. Dinner is almost secondary to the scenery, but the food is generally very good. Steaks, when they are available, are tender and tasty, and fresh seafood is usually listed. Since the restaurant is always crowded, reservations are required. Dinners with wine from either Spain, Portugal, or the Soviet Union will run from $15 to $25.

Tiffany lamps, fern-covered walls, a grand piano, and massive dark wooden Spanish colonial furnishings accent the most beautiful restaurant in Cuba, Las Ruinas. Recently constructed in Lenin Park, about fifteen miles south of Havana, Las Ruinas is a testament to good taste. Built around the ruins of a master's home on an old sugar plantation, it encompasses the crumbling stone walls as decorative details and utilizes space in multilevel expanses of eating, drinking, and viewing centers. Great floor-to-ceiling louvered doors admit sunlight and cooling breezes for the families who stop in after spending the day in huge Lenin Park. As in most restaurants, pianists entertain the dinner crowd with pre-1959 U.S. tunes, still the favorite quiet music throughout Cuba. If lobster and shrimp (which are never sold in stores) are available in Cuba, they will likely be served at Las Ruinas. However, in line with other good restaurants, the prices are high. Dinner for four, with lobster or steak, drinks, dessert, and wine, will cost between $80 and $100.

Many other good restaurants are scattered throughout Havana. The "1830" is located just west of the Riviera, directly on the ocean. Housed in an old mansion, it is quiet, usually empty, and offers dependable meals. The Conejito, just down the street from either the Capri or Havana Libre, specializes in rabbit main courses. Directly on Cathedral Square in Old Havana, El Patio offers a Spanish flavor with a central fountain, garden area, and open-air-sidewalk dining out front. Inside, air-conditioned rooms have full meals with delicious seafood. Around the corner is an old Hemingway favorite, the Bodeguita del Medio, an intimate place whose owner for thirty-six years, Angel Martinez, stayed on after the Revolution to be manager. He proudly conducts tours around the walls crammed with pictures and signatures of the many people who have enjoyed good food here.

Nearby, another prerevolutionary vision emerges on a quiet corner. None of the people waiting on buses give the building a second look. It has no special meaning. A window is cracked, the paint is peeling from a faded sign across the glass, and the wooden doors are badly in need of attention. Inside, plaster drops from a decaying ceiling, a few bare bulbs cast their shadows onto empty, fragmented display cases, while four lonely customers sprawl against the once elegant polished bar, its wood a stranger to care for over a decade. Linda Darnell, Tyrone Power, Victor Mature, and Alice Faye all stare from behind glass under a sign that says in English, "You should have your picture taken at Sloppy Joe's, the best souvenir of Havana." The famous old watering hole, which hosted America's rich and celebrated, is only a shell now, just a corner bar that didn't even have a bottle of beer to sell.

Better cared for is the Floridita, a bar made famous by Hemingway when he said it made the best daiquiris in the world. The reputation still holds—the drinks are good. More importantly, the Floridita provides the proper atmosphere for getting the tourist in the right frame of mind to see more of Ernest Hemingway's life in Cuba. More remembrances of "Papa" exist around Havana than anywhere else in the world. Curiously, the government, while berating the United States generally, has always reserved a special place for Hemingway, accepting him as one of its own.

From the 1930s on, Hemingway divided his year among the United States, Spain, and Cuba. For $18,000 he bought the "Finca Vigia," a small villa on a hill with a pool, about forty minutes outside Havana. From there, he would drive to Cojimar, on the ocean, where he kept his boat, and would fish in the Gulf Stream. Customarily, Hemingway spent six months each year living and working in Cuba. When he left in 1960 and went to Spain briefly, it was to be his last stay. At home in Idaho, whatever demons tormented him finally won, and he killed himself with one of his shotguns in 1961.

The home is now maintained as the Hemingway Museum, open to the public. Everything is just as he left it on that last visit. Old *Times* and *Newsweeks* lie across the bed in his corner bedroom, while across the room his glass-topped desk remains covered with souvenirs, snapshots, military patches, shotgun shells, and wood carvings. A bullfight painting dominates the living room along with a table of partially filled bottles: Bacardi, Gordon's, Schweppes. Two walls of books fill the library, overpowering a small Picasso plate with a bull's face. Mounted African animal heads attest to his lifelong passion for hunting. Beside his toilet, a complete bookshelf holds contemporary reading matter, and on the opposite wall, penciled diary entries record his morning weight, one of the fights he was always losing.

For Hemingway fans, a worthwhile side trip is to the little fishing village of Cojimar, only four miles east of Havana's harbor entrance. There the men of the fishing cooperative paid for and erected a memorial to their friend, who made them and their town world famous as the home port and site for *The Old Man and the Sea.*

For most visitors, the principal attraction of Havana will be the opportunity of seeing communism and the Revolution close up. However, there are numerous other possibilities for sightseeing around town. A walk through old Havana is a must to see the remnants of the protective Spanish wall, the aging stone Cathedral, Museum of the History of the City, Fine Arts Museum, and the old capitol, now the Academy of Sciences. Overlooking the water, across from El Morro, the former Presidential Palace, an elegant building in the Spanish style, has a new life as the Revolution Museum. Under President Batista, whom Castro overthrew, the palace became a symbol to the rebels of the opulence, oppression, and thievery they swore to replace. To reinforce the symbolism, Fidel chooses to live in an apartment and suburban home, and work in the government's new central office building. The relics of the struggle against Batista, and much of the visual history of the Revolution, are now housed in the former palace. Photographs depict practically every step of the fight, a large model illustrates the precise movements of all participants in the Moncada Barracks attack in 1953, and guns, uniforms, hats, souvenirs, books, patches, stamps, and keepsakes are arranged under plastic domes, to be viewed in reverence by the populace as if they were splinters from the "True Cross." Out back, tanks, airplanes, and a miscellaneous collection of war machines chronicle the Revolution's progress from ragtag guerrilla bands to Third-World leaders. And, incredible though it may seem, the world's largest pheasant under glass, the original *Granma,* that creaking yacht that transported Fidel, Ché, and their eighty followers from Mexico to the Sierra in 1956, rests in its new transparent home, viewed in silence by constant lines of people reminiscent of the Lenin tomb crowds. For a museum utilizing photographs for over half of its displays, the height of inconsistency is prohibiting cameras in the presence of *Granma.*

Cameras and all types of fun are allowed and encouraged at Havana's weekend recreation center, Lenin Park, located about fifteen miles south of town. A recently completed amusement park, purchased for over a million dollars from Japan, is the big draw for children with its colorful ferris wheel, carrousel, flume ride, and tiny cars. Picnic areas, rowboats, a rodeo, aquarium, rental horses, narrow-gauge railroad, and amphitheatre are just some of the numerous features at this unique Cuban park. For tourists, it is the ideal place to see residents at play. After a leisurely Sunday afternoon of activities, dinner at the nearby Las Ruinas completes a full and interesting day.

Entertainment is more than daylight walking and looking. Cubans like to have a good time and will gladly spend their few pesos for live entertainment and drinks. Fortunately, tourists are welcome to join in. By far the most elaborate club is the flamboyant Tropicana.... Two bands, dancing girls in the trees, flashing lights, aerialists, singers, and a fast-moving show all blend to create a magic night under the stars. Although reservations are always requested, the huge club is seldom fully booked. Dinner is about 9 P.M. with the show at 11 P.M. For visitors, the meal with a couple of drinks and the show costs approximately sixteen pesos. Usually half the audience is composed of workers paying a fixed eight-peso price, rewarded by their unions for outstanding achievements. Each of the large city hotels has a nightclub with late night entertainment and variety shows. The best is at the Riviera's Copa Room. There contemporary Cuban television and recording personalities perform in a Miami Beach or Las Vegas style revue that is loud, bouncy, and fun. Show times are at 11 P.M. with dancing afterwards until very late.

Shoppers accustomed to bringing home presents will find few places to spend their Cuban allowance. By far, the most desirable products for Americans will be rum and cigars. One of the problems Cubatur is trying to solve is how to separate tourists from more of their money when rationing restricts purchases outside the approved hotel shops and the island society is so short of hard and soft goods even for its own people. Various souvenirs are being tried, but so far the results are dismal. Tee shirts emblazoned with a sun and a "Cuba Sé" are the current rage, while posters are consistent sellers. Attempts at cheap Mexican-style pottery, wooden desk sets with Lenin's portrait, and three-dimensional postcards with rum bottles have not caught on with the foreigners. There is no indigenous craft industry, and all efforts in the economy have been addressed to struggling with domestic consumer demands. There are a few sales of guayaberas, the open Cuban shirts, but the $25 price tags discourage many travelers. Cuba should be seen and enjoyed for what it is, with shopping best left for other islands.

For any tourist, a chance to see Fidel in action would be the best souvenir of all. It is easier and more predictable to see the Maximum Leader than in most countries. So many mass public rallies are held in the Plaza de la Revolución that visitors can often join in with the half million Cubans for a look at civics in action. All such events are free and accessible without tickets. On January first, the Revolution celebrates its takeover in 1959 with a military parade and foreign policy speech. May Day is the international day for Communists and brings a grand parade. July twenty-sixth is the anniversary of the Moncada attack and an important event. September twenty-eighth commemorates the founding of the Committees for the Defense of the Revolution and usually produces another foreign policy address, while December second marks the landing of *Granma* and the founding of the National Assembly. While Fidel may not talk at every event, he is always present when in the country, and usually speaks publicly on several other occasions during the year.

Although the emphasis now is on international tourism and its inherent "hard currency" bonus, most of INIT's time and facilities are utilized by domestic Cuban travel. Only 60,000 foreigners visit the island while over 3 million Cubans use hotels and other accommodations throughout the average year, a new business resulting from paid month-long vacations for workers, more excess money, and a substantial construction program to diversify resorts throughout the country. Until the package tours are expanded or individual travel is allowed, most tourists will see only the Varadero or Havana hotels. From one viewpoint, that will be fortunate, because service and quality vary widely outside the two areas. Accommodations in the old "commercial" hotels are inferior in every way. The new hotels, planned for each province, are still meant for business rather than resort use, but are clean and attractive. For instance, the

Hotel Camaguey has a pool, serves good fresh fish meals, and is several grades above the aging Grand Hotel in the middle of town.

No matter where one travels in Cuba, the general level of accommodation will be more closely related to what we accept as motels. Services are limited, there are no laundry facilities, hot water is rare, the restaurants have fixed meal hours, and interruptions of electricity and water should be expected. Still, there are some visually exciting and interesting places that give a fuller flavor of Cuba than that found in Havana.

Among the most popular short excursions from the capital is the three-hour drive to the Bay of Pigs, where Cubans refer to the fight as Giron, after the town where it began. Cubans sign up for regular bus tours of the area, located on the island's southern, or Caribbean, coast in Matanzas Province. Beginning about twenty-five miles north of the principal landing site, stone markers record the names of Cuban defenders who gave their lives on the spot. At Giron, a museum displays some of the captured U.S. equipment, airplane parts, a tank, photographs, and memorabilia from the reported 160 "martyrs" who perished in the April, 1961, fight. Over 200 of the exiles, called mercenaries here, died in their struggle to "liberate" Cuba from Castro and communism, while 1,100 were captured. Later President Kennedy agreed to pay a ransom of over $25 million for their release.

One of Cuba's most interesting motels, Guamo, also commands one of its more unusual natural sites. Access to this honeymooner's dream is about thirty miles north of Giron, from a parking lot that serves the motel as well as the country's only working crocodile farm. (The idea is to see if the reptiles can be grown economically for their meat and hides. About 37,000 of them wallow around in huge pens beside the road.) There a boat takes guests on the twenty-minute ride first through a manmade canal and then across Treasure Lake. On its eastern shore, looking just like the Indian village they were designed to duplicate, individual units rise on stilts above the interlocked series of islands. Each guest has his own thatched-roof home and a boat, in case he would rather paddle to dinner instead of walking over the arched wooden bridges. To complete the decor, a real Indian village with life-size statues shows how the original inhabitants of the region conducted their daily activities.

Another two hours to the east, backed up against the Escambray Mountains, is Cuba's real live outdoor Spanish colonial museum, the city of Trinidad. Long forgotten and isolated, the town failed to change. From its founding in 1514 by Diego Velázquez, Trinidad developed as Cuba's third city, until Havana was settled and became Spain's treasure port. Most of the remaining center of town was built between 1715 and 1780. Now declared a national treasure, the city must maintain its exterior appearance, with cobblestone streets built of ballast brought by Boston traders, grand stucco façades fronting directly onto narrow walkways, and captivating children playing in the barred and glassless "bay windows." The city museum, housed in a stylish home built in 1705, features a typically Andalusian entry, great open patio, and articles indicative of the wealth of the period, cosmopolitan furnishings from Spain, the United States, France, and Germany. A walk through the streets at dawn is a step back through time.

Another full day's drive to the east brings the hardy Cuban visitor to Santiago, the island's second city in size and importance. This hot Oriente port town is perfect as a jumping-off point for the rugged Sierra Maestra Mountains, within view of the harbor, and smaller ranges to the north and east. Around the industrial city, rum is still made at the old Bacardi plant (now called Caney); the Moncada Barracks are now a school and museum displaying the early Revolutionary Struggle; El Morro, the sixteenth-century Spanish fort, is open for touring; and tiny Siboney Farm shows where Fidel and his 1953 rebels trained and gathered for their first fight. The Las Americas Hotel, constructed in the new concrete style, offers in-town accommodations, while the more stylish Versailles Motel has a fine swimming pool, attractive rooms, and a wide dinner menu choice.

Thus far, all the sightseeing locations have been east of Havana. Two attractions should get the mobile tourist out to the west, to Pinar del Río Province. It is here that Cuba's best tobacco is grown and dried. For the cigar enthusiast, Pinar del

Río is like coming home to the mother lode. Thousands of farmers tend their small plots more as gardens than commercial crops. Heavy thatched drying barns, windowless and closed, are almost overpowering with their constant tobacco aroma. The other sight is one of Cuba's grand natural wonders, the area around Viñales. Great mountainous clusters appear to have been tossed about by some giant hand, with sheer rock walls appearing to leap straight up from the valley floor. In this peculiarly limestone region, said to be duplicated in Puerto Rico and China, centuries of erosion have left only hard caps on the soft mountains, eliminating the slopes. As a result, cracks and caves texture the towering cliffs, with palms and other trees growing directly from the sharp walls, hundreds of feet up. Remarkable views of the valley are available from north-facing rooms at the Motel Jasmines, a delightful new facility done in neo-Spanish style. As with all the motels away from Havana, rooms average $15 nightly, and only occasionally will top $20.

From this brief description, it should be obvious that there is more to see and do on the 759-mile-long island than can possibly be accomplished on a brief vacation. Cuba should be experienced piecemeal to fully appreciate its potential. For Americans, the first accomplishment will be just to get there. Afterwards, as relations stabilize, additional visits can bring out the lesser-known details of Cuba's geography. Columbus may have been correct when he looked ashore in 1492 and called it "the most beautiful island ever seen."

HUGH O'SHAUGHNESSY

Train Number One: Havana to Santiago and Guantánamo Bay, 1980s

" 'SANDWICH OR CHICKEN?' SAID THE WOMAN FROM THE
RESTAURANT CAR. 'BEER OR SOFT DRINK?' ARMED WITH
THE SLIPS OF PAPER SHE GAVE US OUR CARRIAGE FILED
DOWN THE AISLE TO THE ADJOINING CARRIAGE WITH ALL
THE CONFIDENCE OF JUST SOULS ON THE DAY OF
JUDGEMENT. "

*Journlist Hugh O'Shaughnessy has written about the Caribbean
and Latin America for the* Observer *for more than three decades. He reported from Havana at the time of the 1963 missile
crisis.*

*The Cuban railroad, built initially to serve the island's huge
sugar plantations, was the first in all of Latin America. It has suffered badly from the country's lasting economic crisis. The principal service is the train O'Shaughnessy rode, Number One, from
Havana to Santiago de Cuba, at the eastern end of the island.
This is nominally a trip of seventeen hours, but don't count on
that, as unexplained delays are the order of the day. Or, rather,
of the night. Number One leaves Havana in the evening, officially at 5:00 P.M., and reaches Santiago in mid-morning. Train
Number Two departs Santiago for Havana each evening. Comforts are minimal and, while the trip may be an adventure, it's
not very good for sightseeing, as most of it takes place at night.*

During his six-month visit in 1990, Tom Miller announced

that he was going to visit the city of Cienfuegos and that he was going to go by train. All his Cuban friends thought this was an excellent idea, despite the terrible condition of the railroad, but they changed their minds when he said he intended to take the lechero, *the milk train "that stops in every two-bit* pueblito *en route." Then they thought he was out of his mind.*

"The cars had slightly padded plastic reclining seats," he writes, "an overhead luggage rack onto which I tossed my bag, and windows so filthy they could only have been washed a few times since Fidel entered Havana. The aisles were clean."

The humble lechero *fooled all of its detractors. It left Havana right on time, provided nearly eight hours of picturesque rural scenery, and reached Cienfuegos precisely on schedule. "I could report," Miller writes, "as Edwin Atkins did 106 years earlier, 'I have arrived safely at this city without being captured by any rebels.' "*

THE TWENTIETH CENTURY ARCHITEC-ture of Havana is unlikely ever to get the attention the earlier buildings are now enjoying, at least while Castro has any say. The last two years of the last century and most of this are not edifying objects of contemplation for a proud Cuban revolutionary. To restore twentieth-century architecture would run the risk of reminding Cubans of the degradation of the neo-colonialism of Spain.

Cuba, freed from Spanish rule by the intervention of the United States in 1898, became a nearly independent republic in 1902. In its early years until 1932 it was subject to the so-called Platt Amendment by which the government of the United States formally arrogated to itself the right to intervene in the affairs of the island.

One part of the island was to belong for ever to the United States. Guantánamo Bay in the far south-eastern corner of the island is among the finest and deepest in an island of fine, deep harbours. Semi-independent Cuba ceded the place to the United States in perpetuity.

The sight of a tropical equivalent of the Berlin Wall

manned by the soldiers of two countries whose governments hated each other was, I convinced myself one self-indulgent day in Havana, so unutterably exotic that it was not to be missed. I had to see on the ground the clash of Latin and Anglo-Saxon, of the imperial and the anti-imperialist, of Ariel and Caliban. And the visit there would be combined with that most delicious and instructive method of travel, an overnight train journey, one which in this case would take me the long snaky length of the island to Santiago, capital of the Oriente.

Friends and acquaintances in Havana, members of that incomprehensible worldwide conspiracy against train travel, warned against the Cuban railways. The trains, they said, were plagued by thieves. The accepted wisdom in the capital was that many of those who boarded in Havana never reached their destination but were horribly mangled in dreadful disasters on the line. Those males who embarked cleanshaven in Havana, if they survived, alighted in Santiago, they said, with long white beards.

The Cuban state itself seemed little more sanguine about the rail system. "The Most Expensive Breakfast in the World," an award-winning short at that year's Havana Film Festival, told the true story of the driver of a shunting engine who so lusted after a tomato sandwich for breakfast that he left his locomotive switched on, allowing it to move off, career for miles, and finally cause an expensive accident. I was not, however, to be put off.

Train Number One leaves the Havana Central Station every evening at ten minutes past six. It is due in Santiago, 860 kilometres away on the far side of the Sierra Maestra, the mountains in which Castro and his comrades started the war which was to overthrow Batista, thirteen and three-quarter hours later at five to eight in the morning. That is the theory: the practice, as I was to find out, is other.

Shortly before six o'clock one evening I boarded Train Number One and settled in my comfortable but dusty first-class seat in an air-conditioned open carriage beside a young man who was already asleep. It was drizzling and my spirits sank. The rain combined with the grime on the outside of the window to produce a film through which it was impossible to see clearly.

Was the countryside going to go by in a disappointing muddy blur? Was there going to be no one to talk to?

As the train started, punctual to the second, the carriage was addressed by a very beautiful brunette in her late twenties.

"I am Marta, your *ferromoza*," she said starting her short evening lecture on civics and the proper socialist attitude to travel by rail with a flirtatious giggle.

"Children must not be allowed to run up and down the aisle. Your seats, which are adjustable, have ashtrays in the armrests. Use them. When you brush your teeth tomorrow morning do it in the lavatories provided. The restaurant car is next door." Sensing from long practice that her audience knew the difficulties of getting into stationary restaurants in Cuba without foreign currency, she added "Tickets will be handed out for dinner and breakfast."

Another giggle and she was gone.

Gloom returned.

By now Train Number One had come to a halt at Gas Works Junction, a piece of suburban wasteland such as can be viewed at some moment from every long distance train on earth. Marta was succeeded by two policemen who asked everyone which were their bags, presumably to frighten the more timorous thieves.

Things began to get better. The train picked up speed to fifty miles an hour across the green plain surrounding Havana. The speed and the evening sun dried the film of dirt on the windows allowing sight of neat carpets of sugar cane punctured every few miles by the tall smoking chimney of a *central* or sugar factory.

The man beside me awoke. He was a soldier who was serving in Havana but travelling back home to Camagüey, the cattle capital of Cuba a few hundred miles to the east. But he was also a member of the Cuban national cycling team and so did more time training for races than for battle.

Like me, he preferred train travel to going in some cramped bus. You were not boxed in, you could stretch your legs and have a meal.

It got dark quickly and the horizon glowed a beautiful red here and there where they were burning the cane fields to reduce the foliage and make the task of cutting the cane a lighter, though dirtier, job.

We were in the port of Matanzas by eight o'clock and as our diesel pulled us out of the station and away from the sea I thought of what Alberto Korda, the veteran Cuban photographer and underwater explorer, had told me in Havana about the treasure he had found at the bottom of the bay and how it came to be there.

In 1628 the Protestant Dutch made the greatest effort they were ever to mount to break Catholic Spanish power in the Caribbean and South America. One Dutch fleet was sent to Brazil with the ludicrously unrealistic task of attempting to capture Potosí, the immensely rich silver mine in the Andes of Upper Peru.

Two fleets were sent to Cuba to intercept the convoys ferrying home the treasure to Spain from the New World. One of them under the famous admiral Piet Heyn, whose father had been enslaved in a Spanish galley, was stationed off the north coast of the island. Despite frantic attempts by the Cuban governor to warn him of the danger he faced in Cuban waters, Juan de Benavides sailed from the Mexican port of Veracruz with a convoy of treasure. On 5 September the two met, Heyn's more powerful fleet blocking Benavides' entry to Havana. The twenty-two Spanish ships ran for cover in Matanzas Bay but many were captured. Those which ran on the rocks were sacked by Heyn's men who brought back enough loot to allow their masters, the Dutch West India Company, to declare a fifty per cent dividend. The Spanish king Philip IV had lost 1,000,000 ducats in silver and three times that value in ships and guns. Losses by private merchants came to 6,000,000 ducats. It was a major disaster for Spain, rocking the throne, halting payments to the army fighting Heyn's compatriots in Flanders, and plunging the fleet's home port, Seville, and Andalusia even deeper into economic depression. Benavides was put to death on his humiliating return.

But, according to Korda, among the vessels which went to the bottom there was still a fortune to be brought up. And there on the other side of the carriage was where it had all happened.

It was now time for supper. "Sandwich or chicken?" said

the woman from the restaurant car. "Beer or soft drink?" Armed with the slips of paper she gave us our carriage filed down the aisle to the adjoining carriage with all the confidence of just souls on the day of judgement. We queued at a hatch where we were handed fat sandwiches, roughly wrapped in thick greaseproof paper, or big pieces of roast chicken and warm chips in plastic containers acquired from Cuban airlines. The drinks came in anonymous bottles. We paid our *pesos* at the checkout and sat satisfied and happy on stools at counters along the sides of the carriage, without benefit of knives and forks, gnawing and slurping. The chicken bones and paper went into cardboard boxes on the floor. It was a far cry from the ordered atmosphere of *Wagons-Lits* in Europe but the enjoyment was the same.

Back in our seats we did not have to wait long for the dining-car staff to come round offering the strong sweet black coffee in tiny cones of brown paper for a few cents. The cycling soldier offered me some boiled sweets. My evening was made and I dozed off.

At about three o'clock we reached Camagüey. The soldier said goodbye and I went back to sleep. It must have been more than an hour later when I woke up to find we had not moved an inch. The locomotive which was due to take us the remainder of the way had broken down and a new one was on its way from Santiago. Sometime after four we were on our way eastward into the Sierra Maestra.

Breakfast was a sandwich and a soft drink as we lumbered cautiously through the Sierra. Having heard frequently over the years of the heroic revolutionary battles in the mountains, it was something of a disappointment to see how gentle the contours were. Outside the town of Mella there was another long delay, long enough to allow those of us who wanted to to get out on to the track, stroll about, and watch the farmer carefully ploughing behind two slow oxen.

As we bowled downhill towards our destination I encountered a jolly group of *ferromozas* sitting with their foreman in an empty carriage. They explained to me banteringly how useless he was, while he warned me against ever having to supervise the work of a group of flighty women. The foreman added proudly that he had come from a long line of railway workers. The women seemed equally keen on their jobs. One said she had spent years in Czechoslovakia studying textile design but was now much happier away from the cold, stiff-necked city of Prague and Czechs' attitudes of patronizing racial superiority to Cubans. Seeing my camera they all wanted their photos taken.

At precisely half past ten we pulled into Santiago station exactly two hours, thirty-five minutes late.

The Oriente is a rougher, tougher, poorer part of Cuba than the flat lush land round Havana. It is a land of rock and cactus, not of palm trees and sugar cane. In the nineteenth century when virtually all Spain's empire in America had fallen away and only Cuba and Puerto Rico were left, the rich, slave-owning sugar growers of the west of Cuba were reluctant to risk their fortunes in a war of independence with Spain. The estate owners of the Oriente, Ignacio Agramonte and Francisco Manuel de Céspedes, who were later to become bourgeois nationalist heroes in the pantheon of a Leninist Cuba, had less to lose and were more radical.

With few roads and more difficult communication, the Oriente gave the advantage to the nationalist guerrilla bands who, in 1868, proclaimed an independent Cuba. They fought 100,000 Spanish troops for ten years but were in the end unable to defeat them.

Finally, and for its own ends, the United States intervened and in a few weeks in 1898 routed the Spaniards, put an end to their empire, and consolidated its own. The final battle took place in the waters off Santiago.

At half past nine on the fine sunny morning of Sunday 3 July of that year, the Spanish commander, Admiral Pascual Cervera y Topete, steamed his ill-maintained fleet—which he had just navigated groggily across the Atlantic and for which the Spanish government could not afford to buy ammunition—out of the narrow entrance of the Harbour of Santiago de Cuba. He was attempting to break the naval blockade imposed by an overwhelmingly powerful U.S. fleet moored in a semicircle outside under the command of Admiral William Sampson.

It was the culmination of months of agony for a man who seemed to have had foreknowledge of his fate. A year before in Cadiz, when war with the United States seemed a distinct possibility, an acquaintance said to him that he looked likely to be given the command of the squadron in battle.

"In that case I shall accept, knowing however that I am going to a Trafalgar," he replied.

Knowing how ill-trained the Spanish navy was, the admiral added that only the expenditure of 50,000 tons of coal on manoeuvres and the firing of 10,000 shells in gunnery practice could halt the disaster he foresaw.

The government had already lost the Philippines to the United States that year and was desperate to save some shred of military honour. It ordered him to the Cape Verde Islands. Fearing for the ships if he were sent across the Atlantic he made his position plain to the navy minister in Madrid. But there was no going back. Stopping to take on some coal in Curaçao he reached Santiago in the early morning of 19 May. Ten days later his ships, his flagship the *Infanta María Teresa,* the *Vizcaya,* the *Almirante Oquendo,* and the *Cristóbal Colón,* all armoured cruisers, and the destroyers *Furor* and *Terror,* were bottled in the harbour of Santiago by a much more powerful U.S. naval force waiting outside the narrow entrance to the port.

The city of Santiago itself was also under siege by land from the U.S. army and the population was slowly starving to death. As horses disappeared off the streets of the city and into the stew-pots, Cervera, a skilled, respected, and popular commander, fired off appeals for supplies.

On 22 June he appealed to the navy yard in Havana,

> *Six-sevenths of the 5.5-inch ammunition is useless, the fuses not reliable, and we have no torpedos. These are the main deficiencies. If the government could send supplies so that they could arrive this week, it might still be time.*

Meanwhile there were not enough Spanish soldiers to maintain any proper defence of the city and his friend General Linares pleaded with him to order his men from their hammocks into his trenches. The same day as he appealed to Havana, Cervera cabled Madrid.

As the question is going to be decided on land, I am going to send ashore the crew of the squadron as far as the rifles will go. The situation is very critical.

The next day his cable to the navy ministry reported,

I have disembarked crew to aid army. Yesterday five battalions went out from Manzanillo. If they arrive in time agony will be prolonged, but I doubt much whether they will save city.

As it is absolutely impossible for squadron to escape under these circumstances, I intend to resist as long as possible and destroy ships as last extreme. Although others are responsible for this untenable position into which we were forced in spite of my opposition, it is very painful to be an actor therein.

On 24 June he cabled Havana,

With provisions we can hold out until end of July but I believe the siege will be over before then.

A day later he told the Captain-General in Havana,

I believe it my duty to set forth condition of squadron. Out of three thousand rounds for the 5.5-inch Hontoria guns only six hundred and twenty reliable; rest have been pronounced useless, and were not replaced by others for lack of stores before we left. Two 5.5-inch Hontoria guns of Vizcaya and one of Oquendo defective; they had been ordered to be changed for others. Majority of fuses not serviceable. We lack Bustamante torpedoes. Colón is without heavy armament. Vizcaya is badly fouled and has lost her speed. Teresa does not have landing guns, and those of Vizcaya and Oquendo are unserviceable. We have little coal; provisions enough for the month of July. Blockading fleet is four times superior; hence our sortie would be positively certain destruction.

The same day he called Linares,

> *I state most emphatically that I shall never be the one to*
> *decree the horrible and useless hecatomb which will be the*
> *only possible result of the sortie from here by main force, for*
> *I should consider myself responsible before God and history*
> *for the lives sacrificed on the altar of vanity, and not in the*
> *true defence of the country.*

From Havana at 10:45 P.M. on 1 July the Captain-General gave Cervera explicit instructions to sail out of Santiago.

One by one they emerged from the very narrow mouth of the harbour, already partially blocked by the *Merrimac*, a vessel the U.S. sailors had sunk in the channel, at the foot of the crag on which was built the fortress of El Morro. Then they turned westwards in a dash for freedom. Each was destroyed, crippled by shellfire and rammed by its captain on to the beach. The *Furor* and the *Plutón* were gone well before an hour had passed. The *María Teresa* and the *Oquendo* by about ten-thirty. The *Vizcaya* by eleven o'clock.

As the U.S.S. *Texas* passed the stern of the *María Teresa* stuck on the rocks, her crew began to exult. Captain John Philip, the *Texas'* commander, seeing the horror of the burning Spanish ship, shouted, "Don't cheer. The poor devils are dying."

Cristóbal Colón, the warship which some malicious fate had decreed should bear the name of the discoverer of America, made a run for it but was eventually overcome by the combined guns of *Oregon*, *Texas*, and *Brooklyn* shortly before two o'clock. She beached herself and ran down her flag seventy-five miles to the west of Santiago.

In a battle which lasted less than four hours the U.S. navy lost one man dead and one wounded. The Spaniards lost 350 of their 2,227 men dead, 160 wounded, 1,670 prisoner. They lost their fleet and in the waters off the Oriente they lost their empire. Under the U.S.—Spanish peace treaty, to which the Cuban insurgents were not permitted to be a party, not only Cuba, but neighbouring Puerto Rico, the Philippines, and Guam in the Pacific, were ceded by Spain into the hands of the United States or, briefly in the case of Guam, to the German Empire.

Captain Victor Concas, commander of the *María Teresa*, recalling the victory of Ferdinand and Isabella over the Moors in 1492 when Spain began to rise to greatness, later wrote,

> *The bugle gave the signal for the start of the battle, an order which was repeated by a murmur of approbation from all those sailors and marines who were anxious to fight; for they did not know that those warlike echoes were the signal which hurled their country at the feet of the victor, since they were to deprive Spain of the only power still of value to her, without which a million soldiers could be of no service . . . The sound of my bugles was the last echo of those which history tells us were sounded at the capture of Granada. It was the signal that four centuries of grandeur were at an end and that Spain was becoming a nation of the fourth class.*

"WE WANT THEM OUT OF HERE."

The Cuban major in the Frontier Guard Brigade helped me train the telescope on the gate in the fence miles away over which the Stars and Stripes still flew. This was the tropical Checkpoint Charlie. A dozen tiny figures ran from the yellow bus which had brought them to the fence to the checkpoint and into the Cuban bus which was waiting for them the other side. It was four o'clock on a blindingly hot afternoon and work at the U.S. base was over for the day for those Cubans who still clocked on there.

Guantánamo Bay, an hour or so by road from Santiago, lay buzzing in the haze in a great natural amphitheatre of mountains twenty miles across. The hundred square miles of Guantánamo Bay is one of those superb, almost landlocked natural harbours surrounded by protective mountains which are to be found in the Caribbean and which offer seafarers some compensation for the cruel storms and hurricanes which sweep it. The base, "Gitmo" to the U.S. troops, is a rectangle of land and water which embraces the mouth of the bay and the two adjacent promontories. Vessels moving in and out of Guantánamo Bay have therefore to pass through waters controlled by United States forces.

With the major and a disagreeably arrogant young man from the local Communist Party as my guide and minder we had toiled up a long track in a Russian jeep to the eyrie at the top of the mountain. On each side of the track organ pipe cactuses stretched up their fleshy green trunks filled with water they had miraculously sucked from the rock. From time to time we passed a scrawny cowboy on a lean horse herding a few lean cattle. Goats somehow found a meal in the thorny bushes. There were iguanas the size of a strong man's arm. The flat carpets of sugar cane I had seen from the train might as well have been in another country.

From our vantage point, a post from which the Cuban army had been observing for thirty years, the forty-two square miles of the base were spread out distantly below us. The major pointed to U.S. naval vessels at the docks and quays on the eastern promontary and across the bay on the western promontory to the airfield, firing ranges, and a golf course. On the seaward side behind a hill bristling with antennae there was, he said, a bathing beach. Far away in the heat haze the lines of a large warship could be seen.

"A helicopter carrier," said the major shortly.

At an early stage Fidel Castro decided that the continuing military presence of the United States on a corner of the motherland was an affront which was not to be tolerated. The annual cheque for rent of the base was refused and the United States government was left in no doubt that its troops were unwelcome. But while the nationalist point was clear and unequivocal the practical politics on the ground were more difficult.

The base provided many jobs in a region where there was not much employment. People from all over the Oriente came to Guantánamo to earn good money working for the *gringos*.

"Before the Revolution Caimanera was one big bar and brothel," said the disagreeable young man primly.

The decision was taken to allow Cubans already working there to continue to work at the base and to continue selling the base water and power. At the same time the two villages of Boquerón and Caimanera were given special privileged treatment. Wages paid by the state in the area were a third higher than the average and the two villages were the first to be given colour television sets. The government tried to push up employment opportunities by reviving one of the world's most rudimentary industries by building saltpans on flat ground near Caimanera.

There was trouble in 1965 when Cuban fishermen were arrested and held as they sailed through U.S. controlled waters. Castro cut off the supplies of Cuban power and water and since that day the Washington government had to produce its own electricity and procure water either from desalination plants on the base or via tankers bringing water from Puerto Rico.

Now the Guantánamo situation was being turned into a tourist attraction. Behind our lookout post the underground installations, which had presumably once housed an artillery command post, were being painted and spruced up and provided with maps and photographs which would instruct the visitor in the affront to Cuban national pride caused by the U.S. presence on the soil of Cuba.

At the bottom of the mountain hard up against the wire was the fishing port of Boquerón. Why didn't we find some people who worked inside the base to talk to? I asked. With reluctance the disagreeable young man assented and we asked round the village.

"*Hay que bu'car a Dufu,*" said a villager.

Obediently we went in search of Dufu.

Dufu turned out to be Vincent Duffus, a tall, relaxed man with an easy smile sitting in the sun on the porch of his small house who had just retired from working at the base. He had been one of the many Jamaicans who had been taken on there because they spoke English. He was a living reminder of how, in the not too distant times of formal slavery, black labour used to be siphoned around the Caribbean as though it was one labour market. His easy manner and humanity seemed tacitly to ridicule the international ideological quarrel which kept the village where he lived fenced off from the military base where he had worked.

The major and the disagreeable young man were very unwilling to allow me to speak to him alone. But I did.

"I don' remember when I started to work at the base," he

said in a gentle Jamaican accent. "It coulda been before the Revolution."

Vincent's brother still worked at an office in the base and regularly brought out Vincent's pension for him in dollars. Despite the straitened circumstances in Cuba the elderly Jamaican seemed perfectly happy to end his days at Boquerón in the shadow of the base where he had worked for decades.

On the way back to the nondescript town of Guantánamo the disagreeable young man started to talk politics and I told him I was a member of the British Labour Party.

"Now the Labour Party, they tell me, is one of the less reactionary of the political parties in England," he said. His remark recalled the succession of arch references to the "bourgeois democracies" of Western Europe that I had heard in Havana in speeches and in conversations with the narrow members of the Party in Havana. His patronizing tone was no less insulting for being unthinking.

"The Labour Party was working for democracy in Britain for years before your Cuban Communist Party was thought of," I replied with all the forcefulness I could muster in the heat. The rest of the journey was passed in silence.

It was not fanciful, I felt, to detect in the disagreeable young man's tone a not uncommon Cuban arrogance. This is an arrogance that may be compounded of centuries of Spanish imperial pride, native to the biggest island in the Caribbean. It is an arrogance compounded with the intellectual certainty given to those mean spirits whose horizons are bounded by a literal interpretation of Marxism-Leninism, an arrogance tested and tempered by the need to outface a powerful and implacable neighbour to the north. But I was not pleased.

MARTHA GELLHORN

Havana and the Finca Vigia, 1985

"I WAS STAYING AT THE HOTEL DEAUVILLE, A POST-WAR,
PRE-REVOLUCÍON BLIGHT ON THE MALECON. IT IS A PLUM-
COLOURED CEMENT BAUHAUS-STYLE TOWER. I CAME TO
DOTE ON THE HIDEOUS DEAUVILLE BECAUSE OF THE STAFF,
JOKEY AND FRIENDLY WITH EACH OTHER AND THE GUESTS."

Martha Gellhorn is a distinguished novelist and journalist in her own right, but she will certainly also be remembered as the third wife of Ernest Hemingway. They were together in the 1940s when they bought and set up housekeeping at the Finca Vigia, just near the southwestern outskirts of Havana.

There is a famous photo that shows Ernest Hemingway and Fidel Castro together, but it was taken in 1960, on the one occasion when they met. Hemingway has long been a major presence in Havana, and he remains so three and a half decades after his death. He has been warmly adopted by habaneros, and the places associated with him are powerful tourist attractions.

The little fishing village of Cojímar, where Hemingway docked the Pilar, *is six miles or so east of central Havana, and tourists find it an attractive place for lunch and a day's outing. La Terraza, the restaurant Hemingway wrote about in* The Old Man and the Sea, *is still there, and a bust of the writer decorates the town square. As a further attraction, just past Cojímar* are the *Playas del Este*, the eastern beaches that offer habaneros and tourists alike miles of white sand and turquoise water.

Back in *Habana Vieja*, the old city, Hemingway fans have to visit two of his favorite bars and taste his favorite drink at each, a daiquiri at El Floridita (on Calle San Rafael) and a mojito at La Bodeguita del Medio (on Calle Empedrado). The truly determined will also want to see room 511 at the Hotel Ambos Mundos (at the corner of Mercaderes and Obispo), preserved as it was (sort of) when he stayed there in the 1930s.

Also preserved is the famous Hemingway home, *La Finca Vigia*, about seven miles southwest of central Havana. It's been tidied up recently, but visitors are not permitted inside. Instead, they can walk around the outside and peer through the windows at rooms, familiar to fans from many photographs, that are much as he left them, filled with books, papers, magazines, and hunting trophies. The separate tower where he wrote each day is here, as is, rather incongruously, the *Pilar* itself.

The modern and flashy Marina Hemingway, west of Havana, has no connection to the writer other than the name. Marina Hemingway is a playground for foreign visitors and for Cubans with plenty of dollars, offering stylish boutiques, restaurants and nightclubs, condos, hotels, tennis courts, and, of course, the marina. Each May since 1962, the Ernest Hemingway International Billfish Tournament is held here. The competition began in 1950 at Cojímar.

A Cruising Guide to Cuba, by Simon Charles, was published in 1994. Reviewing it in the October 1995 issue of *Cuba Update,* David Bregman, who is both senior heart surgeon at the Columbia Presbyterian Medical Center in New York and a veteran of many (legal) waterborne arrivals at Marina Hemingway, warns readers to bring plenty of extra everything. "The quality of the U.S. fuel is a significantly better grade than the Cuban fuel," he notes. "You always run the risk of fouling your engines and filters with Cuban fuel." And there's another danger one might not anticipate: "When arriving in the Cuban marina, have plenty of spare lines and especially bumpers. Most Cuban marinas are concrete, and therefore you will need a lot of protection."

THE FIRST MORNING IN HAVANA, I STOOD by the sea-wall on the Malecon, feeling weepy with homesickness for this city. Like the exile returned; and ridiculous. I left Cuba forty-one years ago, never missed it and barely remembered it. A long amnesia, forgetting the light, the colour of the sea and sky, the people, the charm of the place.

The Malecon is a nineteenth-century jewel and joke. Above their arcade, the mini-mansions rise three storeys, each house exuberantly different from the next: windows garlanded with plaster roses, Moorish pointy windows of stained glass, caryatids, ornate ironwork balconies, huge nail-studded carved doors. The paint on the stone buildings is faded to pastel, a ghostly reminder of former brilliance: pink trimmed with purple, blue with yellow, green with cobalt. Whoever lived here, when Cuba was my home from 1939 to May 1944, had departed: fluttering laundry suggested that their rich private houses were now multiple dwellings.

A delightful little black kid bounced out of somewhere, in spotless white shirt and royal blue shorts. He smiled up at me with a look of true love and undying trust. *"Rusa?"* he asked. I was mortally offended. Russian women of a certain age, seen in Moscow, had bodies like tanks and legs like tree trunks.

"No," I said crossly, *"Americana."* I should have said *"Norteamericana."* South of the U.S. border, people do not accept Americans' exclusive ownership of the continent.

The loving smile did not change. *"Da me chicle,"* he said. Give me chewing-gum. Cuba does not manufacture chewing-gum. In due course, I gathered that kids admire gum chewing as seen in American movies, still the most popular.

The Prado is a stylish old street with a wide central promenade: live oak trees, big light globes on wrought iron lampposts, benches. The benches were occupied by old women knitting and gossiping, old men reading papers and gossiping, poor people by our standards, looking comfortable and content. Now in the lunch-hour, groups of school children—from gleaming black to golden blonde—romped about the promenade, healthy, merry, and as clean as if emerged from a washing-machine. The little ones wear a uniform of maroon shorts or miniskirts, short-sleeved white shirts, and a light blue neckerchief;

the secondary school children wear canary yellow long pants or mini-skirts and a red neckerchief. The neckerchiefs show that they are Pioneers, blue for the babies, like Cubs and Scouts in my childhood.

Before, street boys would have drifted around here, selling lottery tickets or papers, collecting cigarette butts, offering to shine shoes, begging. They were funny and talkative, barefoot, dressed in dirty scraps, thin faces, thin bodies, nobody's concern. They did not attend school. Nor were they Afro-Cubans.

I had never thought of Cubans as blacks, and could only remember Juan, our pale mulatto chauffeur. Eventually I got that sorted out. A form of apartheid prevailed in central Havana, I don't know whether by edict or by landlords' decision not to rent to blacks. Presumably they could not get work either, unless as servants. But of course there were blacks in Cuba as everywhere else in the Caribbean, descendants of African slaves imported for the sugar-cane plantations. In my day, they must still have been concentrated in the eastern provinces, still cutting cane. Roughly one third of Cubans are of African or mixed blood, two thirds Caucasian.

Calle Obispo, formerly my beat for household supplies, had been turned into a pedestrian street. At one of the cross streets I saw the only cops I noticed in Havana, trying to disentangle a jam of trucks, motorcycles, and hooting cars. The shops were a surprise: bikinis and cosmetics, fancy shoes, jewellery, a gift shop with china and glass ornaments. Not high fashion, but frivolous. And many bookstores, a real novelty; I remembered none. And a neighbourhood store-front clinic.

Faces looked remarkably cheerful, unlike most city faces, and the street was enveloped in babble and laughter. Men met women, kissed them on the cheek, talked, moved on. That public friendly cheek-kissing astonished me; I had never seen it in a Latin American country, and never here in my day. Most of the women wore trousers made of a stretch material called, I think, crimplene; and most women were amply built. Their form-hugging pants were lavender, scarlet, emerald green, yellow, topped by blouses of flowered nylon. The young, boys and girls, wore jeans and T-shirts. T-shirts printed with Mickey

Mouse, a big heart and LUV, UNIVERSITY OF MICHIGAN. Presents from relatives in the U.S.? Grown men wore proper trousers of lightweight grey or tan material and white shirts. These people were much better dressed than average Cubans before, and much better nourished.

At the top of this street, Salomon, a very small tubercular man of no definite age but great vitality sold lottery tickets. Salomon was a communist and lived with the certainty of a glorious communist future, when everyone would eat a lot and earn their keep by useful work. I remembered him out of nowhere, and hoped with all my heart that he lived to see his dream come true, but doubted it; Salomon didn't look then as if he had the necessary fifteen years left.

I was staying at the Hotel Deauville, a post-war, pre-Revolución blight on the Malecon. It is a plum-coloured cement Bauhaus-style tower. I came to dote on the hideous Deauville because of the staff, jokey and friendly with each other and the guests. The Deauville is classed as three-star, not suitable for rich dollar tourists. My room with bath cost $26. Like all tourist hotels, the Deauville has its own Duty-Free Shop. Tourists of every nationality pay for everything in U.S. dollars. You are given your change, down to nickels and dimes, in American money. For practical purposes one dollar equals one Cuban peso, a parallel economy for natives and tourists. President Reagan has tightened the permanent U.S. economic embargo to include people. Cuba is off limits to American tourists. But that year, 1985, 200,000 capitalist tourists, from Canada, Europe, Mexico, South America, uninterested in or undaunted by communism, had caught on to the idea of the cheapest Caribbean holiday.

At the Deauville, I had my first view of the amusing and economical national mini-skirt: above-the-knee uniform for women employees, different colours for different occupations. And was also plunged into the national custom of calling everyone by first names, beginning with Fidel who is called nothing else. I was rather testy, to start, hearing "Marta" from one and all and the intimate *tu* instead of *usted*, a disappearing formality. But I quickly adjusted and was soon addressing strangers as *compañero* or *compañera*. You cannot say comrad (American) or comraid (British) without feeling silly, but *compañero* has the cosy sound of companion.

I wanted to be on my way. I had not come to Cuba to study communism but to snorkel. At the Cuban Embassy in London, I found some tourist bumf, describing a new glamorous hotel at Puerto Escondido, which included the magic word, snorkelling. I was going to Nicaragua, serious business, and meant to treat myself *en route* to two weeks mainly in the lovely turquoise shallows off the Cuban coast. A couple of days in Havana, to retrace my distant past; then sun, snorkelling, thrillers, rum drinks: my winter holiday.

You can go anywhere you want in Cuba, except to the American naval base at Guantanamo on the eastern tip of the island—an extraordinary piece of property which most foreigners do not know is held and operated by the United States. You can hire, with or without driver, a small Russian Lada sedan belonging to INTUR, the Ministry of Tourism. The Lada is as tough as a Land Rover, Third World model, with iron-hard upholstery and, judging by sensation, no springs. I asked INTUR for a car with driver, intending to look over the hotel at Puerto Escondido, the goal of my Cuban trip.

The driver, rightly named Amable, said that Puerto Escondido was half an hour from Havana; my introduction to Cuban optimism. "No problem" might be the national motto; it is the one English phrase everyone can say. We drove through the tunnel under Havana harbour, new to me, and along the superhighway, adorned with billboards, very depressing: progress. The billboards are exhortations, not advertisements. A light bulb, with ENERGÍA in huge letters and a plea to save it. A bag of coins and a single-stroke dollar sign for the peso, recommending the public to bank their money at two-and-a-half percent interest. Many patriotic billboards: "WE WOULD DIE BEFORE WE GIVE UP OUR PRINCIPLES." Two hours from Havana found us bumping on a mud road through lush jungle scenery. A solitary soldier stopped us where the track ended. Puerto Escondido was not finished; it would be ready next year. More Cuban optimism. The soldier suggested a tourist resort at Jibacoa further on.

Amable managed to find Jibacoa—small brick houses, newly landscaped—and a bar and a restaurant. At the bar two Canadian girls, secretaries from Toronto who had arrived yesterday, were full of enthusiasm and information. They had a nice double room; the food was "interesting"; rape was punished by shooting; Cubans were lovely people; and they looked forward to a night out at the Tropicana, Havana's answer to the Paris Lido. Goody, but what about snorkelling? A man in a wetsuit was coming up from the beach; the girls said he was Luis, in charge of water sports. Luis guaranteed that the snorkelling was fine and we both stared to the north where clouds like solid black smoke spread over the sky.

"*Un norte?*" I asked with dismay. I remembered only perfect winter weather.

"Yes, come back in a few days when it is passed."

But it did not pass.

By morning, the sea was greenish black, matching the black sky. Waves smashed across the Malecon, closed to traffic, and drove sand and pebbles up the side streets. The wind was at gale force; it rained. A gigantic storm and worsening. I was cold and slumped into travel despair, an acute form of boredom. With no enthusiasm, I arranged to fill time, meeting people and seeing sights, until the storm ended.

The distinguished Afro-Cuban poet and I talked in the crowded lobby of the Hotel Nacional, an old four-star hotel. Suddenly she made a sound of disgust and said, "I hate that stupid out-of-date stuff." She spoke perfect American. The object of her disgust was a wedding party: bride in white with veil, groom in tuxedo, flower girls, bridesmaids, beaming parents and guests, headed for the wedding reception. I was pleased that the out-of-date could be freely practised by those who wanted it.

I had an important question to ask her but was very unsure of my ground. "Something puzzles me," I said. "Fidel made a decree or whatever, as soon as the Revolución started, forbidding racism. I mean, he said it was over; there wouldn't be any more. And there isn't. Surely that is amazing?" It sure is. Even more amazing, it seems to work.

"Of course you can't change people's prejudices by law; you can't change what they feel in their hearts. But you can make any racist acts illegal and punish them. We hope that as we live together more and know each other better as human beings, the prejudices will disappear."

We had no racist problem, she and I, just the wrong vibes. She thought me too light; I thought her too heavy.

I was interested in how writers earned their livings. Very few of the 600 members of the Writers' Union can live by books alone, like us. There are many publishing houses, state-owned but managed by distinct staffs for a varied public. You submit your manuscript; if accepted, you get sixty percent of the retail price of the first edition, whether the books are sold or not; then forty percent of further editions. Cubans love poetry, so poets abound and are widely read.

Feeling dull but dutiful, I went to look at Alamar—a big housing estate, white rectangular factories for living spread over the green land off the highway outside Havana.

"Marta, why do you say you do not like such a place? I have friends there. They have a very nice apartment." Today's driver, called Achun, part Chinese, had served in Angola. He said he was truly sorry for those Africans; they were a hundred years behind Cuba.

I asked, "How big?"

"Two bedrooms, three, four, depending on the number of the family."

I told him about vandalism as we know it. Achun was dumbfounded.

"Why would people ruin their own homes?"

Close-up, Alamar was not bad; no graffiti on the white walls, no broken windows—on the contrary, shined and curtained—a skimpy fringe of flowers around each building, and thin new trees. The buildings are four storeys high, widely separated by lawn.

"The cinema is behind those buildings," Achun said.

Here the bus stopped; a few weary people were piling out. The forty-minute ride to and from Havana in the always overcrowded buses has to be a trial. (Havana is about to get a needed metro system.) This central shopping area reduced me to instant gloom. I thought at first it was filthy. The impression of grime was not due to dirt but to unpainted cement. Of course Cuba is poor and needs many things more vital than paint, yet it distresses me that these people, who adore bright colour, must be denied it.

The bookstore was attractive because of the gaudy book covers. A soldier and a child were the only customers in the middle of a chilly grey weekday afternoon. A corner of the room had been set aside for children's books. The paper is coarse, the covers thin, but books cost from forty-five to seventy-five cents.

"Every year we have a quota," said the middle-aged saleslady. "And every year we exceed it."

"How can you have a quota? You can't force people to buy books, can you?"

"Oh no, it is not like that. Every year we are sent a quota of books and every year we must ask for more, because they are sold. All ages buy books. Fidel said 'Everything basic to the people must be cheap. Books are basic.' "

"What is most popular?"

"Detectives and romantic novels."

I drove around Havana, sightseeing, half-curious, and wholly sick of the miserable weather. I chatted in the dingy main market where the toy counter and meat and poultry counter were the busiest. I asked about fares at the jammed railroad station, learning that the best fast train to the other end of the island costs $10.50. I cruised through the stylish section of Vedado with the big hotels, airline offices, shops, restaurants, movies, and the large Edwardian houses. I peered at the Miramar mansions. The rich departed Cubans left a bountiful gift to the Revolución, all their grand homes and classy apartment buildings. The big houses are clinics, kindergartens, clubs for trade unions, and whatever has no public use is portioned off for private living space.

Then I decided I needed some action and barged into a secondary school, announcing that I was a foreign journalist and would like to sit in on a class and see how they taught their students. This caused extreme confusion. (As it probably would if I barged into the Chepstow comprehensive.) The school sent me to the local Poder Popular office where I met the very cornerstone of bureaucracy: the woman at the door. Behind a desk/table/counter in every government office is a woman, preferably middle-aged; her job is to keep people out. Poder Popular sent me to the Ministry of Education. There the woman at the door said that Public Relations at INTUR, the Ministry of Tourism, must write to Public Relations at the Ministry of Education. I reported this to INTUR, decrying it as an absurd fuss about nothing. INTUR promised that a school visit would be arranged. "Be patient, Marta," said Rosa, an INTUR director. "Everything is done through organizations here."

To their credit, the Ministry of Education sent me to a very modest school in a poor suburb. The Secondary School of the Martyrs of Guanabacoa. The driver could not find it. We were twenty minutes late. I got out of the Lada and saw school kids in canary yellow lined up along the path to the front door and a greeting committee of adults. I apologized unhappily for keeping everyone waiting and walked past the honour guard, feeling absurd. Instead of a twenty-one-gun salute, I got a shouted slogan. On the school steps a little Afro-Cuban girl stepped from the ranks, shouted something, and behind her the official chorus shouted an answer. This went on for several minutes but I could not decipher a single shouted word. I was then presented with a sheaf of gladioli and lilies in cellophane and began to feel as if I were the Queen Mother.

The man in charge, whose position I never understood, presented the school principal, a large shy Afro-Cuban woman in dark blue crimplene trousers and white blouse. I was shown the school bulletin board with its smiling photographs of the "martyrs"—handsome girls and boys, not much older than the children here, killed by Batista's police for their clandestine work in the Revolución. Asked what I would like to visit, I said the English class. The school was unpainted cement inside and out, built on the cheap in 1979.

The English teacher was nervous and nice and desperately eager for his class to perform well. Each child read aloud a sentence from their textbook, dealing with Millie's birthday party. Offhand, I could not think of a deadlier subject. " 'Toothbrush' and 'toothpaste' " (Millie's birthday presents!) 'are very hard for them to say; also 'room.' " His own accent was odd; the kids were choked with stage fright, rivalling mine.

A bell blessedly rang. Here, the children stay in one room, the teachers move. It was the history hour in another classroom. The children—the top form, aged fifteen—rose to their feet and shouted a slogan, led by the elected class prefect who was always a girl. Hard to understand, but it sounded like promising Fidel to study and be worthy of the Revolución. Each class devised its own slogan, a new one every month, and five times a day, at the start of their class periods, they shouted this at the teacher. The history teacher was a thin intense shabbily-dressed young man who described the sugar crisis of 1921, when prices fell and the people suffered despair and starvation though their work had enriched the bourgeoisie and the American capitalists. I wanted to say that American workers suffered too in times of depression and unemployment, but didn't feel that speech-making was part of my new role.

Biology was taught by a stout mulata compañera in lavender pants, and taught brilliantly. The subject for the day was the renal system, up to that moment a total mystery to me. All the kids raised their hands, competing to answer. This subject—their bodies—clearly interested them much more than history or English. After class, the teacher explained that by the end of the term they would have studied the sexual organs, the nine months of pregnancy, and birth. To finish, they would discuss "the human couple, and the need for them to be equals and share the same ideals and interests." She showed me their laboratory, a small room with a few bunsen burners. Her only teaching-aid was a plaster human torso, open at the front, with all the brightly-coloured alarming organs in place.

There were 579 children, more caucasian than Afro-Cuban, and fifty teachers, about equally divided as to colour and sex. School is compulsory through the ninth grade, age fifteen. After that, children can choose to continue for three years in pre-university studies or technical schools, according to their grades. At eighteen, the boys do military service, but university students are exempt since Cuba needs all the professionals it can train.

Snacks had been laid out in the principal's office. I looked at these poorly-dressed men and women and grieved to think of them chipping in for this party. They were so excited about me because the school had never received a visitor before, no Cuban personage, let alone a foreigner. They spoke of their students with pride; it must feel good to teach such lively and willing children. Never mind that they had no library, no workshop, no gym, no proper laboratory in this bleak building. The staff invented substitutes and got on with the job. I asked to meet the Head Prefect, elected by her peers. She was a lovely tall slim girl, almost inaudible from shyness, blonde with grey eyes. She said that the entire school went on two camping weekends a year and for a week to Varadero, Cuba's famous beach. The top student (this girl) joined all the other secondary school top-graders for a whole summer month at Varadero. Fun and sport as a reward for work. I remember winning a school prize, a richly-bound uninteresting book.

I liked everyone and told them they had a fine school, meaning it, and thanked them for the visit. In the Lada, returning to Havana, I gave my character a shake and became again a normal, not a Very Important, person.

That night, on the thirteenth floor of the Deauville, I listened to the howling wind. The storm had renewed itself with spiteful vigour and would never end. Snorkelling was a dead dream. I gave up. I had no choice; there was nothing left to do except cramp myself into a Lada, drive around the country, and get a general idea of how communism works in Cuba.

For transport on this journey to the Cuban hinterland, I went to Rosa at INTUR, my sole contact with the Cuban government. She is small, brunette, very pretty, very bright, and kind and patient above and beyond the call of duty. My manners to her were abominable and in no way deserved. I was rudely determined that nobody was going to show or tell me anything; I would see and question for myself. Rosa assigned Rafael as my driver. Rafael is grey-haired, mid-forties, overweight, racked by a cigarette cough, intelligent, good, and a charmer. We drank a lot of delicious ice-cold Cuban beer and he laughed at my disrespectful jokes.

Rafael's story is one example of how the Revolución has changed lives. His wife works as an accountant in some ministry. Rafael is an official of the drivers' trade union, bargaining on his members' behalf with another ministry. "Whoever gets home first cooks the dinner." One son is reading English at Havana University. Another, having failed his exams, is doing military service and expects a place in medical school afterwards. Rafael pays thirty-five dollars monthly rent for an apartment in Vedado, formerly the chic section of Havana, and soon will own it. Rents pile up like down payments year after year, until the sale price of the flat is reached, whereupon bingo, you become an old-fashioned capitalist owner. Mrs. Thatcher's vision of a home-owners' society coming true in communist Cuba.

Rafael left me strictly alone whenever we stopped. I stayed in several sumptuous hotels; these were the Mafia's legacy to Cuban tourism, built with Mafia money because they included casinos, now closed. It was all new to me; I had never bothered to travel in Cuba when I lived here and had no sense of its size—730 miles long by an average of fifty miles wide—or of the variety of the towns and the landscape. We drove without any previously arranged plan—wherever I felt like going—and covered 1,500 miles in the backbreaking Lada, a partial look at about a third of the country. Our first stop was Trinidad.

Trinidad is a beauty; Cubans are very proud of it. It is an unspoiled colonial town, most of it late eighteenth- and early nineteenth-century, but inhabited from the sixteenth century. The streets are cobbled, the houses one storey high, with vast, handsome wood doors, wide enough for a carriage, and bowed iron grille-work on the front windows. Every house is painted, and paint makes the difference—pale green, pink, blue, yellow. The Cathedral, at the top of the town, is yellow trimmed in white, and fronts a flowery square that descends in steps to the houses.

The Museo Historico was the home of a nineteenth-century sugar baron. The enchanting girl in charge, aged around twenty, with blonde hair in a pony tail, wore the museum uniform, immaculate white shirt, dark blue jacket, and mini-skirt. "He had thirty slaves," she said. *Thirty.* They lived in that one big room at the back." The idea of slaves horrified her. Earlier, when she had collected my entry centavos, she said, "Cuba was under Spanish domination for three centuries, until 1899. After that, it was under American domination until 1959." It had sounded pat and off-putting, straight Party line, until I thought it over and decided it was true, no matter how it sounded.

The U.S. actually ruled Cuba twice, and the Marines had been around in the usual Monroe Doctrine way. Until 1934, the United States government had the right by law to interfere in internal Cuban affairs. But American domination was mainly felt through its support of whatever useless Cuban government protected American investments. In my time, no one ever talked politics or bothered to notice which gang was in office and robbing the till. I cannot remember any elections, though I think the government did change, perhaps by palace coup. One day driving in to Havana, I heard shooting and Salomon or the street boys advised me to settle in the Floridita and drink frozen daiquiris until it was over; the noise was farther down towards the harbour. This was taken lightly as a joke: who cared which crooks got in, the results would be the same. The poor would stay poor; the rich would stay rich; a different bunch of politicians would grow richer. After World War Two, during the Batista dictatorship, apart from the standard horrors of such rule—arrest, torture, executions—corruption must have been out of control, thanks to Batista's faithful friends, the Mafia.

At the Museo Romantico, said to be the former home of a Count, a bunch of noisy young people was clattering up the stairs to the salons and bedrooms. In the hall, a white-garbed nun waited, saying that she had seen it before. "If you have lived in Spain," said the little dark Spanish nun, "there is nothing to look at in this country." She seemed about thirty years old and had a sharp, severe face. She had come to Trinidad from Cienfuegos with the young people to attend the cathedral wedding of two of them, tomorrow. Her order has two houses, in Cienfuegos and Havana. There are eight Spanish, three Mexican, and three Cuban nuns in all.

"People must be very brave to go to Mass," she told me. "We do not go out in the street with the young for fear of compromising them. There is much fear."

"Fear? You mean fear of prison, fear for their lives?"

"No, no," she said impatiently. "Fear of losing their jobs or not getting a good one, if they are seen to be practising Catholics." Mass is celebrated here in the Cathedral and in another church "down there," twice on Sundays and that is all. She felt outraged by this. "No, nuns are not molested in any way but we are not allowed to do our pastoral work in the streets." As far as I was concerned, that was great: I don't want anyone of any religion, secular or spiritual, haranguing me in the streets. "Still, people do talk to us."

I pointed out that she had come here with these young people, a whole band of them, to take part in a church wedding.

"Yes, they are very loyal," she said.

The stern Afro-Cuban museum lady, the ticket collector, stared at us with plain dislike. The nun remarked on it. "She does not want me to talk to you." Even so, it did not stop the nun from talking to me, an obvious foreigner.

Cuba is awash with museums. Museums for everything, past and present. The museums are scantily furnished—no great art treasures—and are visited with interest by all kinds of Cubans, young and old. I don't think I've ever raced through so many anywhere and I think I understand them. This is consciousness-raising on a national scale. The mass of Cubans had no education and no real sense of identity. Being Cuban meant being somebody else's underling, a subordinate people. I knew a few upper-class Cuban sportsmen; they spoke perfect English, had been educated abroad, and were considered honorary Americans or Europeans, not in words, nor even in thought, but instinctively: they were felt to be too superior to be Cubans. Now, through these innumerable museums, Cubans are being shown their history, how their ruling class lived and how the people lived, the revolts against Spanish "domination," and everything about the Revolución. They are being told that they have been here a long time: they are a nation and they can be proud to be Cubans.

BETWEEN TRINIDAD AND SANCTI SPIRITUS, the country looked like Africa: hump-backed, bony cattle, like Masai cattle; palms and ceibas, the handsomer Cuban form of the African baobab tree; jungle-green hills; brown plains; but where were we going to sleep? We had been turned away at two hotels, full up with Cubans, who travel joyfully and constantly. We set out again, hunting for rooms.

Suddenly loud horns and sirens. Motorcycle cops pushed the traffic to the roadside. Ten first-class buses flashed past, filled with excited kids, singing, shouting, waving. "Pioneers," Rafael said. They were primary school children, the baby Pioneers of the light-blue neckerchief. "They are going to camp at Ismaela. They go for a week with their teachers and continue with their lessons."

Not that bunch, far too elated for lessons.

"Fidel started the idea of camping," Rafael went on. "Nobody in Cuba ever did that, live in a tent, cook over a fire. Now everybody does it. It is very popular." Cubans have two paid vacations a year, two weeks each, and alternate full weekends. Besides camping, many new beach resorts dot the coasts. These resorts are simple, rudimentary—I don't want to give the impression of places like luscious photos in travel brochures— and so inexpensive that most Cubans must be able to afford them. And there are town parks with children's playgrounds, swimming pools, sports grounds. I like the government's decision in favour of pleasure: Cuba's Revolución is not puritanical. Outlawing drugs, gambling, and prostitution eradicated crime as big business, hardly a bad idea. But there remain the delicious beer and rum, flowing freely, and cigarettes and cigars, since Cubans haven't yet heard of the horrors of smoking. But I think that the main cause of a different, open, pleasurable life-style is the change in women. The old Hispanic and Catholic custom of the women at home—isolated, the daughter guarded, the stiffness of that relation between men and women—is truly gone. Women are on their own at work, feeling equal to men, and showing this new confidence. Girls are educated equally with boys and chaperonage is dead. There is a feeling that men and women, girls and boys are having a good time together, in a way unknown before.

Bayamo, said the tourist map, offered historical sights; the church where the national anthem was first sung and other episodes of heroism against the Spanish overlords. I was not interested; I was interested in food. The food is ghastly, apart from breakfast. If Cuba means to earn millions of tourist dollars, it will have to make a culinary Revolución. On a corner of the main square, I saw an ice-cream parlour and bought a huge helping of delicious chocolate ice-cream.

I was enjoying this feast at an outside table when a boy came up, said his name was Pépé, shook hands, sat down, and asked my name and where I came from. I thought he was eighteen; he was twenty-four, good-looking with light brown hair, blue eyes, and a summery smile. He wanted to buy a pack of my cigarettes, Kools from a hotel Duty-Free; I said he could share mine. He wanted to see what a dollar looked like; I showed him. He wanted to know the price of cigarettes, gas lighters, dark glasses, and trousers in England. He then brought out of his wallet a small colour print of a beautiful little bejewelled and bedecked doll, the Virgen de la Caridad de Cobre, patron of Cuba. He handed me this as if he were giving me a family photo.

A young Afro-Cuban in a dark business suit lurked nearby, listening. I said, "Why do you stand there with a look of suspicion? Sit with us." His presence at first annoyed Pépé, then he ignored the newcomer.

Pépé wished to talk about religion, absolutely not my subject. "Are you a believer? Do you go to Mass? Do you believe in Jesus Christ?" By now we had another member of the seminar—an older Afro-Cuban—and slowly the waitresses pulled up chairs around our table.

Hoping to bring an end to this topic, I said, "In our country, people are Protestants." Easy misinformation.

"What religion is that?" said Pépé. "*Protestante?*"

"They are not loyal to the Pope," the older Afro-Cuban said.

"But you believe?" Pépé insisted.

As an untroubled unbeliever, I could not go into a long thing about Jesus as a man and a teacher, so I said, "*De vez en cuando*"—which comes out as "sometimes" and satisfied Pépé.

"There are churches in Bayamo?" I asked.

"Four," they said in unison.

"People go to Mass?"

In unison, "Yes."

"They have trouble if they go to Mass?"

Again in unison, "No."

"I want to see a capitalist country," Pépé said. "I want to go to France. I met some Frenchmen here."

"You want to leave?" the business suit asked, scandalized.

"No, not leave," Pépé said. "Visit. To see. But they will never give me a passport. Only to the socialist countries."

The older Afro-Cuban said, "Artists can go. Musicians, people like that."

I didn't want Pépé to cherish hopeless golden dreams and could imagine the Frenchmen talking about France as the French do. "You know, Pépé, everything is not perfect in our capitalist countries. We are not all rich and happy. We have great unemployment. There is also much crime."

"There is no crime here," said both Pépé and the business suit.

"No unemployment," said the others.

Cubans believe that there is no crime in Cuba. They feel safe in their homes and on their streets. You see very small unaccompanied children going about their business in Havana, and women walking alone at night wherever they wish to go. No one fears mugging. Rape is too unimaginable to think about. But of course there are crimes since there are gaols for common criminals.

We were now talking about education, and the main members of the seminar, Pépé and the business suit, agreed that education was very good here. "And free," Pépé added, "everything is free, even universities."

Business suit, who was a serious young man employed as health inspector for hotel and restaurant kitchens, now departed: end of the lunch-hour. The rest of the seminar drifted back to work.

Pépé, it developed, was a night-watchman at a cement factory, scarcely a demanding job, and had only completed two
years of secondary school. I began to realize that he was twenty-
four going on sixteen, but no less sweet and interesting for that.
"Do people have servants in England? Not here, there are no
servants here. Could I come to England and be your servant,
chauffeur or something? I wouldn't want any money." How he
longed to see the mysterious capitalist world. "If I was going
about in France, just looking, doing nothing wrong, would they
give me difficulties?" Cuban police are notably absent everywhere, and as Pépé had talked openly in front of his compatriots, strangers to him, he must have picked up some ominous
news about police in the free world.

By now we were great friends and he said confidentially, "I
don't like dark girls." I thought: gentlemen prefer blondes. But
no. "I only like girls with light skin." He now produced two
photographs from his wallet, almost identical Caucasian Cubans with a lot of brunette hair.

"Two *novias*, Pépé, isn't that one too many?"

He grinned, then said in a low voice, "I have a brother who
is a racist. He told me."

I imagined an older brother and said, "There is nothing
much he can do about it, is there? You don't have to marry a
dark girl. You aren't obliged to make any friends you don't want,
are you?"

"No. Clearly no."

"Well then. How old is your brother?" I disliked this te-
dious dummy brother, a bad example for young Pépé, and remembered the Afro-Cuban poet and the prejudices of the heart.

"Thirteen," said Pépé. I shouted with laughter. At first he
was bewildered; racism is no joke, an offence in law; then gradually he understood and the summery smile appeared.

I wandered into the square: live oaks, ali baba flower jars,
benches of bright patterned tile, a design in the paving bricks—
the Cubans had luck, architecturally, to be colonized by Spain.
No sign of Rafael, so I sat on a bench in the shade, and an
elderly lady sat beside me. She wore a neat, rather prissy cotton
dress and a hat, unheard-of, a proper lady's hat; I felt she

should have gloves. She said her husband had gone to the "office" to speak about their pension. "We are retired. Our pension is fifty-two pesos monthly. What can you do with that? Some people get seventy pesos. If you have children, they could help. Or else you must do work at home, little work." She was very worried and indignant. "Ridiculous," she said. "Impossible. I hope they listen to my husband."

In the car I asked Rafael about this. He said that pensions depended on how long you had worked. His mother got sixty pesos a month, from his dead father's pension. I pointed out that his brother lived in the same village and would help her and so would he. "Surely it is a bad system, Rafael, if people must depend on their children for money in their old age. It would be a reason to have as many children as possible."

"But people do not want many children; they want few and to give them more. People do not have big families now. Every woman, girl, can get birth control assistance, whether married or not. There is no sense in big families."

I abandoned pensions.

"Stop, Rafael. I want to take a photo." This was a picture of rural poverty. Everywhere, in the villages, along the roads, the sign of new private prosperity was paint. If they could afford no more, people painted their door a brilliant colour and painted a band to outline their windows. Here three small, crumbling, unpainted wood houses stood on bare treeless ground in the middle of nowhere. They were typical peasants' homes; painted, beflowered, they would be picturesque cottages. They are box-shape, one room wide, with a porch on wood pillars. If very poor, the roof is palm thatch, less poor, it is corrugated tin. I chose the worst of the three.

"Did you see that?" Rafael pointed.

I had not. Each of the houses had a TV aerial.

"Marta," Rafael said, "have you seen anyone without shoes?"

"No."

"You say everyone is too fat. When you lived here, how did the *campesinos* look?"

How did the *campesinos*, the peasants, look; how did everyone look? They looked abjectly poor or just everyday poor. Except for us, the narrow top layer. You could live in princely comfort on very little money in Cuba.

There was a farmhouse, barely visible beyond our land, east of the driveway. It was a bit larger than these houses, with peeling paint. The farmer was a bone-thin, unsmiling man; he kept chickens. If I saw him I said good morning. That is all I knew about him; I don't even know if the cook bought eggs there. The village below our place was a small cluster of houses like these; I knew nothing about the village except that it had a post office. The children waved when I drove by, I waved back, lots of smiles. They were in rags, barefoot, and everyone was unnaturally thin.

I did not say to myself: it isn't my country, what can I do? I didn't think about Cuba at all. Everything I cared about with passion was happening in Europe. I listened to the radio, bought American newspapers in Havana, waited anxiously for letters from abroad. I wrote books, and the minute I could break free, I went back to the real world, the world at war. Rafael had asked the wrong question. The right question would be: who looked at the *campesinos*? Who cared? Nobody, as far as I knew; including me.

"I know, Rafael. They were hungry and miserable."

"Those people own their houses and prefer to stay there, not move themselves to a new co-operative building which is like an apartment block."

"So would I."

"Good, if they prefer television to making their houses beautiful, that is their business. When they get more money, maybe they will improve their homes. My mama lives in a house like that. I was born in a house like that. Clearly it is better repaired."

I RETURNED TO HAVANA FROM SANTIAGO DE Cuba by air; the Lada had destroyed me. As I was about to leave Cuba, the sky cleared. On a sunny morning I collected Gregorio and we went to visit my former home, the Finca Vigía, fifteen miles outside Havana, now a museum or indeed a shrine. Gregorio is eighty-seven years old, the only link to my Cuban past and the only Cuban repository of Hemingway lore, as he was the sailor-guardian of Hemingway's boat, the *Pilar*, for twenty-three years. People come from far and wide to hear his verbatim memories, which he quotes like Scripture. Hemingway and he were the same age. His devotion to his patron-hero is genuine and time has added lustre to that devotion. The *Pilar* years were surely the best for Gregorio. He is a tall thin weather-beaten man, with calm natural dignity. He was liked and respected—thought, typically, to have the finest qualities of a Spaniard. Not that anybody troubled about his separate existence; I had never seen his house.

The Museo Hemingway, temporarily closed to the public for repairs, is wildly popular with Cubans. They come again and again, bringing picnics to spend the day, after a respectful tour of the house. The long driveway is flanked by towering royal palms and sumptuous jacaranda trees. I couldn't believe my eyes; I remembered nothing so imposing. The driveway curved to show the house, now glaring white and naked. "It looks like a sanatorium," I said. "What did they do to the ceiba?"

Forty-six years ago, I found this house through an advertisement and rented it, for one hundred dollars a month, indifferent to its sloppiness, because of the giant ceiba growing from the wide front steps. Any house with such a tree was perfect in my eyes. Besides, the terrace beyond the steps was covered by a trellis roof of brilliant bougainvillaea. Flowering vines climbed up the wall behind the ceiba; orchids grew from its trunk. All around the house were acres of high grass, hiding caches of empty gin bottles, and rusty tins, and trees. The house was almost invisible but painted an unappetizing yellow; I had it painted a dusty pale pink; the Museo changed it to glaring white. The great tree was always the glory of the finca.

"The roots were pulling up the floor of the house. The Museo had to cut it down," Gregorio said.

"They should have pulled down the house instead."

I never saw a ceiba like it, anywhere. The enormous trunk, the colour and texture of elephant hide, usually dwarfs the branches of a ceiba. But this one had branches thick as other tree trunks, spreading in wide graceful loops; it was probably several hundred years old. The house is a pleasant old one-storey affair of no special style; the six rooms are large and well proportioned, full of light.

The members of the museum staff have their office in the former garage; they are earnest, devout keepers of the shrine. I recognized all the furniture I had ordered from the local carpenter, and lapsed into giggles over the later addition of stuffed animal heads and horns on every wall. In the master's bedroom, the biggest buffalo head I had ever seen, including hundreds on the hoof, glowered over the desk. True, I had never been so close to any buffalo, living or dead. "He did not write here," said one of the staff. He wrote *For Whom the Bell Tolls* at this desk, but that was pre-buffalo.

The house depressed me; I hurried through it, eager to get back to the trees. How had I taken for granted this richness? Then it struck me: time, the years of my life at last made real. The trees had been growing in splendour for forty-one years — the immense mangoes and flamboyantes and palms and jacarandas and avocates were all here before, but young then like me.

I had definitely forgotten the size and the elegant shape of the swimming-pool. Gregorio was interested in two large cement cradles, placed where the tennis court used to be. The *Pilar* was his inheritance, he had cared for it and given it to the state, and it was to be brought here and placed on these cradles.

"Like the *Granma*," I said, and everyone looked slightly shocked at the irreverence. The *Granma* is the large cabin cruiser that bore Fidel and his followers from Mexico to Cuba in 1956: the transport of the Revolución. It is enshrined in a glass case in a small park in Old Havana. As an object of patriotic veneration, a lot jollier than Lenin embalmed. It seems that *Granma*, now the name of a province and of the major national newspaper, is simply a misspelling of Grandma, which is delightful.

The visit was as fast as I could make it — handshakes, compliments standing under a beautiful jacaranda by the garage —

and we were off to Gregorio's house in the fishing village of Cojimar. The visit to the Museo had been a duty call; it was expected. I wanted to listen to Gregorio.

In the car, I began to have faintly turbulent emotions. I remembered with what gaiety I had come to this country and how I had left, frozen in distaste of a life that seemed to me hollow and boring to die. Looking after the finca ate my time, but was worth it because of the beauty. Then Cuba became worth nothing, a waste of time. Cuba now is immeasurably better than the mindless feudal Cuba I knew. But no place for a self-willed, opinionated loner, which is what I suppose I am. Never a team-player—though I wish this team, this people, well, and hope it improves, as it has, year by year.

"Gregorio, it is a comfort that nobody is hungry."

Gregorio looked at me and smiled. "You remember that?"

"Yes."

"*Pues sí*, Marta, nobody is hungry now."

Gregorio has owned his small cement house since 1936 and it is freshly painted, sky blue and white. Gregorio was still anxious about his wife, *mi señora* he calls her in the old way, who fell off a ladder weeks ago and broke her thigh. She was waiting for us indoors, in a chair, her leg in plaster. She kissed me, told me I was "very well preserved," and they both recounted the saga of the leg. They have a telephone; the ambulance came at once; she was taken to hospital and operated on. " 'A big operation,' the doctor said." Gregorio's turn: "Very big. He said at our age the bones are like glass." She stayed twenty days in hospital, then the ambulance brought her home. The doctor from the local polyclinic came every day to check her condition, now he only comes once a week. "Not a cent, Marta, you understand. It did not cost even one centavo."

Gregorio has a monthly pension of 170 pesos (call it pre-inflation dollars); actually a large pension, due to his long work years. Still, I thought this a skimpy sum until they told me the price system: six dollars a month flat for the telephone, which is a luxury; three dollars flat for electricity—and they have an electric fridge and cooker and water heater; the colour TV is bought on the never-never, at ten percent a month of salary or pension. The food ration is extremely cheap.

"Is it enough food?"

"Yes, yes, more than enough, but if you want different things you buy them. It costs more." Clothes are also rationed and cheap; they would not need or want more than the yearly quota of shoes, shirts, underclothes, etc. "Young people care for clothes, they buy more off rations. And education is free too, Marta."

His middle-aged daughter now arrived; she is volubly enthusiastic about the new Cuba. Then his grand-daughter appeared with a pink and white baby in her arms, Gregorio's great grandson, on her way to his weekly check-up at the polyclinic. Each generation owns its little house in this village.

I felt that Gregorio was getting a trifle restive among all these females so we moved to the front porch to smoke. He brought out a bottle of Cuban rum. "As long as I have this," he said, pouring me a hefty slug, "and my cigars, I am content." Now talking soberly he said, "Marta, all the intelligentsia left, all of them." I was baffled by that word: what would Gregorio know of intelligentsia? Then I guessed he meant the world he had known with Hemingway, the Sunday parties with the jai-alai players at the finca, parties at the Cojimar pub, the carefree company of the rich and privileged, the big-game fishermen, the members of the pigeon-shooting club, and though I had never seen the Country Club he meant that circle too, since the *Pilar* was berthed there in later years. He may have missed the glamour of a life he shared and did not share. But he had met Fidel. "I think he is a good man," Gregorio said. After Hemingway left in 1959, Gregorio returned to his old profession of fisherman, then retired and became unofficial adviser to the Museo Hemingway. "I have never had any trouble with anyone."

I asked about the few Cubans I could remember by name; they had all long decamped. I asked about the Basque jai-alai players, exiles from Franco's Spain, who had fought for their homeland and lost. I loved them, brave and high-spirited men who never spoke of the past, not expecting to see their country and families again.

"They left when Batista took power. They did not like dictatorship. There was much killing with Batista, in secret. I heard that Patchi died."

"Patchi!" I was stunned. "And Ermua?" Ermua was the great *pelotari* who moved like a panther and was the funniest, wildest of them all.

"Yes, he died too."

"How could he? Why? So young?"

And suddenly I realized that Patchi was probably my age, Ermua maybe five years younger; they need not have died young.

"Gregorio, I am growing sad. Cuba makes me understand that I am old."

"I too," Gregorio laughed. "*Pues, no hay remedio.*"

My bag was packed, my bill paid, and I had nothing to do until two A.M. when I took the plane to Nicaragua. I went back to Jibacoa where I had gone in hope of snorkelling on my first day. Now the weather was the way it ought to be, brilliantly blue cloudless sky, hot sun. I went to the Cuban resort, not the foreigners' tourist domain on the hill. There were dozens of small cabins for two or four people, a boat-yard with rentable pleasure craft, an indoor recreation room, ping-pong and billiards, a snack bar to provide the usual foul American white bread sandwiches and a restaurant. The main feature was a beautiful long white sand beach, bracketed by stony headlands. Where there are rocks there are fish. I was loaned a cabin to change in and a towel: No, no, you pay nothing, you are not sleeping here. I could never decide whether I was treated with unfailing kindness because I was a foreigner or because of my age.

There were many people on the beach, looking happy in the lovely weather, all ages, sunbathing, swimming, picnicking. A young man offered me his deck-chair so that I could read and bake comfortably between swims. I put on my mask and plunged in, feeling the water cold after the storm, but bursting with joy to see familiar fish, special favourites being a shoal of pale blue ovoid fish with large smiles marked in black on their faces. In my old Cuban days, I wore motorcyclist's goggles; masks and snorkels had not been invented.

When I returned to my deck-chair at the far end of the beach, I found two small fat white bodies lying face down near me. After a while they worried me, and I warned them in Spanish that they were getting a dangerous burn. A grey-haired man sat up and said, "Spik Engleesh?" They were "Greek-Canadians" from the tourist resort above; they liked the place, they even liked the food. He said, "They work slow. No, lady, I don't think it's the climate. But they're happy. The guy who looks after our group is doing double time. For that, he gets a month off." He smiled, he shrugged.

From nine to five, the tour guide would be on hand to interpret if needed, to coddle the old if they wanted it, swim with the girls, play table tennis, eat, drink. Maybe he would take them on a day sight-seeing tour of Havana. And then, from five to one in the morning, if anyone was still awake, he would do the same, except he would drink more than swim, and dance with the girls to radio music in the bar, and of course escort them all on the big night out at the Tropicana. The Greek-Canadian's shrug and smile said clearly that he did not consider this to be hardship duty. Here was a small-scale capitalist deriding the easy life of communists. Soft communism, a comic turn-around from the dreaded American accusation: "soft on communism." I thought it the best joke yet.

GRAEME GIBSON

Santiago and beyond, 1987

"IN THE RESTAURANT OF THE HOTEL DE LAS AMERICAS. DARK
WOOD PANELLING, BIG WINDOWS THAT OPEN, WORN WHITE
TABLECLOTHS, AND A CEILING FAN. THERE'S NO BEER, BUT
A WIZENED FELLOW IN A SHINY, DARK (PROBABLY PRE-
REVOLUTIONARY) SUIT IS PLAYING NAT KING COLE SONGS
ON THE PIANO. HE'S GOOD, TOO."

*Canadian writer Graeme Gibson is the author of four novels, in-
cluding 1993's* Gentleman Death. *A past president of PEN Canada, he has won the Toronto Arts Award, the Order of Canada,
and the 1993 Harborfront Festival Prize.*

Santiago de Cuba, with a population of four hundred thousand, is Cuba's second city, located at the far eastern end of the
island. As part of the government plan to make Cuba a multi-
stop destination for visitors, Santiago has seen considerable development in recent years, with a profusion of new hotels being
built.

Santiago has much to offer. The Casa de la Trova, on Calle
Heredia, is a living shrine that preserves traditional Cuban music. Many cities have a Casa de la Trova, but Santiago's is considered the best. For a very different kind of music and evening's entertainment, there's the Tropicana, a country cousin of
the famous Havana nightclub. The cathedral, facing the tree-
shaded Parque Céspedes, is now a museum documenting the history of the Catholic church in Cuba. Next to the cathedral, the

Casagrande Hotel is the setting for a scene in Graham Greene's Our Man in Havana, *and Greene stayed here himself.*

Not far away is the Moncada barracks. Most of the space here is now a school, but part of the former military barracks is maintained as a museum documenting the revolutionary force's attack on July 26, 1953. The bullet marks are still in the walls, and the displays inside are vivid, if a bit on the bloody side. Many of Cuba's revolutionary martyrs met their deaths here.

There are beautiful beaches near the city, and Playa Daiquirí, just east of Santiago, is especially popular with Canadian visitors.

The Hotel de las Américas, where Graeme Gibson heard the piano player, is at Avenida de las Américas and General Cabreco. It has sixty-eight rooms and a swimming pool, and, as the 1996 Fodor's guide notes, "there is usually piano music."

Sunday, April 5, 1987

After a crazed seven-hour drive westward from Santiago de Cuba (the last three of them in darkness on an unfinished road), I'm writing this in a reassuringly commonplace seaside resort called Marea de Portillo. It was built, in partnership with Canadians, for tourists who fly into Manzanillo; as a result my generic room (with about as much character as transnational lite beer) could be in Brisbane, or Mobile, Alabama—or Algonquin Park. Dinner was surprisingly good, but the greyish beach at dusk looks narrow.

The Sierra Maestre, which sheltered the young Fidel and his followers, rises like a jagged black wall behind us. Much of the staff is clustered around various televisions, watching an older *El Jefe* deliver a speech at some Congress in Havana. One or other of them periodically trots out with drinks for the tourists, who are boisterously shouting and laughing by a huge bonfire on the beach. This has been going on for some time. Fidel's still a striking man, but the grainy, black-and-white images make him look washed-out and tired. None of us, however, is getting any younger.

I am here, where the Revolution began, with the hope of

finding enough spots for a series of birding trips to complement those I've been running to Zapata, by the Bay of Pigs. Or at least that's the excuse, the justification.

Three Cuban scientists are travelling with me. Orlando Garrido, whom I've known for several years, is a complex man and an indefatigable, quite remarkable ornithologist. An athletic sixty year old, he was a member of Cuba's Davis Cup team before the Revolution and runner-up, in the Canadian Open, to his brother—who is now a golf pro in Florida. Although I've seldom met a man so dedicated to his country and the work to be done, Garrido seems to have little, if any, political interest.

Dr. Gilberto Silva, an authority on bats and Director of Research at the newly established Cuban Museum of Natural Sciences in Havana, is clearly our leader. A very bright, engaging man, he's a fellow cigar lover—who enjoys a dram or two from my bottle of duty-free Famous Grouse. Clearly a fine companion.

Luis is a younger, brasher fellow. I haven't yet figured out what he does, but his cool and shadowed little house (in Santiago de Cuba) is cluttered with dusty pinned and mounted butterflies, with glassy-eyed stuffed birds and reptiles. Finally there's Pablo, our driver. Strong and paunchy, with formidably hairy forearms, he combs his hair a lot. Moreover he has a vaguely hysterical giggle and drives badly.

Because I'm on tourist business, we were assigned a "protocol" host in Santiago de Cuba. His name is Calvo, and both breast pockets of his immaculate blue shirt were filled with pens which glinted in the sun like decorations, like medals.

Clearly he had no idea of who I was and what a picayune enterprise I run, because he behaved as if I had authority or money. As if I were a potential investor. His task was to introduce me, with his persistent gravelly voice, to the wonders of Bacanao, La Riviera del Caribe. This impressive development, of eighty thousand hectares, sprawls just outside the city of Santiago. As a result we didn't escape until late afternoon. Still, Plan Bacanao is undoubtedly paying for much of this trip. So fair, I suppose, is fair.

Quick as my visit was to the city itself, I warmed to Santiago. Wooden houses with balconies and fine, lacy grilles. An impression of liveliness in the streets. A handsome cathedral and the celebrated Moncado barracks (now a school), where Fidel and his rebels made their first, abortive assault.

The city also celebrates Cuba's finest carnival. Despite the Revolution's organized seriousness, the locals have apparently managed to hang onto the spirit of chaos that properly underlies all the best carnivals. Such independence may help explain why most Cuban revolutions have found their earliest support here. . . .

Although not so widespread as in Havana, there's a helluva lot of people in the streets wearing T-shirts that advertise Capitalist Wonders from abroad. BMW, Adidas, Firestone, UCLA, European Soccer Final. It's weird the way clothing has been substituted for the actual objects. It happens at home, of course; we're all subject to the hunger for objects. But in Cuba there's no chance of owning most of what is being advertised.

Our big white American van (made in Mexico!) attracts much attention. Staring as we pass, certain men (most of them young) absently pick at their crotches. I've noticed a tendency to do this, unthinkingly, as a kind of macho gesture. It isn't clear, however, whether it is a sign of vulnerability or aggression. Perhaps both?

Finally escaping Calvo, we drove westward along the coast towards the sun. Clint Eastwood cowboys (without the guns) herded cattle among bare, thorny bushes on the flat lands between us and the mountains. Few cars, but many horseback riders on the road; some were women in straw hats and bright kerchiefs, who cantered past us with a seductive abandon. It strikes me, once again, that women here dress well, stylishly, with very limited resources.

Beyond gravel beaches slipping by to our left, the sea was a sombre oily blue. Sprawling arid streambeds were filled with dry stones. Fewer buses in Oriente, and those we've encountered are ram-jam full, so people walk long distances in the sun, often with heavy loads. Men and women wander in the shade of umbrellas, and there are lots of school kids in maroon or mustard-coloured shorts or skirts. Striking billboards encourage, cajole (demand?)—with all the optimism this beleaguered country can muster—the Power of Positive Thinking. THE

BLOOD OF HER SONS FOUNDED THE SOCIALIST STATE, and so forth. USE YOUR TIME CONSTRUCTIVELY, and VOLUNTARY WORK IS A SCHOOL FOR TRAINING THE CONSCIENCE. Then a series of five signs about fifty yards apart—like the old Burma Shave ads in the States:

THE REVOLUTION IS NOT ONLY IN YOUR HEART,
AND IN THE LIVES AND FUTURE OF YOUR CHILDREN,
IT IS IN YOUR ARMS AND HANDS,
AND IN YOUR VALLEYS AND CAVES;
AND IN ALL OF AMERICA.

My companions all talked at once, and loudly. After months establishing the new museum, doing administrative and theoretical work, they're thrilled to be in the field. Both Silva and Garrido were among a group of natural scientists who resigned from the Academy of Sciences in protest at what they believed to be a damaging lack of support for their disciplines. As a consequence (and for other reasons), there was a long stretch of time when neither man could make field trips. Or, indeed, do any "official" scientific work. The fact they are here, as senior members of the newly established museum, is a clear sign of the improvements taking place in Cuba's intellectual life.

Garrido, in particular, was high and urgent with talk, with excitement. Waving his hands and staring straight ahead, he got louder and louder, repeating phrases, almost shouting. I gather he was speculating about relationships among various species and sub-species of local reptiles. In particular, there's one that lives in the grass which might be a new species.

Eastern Cuba has been little explored scientifically. These mountains are dramatic as hell. Very dry, at the moment, they're piled close to the shore, and rise one behind the other as they progress inland. Wild and largely uninhabited, they are shot full of isolated valleys. Such terrain, like islands, can be a rich source of endemic plants and animals.

Because of the coffee and beer consumed at Bacanao, we stopped to pee. The driver did so with a macho flourish, as if putting out a four-alarm fire. After this spectacle Silva crossed the road to sit and smoke by the shore, and Garrido searched for reptiles. Rooting among logs and stones, Luis was after insects. Meanwhile I poked happily about with my binoculars in desiccated scrub bush and wonderful cacti, hoping for the Cuban gnatcatcher, or Oriente warbler, endemic species that don't occur in Western Cuba. The silence was abruptly broken by exultant shouts from Garrido. Jumping up and down, waving his arms, he appeared to be hurling rocks into an almeciga, a lovely reddish tree that reminds me of the arbutus in B.C. "Gibson!" he shouted. "Quick . . . Gibson, quick!" By the time I lumbered up he'd lost sight of what would turn out to be a very handsome giant lizard. Circling the tree, staring excitedly into the foliage, Garrido had a fist-sized stone in either hand. When he briefly caught sight of it again, with another series of shouts, he fiercely hurled his rocks, one after the other, dodging away as one rebounded almost to his feet.

I know the rationale for scientific collecting. Garrido is an indefatigable student of Cuban fauna. A legendary ornithologist, he's also discovered hitherto unknown lizards, mammals, and fish. Obviously, in order to be certain he'd found a new species, and in order to describe it adequately, he'd have to have the wretched creature in hand. On top of this, as a Cuban, often working on his own, Garrido would not have been believed without well-documented specimens. Still, I find myself troubled by the way these men must kill like small boys.

From where I stood I could see the extraordinary beast poised with heaving sides in the crotch of a bare limb. Maybe ten inches long, and chunky, it was an exquisite green, with a brilliant yellow band along the side. After a few heartbeats it crept from sight, and I should have told Garrido where it had gone, when I had the chance, but I didn't.

All that was left of the sun, when we stopped for supper in a tiny village by the sea, was a blood-red band along the horizon. Men wearing sombreros were clustered laughing and smoking in darkness beneath a pale ceiba—that great tree which the Mayans venerated because it best understood human sorrow. Unbelievably loud and terribly distorted dance music blared from a pole behind us as we filed into the restaurant, which was crowded with others watching a ball game on television. Cubans are crazy about baseball. League games are free, by the way. Whenever there's a game, men crowd intently around public televisions, and the commentary can be heard everywhere in the streets. There's almost as much interest as I found in St. Vincent, when the West Indies hosted an International Test in cricket. . . .

No choice for dinner: beef ribs, black rice, and an odd mushed banana as vegetable. Then mango marmalade and cream cheese for dessert. The beer and coffee were both welcome and good. But the noise was appalling.

Emerging, we discovered the van's battery was dead. However, since we'd parked on an incline, we managed to get going with a rolling start.

Tuesday, April 7, 1987

6:15 A.M.: A fresh but already warm breeze is blowing off the sea, and a sleepy waiter has just given me an orange, a curious sweet bun, and a demitasse of very strong coffee—which is syrupy with sugar. I'm waiting for the others before our six-and-a-half-hour drive back to Santiago de Cuba. Then it's on to Guantanamo.

My growing suspicion that this first part of the trip will prove useless, so far as birding trips are concerned, is being confirmed. We're obviously here so my companions can collect specimens for the museum. Yesterday we drove for several hours, to a village with a fine old lighthouse and a straggle of shacks along the shore. Each with a wooden privy on rickety stilts over the water. In front of one house, an ancient woman was methodically sweeping her dirt yard, with a homemade broom. Chickens and a tawdry rooster followed stupidly in her wake. Although a common-enough sight throughout Latin America and the Caribbean, there was a difference—this old soul was wearing a pair of shiny new, government-issue spectacles.

No birds to speak of, but my companions scampered happily off in search of whatever. Mostly they were hoping for slender, elegant-looking lizards called anoles. These are delicate little creatures with—depending on the species—different coloured dewlaps, or loose folds of skin, at the throat, which can be expanded when they want to show off. There have been more than twenty species of anole identified in Cuba, and Garrido is convinced there are more.

Garrido and Luis catch many of the animals by stunning them with rubber bands, expertly shot from the tip of their thumbs as kids do, then store them in carefully marked plastic bags.

I wish the tiny corpses didn't continue to bother me. . . .

Although troubled and frustrated by the relative shortage of birds, I'm delighted by the landscape. Especially by the trees. The almacigo with its graceful, often twisting cinnamon trunk and bark peeling like coloured paper. The Mayans' ceiba, a large pale creature filled with air plants that look like enormous dream porcupines. And a myriad others that I don't know. Some with heavy, elegant canopies—at a distance they resemble green mushrooms. And pine trees in the hills. With my eyes closed, hearing the wind in their branches, I could be in northern Ontario; however, when I look I see palm trees among the evergreens, and cacti among spiky scrub bush that is totally unrecognizable. The overall effect is prehistoric.

Mid-afternoon, Santiago de Cuba: In the restaurant of the Hotel de las Americas. Dark wood panelling, big windows that open, worn white tablecloths, and a ceiling fan. There's no beer, but a wizened fellow in a shiny, dark (probably pre-Revolutionary) suit is playing Nat King Cole songs on the piano. He's good, too, although lunch was mediocre. Despite the shortages and generally run-down atmosphere, I like these older hotels. If only because they're frequented by Cubans. The Havana Libre and the Riviera (Meyer Lansky's old money-maker on the Malecón) service organized tourists and businessfolk who fume in lines by the erratic pay telephones. Most of the others, the big official ones, places like the Triton or the Commodoro, in Havana, have their lobbies and elevators filled with stolid Russians or Poles, with athletes from Nicaragua or Mozambique, and all sorts of "officials" from Cuba, and God knows where else, stocking up on consumer goods in "tourist" shops. In none of them can an "ordinary" Cuban venture above the ground floor.

Still, even these hotels have their charms. I once watched a group of Russian men wrapping their companions in toilet paper on the dance floor after dinner. The women stood absolutely still, like vertical mummies, while the band played a gallumphing, repetitive melody and the men pranced about them unrolling the toilet paper. There didn't seem to be a winner, or any losers, although some did a much better job of it than others.

Nothing like that here, though. Lunch is over and most of the other patrons have left. We're waiting for the van to be returned from "an electrical specialist" because it failed us once again. We'd stopped where another ceiba burst evocatively above weedy brush. There I was delighted to find, among a mixed flock of migrants between the sea and the road, my two Oriente endemics, the Cuban gnatcatcher and the Oriente warbler. When the time came to leave, however, the van was dead. Forty-five minutes later a passing military jeep, carrying a pair of Czech geologists, gave us a boost. It turned out to be a fortuitous delay, because Garrido found only the third nesting colony of tropic birds in Cuba. . . .

Still, it's a drag.

Evening, Hotel Guantanamo: More drama with the van. After we'd waited three hours, first in the hotel, then at the protocol office, it finally appeared and we set off for Guantanamo. About thirty kilometres along the road, Luis discovered that he'd forgotten his briefcase. Much consternation and elaborate talk, until Garrido and I got out to explore while the others returned to fetch it.

We were wandering past some casuarinas (an extraordinary Australian tree that seems bent on world conquest), with a motley collection of wood warblers, indigo buntings, and local green and red-bellied woodpeckers flitting about, when Garrido suddenly bellowed and dropped to his knees. Staring as he shouted—while furiously bashing his palms against the earth— it occurred to me that he'd gone mad, or taken a fit. But it was the lizards, his grass anoles. He'd seen one, no doubt about it, and there were others. Crawling on my knees beside him, I also saw quick, dainty little forms, but we couldn't catch any. Eventually, because the others would soon be returning, I left him creeping about and returned to the road.

Waiting for the van, I smoked a cigar with my back against a post. Obviously this is not a part of the country that sees many tourists. Worn, hard-looking little men and women in faded clothing slowed down, then paused just up the road to get another look. Others peered suspiciously from nearby houses, wondering what the big gringo was doing. I remembered, with some unease, my arrest in Havana. This happened in 1984, during my first visit to Cuba. Poking about the suburbs, again with my binoculars, I apparently circled close to one of Fidel's safe houses. As a result some local worthy, a gardener I think, collared me with a "citizen's arrest." It was five hours before I was released from a large and busy police station. How long would it take down here?

Garrido finally joined me with three small, limp bodies. No longer quick and graceful, they were deflated, nondescript. He was hugely excited. And oddly tender. Picking at them, extending a leg, the tail, staring at the adhesive pads on their delicate feet, he decided they were almost certainly new to science.

It was more than two hours before Silva and Luis returned, this time in a small Alfa Romeo with a new driver. It wasn't their tales of a broken distributor and the van bursting into flames, but Garrido's discovery that preoccupied them as we sped off at breakneck speed.

Wednesday, April 8, 1987

At Rio Yumuri in the mountains between Guantanamo and Baracoa, after a dramatic drive up a good, steeply curving road among red hills shot through with green basalt. The gang is off, once again, searching for insects and reptiles. They're well pleased with the trip so far, and seem to be making a good haul—which they keep on ice in the trunk.

In the first town where we stopped for lunch, back down there on the plain, there wasn't a restaurant. In the second there was, but it didn't open until 12:30. At the third, half an hour further on, we were presented with a choice of tinned

fish, or eggs, and rice, bean soup, and the ubiquitous marmalade with cheese. No beer or soft drinks, and no ice. . . .

Although I've searched, there are few birds, and time runs
on. No cars pass on the road, and only a couple of trucks have
laboured by. A worried hen tries to supervise her insanely peeping chicks behind me, and a plump turkey revels in its dust
bath to my right. There's a breeze up here, but the sun is extremely hot and I'm surrounded (but ignored) by brown-eyed,
slow moving men. All of them very short.

I wish I could relax and enjoy myself. It's an intriguing,
complex, and lovely country. My companions are terrific. But
the dreaded "business" meeting with the director of Plan Bacanao at the end of the week preys on my mind. Unless we're
surprised by something very good, it will be difficult, if not impossible, to put a positive face on our "business" discussions.
What can I say to justify his investment?

Moreover the van seems gone for good. Kaput. The Alfa
Romeo is too small to be comfortable, too close to the ground,
and much too old for rough roads. So we've had to abandon
what might have been a rewarding side trip.

Baracoa, late afternoon: Baracoa, which was Cuba's capital
from 1512 to 1515, is lusher, much more tropical, more "Caribbean" than the rest of the country. A punishing sun, and great
humidity, but here on a hill overlooking the glistening town,
with its red-tiled roofs and masses of flowering trees and
shrubs, there's a fine breeze.

On October 27, 1492, Columbus first landed, in Cuba, on
the unprepossessing crescent of sand that curves just below our
hotel. This was, he said, "the most beautiful land ever seen."
Even now it is hard to disagree. Only twenty years after Columbus, a certain Diego Velázquez arrived with three hundred conquistadores and orders from Spain to conquer the island.
Among his company were Hernando Cortés, and the remarkable priest—known as the "Apostle of the Indians"—Barto-
lomé de las Casas. On the other side was Hatuey, an heroic
but doomed leader of the resistance, who managed to pin the
Spaniards down for three months before being captured, then
burned at the stake. The rest, as they say, is history.

There's a predictably good Cuban beer called Hatuey.

It is now raining gently. A radio plays rhumbas in one of the public rooms to my left. I'm drinking a glass of Cuba's great seven-year-old dark rum while smoking a cigar under the sheltered walkway facing a garden full of brilliant flowers and small coconut palms. At its far end there's a living fence, which was made (according to Silva, who just left me to shower before dinner) by planting lengths of *piñon flordito,* close together, in the earth. The sticks soon take root and grow interlocking branches, thus providing an almost impenetrable wall.

Beyond the fence rises a massive hill called El Yunque, or Sleeping Beauty, and behind it another forbidding range of mountains. Dispossessed Indians, runaway slaves, along with all sorts of rebels and renegades, have, for centuries, sought and found sanctuary in those hills. For all I know there are fugitives up there now.

I've really taken to Gilberto Silva. He's elegant, smart, humorous, very experienced, and sad. Wonderful talks about Cuban history, and what the Revolution has meant for this country. The profound gains it has made. Silva was here in Baracoa before the Revolution. There were no roads over the mountains then; he had to come in by boat. It was poor, he said. Terribly poor and without schools. Because the people were so exploited by the landowners, they took to the Revolution right away.

I have been told (although not by him) that Silva was invited to a conference in the States in the early sixties. The American authorities immediately seized him. After being interned for several months, in Florida, he was deported as an "undesirable alien." Back in Cuba it was decided, because he'd been locked up by the CIA and FBI, that he must have been "turned around." So he was sent to prison on the Isle of Youth.

Great stuff, too, about Cuban natural history. Especially the bats—one of which catches fish at night. It has developed a sonar that adjusts to the distortion created by water. And the extraordinary caves found in Cuba. Both the longest and the second deepest caves in Latin America are here.

In my half-a-dozen visits during the past three years, I've encountered others who have suffered within Cuba's defensive, ideological, and often arbitrary political culture. Most have been punished with "under-employment" and/or a loss of privileges. Some have been imprisoned. Despite this, the majority I know remains committed to the ideals of the Revolution. To the best that it has accomplished. Whatever it is they want for the country's future, it's not a return to the status of a de facto, neo-liberal American colony. They retain real affection for Fidel. And a puzzled, spine-stiffening resentment at the intensity of American opposition—the prospect of what Washington seems to want for their country.

I guess our equivalent would be Joe Clark's remarkably sustained loyalty to the Conservatives, his willingness to beaver away on the party's behalf after its cruel treatment of him. Which says something about faith, I suppose, and conviction.

Thursday, April 9, 1987

I'm sitting on an orange, fifties-style, free-form chair in the lobby. Garrido and Silva talk energetically, a telephone rings unanswered, a woman is calling for someone loudly, and there's a radio playing around the corner.

I'm intrigued by the way Cubans repeat themselves in free-flowing conversations. Instead of "yes," it's "yes-yes-yes," and they come back to phrases. Someone's name, for example: "Roberto, yes-yes-yes, Roberto Sendina. From Havana. Sendina . . . I remember him. Roberto Sendina."

Wonderful visit with Anfiloquio Suarez Castillanos; an older man (seventy-two, or something) who was having a bit of trouble with his false teeth. Known as *El Rubio,* he's a farmer. Also an amateur but expert naturalist who started Baracoa's zoo—donating many animals from his own collection. Professionals in Havana, people like Silva and Garrido, have long depended on him for information about the region—as well as for useful specimens, of course. At the same time, he's a fierce conservationist, one who has evidently converted many of the local kids. Returning from a guided tour of his property, we encountered a trio of ten-year-old boys, who were studiously watching a small pink constrictor—a rubber boa—entwining itself around a fence rail. Few snakes are fortunate enough to survive such encounters with young human males. . . .

Robust and genial, *El Rubio* is a fascinating guy. Although a landowner, he was quick to join the revolutionaries, whereupon Batista's forces razed his home and farm. A deadly shot, he distinguished himself, and after the triumph of the Revolution he returned to rebuild everything. Not long after, discovering the revolution had turned Communist, he dashed back into the hills to join the fight against his former comrades. The rebels were eventually captured. *El Rubio* spent a number of years in jail, then returned to his farm. There's a prominent, most engaging picture of Fidel on his sheltered verandah; an equally large painting of the Virgin is displayed just inside the living room door.

Friday, April 10, 1987

Santiago de Cuba: Last night, after some delay, we flew back here in a Russian Yak 40, which carries maybe forty-five passengers.

This evening I return to Havana. In the morning it's back to Toronto.

The dreaded meeting with the Director General of Plan Bacanao, which was scheduled for last night at nine o'clock, didn't start until he arrived, from another meeting, just after ten. A strong-looking, tough-looking man with a palpable air of authority, he put me very much on guard at first. Poor, worried Calvo and a small-moustached, expressionless middle-level bureaucrat hovered about while we trudged through the preliminary talk. We explained that we hadn't found an effective focus for my trips. He said there were lots of birds. We said the reserve at Zapata (where my other trips go) had been thoroughly studied and explored, but there hadn't been enough work done here to find the "hot spots." The mood got a bit dicey, a bit sharp and persistent. Meetings with Cubans often begin like this, especially when you're dealing with those in authority. At first there's an obligatory formality, all masks and ceremonious talk, but with many people that soon collapses and the individual reveals himself. It's almost as if Cubans are too gregarious, too curious, to maintain the bureaucratic pose—although, God knows, I've met some who revelled in their abstract power!

In any event, while we were sipping our second glass of rum and nibbling small canapés prepared by Calvo, the Director General abruptly, and quite wistfully, confessed the delight he finds in nature. He'd love to go birding with us, to wander and learn from people like Silva, he said. But his boss didn't understand anything except work and more work. It seemed a wonderful, disarming gesture, and it won us all over. I have begun to sense there's a whole bunch of upper-middle bureaucrats in Cuba who work compulsively, trying to carry the country on their backs. In their late forties or early fifties, they look a decade older. Below them, it often seems, there's inertia; above them an entrenched officialism. In Havana I was told by a serious man that it's not the Party that runs Cuba, but the bureaucracy. The Party, he said, is the opposition. . . .

The Director General is also a problem-solver. As a result we came away with a perfectly respectable proposal for a series of nature cruises, in a good-sized yacht they own. Although it may or may not work out, it's a terrific idea. In the event, we'll see.

A touching moment at dinner, just before we left Baracoa last night. Casually but studiously, Garrido and Silva told me that, should the little grass anole prove to be a new species, they were going to name it after me. *Anolis gibsoni,* or whatever the Latin might be. I was utterly taken aback. We've travelled a long way together, and I've come to admire and love these men. And their country. Perhaps as a result, I was surprisingly moved by their gift. And secretly embarrassed by my unspoken and sentimental difficulties with the collecting of animal specimens. Even now, remembering three little corpses in Garrido's hand, I find it ironic, curious to say the least, that these lizards (and their kind) might carry my name. The trio, which are somewhere still on ice, will have paid heavily for that unlikely honour.

CARLO GÉBLER

At the beach, Santa Maria and Varadero, 1987

"A CHEVROLET, A RED 1952 DELUXE STYLELINE SPORTS
COUPÉ, RUMBLED PAST. THE SHADOWS OF THE PALM TREES
LAY ACROSS THE CROPPED GRASS AS IF THEY'D BEEN
PAINTED THERE. THERE WAS A DISTANT VIEW OF TWO MEN
SWINGING THEIR GOLF CLUBS. IT WAS LIKE STUMBLING
INTO A RICH MIAMI SUBURB IN THE 1950S."

*Varadero Beach, sixty miles or so east of Havana on Cuba's
north coast, facing the Florida Strait, is Cuba's oldest and best-
known resort area. Varadero is actually on the narrow Hicacos
Peninsula, twelve miles of white sand beaches jutting out north-
eastward from the coast.*

*Varadero has seen four periods of concentrated growth. At
the end of the nineteenth century, wealthy people from the
nearby city of Cárdenas began building luxurious summer villas
on the beach here. Then, in the 1920s, the millionaire Irénée
Du Pont bought a very large piece of beachfront property here,
large enough for a dock to accommodate a yacht and a seaplane,
a landing strip for another aircraft, a golf course, gardens, and a
mansion rich enough in size and decor to be suitably named,
with a nod toward Samuel Taylor Coleridge, Xanadu. It boasted
a sumptuous dining room, a wine cellar, a library, nine bedrooms, and a top-floor ballroom, all of it done up properly with
marble from Carrara, Italy, and Cuba's own Isle of Pines and
with walls of ebony, cedar, and mahogany. And there was*

enough land left over for Du Pont to sell to other millionaires, who soon put up nice places for themselves nearby.

With tourism reaching grand heights after World War II, another major building period, geared to less ostentatiously wealthy visitors, began in 1950 with the opening of the Internacional Hotel right on the best beach on the peninsula. Among the Internacional's attractions, of course, was a gambling casino. Throughout the next four decades, new hotels continued to rise along the beaches, the Kawama, the Siboney, the Atabey, and the Bellamar, among others. And as the resort developed, the private villas along this same stretch of beach were converted into additional luxurious hotels.

And now, in the 1990s, Varadero is booming again. In 1990, the Spanish hotel chain Grupo Sol-Meliá, which owns nearly two hundred properties around the world and is well represented in Latin America, opened the six-hundred-room Sol Palmeras. And, repeating their successful policy in Cancun, Mexico, they have since opened two additional hotels at Varadero. Other international hotel chains, in joint ventures with the Cuban authorities, are doing likewise, and by the time this book is published, Varadero will have Cuba's first Club Med.

THE BEACH

The next morning, when I woke up, the sun was shining behind the half-closed shutters. Pulling open the drawer of the bedside bureau, I saw a telephone directory lying there. Idly I started leafing through, expecting names which were African, French, and Chinese, a summary of the racial history of the country, but they were all disappointingly Spanish. I put it away and made a telephone call to a friend of a friend.

We were invited to the beach for the day and met Eleanor in the foyer. She was about forty years old and had a long face. She was a journalist.

Outside Eleanor had a black Volga, the Soviet motor industry's equivalent to the Oldsmobile. There were no number plates but an enormous cardboard sign stuck to the windscreen announcing, "Number plates coming."

She drove us all slowly down the street. No longer unfamiliar, Vedado, with its mess of colonial houses, Gaudi-inspired apartment blocks, and skyscrapers, suddenly looked fake; fake like the buildings in Californian cities. One good strong wind and the whole lot would blow into the sea, I thought.

At the end of the street, some half dozen blocks away, was the sea. We turned onto the Malecón, the wide highway which runs parallel, carrying Havana's traffic from east to west, and drove out of the city.

Santa Maria was about twenty-five miles from Havana. Because it was Sunday, the beach was crowded.

We spread our towels on the white, coarse, spotless sand. It was an overcast day but the heat of the sun seeped through the cloud. The ocean was an inky blue.

One of the most memorable passages in *Our Man in Havana* is the description of the city as a conveyor belt for the manufacture of beauty. Even the most cursory glance around showed this to be true. What was also remarkable, as Greene had also said, was the racial mix. On the beach the colour of the people stretched from purest white with blue eyes and blonde hair to deepest black with olive eyes and curly hair and with every possible shade and combination of features in between. A sense of the island's racial history and its diversity wasn't to be culled from the telephone directory, but was to be seen at first hand on the sand by the edge of the sea.

A young man splashed out of the foam in front of us and stopped a few feet away.

He took a comb from the side of his tiny trunks and carefully started grooming his hair.

A girl came out of the ocean and led him past us. She wore a swimsuit with an enormous open "V" from between her breasts to just above her groin.

The couple went up to a crowd of young people. They sank down and he put his head on her lap. She took the comb and started on the thick black hair—first his head, then his chest.

Looking around the group, it was evident that everyone had paid close attention to their own appearance, especially the girls. Bikini, lipstick, handbag, jewellery, shoes: everything was matched.

"Cuban girls are lovers of glamour," Eleanor said. "They

melt down toothbrushes to make pendants, horrible, lumpy, green blobs, and from the cardboard inner linings of bottle tops, they make earrings."

Someone in the group had a ghettoblaster, with plastic bags around the base to protect it from the sand. It was tuned to a radio station in Miami, only eighty miles away to the north. From the speakers drifted the voice of Paul McCartney, followed by details of an accident in the Miami suburb of Coral Gables. A young black of fifteen or sixteen asked me to sell him some dollars. I said no and he slid away, diffidently wiping the sand off that had stuck to his body.

We ate in a restaurant overlooking the sea, flaky salty fish with the texture of mullet, and drank Hatüey beer. There were no salads or vegetables, barring potatoes.

"The lorry with them didn't come this morning," the waitress explained.

Eleanor told the story of Rosa, a young student who was having an affair with a foreigner. The relationship was frowned upon at the university by the tutors, and so Rosa started carrying around the Cuban constitution. Whenever any criticisms were levelled, she would brandish it and say, "Tell me . . . where it is written, it is forbidden to love a man who isn't Cuban . . . ?"

"If the government wants more tourists," I said, "fraternisation is inevitable."

"It will be discouraged," said Eleanor.

"By whom?"

She pointed at the policeman in the corner in a tight blue uniform. He was eating a large, pink ice-cream.

"Cubans can be called to account for what they are doing," she added mysteriously.

We got back to Havana late in the afternoon. As we were coming from the old part of the city towards the Hotel Colina, I noticed a piece of graffiti. It was on the corner of a building opposite the university steps. It said *"Batista Asesino,"* a phrase that needs no translation. It had obviously been the work of a student radical in the 1950s but could it be original after so many years?

"Is it genuine?" I asked.

"Yes, it is."

"Are you sure?"

"Oh yes, it's genuine." There was a pause and then she continued, "Of course, they touch it up every year, just the same."

VARADERO

We left Havana on Monday. We drove along the Malecón, took the tunnel under the harbour, and emerged on the eastern side. Our destination was Varadero, a resort about sixty miles further along the northern coast.

A friend had given us advice. On the far side of the tunnel, we would find ourselves on a six-lane highway. We would see a small turning off it, marked Playa del Este. Strange as it might seem, that was the road we were to take for Varadero. If we stayed on the highway, it would take us in the opposite direction, doubling back under the city and ending in Mariano on the other side.

But when we got to the turning marked Playa del Este it looked so small, and there was no mention of Varadero, and the road we were on was a huge six-lane carriageway. Surely there was a mistake? Carry on, I thought.

An hour later we indeed found ourselves in the western suburb of Mariano.

We turned the car on a bridge over a muddy brook where boys were fishing with rods of bamboo.

When we finally got onto the right road, the way east took us past one of the ubiquitous shooting ranges. From the frequency of these I had begun to imagine Cuba as a militarised society. This range had metal cut-outs of tanks, helicopters, and infantrymen in U.S. army metal hats, but the complete picture undercut the first impression because, among the targets, which were painted white, there was a herd of defecating cows, unconcernedly loosing off their stools all over the range. Beyond here the landscape was rolling. There were quarries for red stone, slogans on the old advertising hoardings about Fidel and the party marching towards the year 2000—the same as on the matches—and parked outside a café called the Cafeteria

Americas, a 1955 New Yorker sedan, which was a Chrysler car, with a pillar-box-red body and a cream roof.

Somewhere near Santa Cruz del Norte, a girl was standing by the side of the road trying to thumb a ride. We pulled up in a cloud of dust and she climbed in. She was small and carried an Aeroflot bag.

Her name was Maria, and soon she was telling us about herself and giving us her opinions. There was no order to what she said; everything just tumbled out. The Cuban people were lazy because once they had a job it was forever and there was no incentive to work. She only had the clothes she was wearing, because the night before someone had broken into the room in Havana where she'd been sleeping, and taken her suitcase with everything in it. She was nearly thirty and had studied philology in Czechoslovakia for five years. Now she had returned, she could not find a job in her field, and was working as a translator for Czech geologists. Whatever the government said, there was serious unemployment in Cuba and we weren't to believe otherwise. She was on her way to her parents in Santa Clara for a few days. She had intended to take the bus, but in the Havana bus depot the queues were so long she'd decided to hitch to Varadero and try to pick up a bus there. Her economic situation was terrible. She was paid 190 pesos a month. After contributions to the Federación de Mujeres Cubanas (the Federation of Cuban Women), the CDR (the Committee for the Defence of the Revolution), the Territoriales (the militia), and the Sindicato (the trade union in the workplace), she was left with 176 pesos a month. Food and rent in Havana took 120 pesos a month, which left her with just over 50 pesos a month to go to the cinema, buy cigarettes, and buy clothes. With a pair of jeans costing 150 pesos it was not enough. Life was very hard for the Cuban people and there was much discontent.

"To make ends meet, many Cubans turn to the black market, buying and selling dollars," she said, and leant forward into the front of the car holding one wrist over the other.

"One year for each dollar they are caught with," she added dramatically.

I had no idea what to make of her long, breathless diatribe. I was in the front passenger seat and I looked out of the front window. We were coming into the town of Matanzas (the Spanish word for "slaughter"). Just in front of us was a policeman on his Italian motorcycle, spurs flashing on his heels, rocking backwards and forwards like a metronome as the road curved. There were people beside the road and I thought we'd stumbled into a political parade. Then I realised the crowd was a queue, a long, long queue. Maria saw them too and, catching my attention by squeezing my elbow, archly raised her eyebrows when I turned round to her.

She pulled an airmail letter out of her Aeroflot bag.

"I am learning Italian," she said. "Last year at Varadero I met an Italian couple. They were like you, husband and wife."

She repeated this.

"We became very good friends. This is where they live."

She pointed at the address on the back of the envelope.

"Do you know La Spezia in Italy?"

I said I thought La Spezia was a town where Byron had stayed.

"They invited me to Italy for a holiday," Maria continued. "They sent me money for the ticket. I went to immigration with the money and they said I couldn't go. They said Italy was a capitalist country."

Her brown eyes filled with tears.

We were on a plateau of volcanic rock beside the sea, with oil derricks see-sawing on either side of the road, and pipes flaming in the distance. This was where all of Cuba's indigenous oil was produced.

A few miles later we came to the town of Varadero. The resort lies at the base of a long finger of sand which stretches twenty miles out into the Atlantic, a town of palm trees and big old hotels. A few U.S. cars and a number of holiday-makers on Soviet bicycles cruised along the wide streets. In the 1930s the U.S. industrialist, Irénée Dupont, bought many properties in Varadero and built an estate on the peninsula beyond the town. In the 1950s came the hotels, many U.S.-financed, including the Varadero International, a close relation of Miami's Fontainebleau. After the revolution the speculative hotel-building stopped, and after President Kennedy's "quarantine" in 1961, so did the U.S. tourists.

We went through the town and passed out the other side. Before we dropped Maria at the bus station or found our house, we were going to visit the old Dupont mansion. Maria pointed out Fidel's Varadero house, a guard at the gate and aerials sticking out of its roof, and a moment later we passed through the gateway into the old Dupont estate and started to cruise along a straight road which rose and fell like a roller coaster. There were immaculate, undulating golf links on one side and the blue sea on the other.

A Chevrolet, a red 1952 DeLuxe Styleline sports coupé, rumbled past. The shadows of the palm trees lay across the cropped grass as if they'd been painted there. There was a distant view of two men swinging their golf clubs. It was like stumbling into a rich Miami suburb in the 1950s.

We neared the Dupont house. It was an elegant, white mansion. It overlooked a beach lined with palm trees. The sun was sinking and the crests of the waves were points of silver. All this had once belonged to one family of North Americans. After the revolution the house had been nationalised by the state and turned into an extremely grand restaurant, with the dining room on the first floor in the old library.

"That's where the servants lived," said Maria, pointing to dreary outbuildings which looked like a cross between stables and an almshouse. Of course, I thought, the servants of the Duponts would have lived worse than their masters and every post-revolutionary Cuban would be brought up to know that. But Maria's tone was utterly mechanical and quite unlike the way she'd been talking all afternoon. I sensed she was going through the motions out of habit.

At the top of the entrance steps, there was a flunkey in a Louis Quinze chair whose job it was to keep Cubans out. We spoke English very loudly and brought Maria in. We went to the bar in what had once been the wine cellar. The walls and the niches where the bottles had been stored were covered with new cement, and the customers' voices echoed off these surfaces. There were two or three South American women in flounced gypsy dresses with tight bodices which showed off their bosoms. Their escorts were neat men with impenetrable expressions. They were to go skiing at Easter but the ladies were tired of Bariloche in Argentina. Dupont has gone, only to be replaced with more of the same.

We had arranged to rent a room in a house in Varadero. We dropped Maria off and found it a couple of blocks away from the bus depot, at the end of a short street which ran down to the beach.

Casa C—— was made of yellow stone, two storeys high. Upstairs there were bedrooms with sloping roofs and tiny windows, and bathrooms filled with English sanitary ware, old, heavy, and fed by lead pipes which chattered and rumbled when the taps were run. The atmosphere was similar to a run-down country house in Ireland. Downstairs was different. In the kitchen there was a gigantic U.S. refrigerator, its door corroded by rust but still functioning within; a dilapidated stove missing its bakelite knobs—the gas controls were turned up and down with a knife; and an extraordinary freezer, circa 1950, which had long since been turned off because it gave terrible electric shocks to anyone who went near it. Piled in the cupboard and scattered on the worktops was an amazing array of culinary Americana. Aluminium saucepans, pressure cookers, whisks, ladles, ice-cream scoops, egg slicers, meat hammers, early electric mixers, omelette pans, and plastic beakers, along with a great deal else which I didn't recognise. But whilst as a museum it was interesting, as a place to cook the kitchen was infuriating—only one sharp knife and no vegetable peeler.

The rest of the ground floor was taken up by a huge living room. There were two refectory dining tables with a wooden candelabrum hanging above, bookcases, and immense leather sofas hollowed with use and age. At the end of the room there were buckled french windows. They opened onto the garden with its dribbling shower, washing line, and rickety wooden sun-seats. A low wall split by cracks boxed in Casa C——, and beyond it lay the gentle incline of the beach and finally, a dozen paces away, the sea. The other guests were Raoul, a young Cuban, and Kate, his girlfriend, and her two children. Kate was English and worked for the Cuban press agency, Prensa Latina.

The first morning I woke up and saw a sloping roof above,

and heard the murmur of the sea. A few minutes later I found Raoul lying on the sand, below the garden wall, reading a book. We walked out into the water together and at waist depth slid down and started to float on our backs. Raoul was talking about the Cuban press. "It tolerates no dissent," he said. I noticed how warm the water was and how silky it felt on the skin, it was like no water I had swum in before.

When I came out I found Maria on the beach. She was a tiny figure, sitting on her haunches, her Aeroflot bag beside her, staring out to sea. Uncharitably, I found myself wondering if she had lingered in Varadero in order to attach herself to us. None the less, I asked her to come inside. When she said she wouldn't I sensed she knew what I'd just been thinking. Finally, I insisted she came in out of the sun, and sitting inside at one of the enormous dining tables, she told me there had been no room on the evening bus. She had had to stay overnight in a hotel. "It was horrible," she added. "I had an argument with a policeman." She wouldn't tell me what the argument was about, only that all policemen were awful. It was a verbal giveaway, the tip of an iceberg, there was a huge bulk of story beneath the surface. I kept questioning but I got no further, and I only found out about it all much later.

Towards midday Maria left, having extracted a promise to visit her.

Every morning in Varadero, at around ten o'clock, I would go with Tyga and India to the little *bodega* or grocery store on the corner of the bus-depot building. Here we would buy bread, butter, milk, and eggs, which were all freely available, unrationed. This was what we lived off, along with what Kate gave us.

The woman behind the counter in the shop had a moustache and the curious habit of always serving two or three customers simultaneously. Sometimes we would see her with poor customers, men in filthy, frayed trousers and greasy hats, opening a packet of Popular cigarettes and counting them out ten, five, or even two, and then giving them a few matches to take away.

On the third or fourth morning she gave India four *gallé-*

tas, the ubiquitous sweet biscuits sold loose, and then advised us to buy some.

"If you don't, you'll regret it," she said, "we'll soon be out of them again."

As they were being weighed up and bagged, I looked at the shelves. There were gigantic jars of tomato paste, available only on the ration and essential for eating pasta, bottles of banana liquor, and bags of sugar, vanilla, and macaroni. That was about all. The display under the glass-topped counter consisted solely of Sputnik razors and razor blades.

Our bill was written out on the corner of a coarse brown paper bag and added up twice. We paid* and went next door to the *puesto.* It was a tiny, dark, windowless room which sold fresh produce. As usual there were only potatoes and cabbages.† Because these were white they glowed faintly in the near darkness.

The proprietor was a black man in a straw hat with a gold front tooth. Hearing our appalling Spanish as we ordered, he lifted up a box hidden under the counter. It was filled with green peppers. He didn't need to tell us to buy because soon he'd be out of them. We ordered as many kilos as we thought we decently could without seeming to be greedy.

Outside again we blinked in the sun. We were now in the parking lot of the bus depot. Between two battered coaches, an old green 1953 Cambridge club sedan out of the Plymouth corporation, with the flow-through bumper lines and the one-piece windshield, stood with its bonnet up. Steam poured out of the engine and water cascaded from the radiator onto the tarmac. "Cardenas," the name of the nearest town to Varadero, was painted on the roof above the windscreen, for this was a *maquina,* one of the inter-city taxis. The owner stood nearby with a baseball hat pushed well back on his head, staring in

* We had bought two litres of milk, seventy-five cents each; six eggs, twenty-five cents each; two loaves, eighty cents each; one packet of butter, eighty cents; and a kilo of *galletas,* eighty cents: total, six pesos twenty cents.
† They were in season and cheap. At other times of the year, they might have been expensive, scarce, and/or rationed. During the journey I heard numerous complaints that Cuba's *puestos* offered appalling quality produce and little or no choice.

disbelief and pain and shouting, "Why? Why? . . ." It was like an illustration from a Norman Rockwell cartoon.

A few steps further on brought us to the entrance to the ticket hall. Inside, passengers milled around the counters. A youth showed a friend the numbered ticket he'd been given, and they calculated how many buses before he'd get a seat.

They came down the steps past us and set off towards the *maquinas* standing in a row on the other side of the lot. They approached a bulbous 1950 Lincoln sports sedan distinguished by its sunken headlamps. It had "Matanzas" written on it. We watched as they entered negotiations with the driver. He wouldn't leave until he had six passengers, he said—this was quite normal—and the youths turned away.

When we got home, I found Kate in the kitchen making Russian tea in an extraordinary strainer shaped like an auto-da-fé hat.

"We've got some peppers."

"Whoopee," she said. "We'll have those tonight, we're going to have some of my meat ration."

Cuba's rationing system can be interpreted—depending on the ideological view of the interpreter—as proof that the government is economically inept, or as proof that Cuba is a just society.

Cuba's per capita income in the 1950s—about $500 per person*—was higher than any other Latin American country except Venezuela (which had oil) and Argentina (which was relatively industrialised). There was plenty of food, and in terms of meat availability—*the* benchmark of prosperity in food terms among developed nations—the island could boast of seventy pounds per person annually, twice Peru's figure.

But for the poor, the landless, and the marginal, perhaps two and a half or three million out of a population of seven million, life was economically harsh. Whilst seventy pounds of meat were theoretically available, in fact only four percent of the families of farmworkers ate meat regularly according to the

* All statistics, unless otherwise stated, are taken from *No Free Lunch: Food and Revolution in Cuba Today,* Medea Benjamin, Joseph Collins, and Michael Scott.

Catholic University Association survey of 1956–57. Only two percent of such families consumed eggs on a regular basis (they had to sell their eggs instead), only eleven percent drank milk on a regular basis, and so on.

In pre-revolutionary Cuba, if you were wealthy you ate well, and if you were not you ate poorly. There are no official figures, but opinions incline to the view that the bottom twenty percent of Cuban society received about six percent of the national income, while the top twenty percent had about fifty percent of it.

The reason for these inequalities of income was the concentration of land, factories, and so on in the hands of a small proportion of the population. In the 1950s this is how Cuban society was organised. First, the countryside. At the top were the owners of the sugar plantations and the cattle ranches. About nine percent of the farm owners possessed about sixty percent of the land. At the opposite end of the ownership scale, a good sixty percent owned seven percent of the land. Next down the ladder were about a hundred thousand tenants who owned no land at all but rented, often for exorbitant amounts. Finally, at the very bottom, there were nearly half a million farmworkers. They, along with their families, comprised about a third of the population.

Only about ten percent of these farmworkers were permanently employed. The rest were only certain of work during the cane harvest from January to May and were usually unemployed for the rest of the year.

In the cities there was a similar unemployed under-class (estimates of their numbers vary) who survived by washing cars, selling lottery tickets, stealing and begging. Above these were about a quarter of a million Cubans who lived off the tourist trade, as shoeshine boys, street vendors, prostitutes, pimps, pedlars, and entertainers. Above them were the urban workers, about 400,000 of them and enjoying good incomes, on average about $1,600 a year, a high sum by Latin American standards. Next, there were those who worked in local or national government, about ten percent of all those employed. In 1950 an extraordinary eighty percent of the national budget was spent on their salaries. This type of work provided—besides a wage—

numerous opportunities for personal enrichment. Finally, at the very top were the tiny majority who enjoyed the lion's share of the national income. Hugh Thomas, in his history, *Cuba,* estimates there were more Cuban millionaires—dóllar millionaires—than anywhere else in the Americas south of Dallas.

In terms of housing, health care, education, and literacy, the pattern in Cuba in the 1950s was exactly what one would expect with the distribution of wealth as it was. There was little food to eat if you were poor. There was nothing of anything else.

In the countryside, two-thirds of the houses were palm-thatched—which was probably not such a hardship considering the semi-tropical climate—and without toilets, which certainly was. Less than three percent of all rural houses had running water, and only one in fourteen families enjoyed electricity.

In the cities, the poor lived as squatters in makeshift shacks, or in cramped tenements. A fifth of Cuba's urban dwellers—and the average family size was five—lived in one room.

Education was dire. According to the World Bank, about 180,000 children started first grade but only about 5,000 entered eighth grade. By 1958 over half of Cuban children of primary-school age (six to fourteen) were not attending school at all. (The Latin American average was about thirty-six percent.) One in four Cubans over the age of ten could not read or write.

Onto this situation, one then has to graft Cuba's particular underdevelopment. Sugar is Cuba's principal industry, principal export, principal employer. Sugar was and is both Cuba's curse and her greatest asset. Cane thrives in Cuba's soil and climate like nowhere else in the world. It grew, and grows still, prolifically and effortlessly. It was a generator of sometimes fabulous wealth. For instance in 1920, the greatest year in the whole history of Cuban sugar production, the world price of sugar rose from nine and one-eighth cents a pound on 18 February, the first day of the harvest, to twenty-two and a half cents a pound on 19 May, the end of the harvest. It made plantation owners and investors rich. For the agricultural workforce on the other hand, it was a capricious provider. During the harvest it offered backbreaking round-the-clock employment, cutting or milling, but the rest of the year was a dead season with almost no work except for a little re-planting. *Sopa de gallo* (rooster soup) formed an important part of the rural diet during the idle months. It was a mixture of water and brown sugar.

At the turn of the century, Cuba was the largest producer and exporter of sugar in the world. By the 1950s she had slipped to seventeenth amongst the world's eighteen top sugar-producing nations. None the less, manufacturing sugar from cane remained the country's largest industry, and the entire economy was inextricably linked to it. For instance, the sugar estates and the mills were the principal customers of the railways. Half of all bank loans went to the sugar industry. Raw sugar and its by-products, alcohol and molasses and so on, accounted for eighty percent of the country's exports. When the world price of sugar fell, the country's economy went into spasm.

In 1955 U.S. interests owned nine of the ten largest sugar mills, produced forty percent of the island's sugar, and controlled fifty-four percent of the total grinding capacity. Standard Oil, Shell, Texaco, Procter and Gamble, Colgate-Palmolive, Firestone, Goodrich, Goodyear, Coca-Cola, Pepsi-Cola, Canada Dry, and Orange Crush all had subsidiaries in Cuba. U.S. firms directly employed 160,000 workers in the country itself. Overall, the U.S. had a billion dollars invested in Cuba—an eighth of the total U.S. investment in Latin America—and Cuba as a recipient of investment was second only to Venezuela. This is not taking into account the considerable *mafioso* involvement in Cuba which is impossible to estimate.

But more important than what the U.S. owned (which in percentage terms had anyway been declining since the nineteenth century) was the fact that each year the U.S. Congress made the single most important decision in relation to the Cuban economy. As they had since 1934, they set the quota of Cuban sugar that could be imported into the U.S. market at the relatively high prices of the U.S. domestic producers. Over the twenty-five years to 1959, Cuba exported about sixty percent of her sugar to the U.S. The economy was thus not only dependent on a single crop, but on a single customer.

The U.S. quota did not come for nothing. In return for preferential entry into the U.S. for some of its sugar (along with some of its rum and leaf tobacco which was tied to the same agreement), import duties on a large variety of U.S. goods were cut; Cuba agreed not to increase existing duties on a number of other products; Cuban internal taxes on U.S. goods were cut or reduced; and there was free conversion of pesos into dollars, which allowed capital to be moved easily out of the country.

In consequence of the quota agreement, Cuba lost the opportunity to compete with the U.S. home industry on an economic basis. The agreement also bound Cuba to the U.S., and to the use of U.S. goods. About eighty percent of Cuba's imports were coming from the U.S. by the 1950s, everything "from corn flakes to tomato paste; from nails and tacks to tractors, trucks, and automobiles; from thread to all types of clothing; from goods from Sears and other department stores to accessories for the home, fertilisers and insecticides for agriculture, and materials for industry and construction,"* as Edward Boorstein, the U.S. economist, put it. This in turn discouraged the development of a home manufacturing base.

Dependency on the U.S. gave rise to a number of ironies. Cuba was an exporter of raw sugar yet imported confectionery. She exported tomatoes yet imported most of the tomato paste she needed. She exported fresh fruit and re-imported it in cans. Cuba produced vast amounts of tobacco and imported U.S. cigarettes. Even Havana cigars were increasingly manufactured in the U.S. in the Fifties. Cuba exported the leaf to Florida for U.S. companies who had shifted there to avoid the high U.S. tariffs on Cuban-produced cigars.

Cuba in the 1950s was a classic underdeveloped nation, and one of the severest symptoms of the malaise was the widespread hunger in the country. When the World Bank sent a study group to Cuba in 1950, Cuban doctors reported that forty percent of urban dwellers and sixty percent of those in the countryside were undernourished. Those who suffered in this way—or a great many of them—supported the Fidelistas because they thought this was a way they would get to eat properly. Those who weren't hungry and supported the Fidelistas did so because they wanted to see an end to the injustice of hunger.

---

* *The Economic Transformation of Cuba*, Edward Boorstein.

The revolution of the Fidelistas achieved fully what was expected of it on the issue of hunger, although no one before the revolution could have foreseen how radical that revolution was going to be in other ways.

The owner of the house in Varadero where we were staying was a tiny, dark woman. She stayed in the small extension at the back, facing away from the sea, while we, her paying guests, had the run of the place. At first the situation struck me as a basis for a West End play: bourgeois type stranded by the revolution, lives on, renting out her once-grand house by the sea while she survives in an outbuilding. This ridiculous fabrication died when I saw her one morning under her porch, curled up on the settee, a novel (I think it was by John Updike) propped open in front of her, and drinking her morning coffee from an exquisite porcelain cup.

Another morning she put her head round the door which connected her section with ours and I offered her some coffee.

"Oh yes," she said, and we sat down at one of the long mahogany dining tables.

Her broad forehead tapered to a pointed chin. She was about fifty or fifty-five years old. She wore cerise-coloured lipstick.

"Oh, I see you have . . ." she said, and pointed to the novel *Infante's Inferno* by Guillermo Cabrera Infante which I was reading. The author was a Cuban and, after the revolution, was briefly head of the National Council for Culture and an executive of the Instituto del Cine, then, after 1966, settled in London an exile.

She continued:

"I can't understand the people who leave. How can they just turn their backs on their country and go? They don't like the system? Well, they should have stayed behind and tried to change it."

"Maybe they didn't think they could change it."

"But just to turn one's back. It's never made any sense to me. One has to be positive."

"The reason most people left Cuba," she continued, "was not because of what they did before the revolution. It was because they didn't want to adapt to a new economic situation. It was very simple."

"And your own family?" I asked.

She gave a marvellous shrug which said: Why ask? You know the answer.

"They didn't want to adapt," she said.

"And you?"

Another shrug.

"When I told my family I wanted to stay they said, 'What! You're crazy. You're a communist.' But do I look like a communist? No, of course I'm not."

She didn't. She was the owner of two houses. She was also sufficiently wealthy never to have to buy her food at subsidised rates on the ration, and she always shopped on the free or parallel market which was more expensive.

"My family said, 'The communists will take everything you have away.' Well . . ."

She pointed around the room, her room.

"They never took anything away which I used."

This had the ring of the Cuban state, with its sincere, avuncular style.

"We had three places," she said. "The house in Havana, here, and the farm. They said, "You can't keep all three places." I thought, 'Well, the beach is better than the country. I get more out of it.' So the farm went and here I am."

"For those who left," she continued, "it has been hard. When the revolution came they thought it would be over in six months. They'd go to Miami, they thought. The children would learn a little English. Then the Americans would come back to Cuba and the country would go back to what it had been. Only the Americans never came back.

"Every ten years I meet my family in Costa Rica. My daughter too, she is in the States as well. When we meet up we have an unspoken agreement that we don't talk about Cuba. It would upset them too much."

She looked at me with her large brown eyes.

"It is hard for them but there are difficulties for me here as well and they are not what you think."

I wanted to ask her about them but at precisely that moment she looked at the wristwatch on her fine, brown wrist.

"My bus," she said, "it is leaving in five minutes," and with that she vanished back to Havana.

Beyond the buckled french windows and the crumbling garden wall lay the sea, smooth and blue. I sat at the table thinking about B—— with her expensive foreign clothes, curled up with her painted toenails showing under the verandah, looking like an affluent member of "the community," as the Cubans in exile are called. I would never know the nature of her struggle. Did she now regret not having left, or was her difficulty the disappointment that life had not turned out as she had expected? She was an optimistic woman who believed that change was possible and any system was malleable, and yet the Cuban one appeared to be immovable.

There was a bookcase in the corner. I went over and, from beside a Spanish edition of John Reed's *Ten Days That Shook the World*, I idly picked out a copy of the autobiography of Stefan Zweig, *The World of Yesterday*. Zweig, a Jew, an Austrian by birth, was a poet, essayist, playwright, novelist, and for a while librettist to Richard Strauss after Hofmannsthal's death. He was one of the best known German-speaking literary figures between the wars. He fled from Austria in 1933 and committed suicide in Petropolis, Brazil, in 1942 along with his second wife. There was a home-made dust-jacket on the book made of wrapping paper, which I later learnt had been put on the edition by B——'s mother.

The book fell open at a passage marked in pencil:

> *I remembered a conversation with my publisher in Leningrad on my short trip to Russia. He had been telling me how rich he had once been, what beautiful paintings he had owned, and I asked him why he had not left Russia immediately on the outbreak of the revolution as so many others had done. "Ah," he answered, "who would have believed that such a thing as a Workers' and Soldiers' Republic could last longer than a fortnight?" It was the self-deception that we practise because of reluctance to abandon our accustomed life.* *

* *The World of Yesterday*, Stefan Zweig.

Here perhaps was a description of the difficulties B—— faced.

The new economic system to which neither B——'s family, nor tens of thousands of other Cubans, were willing to adjust was a socialist economy. It sought to increase the incomes of the poor, so they could buy more and eat better. The First Agrarian Reform law of 1959 was the first move in this direction. It granted some 100,000 tenant farmers, sharecroppers, and squatters tracts of land for their own use, and it freed them from the obligation to pay rent to landlords. Simultaneously, it nationalised just over half of the privately owned land in the country to create state enterprises, and all-the-year-round jobs on these rose from 50,000 in 1959 to 150,000 in 1962. Sugar workers were also able to find work on the construction projects which the government was starting all over the country, during the dead season when the industry was at a standstill. A minimum wage in agriculture was also decreed. These and other measures gave farmworkers higher incomes than before the revolution. Only about a quarter of all rural workers earned more than seventy-five pesos a month in April 1958. By 1960 nearly sixty percent had achieved this.

In the cities, as opposed to the countryside, the government did not need to intervene, as wage increases were achieved by the unions. But, as in the countryside, there was a pattern of redistribution of wealth. By 1962 the lowest forty percent of urban income-earners had enlarged their slice of the national income pie from six and a half percent (the 1959 figure) to seventeen percent.

Simultaneously there was legislation which enabled all households to have more of their income to spend on food and other essentials. The government made basic welfare free for everyone, that is schooling, medical care, and social services. The government also made water, all sporting events, burials, and even the public telephones free (for local calls).* Electricity, gas, and public transport costs were lowered. The lottery and all other forms of gambling were outlawed. In 1960, under its Urban Reform Plan, the government decreed rent reduc-

* This did not last.

tions of up to fifty percent. In 1962 it set the maximum rent that could be charged at ten percent of the income of the head of the household.

These measures, along with fuller employment, led to the transfer of fifteen percent of the national income from property-owners to wage earners in 1960 alone. A good many, but not all, of those who left Cuba in the early Sixties were on the wrong side of this equation.

With more money in more pockets there was a consequent rise in consumption, especially of food. Beef consumption alone went up fifty percent between 1959 and 1961. There were similar rises in the consumption of milk and pork.

The next stage, inevitably, was that supply failed to keep pace with growing demand. Agricultural production was handicapped by the departure to the U.S. of those with administrative and technical skills who weren't prepared to adjust to Cuba's way of life. The newly created state farms and cooperatives produced less than they had done when they had been in private hands. In 1960 the U.S. embargo on the export of most U.S. goods to Cuba caused further widespread disruption to the island's agriculture, completely dependent on the U.S. for machinery, pesticides, fertilisers, seeds, and all sorts of other goods. To make the situation worse, there was also a fairly widespread programme of anti-Fidelista sabotage in the countryside. Fields of crops were burnt, cattle were slaughtered. Then came the invasion in April 1961 at the Bay of Pigs, diverting scarce resources into defence and lowering production even further.

The resultant shortages were felt particularly in the cities. Because there was less to buy after the embargo, small producers (tenants and sharecroppers) had less need for cash and so produced less for sale at the market. Meat began to disappear from city shops, and plantains (cooking bananas) were no longer sent every day from Oriente province to Havana.

Shortages fed further shortages, since the lack of one item led to an increase in demand for others. For instance, in 1961 when the root crop taro became scarce, there was a run on sweet potatoes.

The trade embargo—the single greatest contributing factor to the fall in production—also led directly to a fall in supply because Cuba had imported so much of her food from the U.S.: seventy percent of her wheat, lard, rice, beans, poultry, eggs, onions, and garlic. To find new sources for these products was extremely difficult. Consider pork lard, essential in the cooking of Cuba's national dish of pork, rice, and beans. At the time of the embargo Cuba was importing eighty-five percent of her pork lard from the U.S., and when the government went to find alternative suppliers they found to their dismay that no one could supply as much pork lard and as cheaply. Cuba's food importation was also affected badly by the simple fact that with her principal trading partner, the U.S., being so close, the Cuban dock facilities were designed to handle short-haul craft which had come from New Orleans or Miami and were not geared up to receive ocean trade. During the early years the arrival of long-distance shipments of food often foundered because there was no warehouse big enough to put them in: the food either rotted or had to be given away. Finally, even when there was food available, its processing, packaging, and distribution was often made impossible because the embargo ensured there were none of the machines, materials, or trucks needed for the job:

> For the past few weeks there hasn't been a soft drink to be had anywhere. I never thought that the manufacture of soft drinks could be paralyzed just because there was no cork for the caps. That's what they say. That shitty cork I used to scrape off when I was a boy and then I'd flatten out the tin with a hammer, open two holes with a nail, and with a piece of thread make myself a disk that would spin and spin and was quite sharp. Once I almost lost a finger playing with it. Never, not then or ever after, could I have imagined how many insignificant things are necessary to keep a country running smoothly. Now you can see everything inside out, all the hidden entrails of the system. We're living suspended over an abyss; there are an almost infinite number of details that have to be controlled so that everything can flow naturally; it's overwhelming.*

* *Inconsolable Memories*, Edmundo Desnoes.

In a free market the shortages would have led to higher prices. If this had happened in Cuba, the gains in living standards which urban and rural workers had achieved would have been lost, and there would have been a return to the situation as it had existed before. Those with high incomes would have eaten well, those without would not. Instead the government tried price controls. In March 1959 there were official prices set for milk, rice, bread, and beef. In May, cheese, potatoes, pork, butter, and some other items like soap were added to the list. Simultaneously, profit margins of ten percent and twenty percent respectively were set on wholesalers and retailers. In the following months, all remaining staples were added to the list of price-controlled foods.

It didn't work. Hoarding and profiteering became widespread. The government's next move, intended to stop speculation, was to nationalise the wholesale food business and many retail outlets. By 1961, 8,000 of these had been taken over. At the same time the government set up *tiendas del pueblo,* people's stores, in the countryside, to supply basic goods at official prices. There were 2,000 of these by 1961.

Having started to intervene directly in the economy, the government found itself, rather like the sorcerer's apprentice, with more and more demons to control than it knew how to cope with. The retail nationalisation programme and the *tiendas del pueblo* failed to curtail the black market (if anything, they increased it), and as supply problems multiplied, speculation increased. At this stage the government could have opted to make basic staples available to the poor at low prices. But the consequence of this would have been a dietary "two nations," so instead they plumped for a rationing system for all Cubans.

In mid-1961 lard was the very first product to be rationed, when the government specified that the ration would be one pound per person per week. In March 1962, cooking oil, rice, and beans were also rationed on a nationwide basis; toothpaste, soap, and detergent in the twenty-six principal cities; and fish, eggs, chicken, beef, sweet potatoes, milk, and root crops in Havana only. All these items were eventually rationed throughout the whole country, along with sugar, bread, salt, tobacco goods, cloth, clothing, shoes, and most household items.

When rationing was introduced the government promised it would be short-lived. Officials were optimistic about increases in yield and production in agriculture. Some foreign experts supported them. It was widely believed rationing was an interim measure. It was not to be. Rationing remained (although bread, butter, eggs, and milk did become freely available on the parallel market) and food remained scarce, just like the peppers withdrawn from their secret hiding place under the counter in the *puesto,* and carried home by us in triumph.

Every evening in Varadero, I used to go for a walk.

Towards six o'clock that day, I walked up to the avenue at the top of the road, crossed over to the bus station, and disappeared into the strange, suburban backwater of Varadero, the back part of the town along the fringes of the *autopista* which ran on to the end of the peninsula.

The bungalows here—all the dwellings were bungalows—were smaller than near the seafront. A woman was shouting angrily over a fence at two silent men in paint-spattered trousers, whilst her daughter played around a wooden kennel with a fluffy alsatian puppy. Chickens pecked around crazy-paving pathways. Old couples sat silently side by side on rocking chairs under porches or else the chairs were stood back to front on the porches, tilted against the wall so that any rainwater would drain away. This was one of Cuba's commonest sights. Two neighbours, male, were leaning on their respective gates, admiring a U.S. car parked by the kerb.

Drawing closer, my heart started to race. There were the same fins, pronounced but not outrageous, the same chrome lengths of trim running above the rear wheels and cutting off a third of the way along the flank (a wonderful conceit of the design), and the same rear windscreen which curved on into the body of the roof. Could it be an Eldorado Brougham? I walked quickly up to it, only to find that my powers of distance identification were still hopelessly inaccurate: it was a 1958 Oldsmobile Dynamic 88 Holiday four-door hardtop, from General Motors. Nearly 150,000 of these were made and they had sold for $2,971. The car was red and had the word "Mustang" painted on the door in the sort of script I associate with ghost trains at funfairs.

A young man in a garden, apparently showing a young girl of about fifteen a judo throw, was holding her closely and catching her as she fell, laughing, her skirt riding up her brown thighs. An alsatian watched them. There seemed to be dogs in every other garden, and flapping lines of washing wherever I looked. Youths around the entrance of a *microbrigada*-built block of flats (blocks built by volunteers under expert supervision) looked curiously at me as I passed but went on talking. A line of men were unloading tiles from an articulated lorry, passing the tiles along a human chain with much laughter, while the driver sat in the cab listening to the radio. A boy of perhaps three asked me to take his photograph. He posed, pointing the plastic gun he was holding at the camera. As soon as I had taken the photograph, he demanded to see it and took the camera from me and stared into the lens, believing he would be able to see it inside the body. His mother took him away shyly, almost apologetically. There was another U.S. car at the side of the house under a canopy to protect it from the sun, but as I'd already had one disappointment I went past. In the Los Pioneros, the "Pioneers" playground, there was a U.S. pop song playing over the PA. An attempt was being made to get the children around the flagpole where someone was holding a blue-and-white Cuban flag. The children on the swings all shouted out for Chiclets and made the gesture of pulling imaginary gum from their mouths. The Pioneers all wore blue-and-white scarves over their school uniforms. The movement is not unlike the Boy Scouts or the Girl Guides. It provides primary-school children with recreational opportunities, in this case a playground. It also "introduces Marxist-Leninist theory," and membership is compulsory. "Chiclets, Chiclets, . . ." sounding in my ears, I carried on.

Two fishermen, with enamel buckets filled with silvery fish, were smoking on the kerb outside the house when I got back. The sky above the sea was streaked with purple clouds and red shafts of light from the sun which had just disappeared over the horizon. The sea was silver again, like a vast piece of crumpled silver foil. The mosquitoes were out, large and black and clustered in great swarms, and I had to run through the door so as not to let too many in. In the kitchen I found Raoul pounding the steak with white garlic powder. The green peppers we ate that night, the first we had had for a month, tasted incomparable.

MARK KURLANSKY

Havana, 1990s: *The* Babalawo *and the Birds*

"THE *BABALAWO* BEGAN CHANTING IN YORUBA, THE
CHICKENS STARTED SQUAWKING. THE TELEVISION IN THE
BACK ROOM WAS TURNED LOUDER. I IMAGINED THE KIDS
ROLLING THEIR EYES AND SAYING, 'OH DADDY'S KILLING
MORE CHICKENS IN THE LIVING ROOM.' "

*Mark Kurlansky is a journalist who has specialized in covering
the Caribbean for the* Chicago Tribune *and other publications.
His 1992 book,* A Continent of Island: Searching for the Caribbean Destiny, *draws together his experiences and ideas.*

*In the introduction to that book, he writes, "Caribbeans
have found their history too horrible to show and have tried to
keep it tastefully tucked out of sight, along with their society
and their culture, out of a vague notion that it is all too upset-
ting for foreigners. They even avoid serving local food to foreigners. They have tried to tell us that nothing is going on here, that
they are an easygoing island people enjoying glorious sunshine.
In truth, there has always been a great deal going on: music, architecture, theater, literature, painting—a people formed from a
unique blending of races and cultures with a restless creativity
and a richly ironic sense of humor that never fails them, even in
the worst of times."*

*Officially, Cuba is a socialist state that does not countenance
religion. Historically, Cuba is a Catholic country. Realistically,*

*Cubans hedge their bets, and one of the most popular hedges is
santería, a religion derived from ancient West African practices,
including blood sacrifice. Carried to the Americas by the Yoruba
people of West Africa who came to the New World as slaves,
santería is closely related to the voodoo practiced in Haiti and
the candomblé of Brazil. The religion posits a large pantheon of
orishas, gods and goddesses who will look after the needs of mortals but who are quick to anger and so require steady and frequent devotion. Because Christian slave owners in the New
World forbade the practice of pagan religions, followers disguised the orishas as Christian saints.*

*Santería has entered North America in recent years with
the new wave of immigrants from Cuba, Puerto Rico, and the
Dominican Republic. The statues, candles, herbs, and other materials needed for the practice are sold at shops called botánicas,
and the statue that looks, for example, like the Blessed Virgin
Mary is really the goddess of the seas, Yemanyá.*

FIDEL CASTRO'S FIRST DARING SALVO
against the Batista dictatorship, a quixotic and unsuccessful 1953 attack on the Moncada barracks, is commemorated
every July 26, *veinte-seis de Julio.* It has become a time when
many Cubans think about sacrifice. That is how I ended up
spending a Cuban national holiday riding around the deserted
streets of Havana in the back of a blue 1941 Chevy with a half
dozen terrified birds tied up in the trunk.

To worshippers of Santería this time of year was significant
because, between the Moncada anniversary and carnival, Cubans got time off from work in mid-July. Unlike most Afro-
Caribbean religions, Santería deems daylight essential for its
rituals, which must be practiced before 6:00 P.M. This poses a
problem in a country where people work five and a half or six
days a week. Worshippers sometimes called in sick to get time
for a ceremony.

In revolutionary Cuba, being a *babalawo,* a high priest of
Santería, was a niche of tolerated—not legally sanctioned—
capitalism, in the midst of the socialist state. An initiation to a

major spirit cost $4,000 in Havana, less than a third of the fee in Miami. Miami relatives saved money by having their ceremonies done in Havana when they were visiting their families. For Habaneros wanting ceremonies, Sundays and holidays were the big days, and the *babalawos* complain about their workload in July the way Catholic priests sometimes grumble about Eastertime. "Aye, I'm divining and consecrating from morning to evening," said a *babalawo* in Cayohueso.

Cayohueso is a traditional black neighborhood of central Havana, the kind of neighborhood that in every third building has telltale dolls, flags, or the mysterious stick-filled black iron kettles. Like most of central Havana, the district has three- and four-story buildings, some with wondrous architectural details, from elaborate baroque swirls to bold Art Deco angles. But it was all falling apart. The *babalawo* I knew in the neighborhood lived in a building that inspectors had last visited in 1970. They reported the building "in bad condition" and it was condemned. The residents were told that they would be relocated to new apartments as soon as the construction was completed. Twenty years later they were still waiting.

Believers were making their way to this condemned building with problems of money, health, legal questions, problems in their love lives. A steep, narrow stairway from the street ended without warning in the *babalawo*'s second-story living room. The apartment was a series of small rooms with twenty-foot ceilings. Old Havana buildings often have these high ceilings that, along with tile floors and little direct sunlight, were designed to keep the rooms cool. But they didn't stay cool in July. July in Havana is the hottest weather in the Caribbean. Morning breezes burn into white-hot summer light until the sky turns the color of shiny gray metal every afternoon. Then the cooling rains come to save us. After the rain, the sun dries the pieces of ceiling that the moisture has loosened and small chunks fall. The iron reinforcement rods were beginning to show.

The living room was crammed with cracked and aging furniture. Like many Havana living rooms, this one had on display the colorful icons of Cuban Catholicism. There were two painted wooden statues of the Cuban patron saint, Our Lady of

Charity, *La Caridád,* a mulatto Virgin rising out of the ocean. A dark-skinned doll in a rich, deep blue dress with matching crown and fuchsia plume sat on top of the television. Well-cared-for dolls, representing departed spirits, are commonplace in Havana homes. These spirits, like crotchety ancient relatives, are thought to be demanding, requiring gifts, constant care, and, often, the best spot in the room.

In another room to the right, against the wall, a cabinet painted the same deep blue as the doll's dress contained shelves of soup tureens filled with stones and draped in colored beads. These were the vessels of the spirits, the *orishas.* In the opposite corner of the breezeless ten-by-ten room various pots and vases were displayed on the floor. Old crackers were sitting in some of the pots to feed *orishas.* Oggún, a war god, had been given what appeared to be stale pizza.

A red-and-white-striped wooden pedestal with a vaguely hourglass shape was the sacred pylon on which sat the pot of Changó. This *babalawo* was a priest of Changó. His wife was a devotee of Yemayá, the ocean *orisha* who loves deep blue. Many of the household items, including an antique refrigerator running off an electrical wire that came through the window, had also been painted that same blue.

Babalawos, in spite of a reputation for secrecy, are compulsive teachers. This one had nineteen disciples in training. He was obsessed with his theology and the urge to explain it. I would talk to him for hours at a stretch until late at night, the heat almost unbearable in his humid, decaying room. His dark eyes always looked alert with a mysterious grin lurking somewhere behind the bushy eyebrows. He had a strong, straight nose leading down to a little moustache. In his early seventies, his still strong-looking, stocky body barely reached my shoulders in height. He had thick, self-assured craftsman's hands and a Buddha-like pot belly that friends affectionately patted when they greeted him.

Women, by tradition, could not become *babalawos,* but his wife, small, sprite, with very black skin and hair always worn up in a scarf, stubbornly interjected her own observations. Her husband seemed to only tolerate the interruptions while he sat at his rickety iron table littered with divining chains, cowrie shells, and old cigar stubs. The stool on which he always sat was a sacred pylon of Changó, but he just shrugged when asked and said, "Yes, but it has not been consecrated." He leaned back showing his Buddha belly. "And it is very comfortable."

There were always a pad of paper and several pens in front of him. He illustrated everything by writing notes, charts, or diagrams on the paper. Even as he explained that the religion was in an oral tradition requiring each *babalawo* to store enormous quantities of information in his head and pass it on only by word of mouth, he wrote the word "escritura" on his pad, crossed it out and wrote the word "oral."

There were a number of divining systems. Each functioned like two-sided dice. Four pieces of coconut were dropped. Each landed on the white side or the shell side and the result was recorded in zeros and ones. There was a necklace with eight pieces, each having a light side and a dark side. Each toss was a series of eight zeros or ones. As in the early days of computers, answers were tabulated in binary mathematics. *Babalawos,* the reverse of journalists, are trained to always ask questions that can be answered with no or yes—a zero or a one.

"It is a logical mathematical system which cannot make a mistake," the *babalawo* insisted. He explained the mathematics until deep into those muggy nights—how 16 squares to 256 and, with 4 possibilities each, that leads to 1,024 possible zeros and 1,024 possible ones. When he felt he had finished his point, he would say in that Afro-Cuban Spanish that has no *s,* "*¿Qué má-?*" what else?, and impatiently wait for the next question. He filled page after page with calculations while I struggled to understand until I could try no longer. I left and wandered the dark streets. A man on a doorstep was sharing a glass of water with a small blond-haired doll. The streets were crumbling but always clean.

I looked for the Habana Libre, the one featureless glass highrise that got built before a revolution saved the skyline from the fate of San Juan. It stood like a beacon in old, moldy, low-built Havana, lighting the way to the only well-functioning taxi stand. From there I got a taxi back to my whorehouse-elegant room of brocaded furniture at the El Presidente. Sealed in with the loud but appreciated air conditioning, I worked on my pocket calculator, trying to make some sense of my notes.

Each time I went back to that *babalawo*, the altars looked different. Sometimes there was a stray feather or some brownish spots of blood. One morning a large hand of green bananas sat on Changó's pot, fitting like a leg of lamb on a small mixing bowl, making the whole pylon unsteady. I knew that Changó liked bananas, that he controlled lightning from his perch in the tall Cuban royal palms. I had often seen offerings of ananas left under these elegant plants that grace Havana's parks.

At first I watched simple divinations, the asking of questions, the calculating of zeros and ones. There was a casualness, a banality to the ritual, the way there is in Jewish seders and Catholic confessionals. The *babalawo* sat on a sheet on the floor for these events and the telephone was kept nearby on the unconsecrated pylon so that he could take calls during the divination. He and his wife would get into minor domestic tiffs about how to lay out ritual objects for the next reading.

One day I arrived and found a makeshift white sheet of a curtain covering the doorway to the altar room. I sat in the kitchen by the deep blue refrigerator with the homemade latch while at the table the *babalawo*'s wife and their daughter, the two also not privy to this rite, sifted rice absentmindedly through their hands, occasionally discarding a darkened grain. We made small talk while birds were squawking and clucking in the next room. At one point the *babalawo* came out and called in his wife. Minutes later she emerged, saying nothing, but a fluffy gray feather had landed on her forehead above her glasses. At another point he came out with a basin of blood. Women kept circulating furtively between the altar room and the larder where they washed their hands. But nothing was explained to me nor did anyone react to poultry screams, which resonated in the high ceilings.

When it was over, I went into the altar room. There were traces of feathers and blood everywhere as though mortal enemies had just fought to the death with pillows. The room was also becoming a little too redolent. Changó's, bananas were black. Yemayá had half a rotten red melon, and Eleggúa his favorite, coconuts and corn kernels.

But sacrifice was never mentioned to me. Finally one night, while he was sitting over his pad, pen in hand, I asked him. He answered directly. "*Sin sacrificios, no hay nada.*" Without sacrifices, there is nothing.

"Do you perform a lot of sacrifices?"

"Yesterday alone, I killed nine animals including chickens, doves, and goats." The more questions I asked the longer the list of condemned species became. I tried to sort out some of the rumors I had heard. In Nigeria there is a worrisome line in the annual ceremony for Oggún. "Oggún eats dogs and we give him dogs." Now he confirmed that in Cuba as well, dogs were sometimes sacrificed to Oggún. "Only in very extreme cases," he emphasized. He did say that once at a ceremony he saw a man possessed by Oggún run out into the street with a machete and lop the head off a growling dog, then fall on the body, sucking the blood out of the neck.

While there were few private farms left in Cuba and meat was tightly rationed, its declining presence in the daily diet a common source of grumbling, *babalawos* still managed relationships with small farms that supplied them with sacrificial animals. The *babalawo* agreed to show me such a farm, and the next morning, the *veinte-seis de Julio*, when it seemed most of Havana had been bused to Camagüey to hear Fidel speak, a 1941 Chevrolet puttered up to the condemned building. The small toothless driver was proud of his car—proud of how he started it by stamping hard one time on the accelerator, proud of the fact that the antique had been used in the film re-creation of the Moncada barracks attack. (This car was already twelve years old in 1953 when the real attack took place.)

With only two forward gears, we putt-putted past old Havana to Cerro, an area of fine old crumbling, low buildings with pillared porches. The engine gurgled like a coffee percolator, which is why Cubans call their old jalopies *cafeteros*. To make it up the smallest incline, the driver would have to stop and add water to the radiator, but the Chevy kept running. We stopped at the small one-story house of a tall man with flowing shocks of silken white hair and a kind face. Ushered into the backyard, we were suddenly in a small poultry farm. They raised chickens, doves, ducks, goats, even turtles (Changó likes turtles). The man explained that this private farm had been in his family for seventy years. I asked him if it was secret or if the government permitted it. He shrugged indecisively.

The *babalawo* bought six black hens, six doves, and three young roosters. The roosters, he told me, had very strong blood and were good for ceremonies. The total price was 204 Cuban pesos (at the time officially equivalent to about $255 U.S.). With the doves and hens tied up in a burlap bag in one hand and the three roosters tied at the feet in the other, he went out to the car and stuffed it all into the high but very shallow trunk and we slowly chugged back to his apartment.

The young white man who commissioned the ceremony was patiently waiting back there, watching an ad for the American movie *La Bamba* on the television while the blue-dressed doll, who had clearly just had her hair done, started back from the top of the set. Most of the doomed birds were put in coops that had been built on a rooftop terrace adjoining the altar room. I could see across the alley to a back balcony where there were flags and one of the iron kettles, called *ngangas*, of a different Afro-Cuban religion.

The young man, seeming anxious to get on with his ceremony, grabbed the necessary birds, the three roosters and the dove, and we were off in the Chevy again, he holding the dove in his hand, a tiny, perfectly round, amber eye staring out from above his thumb. We rode to a small house with concrete floors and pressboard walls.

The men all sat on a red plastic couch, taking turns sharpening a very used-looking knife while one of the roosters stretched, stared at the family photos, and defecated on the concrete floor. I could hear that there were other family members—a woman, some children—but they were staying in the next room watching television. The *babalawo* began chanting in Yoruba, the chickens started squawking. The television in the back room was turned louder. I imagined the kids rolling their eyes and saying, "Oh Daddy's killing more chickens in the living room."

The *babalawo* sprayed the makeshift altar by spitting out a

swig of sweet-smelling white rum and started tossing the coconuts. He stretched the neck of one of the roosters and put the
knife through it. While he continued chanting, he dripped
blood in bloppy lines from the rooster body onto the altar and
across the floor at the front doorway.

No knife was used for the dove. The little brown head
seemed to twist off easily. As if squeezing a wine skin, he
poured the blood out of this bird too. He was singing merrily in
Yoruba, haphazardly plucking a few handfuls of feathers. On
television in the next room was a melodramatic movie with a
Tchaikovsky-based soundtrack. The music swelled emotionally
while honey was poured over the blood and feathers.

The Tchaikovsky soundtrack seemed to be reaching for a
climax in the next room as the *babalawo* took the second
rooster, twisted its neck with his thick powerful arms, wrung it
around twice in sudden circles and, placing the head on the
floor under his foot, separated it from the body with one tough
yank. As he poured the blood out of the headless bird I noticed
its talons stiffly splayed outward in a last desperate strain, like
clutching for air.

On the television, Tchaikovsky rolled toward its final or-
gasmic chords and voices in Spanish were swearing eternal
love, while in the front room the *babalawo* was singing "*popo
fun mi*," feathers for me, in Yoruba, as he sprinkled the bloody
mess with feathers, asking the *orisha* to protect the household
as would a soft feather covering.

He finished up at almost the same moment as the movie.
The news came on, paraphrasing the *New York Times*, talking
about Cuba fighting drug trafficking. A cute, spunky little gray
terrier came out to sniff the interesting new smells in the living
room. The initiate cleaned up the feathers and blood but as we
left I noticed that tiny dark puddles of blood remained in the
little flaws in the concrete surface of the living room floor. Still,
the initiate seemed very happy, like a man who had passed a
good *veinte-seis de Julio*.

TOM MILLER

Trinidad, Sancti Spíritus, and the Bay of Pigs, 1990

"A FEW ROYAL PALMS GREW FROM THE SMOOTH SAND.
LAUGHING VACATIONERS TROTTED IN AHEAD OF THE SURF.
I COULDN'T SEE ANY HISTORY. IT WAS A LOVELY DAY AT THE
SHORE."

It may be that few Americans know Cuba as well as Tom Miller does. His Trading with the Enemy: A Yankee Travels Through Castro's Cuba *was published by Atheneum in 1992, and it was reprinted in paperback by Basic Books in 1996 with a new introduction. It's required reading for anyone who proposes to visit— or even to talk about—Cuba today.*

Miller came well prepared to the writing of that book. He had already traveled widely in Latin America, and his The Panama Hat Trail *was already regarded as a modern classic of travel writing, one that, for better or worse, permanently labeled Ecuador "the bus-plunge capital of the world." And he had visited Cuba on several short trips before finally completing the arrangements that made it possible for him to spend six months there in the latter half of 1990.*

To be sure, he was not a mere tourist in Cuba. His way was smoothed everywhere—although it was seldom very smooth per se—with contacts, introductions, and the approval of the Cuban

Writers Union. But, although he had some peripheral contact with the Cuban government and experienced some minor delays associated with paperwork attendant on that contact, he went wherever he wanted throughout the island, and he spoke with whomever he pleased.

In the excerpt that follows, he travels along Cuba's southern coast, visiting Trinidad and Sancti Spíritus on his way to Playa Girón, the name by which Cubans know the Bay of Pigs. Playa Girón takes its name from a French pirate, Gilbert Girón, who came ashore here in the seventeenth century. Trinidad, oddly, gets short shrift. It's the best-preserved colonial city in Cuba and in 1988 was declared a World Heritage site by UNESCO. Residents of Trinidad like to boast that the cobblestones in the city's streets came to Cuba as ballast in trading vessels from New England.

In 1961, only three months after taking office and acting on a policy left over from President Eisenhower's administration, President Kennedy authorized Brigade 2506, a CIA-trained band of mercenaries and Cuban exiles, to go forward with a planned invasion of Cuba whose object was the overthrow of Fidel Castro's government. On April 15, American planes attempted to destroy Cuba's small air force on the ground but failed in their purpose. Instead, the attack warned Cuba to prepare for invasion. That invasion came a little after midnight on April 17, when around 1,300 invaders went ashore at Playa Girón. Within twenty-four hours, they were surrounded and pinned down by twenty thousand Cuban troops. Their air support was shot down by the Cuban planes they had failed to destroy two days earlier. The U.S. naval ships that were standing off the coast sailed away. Fidel Castro personally supervised the Cuban victory; a famous photo showed the dynamic young leader leaping from a tank to the ground. And by the afternoon of April 19, the invaders had surrendered.

The results were devastating. The invaders suffered 107 killed and 1,189 taken prisoner. Of the Cuban forces, 161 men and women were killed. Some observers feel that the attack served to radicalize Castro's view of la Revolución and drive him toward a close alliance with the Soviet Union; it was only a few days after Playa Girón that he first used the term "socialist" in

*describing Cuba's future. A year later, in 1962, it cost the
United States $53 million to bail out the prisoners.*

*Today, near the museum, Villa Horizontes Playa Girón of-
fers 196 bungalows, a restaurant, a bar, a pool, and the usual
amenities of a beach resort.*

THE ROAD TO TRINIDAD IN THE FOOT-
hills of the escambray swung through ranching country.
Twice I had to pull over to let cowboys and their cattle hoof
down the highway from open range to huge pens. High grass
obscured a small billboard that said: TO CARE FOR WILDLIFE IS
A SOCIAL OBLIGATION. A deer and a bird were painted in the
corner.

Diego Velázquez, the Spanish conquistador, founded Trinidad in 1514. At least that's what all the history books say, but
what does that really mean? It has the same clean sweep as
"Abraham Lincoln was born in a log cabin and grew up to be
president." Did Velázquez hammer in a cross, leave some of his
men, round up some Indians, harvest wild crops, or set up a
gold mining camp? Whatever he did, it attracted a fellow Spaniard, Hernán Cortés, who five years later stopped at Trinidad
before sailing for Mexico. There, pitting European might
against indigenous faith, Cortés brought down the Aztec empire.

Carlos Joaquín Zerquera Fernández grew up in Trinidad
learning these building blocks of Latin American history, and
went into banking. I met him at his home, an expansive colonial
place near the middle of town. Trinidad has benefited by generations of benign neglect from Havana; much of it remains unchanged from colonial days. UNESCO has anointed it a
Patrimony of Humanity, not to be tinkered with. In his detailed
and far-ranging account of early nineteenth-century Cuba, Alexander Humboldt observed that "all the streets of Trinidad are
very steep, and the inhabitants there complain, as they also do
in the greater part of Spanish America, of the bad selection
made by the conquerors of sites for the towns they founded."
The Humboldt Museum of Natural Science was closed for re-

pairs, but Zerquera, now Trinidad's historian, waltzed me in and out of all the other museums in town. The cobblestone streets, the thick-walled houses with red tile roofs, the brilliance of the flowers and smoothness of the marble floors and mahogany stairways in the museums, all combined to give a sense of well-preserved wealth.

Lovely vases and porcelain centerpieces adorned elegant dining rooms in a former sugar baron's home, now a museum. Swiss and Austrian utensils hung in the preserved kitchen, Portuguese paintings hung on the walls. "This museum was home to one of the oldest families in Trinidad. They lived here until 1930." A cast-iron bell four feet tall sat prominently on the first floor. It came from Meneely's of West Troy, New York.

We next went to the National Museum of the Struggle Against Banditry, which, like most of the other politically oriented museums in the country, displayed the personal effects of Cubans who died defending their government. One soldier left behind a Remington Roll-A-Matic shaver. Another, a song book. A CIA radio transmitter was on exhibit. So was a poster showing a boy hoisting a rifle. MY MOUNTAINS WILL NEVER BE TAKEN, it said. A booklet said to be financed by the CIA read, *We work as slaves to serve the Russians! Russians get out of Cuba!* A detailed map of the country showed the areas most affected by "*bandidismo.*" The museum was sponsoring an essay contest on the theme, "the struggle against bandits." First prize was three hundred pesos—somewhat more than most Cubans earn in a month.

Carlos Joaquín took me out to sip some *canchánchara* at a long, narrow open-air place named for the locally popular drink. The icy drink is made from raw rum, lime juice, and honey. We talked about the differences between Spanish as spoken in Spain and the same language in Cuba. Musicians played for the sunny weekend crowd, mainly foreign tourists.

The climate was right for a question I occasionally asked Cubans over forty: "What did you do in the Revolution?" It was neither lightly asked nor easily answered. Responses usually came in two speeds: rapid claims of active but unspecific support, or slow-murmured acknowledgment of participation. The former lacked credibility; the latter often concealed dark and intricate activities. Carlos Joaquín's reply was refreshing. "Nothing. I wasn't active. I was an accountant at a bank. You must remember, I come from a very old and traditional family."

I went back to my hotel at Playa Ancón outside Trinidad to take a swim in the sea. On the way I passed a billboard trumpeting UNITY AND IDEOLOGY—TWO PILLARS OF OUR PARTY. Another, common throughout the country, proclaimed THIS LAND IS 100% CUBAN. A tour group from Germany downing Cuba libres monopolized the beachside bar. After a dip I walked west a few kilometers until the hotel was far out of sight. Eventually I came upon small groups of Cubans passing the time on the beach. They were involved in *campismo,* a somewhat supervised outdoorsy retreat for older teenagers. Jorge, the most talkative fellow in a small group I chatted with, asked my nationality.

"Norteamericano. ¿Y tú?"

"Cubano."

"A hundred percent, right?" I said, joking about the ubiquitous slogan.

"No, actually I'm fifty percent Cuban. I'm also fifty percent African." Vladimir joined in: "Me too." They were a comfortable mix of Afro-Cubans, mulattos, and a few whites. Jorge said he was a coral craftsman. He pulled some smoothly polished earrings, necklaces, and bracelets from a bag. Coral, highly prized and easily available from freelance divers, made fashionable and desirable jewelry. So much so that to regulate the endangered supply along Cuba's coastline, independent coral mining was expressly prohibited. When I asked about this Jorge dismissed it out of hand. He sold directly to customers for dollars rather than through state middlemen for pesos.

"Ah, a *jinetero,*" I said, catching Vladimir by surprise.

"How do you know what that is? Foreigners aren't supposed to know."

Jorge ignored our exchange. "I'm a sea merchant. That's what I do. I can sell you lobster, coral, fish; anything from the sea that you want. Also clothes. Just about whatever your needs are." I turned down his offer of a large, polished seashell for ten dollars. He hesitated. "Five dollars?"

"No, gracias."

Jorge conferred with his confederates and walked over to the bench where I had taken a seat for one of the best sunset vistas in the Western world, a 180 degree sweep of the Caribbean at high tide. "Here." He held out the shell. "We want you to have this as a gift."

Vladimir invited me to a dance that evening. "That is, if the guard doesn't mind." Jorge asked about the letter I was using as a bookmark. I asked, "Do you really want to hear it?" They were a hundred percent certain. Evidently afternoon entertainment was at a premium at *campismo*.

"Okay, here goes. It's from a friend at a university." I began to read: " 'A fraternity had a party, and a couple of the invited girls brought along some high school crashers, one of whom was black. They were asked to leave, and I gather the word "nigger" got used by a fraternity kid who later explained that he was from the South and that's the way they do things there. The crasher went and got a pistol out of his car, cops were called, and one cop shot at the armed kid. The bullet went through the kid's arm and killed another cop. Who fired the gun was withheld from the press for two days. A university spokesman said it was not a racial incident.' "

The crowd, about the same age as the partiers, grew to eight or ten. They listened with rapt attention, dead silent even after I finished. Then they flooded me with questions.

"Can just anyone have a gun?"

"Why did the police shoot at him?"

"Why did the other guy call him 'nigger'?"

"You mean at the whole party there was only one black student?"

"Do the police come when the whites have a gun, too?"

"Of course it was a racial incident. Can a university lie like that?"

My interrogators had all grown up in a country where getting an education is far easier than getting a gun, and I was helpless to answer most of their questions. Or rather all of my answers reflected poorly on American society.

An end-run around the uncooperative guard at the dance was impossible, the gang told me when I drove by their campsite that evening. "Let's go into town," one of them suggested, and two girls and a guy from the afternoon crowd climbed into the VW and gave me directions to the Club Las Cuevas.

Las Cuevas was closed for repairs. I wanted to see Trinidad's Casa de la Trova, the center for local musicians. "I don't want to go there," my youngest passenger whined. "Young people don't go to the Casa. We like to go dancing instead." She sulked all the way to the Casa, but her friends seemed happy to go there, or maybe just happy to go anywhere. When we arrived, Los Trovadores de Trinidad, a four-man band, was starting a set of traditional romantic ballads, playing for an appreciative and well-dressed audience of two hundred. The sulker to the contrary, lots of young people had shown up. The crowd had arrived on foot and bicycle; mine was the only car there. A shot of rum at the bar cost fifty centavos. Curiously, cigarettes were sold only for dollars, effectively preventing virtually everyone from buying them. Some men sat and played dominoes. Photos of local musicians going back to the 1930s hung on the walls. There was no admission charge.

We cruised Trinidad some more, just a restless carload prowling for Saturday night kicks. "This book you're writing, it's about Cuba, right?" The sulker again. "In English, right? Well, a lot of Cubans read English." She said this more in fear than pride. She didn't want her name used.

"Don't worry. In delicate situations I won't use names."

"Well this is a delicate situation. My father's a cop and he'd kill me if he knew I was with a foreigner."

Oh.

The town was thick with cops, the sulker said; plainclothesmen were out in force at the Casa de la Trova. "They were wearing white *guayaberas*. They tried to follow us on bicycles." She glanced out the rear window.

Great. This was just what I needed. Picked up on the back streets of a provincial town with the teenage daughter of a local cop on a Saturday night. I started to play "Write That Headline!" in my mind. The two other passengers laughed at this low drama, enjoying the sulker's fear. "Don't you see? Nothing would happen to you. But me—" She patted her wrists together and let out a hyperventilated moan. We headed back to the *campismo* site on the beach.

"My dad's a Communist. My mom has no use for the Party. And my grandmother, she's a gossip. She's got a long tongue." She pouted. "Fidel's a *comemierda*," a shiteater. The sulker was going down the list of people she despised. "I wish he were dead. I wish my father was, too. Why can't we leave this country? Why are we so isolated?"

The fellow in the backseat. "And why are the goods the lowest of the lowest quality?"

This squall blindsided me. "Is this a common view?"

Sulker. "Yes. Well, no. Among the kids it is. Remember that guy this afternoon?" She described a quiet youth who had watched the conversation about the fraternity party. "He said I was a counterrevolutionary because I was talking to a foreigner and that you must be with the CIA. I told him you weren't."

"*Muchisimas gracias.*"

"They keep telling us that foreigners carry infections with them, like AIDS and venereal disease."

"*No, gracias.*"

Back at the road paralleling the beach I pulled over to let my three passengers out. A young man wearing civilian clothes and a military armband walked up to the car. He was a friend of theirs. He had pulled the night shift for beach patrol. His most distinguishing characteristic was the bolt-action rifle he carried. "It's a Winchester," he said. We talked about beaches, stars, and seafood. They had plenty of the first and second and little of the third. "Here." He put his rifle in my hands. "It's heavy, but it hits its target from a great distance." I took aim at a faraway bush and gave it back to him. He was talking with my passengers about the fellow who had called me a CIA agent.

"No, no, no." The beach patrol to the sulker. "He didn't say you were a counterrevolutionary for talking with a foreigner. He said you were an antisocial *gusana*." Within Cuba a *gusano*—literally, a worm—is someone said to contemptuously discredit the government by public words or deeds. More generally, it is the name good revolutionaries slap on evil Cubans who have crawled away from their homeland. At its loosest and most generic, it's applied to everyone in the first tidal wave of exiles, and many in subsequent waves. Castro once defined *gusanos* as "disgruntled bourgeois elements with counterrevolutionary tendencies." (At the Miami airport, the dufflebags visiting Cubans arrive with are called *gusanos* by the baggage handlers.)

The beach patrol came over and motioned me aside. "*No te preocupes,*" don't worry. "The *compañero* who said you were with the CIA? He used to be her boyfriend. He's just jealous." I bid good night to the beach patroller, *la gusanita,* and the other nightcrawlers, and drove back to my hotel.

THE SEVENTY KILOMETERS FROM TRINIDAD to Sancti Spíritus "looked like Africa," wrote journalist Martha Gellhorn, Hemingway wife number three, when she motored the same stretch during a visit in the mid-1980s. "Humpbacked, bony cattle, like Masai cattle, palms and ceibas . . . jungle-green hills, brown plains." When I reached Sancti Spíritus I checked into the Zaza, a hotel whose name I liked far better than its amenities. It was named for the lake on whose west side it was built. The Zaza had a full house; I was its only foreigner. Groups vacationing from job sites in Havana and Cienfuegos filled the bar, swimming pool, and restaurant. The most interesting part of my stay, aside from an afternoon fistfight between two drunken *machos,* was watching a cooking show called *Cocina al minuto* on the television in my room.

Cocina al minuto was hosted by Nitza Villapol, a woman in her sixties erroneously called the Cuban Julia Child. She puttered about her small kitchen fixing a fruit concoction aided by a helper who was less than helpful. When Nitza was annoyed at her assistant she flashed anger; when she was pleased with the dish's progress she smiled; and when she was done she seemed relieved. Nitza Villapol had been on Cuban television before the Revolution, and prior to that, radio. With the possible exception of Vilma Espín, Raúl Castro's wife, who heads the Cuban Women's Federation and sits on the Central Committee and has her face on billboards, Nitza Villapol is Cuba's best-known woman. Three generations of Cubans, many of them abroad, swear by her advice and her cookbooks. When her fifteen-minute show ended, the poolside noise level rose, the lobby filled up again, and people went on with their day.

The center of Sancti Spíritus resembled Trinidad in its age, its cobbled streets, and its long, narrow grilled windows, yet it lacked Trinidad's confidence and vitality. Possibly it was the heat of day, or too much time on the road. Perhaps I was simply colonialed out. Whatever the reason, the enthusiasm I felt elsewhere was missing in Sancti Spíritus. I crisscrossed the town a few times looking for Calle El Llano, reputedly the quintessential colonial street. It lived up to its reputation, yet its most conspicuous feature was not architecture from the Spanish empire but an automobile from the heyday of Detroit: parked on Calle El Llano was a two-tone Plymouth Deluxe made in 1934. Just a few months before that car reached Cuba, Gerardo Machado had been overthrown and Fulgencio Batista began the puppeteer phase of his political career.

The blue-and-white car sat in front of a house, and when I slowly circled it, admiring its well-preserved condition, its owner came out in shorts and thongs to show it off. "It has its original running board. Look." He showed me Detroit's sturdy workmanship. To crank it up he raised half of the hood from the side and tinkered with a few wires, then got inside and finally got it humming. Purring. He took me for a spin around the block. The car would never make it far out of Sancti Spíritus, its owner acknowledged, but then he probably wouldn't either. A whitewall was affixed to the rear. Emblazoned in white paint it said

1 9 3 4 — P L Y M O U T H — 1 9 3 4

A Packard was the first automobile ever to drive on Sancti Spíritus streets. Fifteen years before the blue-and-white Plymouth on Calle El Llano came to Cuba, the Packard Motor Car Company sent E. Ralph Estep and a couple of colleagues to Cuba with a brand-new convertible. Their mission: to drive the length of the country. "We had imagined that Cuba was a sort of national park with an immense system of boulevards," Estep wrote, but soon learned Cuba had only one highway, fifty miles long. Still, emboldened with equal parts bonhomie, determination, and ignorance, Estep and the others set out from Havana to Sancti Spíritus. They traveled through small towns and up and down hills where faint paths became their roads, and seemed to spend most of every day changing flat tires and chopping at tropical growth that blocked their way. "We were not prepared for camping because we had anticipated spending our nights in villages or towns."

The hardships Estep accepted with equanimity, and the surprises with pleasure: "We forded nine shallow rivers and rushed innumerable short steep climbs up their farther banks. Some of these grades seemed to stand the car on end, both going down and coming up. At many of them we were forced to stop and cut out notches in the hard clay or solid rock, to clear the fly wheel, when the car should go over the sharp crown of the hill."

Finally, 313 miles after they set out, the Packard-sponsored crew arrived in Sancti Spíritus. "The town received us boisterously. Each crooked street filled with noisy crowds of men, women, and children who darted from their homes to chase after us to the hotel . . . Sancti Spíritus was innocent in automobiles."

Jorge Daubar had suggested I look up Carlos, a friend in Sancti Spíritus. Carlos lived on the third floor of an old house now home to four families. I introduced myself. He was home alone while his wife was off visiting relatives. He had plenty of time for a visit. I glanced up at an unlighted chandelier that hung forlornly in the foyer. "I only have one working bulb," he admitted, chuckling at the situation. "I've been waiting for bulbs to come to the market for months now."

Carlos's passion was playing chess by mail. He was involved in games with people in Asia, Europe, and Mexico. He was active in the international organization that promoted chess by mail and handed me its most recent newsletter. But he also kept plenty of enthusiasm for his hometown.

"Let's go outside. I want to show you something." We climbed some steep steps to the roof of his building where we had a full view of the city. "See that?" He pointed to a church a block away. "It's one of the oldest churches in continuous use in the country. It goes back to 1680. I was born and raised here and I'm still proud of it. Its bell still rings for Mass every Sunday morning. Over there"—he pointed across a narrow side street—"my neighbor once had an aviary in the backyard, but there are no birds now."

Carlos, a civil engineer by trade, ticked off the local industries—cattle, sugarcane by-products, tiles, construction, and produce. "This is a very calm city. We pay a guard to walk the streets, but we have no juvenile delinquency. I can't even remember the last time we had a robbery or a break-in."

I asked him his source of news. "Well, sometimes radio. I see newspapers at work, but nothing, really. If you don't get news at all, you don't get either good news or bad news, so what does it matter?"

Do you have a bookstore or library here?

"What do you take us for, savages? Of course we do."

By the time my impertinence showed, we were back downstairs. I mentioned that I hoped to interview Fidel before I left the country, and wondered if he had any questions he'd like me to ask. He paused. "Yes. I want to know why we are always the only country voting one way at the United Nations while all the others are voting the other way. And even in Latin America, why are we always right and the other countries always wrong?"

"Are you a Communist?" I still got a kick out of casually asking the question. You just can't do that back home. Carlos shook his head and smiled. "We have a saying—*Tú no eras ni Pionero.*' You weren't even a Pioneer—the mass organization of Cuban youth. Not to have been a Pioneer! You asked if I was a member of the Communist Party—well, it's one thing not to be a Communist, but *everyone* was a Pioneer in his youth." He laughed. "*Tú no eras ni Pionero.*"

We dropped in on some neighbors and sat around the kitchen table where they served thick coffee and talked rabid baseball. The interprovincial league—La Liga Nacional—wouldn't start for almost two months, but the sport held year-round fascination. The North American World Series was up for discussion, and of course José Canseco figured prominently. "Is he worth it?" the man of the house asked about Canseco's salary. "I can't understand that much money." I mentioned some of the Cubans who played for the Washington Senators in the 1950s—Pedro Ramos, Camilo Pascual, Julio Becquer, José Valdivielso. "They were always my favorite players."

"Mine, too," the neighbor said. "We used to follow them very closely."

"Then the Senators moved from Washington and I stopped following the majors."

"Tell me, I don't understand how a club could simply move from one city to another." I tried to explain franchises. He said, "Okay. Say I live in Jacksonville, Florida, and I have the money to buy a baseball club. What do I do?"

"Well, first you'd need to build a stadium to show good intention."

"Okay, I've got a stadium. Then what?"

"Then you have to prove that you can fill it. Finally you have to find a team available in the marketplace that's doing terrible elsewhere and demonstrate that you can make more money for the other team owners than any of the others who also want to buy that club. It takes a few years and costs a lot just to get that far."

"But why can't I simply field a team?"

His twenty-year-old son came in and listened. He asked about George Steinbrenner and the New York, pardon the expression, Yankees.

When Carlos and I were about to leave, the son gave me a book by historian Orlando Barrera Figueroa about Sancti Spíritus. It starts with Spanish conquerors in 1514 and crescendos to late 1958, "The Final Days of the 444 Years of Oppression, Dependency, and Vassalage." Three hundred forty-six years into this O.D.&V., William Walker, the American filibuster who five years earlier had commandeered Nicaragua and declared himself its president, sailed along Cuba's south coast. The freebooter was "leading a powerful expedition . . . in a mood to conquer Cuba." His presence, Barrera writes, made Spanish colonial forces in Sancti Spíritus very nervous. (In fact, though, Walker never docked in Cuba, but sailed past it to Honduras.)

In 1895 a youthful, vacationing British officer named Winston Churchill went to Cuba to write for the London *Daily*

Graphic during the War of Independence. Spanish authorities suggested that if he wanted to see a battle that he should go to Sancti Spíritus. He found it to be "a godforsaken small town, very unhealthy, with a raging epidemic of yellow fever and small pox. . . ." But, adds biographer Robert Payne, "Churchill found that he enjoyed the Cuban cigars." He also liked Spanish officers in uniforms and the bearded, barefoot soldiers they commanded. As for the home team, he "found the guerrillas tiresome," even if they were fighting for their freedom. A few days later, in a small battle at Arroyo Blanco northeast of Sancti Spíritus, a rebel bullet passed within a foot of the future prime minister's head. "There is nothing more exhilarating than to be shot at without result," he wrote.

Barrera's book suggests that Churchill was more than a reporter, perhaps "a spy or here to distort Cuban reality and its just war." Churchill himself gave history little to go by; a staunch fence-straddler, he wrote, "I sympathize with the rebellion—not with the rebels." As historian William Manchester wrote of Churchill's attitude, "The very thought of Cuban independence was as absurd as, say, an independent India." Churchill, Orlando Barrera adds in his history of Sancti Spíritus, was "an enemy of the Soviet people and of Communism to his dying day."

"See?" We were back at Carlos's place. "I left the front door open the whole time we were gone. There's no crime here."

HOW TO KILL A CROCODILE, BY WALTER D. Wilcox, in a 1908 issue of the *National Geographic Magazine*: "An old hat is placed on the end of a short stick, which is held in the left hand and waved over the water. The crocodile rushes blindly at the hat and is struck a sharp blow behind the head with a machete." Wilcox, describing the fauna of some miserable swampland along Cuba's south coast, added that "sharks were originally attracted by the large numbers of dead and dying slaves thrown overboard." Wilcox grew to love the area with its cedar and mahogany trees, parrots, herons, and white egrets, and the poisonous apples, harmless snakes, and royal palms. He was describing the Bay of Pigs.

The Bay of Pigs is a sizable body of water to the people who live nearby, but to the rest of the world it signifies the failed 1961 invasion of a Cuban exile force backed by the U.S. government. It became the pivotal event in relations between the two countries. It sealed official animosity and directly led to bellicose policies that have long outlived their usefulness. To mention "Bay of Pigs" in conversation evokes bitterness or pride, depending on whom you talk with in which country. The goal of the invasion was to provoke civil and military chaos culminating in the overthrow of Fidel Castro. The invasion of about 1,400 men has become increasingly fascinating because so much of its covert planning and operation has since been released and revealed. Through it, attitudes, money, policies, patriotism, and betrayal can all be traced.

In Cuba, the sequence of events that Americans call the Bay of Pigs is referred to as Playa Girón. Whenever I mentioned to Cubans that I planned to visit Playa Girón, I looked in their eyes for the faintest flash of anger, pride, or smugness. Instead, I got, "You'll like it there. It's very pretty."

I liked it there. It was very pretty. To reach this international shrine to intransigence I had to drive along a major highway, through small towns, and finally into swampland thick with marshy reeds along a road paved with potholes. My riders included two twelve-year-olds in Pioneer uniforms on their way to school, a man in his thirties who didn't say a word, large ladies going from one little town to another who acknowledged me only when they squeezed in and out of the VW, and near the end, Alejandro, who looked every one of his seventy years and then some.

Alejandro was on his way home from work as a guard at a nearby settlement. He wore a slightly dirty loose shirt over somewhat dirtier pants, and a peak-billed cap. He carried a bucket of eggs. His words surrounded his tooth and came out the side of his mouth. Through his thick doo-wah-diddy I learned that he was a retired *carbonero,* a charcoal worker. He had lived in the Zapata Swampland all his life. He hadn't taken advantage of government programs over the years to train for a new job, achieve literacy, or move to better housing. I understood why this last offer had been made when I saw his home.

He lived in a one-room wooden shack with thatched palms for a roof and earth for his floor. He cooked on a crude stove and slept on a blanket that lay on a raised plank. It looked like a "before" picture touting the benefits of the Revolution. "I could live better if I was willing to move." Chickens and goats meandered around his home.

He had lived there at the time of the invasion. His home was fifty feet from the main approach to the Bay of Pigs, beneath U.S. bombers disguised as Cuban aircraft, smack in the way of Cuban troops rolling toward the beach on what would have been the road north for the invaders.

"What was it like?"

He flailed his arms wildly over his head and to his side.

"What did you do?"

"I did what the soldiers told me to do."

"What did they tell you to do."

"Stay inside."

Had I taken a wrong turn? Over the years I had so immersed myself in the literature and mythology of the Bay of Pigs that by the time I drove the last few miles, my head was swimming in background, strategy, images, and numbers—2506, 1,189, 114, $53 million (brigade number, invaders captured and killed, and value of food, medicine, and tractors the U.S. traded for prisoners the following year). Artful propaganda, still photographs, documentary footage, fictionalized accounts, belligerent veterans, interminable analyses, Sunday morning pundits, and Monday morning quarterbacks—their cumulative accounts inspired powerful preconceptions. Yet when I arrived at the Bay of Pigs I found . . . a nicely landscaped resort complex. Sidewalks weaving around comfortable *casitas*. A gift shop. Restaurant. Disco. Equipment for fishing, scuba diving, water sports. Swimming pool. Cabanas near the beach. Ramadas on the sand. Cubans and foreigners playing in the tide.

This was not the Bay of Pigs of my fantasies. It was contemporary reality. What had I expected, hourly reenactments? Life-sized papier-mâché battle replicas? Bay o' Pigs video games? If the invaders had won, by now there would be T-shirts saying:

To find my wistful Bay of Pigs I dashed to the shelter of the Playa Girón Museum, where I met Petra George Caro.

Petra was my guide, a twenty-seven-year-old Party member well versed in the thrill of the victory, the litany of defeat. She slowly walked me through the professionally displayed artifacts, maps, pictures, and captured arms. Photographs of the Zapata Swampland went back to the turn of the century (but none of Federico García Lorca, who hunted crocodiles there in 1930). Charcoal workers lived in hovels before 1959, one caption said. "They sold their products to intermediate exploiters. The people were generally illiterate. The only transportation was a train to Covadonga. They had no way of getting to *zonas civilizadas.* No medical workers served the area. At the time of the Revolution the CIA was trying to subvert Cuba."

Petra led me to the next exhibit. With the Revolution came agrarian reform. Large tracts were broken into small ones. "The Revolution built two new highways," a sign related, "also rural roads, schools, clinics, and tourist centers. Banks and the property of Yankee monopolies and Cuba's bourgeoisie were nationalized." Photos showed fourteen-year-olds in militia uniforms and teachers working in the region's largely successful literacy campaign.

"Fidel came and asked the *carboneros,* 'How many families live here?' " Petra speaking. "He was told seventy. So he asked for seventy houses to be built." Recent Cuban history is filled with parables of progress with Fidel at both ends and the people in the middle, an observation I kept to myself.

The next room showed a virtual hour-by-hour account of the days just before the attack, when a major department store burned down (the CIA) and airbases were bombed (likewise). A detailed organizational chart of the invading Brigade 2506 was part of the permanent exhibit.

We arrived at a set of elaborate maps with arrows and emblems, accurate down to individual buildings. "They disembarked here." Petra outlined troop movements with a pointer. "We advanced here. Their parachutists landed over here"—she indicated a marshy, unpopulated area—"but our forces came down here." She had a no-nonsense way of describing the clash. "Our navy was very weak. It had no chance of a defense at sea." She could have been a general teaching military history at the war college. "We asked the captured mercenaries why they came. None of them admitted they were part of the brigade." She wore an embroidered shift from Pinar del Río and stylish jewelry from Guantánamo. "One said, 'Me? I came as a cook.' Then Fidel asked some of them why they took part in the attack. They said, 'We wanted to reclaim *nuestra patria*.' The mothers of some of the mercenaries came to see their sons in captivity."

Captured hardware took up most of another room: a recoilless .75 millimeter antitank rifle, mounted machine guns, and outside, planes and boats shot down or abandoned by the visiting team.

Mug shots of all the Cubans killed in action hung on one wall. Petra was especially moved by Eduardo García Delgado. García, mortally wounded in Havana during a coordinated attack, wrote FIDEL in blood as he lay dying. In a country with a surfeit of martyrs, García's final act afforded him instant status. A photograph of his body, facedown, his hand on the L, hung next to the clothes he wore at the time.

"The museum opened in 1964, but it was redone in 1976. We get lots of visitors every year in April." Petra told me this in the guest room, where we met after lunch. Vladimir Lenin looked at us from every wall. A medallion carried aboard a joint Cuban-USSR space shot rested on one table.

The man who ran the Centro Cultural in the nearby town joined us. I was curious how the invasion had been absorbed into mainstream Cuban culture. "What music has been written about the invasion?" He seemed a bit confused.

"Have there been any songs about the invasion or poetry commemorating the invasion?" He began to stammer an answer. Petra tapped me on the shoulder and leaned over. "We don't call it the invasion," she whispered. "Here, we call it *la victoria*."

He brightened up when I corrected my question. He and Petra came up with "Preludio a Girón," by Silvio Rodríguez, "La

Victoria," by Sara González, and "XX Aniversario," by Oswaldo González. "You can probably find them at the record store on Boulevard San Fernando in Cienfuegos."

Petra gave me a copy of a 1983 book *Bravery and Fraternity: Internationalism and Solidarity Between the Armed Forces of Cuba and the USSR.* I asked her to show me the invaders' initial landing site. I waited for her outside, where a shiny blue '48 Studebaker Commander sat parked next to the provincial bookmobile. We drove a short distance to a peaceful beach. Petra swept a hand through the air. "This is where they came ashore that first morning." A few royal palms grew from the smooth sand. Laughing vacationers trotted in ahead of the surf. I couldn't see any history. It was a lovely day at the shore.

PICO IYER

Holguín, Santiago, Havana, and the beach:
1987–1992

"SOMETIMES, WHEN I GO OUT AT NIGHT AND SIT ON THE
SEAWALL ALONE, FEELING THE SPRAY OF THE SALT, THE
FAINT STRUMMING OF ACOUSTIC GUITARS CARRIED ON THE
WIND, AND THE BROAD EMPTY BOULEVARDS SWEEPING
ALONG THE LOVELY CURVE OF HAVANA BAY, I FEEL THAT I
COULD NEVER KNOW A GREATER HAPPINESS."

Pico Iyer's first three books covered a lot of miles: Video Night
in Kathmandu: And Other Reports from the Not-So-Far East
(1988), The Lady and the Monk: Four Seasons in Kyoto
(1991), and Falling Off the Map: Some Lonely Places of the
World *(1993).* Cuba and the Night, *his first novel, was published in 1995.*

*Because Iyer specifically refers to guidebook comments on
hotels he patronized, I consulted my own collection of guide-
books for comments on the Hotel Pernik in Holguín. They all
agree on three points. First, it is the best Holguín has to offer.
One calls it "the biggest and best in town," another "Holguín's
best tourist accommodation," another says that it is both "modern" and "four-star," another merely that it is "modern," and yet
another calls it "the best hotel in the city" even as it refers omi-
nously to "scarcity of supplies" and "poor maintenance."*

*The second point of general agreement is that the hotel's
name honors the homeland of the Bulgarian national hero*

Geogry Dimitrov, whose country aided with its construction—a bit of information that will no doubt spark either pride or fear in the hotel's guests, depending on their place of national origin.

And, finally, there is agreement on the hotel's lobby. One book declares that the hotel has a large pool "and even larger lobby." That doesn't sound very large, it's true; doesn't a two-hundred-room hotel usually have a lobby larger than a swimming pool? But the other books elaborate a bit more. One refers to the "impressive marble foyer," while another sings of the "marble lobby as big as a skating rink."

Only one of my books, however, characterizes the hotel's restaurant, calling it merely "good." Alas, it didn't merit even that modest description when Iyer stayed there.

Still, Iyer's observations of Cuba are representative of many reactions. He doesn't hesitate to catalogue the country's flaws, but he doesn't miss its attractions either. Note his praise, for example, of Havana's beautiful oceanfront boulevard, the Malecón, which Norman Lewis, in another selection in this book, calls "the greatest sea promenade in the world."

ANOTHER CHEERFUL DAY IN CUBA. I wake up in the Hotel Pernik in Holguín and get into an elevator to go to breakfast. The elevator groans down a few feet, then stops. I press a button. The button falls off. I ring a bell. There is silence. I kick the door. The elevator groans up to the floor just left. Outside, I can hear excited cries. "Mira!" "Dime!" "El jefe!" A little later, the doors open, just a crack, and I see a bright-yellow head, and then a black face with a beard. "Don't worry," the face assures me. "You cannot move." The doors clang shut again, and I hear a crowd gathering outside, more "Psssts" and cries. Every now and then, the doors open up a few inches and a new face peers in to wave at me and smile. Then I hear a voice of authority, and as a chain gang of men strains to push open the doors, a teenager gets up on a stepladder and, methodically, starts to unscrew the whole contraption.

Twenty-five minutes later, I am released upon the Pernik dining room. My British guidebook, not generally bullish on things Cuban, waxes rhapsodic about the hotel's fare. "Eat and drink extremely well," it says. The Pernik, it adds, has "a long and appetising menu featuring steak in many forms, good fish and chicken, and fresh fruit and vegetables—even including avocado." Not today, it seems. "What would you like?" a smiling waitress asks. "What do you have?" "Nothing." "No eggs, no tea, no avocado?" "Nothing. Only beer." At the next table, a waitress is prizing open a bottle top with a spoon. The "typically cavernous Eastern European dining hall" is full of happy diners this morning, but not, it seems, of food.

Outside, my school friend Louis and I run into a woman from Aruba who is here to find her grandmother. The grandmother, unfortunately, is lost, but the Aruban has decided in the meantime to smuggle out a '56 Chevy. "Here the people have no salt, no sugar, only one piece of bread a day," she informs us as she gets into our car, "but this is a paradise compared with Aruba." Where are we from? England. "Ah," she sighs, "like Margaret Snatcher, the crime minister." Louis, a Thatcher devotee, accelerates. We drop her off at the airport and head for Santiago. Only four hours as the Nissan flies.

Driving along the one-lane roads, past sunlit fields of sugarcane, we pass billboards honoring the great revolutionary heroes (Martí, Guevara, O'Higgins), signs declaring SPEED IS THE ALLY OF DEATH, lonely ceiba trees, and goat-drawn carts. Flying Pigeon bicycles are everywhere, and vintage Plymouths, and hissing, rusted buses. Sometimes we stop to pick up hitchhikers, and Louis serenades them with passages from *The Waste Land,* ditties from the Grateful Dead, and—his latest attraction—manically pantomimed scenes from *The Jerk.* Bicycles, chickens, children swarm and swerve across the roads. I remember the time in Morocco when, on our way to the airport, he hit a dog. The dog bounded off unhindered; our Citroën limped to a halt.

Then, suddenly, out of nowhere, a bicycle swerves in front of us, there is a sickening thud, and our windshield shatters, splattering us with glass. I cannot bear to get out to see what has happened. But somehow, miraculously, the boy on the bicycle has been thrown out of the path of the car and gets up, only shaken.

A crowd forms, and, a few minutes later, a policeman appears.

"We're so sorry," I tell him. "If there's anything we can do . . ."

"No problem," he says, patting me on the shoulder. "Don't worry. These things happen. We're sorry if this has spoiled your holiday in Cuba."

Spoiled our holiday? We've almost spoiled the poor boy's life!

"Don't worry," he assures me with a smile. "There is just some paperwork. Then you can go on."

A car comes up, and two more imposing cops get out. They take some notes, then barrel up towards us. "These boys," says one. "No, no. It was entirely our fault." "These young boys," he goes on. "You will just have to fill out some forms, and then you can be on your way."

Soon we are taken to a hospital, where a young nurse hits me on the wrist. Then she asks me to extend my arms, to touch my nose, to touch my nose with my eyes closed. Luckily, it is a big target: I pass with flying colors.

Then we are taken to the local police station, a bare, pink-walled shack in the town's main plaza. Inside, a few locals are diligently observing a solitary sign which requests them to SPEAK IN A LOUD VOICE.

Across from us sits our hapless victim, next to a middle-aged man. Sizing up the situation, we go over to him. "Look, we can't apologize enough for what we did to your son. It was all our fault. If there is any . . ."

"No, no, my friends." He smiles. "Is nothing. Please enjoy your time in Cuba." Louis, overwhelmed, presents the family with a box of Dundee Shortbread, purchased, for just such occasions, at the Heathrow Duty-Free Lounge. A festive air breaks out.

Then we are ushered into an inner office. A black man motions me to sit before his desk and hand him my passport. "So, Señor Pico." "My surname, actually, is Iyer." "So your father's name is Pico." "No, my father's name is Iyer." "But here it says Iyer, Pico." "Yes. My family's name is Iyer." "So your mother's name is Pico." "No. My father's name is Iyer." "So your mother's name is . . ." This goes on for a while, and then a baby-faced cop with an Irish look comes in. He claps a hand on Louis's shoulder. Where are we from? England. "No wonder he looks like Margaret Thatcher," he exclaims, and there is more jollity all around. Then he leans forward again. "But you are from India, no?" Yes. "Then tell me something." His face is all earnest inquiry. "Rajiv Gandhi is the son of Indira Gandhi?" Yes. "And the grandson of the other Gandhi?" "No. He is the grandson of Nehru. No relation to the other Gandhi." "No relation, eh? Not a grandson of the other Gandhi?" The Irishman shakes his head in wonder, and the black man sits back to take this thunderbolt in. Then he resumes typing out his report six times over, without benefit of carbons.

Finally, he turns to Louis. "So your family name is Louis," he begins. "No, no," I break in, and add, "He cannot speak Spanish." There is a hasty consultation. Then the Irishman pads off, only to return a few minutes later with a trim, round-faced boss with glasses and a tie. "*Guten Tag*," cries the police chief, extending a hand toward me. "No, no," I say. "It's him." The police chief spins around. "*Guten Tag*," he cries, greeting Louis like a long-lost friend and proceeding to reminisce about a "*Freundin*" he once knew in Leipzig. Things are going swimmingly now. "Margaret Thatcher, very sexy woman!" exclaims the Irishman. "Rajiv Gandhi is not the grandson of the other Gandhi," explains the black man to a newcomer. "*Aber, diese Mädchen . . .*" the police chief reminisces. We could almost be at a Christmas dinner, so full of smiles and clapped shoulders is the room. "If this were anywhere else," Louis whispers, "if this were England, in fact, and a foreigner hit a local boy, they'd probably be lynching him by now."

At six o'clock—it is clear that the police plan to make a day of it—the police chief invites us to dinner at the town's only hotel. Guests of the police, he says. We sit down, and Louis spots a glass of beer. He orders one, and drinks it. Then another. Then another. The chief orders more beers all round, then proposes a toast to *Die Freundschaft*. The waitress drops off a few beers. "She worked in Czechoslovakia for four years," the chief proudly informs us. "How is the weather now in Prague?" Louis asks her in Czech. "I worked for four years in a

Trabant factory," she answers. The police chief, exultant, proposes more toasts to *Die Freundschaft*.

"Paraguay is the only place in the world where you win at blackjack even if you're only even with the bank," offers Louis.

"*Gut, gut, sehr gut!*" cries the chief, more animated than ever.

We renew a few pledges to eternal friendship, then get up and return to the police station, which is sleepy now in the dark.

Louis sits down and promptly slumps over. A group of policemen gathers round him to peer at his handless watch.

Then, suddenly, he sits up. "I'm feeling really terrible," he announces and, lurching out to the terrace, proceeds to deposit some toasts to *Die Freundschaft* in the bushes.

The police chief, anxious, comes over. "I'm sorry," I explain. "We haven't eaten properly for a few days, we were somewhat dehydrated already, and he's probably anyway in a state of shock." With a look of infinite tenderness, the chief summons a lieutenant, and, one on either side of Louis, they take him to the hospital.

Ten minutes later, the team returns, all smiles.

"How are you feeling?"

"Great. All better now."

"Good."

Louis slumps over again, and I maintain our vigil for the man from the car rental firm who is due to take us to Santiago. He was expected at two-thirty. It is now nine-fifteen.

Suddenly, a policeman walks into the room and summons me urgently over. I hurry to his side. Maybe he will give us a lift? "You are an Indian?" he says.

"Yes."

"Then tell me something." He points to a TV. "Two months ago, we saw Rajiv Gandhi being burned. Why did they not put his body in the ground?"

What is the Spanish word for "cremation"? I wonder wildly. "*Cremación*," I try.

"Cremation, eh? Is that right? Thank you," he says, and walks out.

A little later, Louis gets up again and staggers to the terrace. More toasts to *Die Freundschaft* go down the drain.

"I'm really sick," he says. "I can't move. Just get me a bed."

I relay the request to the police chief.

For the first time all day, his commitment to our friendship seems to flag. "*Hier gibt es kein Bett!*" he barks. "*Das ist nicht Hotel! Das ist nicht Krankenhaus!*"

"*Jawohl, mein Herr,*" I say, and we go on waiting for the car rental man.

Suddenly, headlights sweep into the plaza, and a car pulls up. I hurry outside. A man gets out, with an air of great briskness, and I hurry over to him. "So you are Indian?" he says. "Yes." "Then tell me something, please. When Rajiv Gandhi died, why did they not put his body in the ground?"

"Cremation," I reply with tired fluency, and, satisfied, he gets in his car and drives away.

Watching this open-air university in action, the police chief is shamed, perhaps, by his earlier brusqueness. "Once," he tells me in German, "I traveled for six hours by train to Dresden to meet my roommate's sister."

"*Ach ja?*"

At 11:15 P.M., the car rental man appears, and we return to the inner office to do some paperwork. "So—your name is Pico?" "Well, my family name is Iyer." "So your father's name is Pico." "No . . ."

At 1:15 A.M., we pull up at last in front of the Casagranda Hotel in Santiago ("simultaneously dirty and suffocating," sings my guidebook), a famous old joint recently closed for fumigation, where we have a four-day reservation, paid for in advance in London. I leave Louis comatose in the back of our new car, sundry revelers singing and banging drums around him in the street. Inside the hotel, an enormous man is sitting next to a wooden cash register. When he sees my voucher, he looks unhappy. Party girls in backless dresses and well-coiffed boys stroll down the pitch-black staircase from the rooftop cabaret. A couple of them sit on a couch in the lobby and gaze expectantly in my direction. The enormous man looks desperate. I look worse. He picks up a telephone and starts dialing.

Thirty minutes later, he has found us alternative accommodations. At 2:15 A.M., a convoy of two cars, including one spokesman for the house of Gandhi, one new rental car, and one immobile investment banker, pulls up at the Hotel Gaviota. As soon as it does, a young boy rushes out. "Welcome," he cries, in English. "How was your trip? Welcome to the Hotel Gaviota! It's great to see you!"

"Thanks."

"We have some Welcome Cocktails all ready for you! What will it be? A cuba libre? A daiquiri? Some *ron*? What would you like?"

"My friend cannot move."

"No problem. A Welcome Cocktail will help. It's on the house!"

"But he's already heard Margaret Thatcher impugned, almost killed a boy, and been taken to a hospital by a police chief speaking German."

"Sure!" says the boy. "That's why he needs a Welcome Cocktail. Please! My friends are waiting!" He points to the bar, where two young bloods are sitting hopefully in the dark.

I go over to Louis, now propped up in the lobby, and break the news to him.

He does not look overjoyed.

"The thing is, unless you order a Welcome Cocktail, I don't think you'll get a room."

"Okay, okay, just get me some mineral water." Realizing that this could entail a long wait—yesterday we had stopped in a small town to ask two boys for water and been told, "For water you must go to the next town! Only forty-five kilometers away!"—I go to the desk to do some paperwork. On one side is a sign that advises, CRAZY LOVE IS NOT TRUE LOVE. On the other, a stack of Cubatur brochures. "*Ven a vivir una tentacíon!*" Come to live out a temptation!

Proprieties observed, we follow our host on the ten-minute walk to our suites, made-for-mobster caverns from the fifties, with mirrors all round, and enormous makeup areas for showgirls.

"This is okay?" the young boy asks.

"Sure," I say. But one thing still bothers me: why doesn't he care about the fate of Rajiv Gandhi?

COME TO LIVE OUT A TEMPTATION! EVERY time I return from Cuba, I find myself sounding like a tourist brochure. Cuba is one of the biggest surprises in the modern world, if only because it has occupied a black hole in our consciousness for so long. If people think of the island at all these days, they probably think of army fatigues, warlike rhetoric, and bearded threats to our peace. Few people recall that Cuba is, in fact, the largest island in the Greater Antilles and, as even my sour guidebook admits, "the most varied and most beautiful." That it has 4,500 miles of beach, nearly all of them as empty as a private hideaway. That there are more than eleven hours of sunshine on an average day, and the air is 77 degrees, the water even warmer. That it vibrates with the buoyancy of a late-night, passionate, reckless people whose warmth has only been intensified by adversity. And that it is still, apart from anything, a distinctly Caribbean place of lyricism and light, with music pulsing along its streets and lemon-yellow, sky-blue, alabaster-white buildings shining against a rich blue sea. Havana days are the softest I know, the golden light of dusk spangling the cool buildings in the tree-lined streets; Havana nights are the most vibrant and electric, with dark-eyed, scarlet girls leaning against the fins of chrome-polished '57 Chryslers under the floodlit mango trees of Prohibition-era nightclubs. Whatever else you may say about Cuba, you cannot fail to see why Christopher Columbus, upon landing on the soft-breezed isle, called it "the most beautiful land ever seen."

In Communist Cuba, of course, you will find shortages of everything except ironies. The Bay of Pigs is a beach resort now, and San Juan Hill is most famous for its "patio cabaret." The Isle of Youth, long the most dreaded Alcatraz in the Caribbean, entices visitors with its International Scuba-Diving Center. There is a "Cretins' Corner" in the Museum of the Revolution, featuring an effigy of Ronald Reagan ("Thank you, cretin," says the sign, "for helping us strengthen the Revolution"). And one

beach near Matanzas (the name means Massacres) has, somewhat less than romantically, been christened Playa Yugoslavia.
Cuba, in fact, has edges and shadows not often found in other
West Indian resorts: the billboards along the beach offer stern
admonitions ("The best tan is acquired in movement"), and the
gift stores in the hotels sell such deck-chair classics as *The
C.I.A. in Central America and the Caribbean.* Everything here
takes on a somewhat unexpected air. "Cuba's waiting for you,"
runs the official tourist slogan. "We knew you were coming."

Cubatur's most intriguing attraction is undoubtedly its
four-hour excursion each day to a psychiatric hospital. But
when I asked one day if I could sign up for the tour, the laugh-
ing-eyed girl at the desk looked at me as if *I* were the madman.
"It isn't happening," she said. "Does it ever happen?" "No," she
replied, with a delighted smile.

Yet the seduction of Cuba, for me, lies precisely in that
kind of impromptu roughness, and in the fact that its streets
feel so deserted; the whole island has the ramshackle glamour
of an abandoned stage set. Old Havana is a crooked maze of
leafy parks and wrought-iron balconies, where men strum guitars in sun-splashed courtyards, inciting one to the pleasures of
a life *alfresco*; its singular beauty, unmatched throughout the
Caribbean, is that it feels as if it has been left behind by history,
untouched. Here, one feels, is all the quaintness of New Orleans, with none of the self-admiration. And the freewheeling
gaiety of a Sunday afternoon in Lenin Park, where soldiers twirl
one another about to the happy rhythms of steel bands, is all
the more intoxicating because it is so spontaneous; here, one
feels, is all the hedonism of Rio with none of the self-con-
sciousness. Everything in Cuba comes scribbled over with the
neglected air of a Lonely Place; everything feels like a custom-
made discovery.

The other great achievement of the Castro government, of
course, is that its overnight arrest of history has left the island
furnished with all the musty relics of the time when it was
America's dream playground, and many parts of Cuba still look
and feel like museum pieces of the American empire. Yes, there
are troubadours' clubs, bohemian dives, a film school run by

García Márquez, and a Humor Museum. But the most aromatic of the culture's features are, in many respects, the backward-looking ones: the savor of rum in the bars that Hemingway once haunted; the friendly dishevelment of the sea-worn old Mafia hotels, crowded now with Oriental-featured tourists from Siberia; the rickety charm of white-shoe bands playing the theme from *The Godfather* in red-lit Polynesian restaurants that must have looked modern when first they were built, half a century ago. You can almost feel the city where typical honeymooners from Connecticut could stay at the Manhattan (or the New York) Hotel, take care of their needs at the Fifth Avenue Shoe Store, and cash their checks at one of the First National Bank of Boston's six local branches, before whiling away their evenings at the Infierno Club (or, in better circles, the Country Club). You can almost taste the tropicolored island where the Dodgers used to hold spring training and Fidel Castro was just another pitching prospect for the Washington Senators. You can almost hear Basil Woon exclaim, in his 1928 book, *When It's Cocktail Time in Cuba,* " 'Have one in Havana' seems to have become the winter slogan of the wealthy."

Yet it is something more than poignant memories, and something even deeper than sun-washed surfaces, that keeps me coming back to Cuba, and it is, I think, the fact that every moment is an adventure here, and every day is full of surprise. I never want to sleep in Cuba. And even after I have returned home—and the place has disappeared entirely from view—I find that it haunts me like a distant rumba: I can still hear the cigarette-voiced grandma in Artemisa who took me in from the rain and, over wine in tin cups, spun me family tales strange with magic realism, before leading me across puddles to hear Fidel; I can still taste the strawberry ice creams in Coppelia, where languorous Lolitas sashay through the night in off-the-shoulder T-shirts, beside them strutting Romeos as shiny as Italian loafers; I can still see the round-the-clock turmoil of carnival, and the Soviet doctor who sat next to me one year, blowing kisses at the dancers. Sometimes, when I go out at night and sit on the seawall alone, feeling the spray of the salt, the faint strumming of acoustic guitars carried on the wind, and the broad empty boulevards sweeping along the lovely curve of Havana Bay, I feel that I could never know a greater happiness.

Cuba, in fact, is in many of its moods the most infectiously exultant place I know: it sometimes feels as if the featureless gray blocks of Marxism have simply been set down, incongruously, on a sunny, swelling, multicolored quilt, so that much of the sauce and sensuality of the louche Havana of old keeps peeping through. "Every step I took offered up a new world of joys," wrote Thomas Merton, the Trappist monk, who felt himself a prince surrounded by graces "in that bright Island [where] kindness and solicitude surrounded me." Norman Lewis, after sixty-five years of traveling, told me that he had never found a place to compare with Havana. And even during these days of post-*glasnost* privations, the fact remains that windows are thrown open so that reggae floods the streets, and passengers waiting for a plane draw out guitars and improvise sing-alongs in the departure lounge. Many Cubans have made an art form of their appetite for wine, women, and song—all the more precious in the absence of everything else; one young friend of mine in Havana knows only four words of English, which he repeats like a tonic each day, accompanied each time by a dazzling smile: "Don't worry! Be happy!" Very often, in fact, the island reminds me of that famous statement of the eighteenth-century Englishman Oliver Edwards: "I have tried, too, in my time to be a philosopher; but I don't know how, cheerfulness was always breaking in."

This exhilarating sense of openness hit me the minute I landed in Havana on a recent trip: the customs officials in the airport were dressed in khaki but winkingly turned the other eye whenever they saw cases piled high with fifteen pairs of new ready-for-the-black-market jeans; the immigrations officials, when not cross-questioning tourists, made kissing noises at their female colleagues. Out in the streets, I was instantly back inside some romantic thriller, with crimes and liaisons in the air. Dolled-up señoritas looked at me with the sly intimacy of long-lost friends; rum-husky men invited me into their lives.

By the following night, I was sitting along the seawall with a group of earnest students eager to thrash out Hermann Hesse, Tracy Chapman, yoga, Henry Fielding, and liberation theology. Later, walking past the commercial buildings of La Rampa, I heard the joyous rasp of a saxophone and, following my ears through the video banks and rainbowed portraits of the Cuba Pavilion, found myself in a huge open-air disco, free (like most museums, concerts, and ball games in Cuba) and alive with teenagers jiving along to a Springsteenish band in WE STICK TO FIDEL headbands and Che Guevara T-shirts; thus—the government hopes—are party-loving kids turned into Party-loving comrades. When the concert ended, round about midnight, I walked over to the ten-stool bar in the old Hotel Nacional, where four cheery, red-faced Soviets were singing melancholy Russian ballads to a flirty *mulatta* of quick charm. The girl counted off a few numbers on her long pink nails, then swiveled into action. "Ivan, Ivan," she cooed across at a lugubrious-looking reveler, "why don't you dance with me? Ivan, don't you like me?" At which Ivan lumbered up, popped a coin into the prehistoric Wurlitzer, and, as "Guantanamera" came up, threw his hands in the air and began wriggling in place with all the unlikely grace of a bear in a John Travolta suit. This, I realized, was not Club Med.

The country's beaches—289 of them in all—start just twenty minutes from the capital. At Santa María del Mar, a virtual suburb of Havana, lies one of the loveliest, and emptiest, strips of sand you'll ever see, with only a few old men—salty castaways from Hemingway—standing bare-chested in the water, trousers rolled up to their knees, unreeling silver fish. Behind them, across a road, reclines a typical Cuban seaside hotel, filled as always with something of the plaintiveness of an Olympics facility two decades after the games have ended. Inside its once-futuristic ramps, bulletin boards crowded with eager notices as happily crayoned as a child's birthday card invite foreigners to "Workers Shows" ("a very nice activity," offers the unread board, "where you will see the workers become artists for your pleasure") and "Happy Shows." Every Monday, at 4:30, there are "Cocktail Lessons," and every afternoon, "Music, Dance and Many Surprises." But when I looked at my watch, I realized it was 4:45, and Monday, and not a single cocktail student, not a sign of music or dance was in sight; somehow, in Cuba, it is always out-of-season.

The proudest attraction of the Cubatur office—and its brightest hope for gaining needed dollars—is the string of coral keys that sparkle like teardrops off the coast. One day I took the flight to Cayo Largo, an absurdly beautiful stretch of fifteen miles of open beach, graced with every enticement this side of Lauren Bacall. As soon as I got off the plane, at 8:45 A.M., I was greeted with a frenzied Cuban dance band and—what else?—a Welcome Cocktail; for the rest of the day, I simply lay on the beach and gazed at the cloudless line of primary colors—aqua and emerald and milky green, flawless as a Bacardi ad. There is nothing much to see in Cayo Largo, save for some basins full of turtles and an island featuring 250 iguanas; but, as with all the most delectable resorts in Cuba, the place is utterly empty, even of Bulgarians in string vests. (This is, in part, because locals are not permitted on the beach—this is, alas, no legal fiction: I, too, while walking along the beach one drowsy Sunday morning, was hauled over, by a policeman hiding in the bushes, on suspicion of being a Cuban.)

In recent years, in a bid to rescue its shattered economy, Cuba has begun refurbishing its old hotels with tiled patios and stained-glass windows, and trying to entice visitors with "Afro Shows" and "Smashed Potatoes"; but even now, thank Marx, the island remains roughly 90 percent tourist-proof: one still needs two chits and a passport to buy a Coca-Cola, and as in some loony lottery, Visa cards are accepted only if they contain certain numbers. This, though, is part of the delight of the place: whenever one goes out at night, one never knows how the evening will end, or when. Days are seldom clearer. One sleepy Sunday not so long ago, I waited for a taxi to take me back to Havana from the beach; and waited, and waited, and waited, for three and a quarter hours in all, under a tree, on a hot afternoon. Finally, just as I was about to lose all hope, up lurched a coughing red-and-white 1952 Plymouth, with "The Vampire Road" written across its back window. Seven exhausted souls piled into the wreck, and the next thing I knew, the quartet in back was pounding out an ad hoc beat on the seat and breaking into an a cappella melody of their own invention—

"Ba ba ba, we're going to Havana . . . ba ba ba, in a really sick old car . . ." For the next two hours, the increasingly out-of-tune singers unsteadily passed a huge bottle of rum back and forth and shouted out songs of an indeterminate obscenity, while the mustachioed driver poked me in the ribs and cackled with delight.

In Santiago de Cuba, the second city of the island and the only officially designated "Hero City" of the Revolution, I spent a few days in the gutted home of a former captain of Fidel's. From the hills above, where Castro and his guerrillas once gathered, the city looked as it might on some ancient, yellowing Spanish map; down below, in a peeling room that I shared with a snuffling wild pig who was due to be my dinner, things were somewhat less exalted. Every night, in the half-lit gloom of his bare, high-ceilinged room, decorated only with a few black-and-white snapshots of his youth, my host took me aside ("Let me tell you, Pico Eagle . . .") and told me stories of the Revolution, then delivered heartbroken obituaries for his country. Next door, in an even darker room, one of his sons prepared dolls for a *santería* ceremony, the local equivalent of voodoo. And when it came time for me to leave, the old man asked for some baseball magazines from the States. Any special kind? I asked. "No," he said softly. "But I like the ones with Jackie Robinson in them."

That sense of wistfulness, of a life arrested in midbreath, is everywhere in Cuba: in the brochures of the once-elegant Hotel Riviera, which now, disconcertingly, offers a "diaphanous dining-room"; in the boarded-up stores whose names conjure up a vanished era of cosmopolitanism—the Sublime, the Fin-de-Siècle, Roseland, Indochina; in the Esperanto Association that stands across from a dingy, closed-off building under the forlorn legend R.C.A. VICTOR. Hemingway's house in the hills is kept exactly the way he left it at his departure almost thirty years ago—unread copies of *Field & Stream* and *Sports Illustrated* scattered across his bed—and the buildings all around, unpainted, unrepaired, speak also of departed hopes. One reason so many Cubans ask a foreigner, *"Que hora es?"* is to strike up a conversation—and a deal; another, though, is that they really do need to know the time in a place where all the clocks are stopped. Perhaps the most haunting site in the beach resort of Varadero is Las Americas, the lonely mansion above the sea built by the Du Ponts. Nowadays it is a dilapidated boarding school of a place, all long corridors and locked doors. The Carrara marble floor is thick with dust, and the photos in the drawing room are hard to make out in the feeble light. But along the mahogany and cedar walls there still hangs a tapestry poignantly transcribing all the lines of the poem that once contained the hopes the home embodied: "In Xanadu did Kubla Khan a stately pleasure dome decree . . ."

It is that mix of elegy and carnival that defines Cuba for me, and it is that sense of sunlit sadness that makes it, in the end, the most emotionally involving—and unsettling—place I know; Cuba catches my heart, then makes me count the cost of that enchantment. Cuba is old ladies in rocking chairs on their verandas in the twilight, dabbing their eyes as their grandchildren explain their latest dreams of escape, and the azure sea flashing in the background; it is pretty, laughing kids dancing all night in the boisterous cabarets and then confiding, matter-of-factly, "Our lives here are like in Dante's *Inferno*." It is smiles, and open doors, and policemen lurking in the corners; lazy days on ill-paved streets and a friend who asks if he might possibly steal my passport.

In Cuba, the tourist's thrilling adventures have stakes he cannot fathom. And every encounter leaves one only deeper in the shadows. My first night in a big hotel, a girl I had never met rang me up and asked, sight unseen, if I would marry her. The next day, in the cathedral, a small old man with shining eyes came up to me and began talking of his family, his faith, his grade-school daughter. "I call her Elizabeth," he said. "Like a queen." He paused. "A poor queen"—he smiled ruefully—"but to me she is still a queen." When we met again, at an Easter Sunday mass, he gave me Mother's Day gifts for my mother and, moist-eyed, a letter for his own mother in the States. Only much later, when I got home, did I find that the letter was in fact addressed to the State Department, and the kindly old man a would-be defector.

And one sunny afternoon in a dark Havana bar, so dark that I could not see my companion's face except when she lit a match for a cigarette, I asked a friend if I could send her anything from the States. Not really, she said, this intelligent twenty-three-year-old who knew me well: just a Donald Duck sticker for her fridge. Nothing else? I asked. Well, maybe a Mickey Mouse postcard: that was quite a status symbol over here. And that was all? Yes, she said—oh, and one more thing: a job, please, with the CIA.

PERMISSIONS
ACKNOWLEDGMENTS